AF262904

AGNÈS VARDA

AGNÈS VARDA

DIRECTOR'S INSPIRATION

Edited by Matt Severson

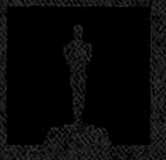

ACADEMY MUSEUM OF MOTION PICTURES
LOS ANGELES

DELMONICO BOOKS · D.A.P.
NEW YORK

DIRECTOR'S FOREWORD

I am so proud to share this publication celebrating the second exhibition in the Academy Museum's Director's Inspiration series, focused on the formidable French director Agnès Varda (1928–2019). The Director's Inspiration gallery, part of the museum's core exhibition *Stories of Cinema*, highlights prominent directors by comprehensively exploring their bodies of work and surveying the influences that shaped their oeuvres. The inimitable Spike Lee was the first subject of this series. Now, with *Agnès Varda*, the museum introduces visitors to the abounding life and art of this exceptional filmmaker whose career spanned seven decades.

Varda started out as a photographer for the French theater director Jean Vilar at the Festival d'Avignon. With her first film, *La Pointe Courte* (1955), she immediately distinguished herself as a writer and director with a unique female voice. She created more than 30 films, demonstrating a penchant for stylistic experimentation and documentary realism. Toward the later part of her life, she began a third career as a visual artist, producing innovative museum installations for venues such as the Venice Biennale, the Cartier Foundation for Contemporary Art in Paris, and the Los Angeles County Museum of Art.

First and foremost, I want to thank and praise the team at Ciné-Tamaris, especially Rosalie Varda, whose commitment to preserving her mother's work makes exhibitions like this possible. I am grateful to Exhibitions Curator Jessica Niebel, former Assistant Curator Ana Santiago, and Research Assistant Manouchka Kelly Labouba for their tremendous work on this elegant show, which deftly captures the various phases of Varda's multifaceted career. I also thank Vice President of Curatorial Affairs Doris Berger for her leadership in initiating and overseeing the exhibition's development.

This accompanying publication expanding on Varda's significance in film history is edited by Matt Severson, Director of the Margaret Herrick Library, who has been a valued collaborator on this project from the beginning. I extend my warmest gratitude to Matt and to Director of Publications Stacey Allan, whose mutual love of Varda is shared by the many talented contributors to this volume: Sasha Archibald, Jane Birkin, Sandrine Bonnaire, Manohla Dargis, Peter Debruge, Mathieu Demy, Julia Fabry, JR, Lynne Littman, Didier Rouget, Martin Scorsese, Rosalie Varda, Viva, and Chloé Zhao.

Finally, I am extremely grateful to the many funders who have supported *Stories of Cinema*, namely Gerald Schwartz and Heather Reisman, Barbara Roisman Cooper and Martin M. Cooper, Jocelyn R. Katz, John Ptak and Margaret Black, Lauren Shuler Donner, Randy E. Haberkamp, Kevin McCormick and A. Scott Berg, and John and Lacey Williams. I am also indebted to our corporate and foundation partners PwC, Metro-Goldwyn-Mayer Studios, FotoKem, Panasonic, Dolby Laboratories, Sony Electronics, Bloomberg Philanthropies, Chanel, and the Ruderman Family Foundation. Their generosity enables our museum to explore and celebrate cinema in all its rich diversity.

Jacqueline Stewart
Director and President

ACKNOWLEDGMENTS

Throughout her nearly seven-decade career, Agnès Varda created work on her own terms: what should be made, how it should be done, and with whom. She set an example for a new approach to filmmaking and became a model for those who followed. Varda took inspiration from the world around her; her experiences with people were the foundation of her art, encounters she would collect and later reassemble into masterful achievements. Her genuine interest in real people and in the everyday, paired with her exploration and interrogation of traditional cinematic language, led to a body of work that is both subjective and reflective of her time.

Director's Inspiration: Agnès Varda was originally curated by Ana Santiago. When Ana left the museum in the summer of 2022, I finalized the exhibition together with Research Assistant Manouchka Kelly Labouba, whose expertise and reliability made the transition smooth. I am grateful for the wonderful groundwork laid by Ana and Manouchka; it can be challenging to embrace another curator's approach, but Ana's vision made the process easy and enjoyable.

The exhibition comprises three sections reflecting on Varda's lives as a photographer, filmmaker, and visual artist. At its heart is an immersive triptych film montage, the triptych being a form Varda liked to work with. It begins with Varda, in *The Beaches of Agnès*, saying, "If we opened people up, we'd find landscapes. If we opened me up, we'd find beaches." Ana and the museum's exhibitions team, led by Executive Vice President Shraddha Aryal, took Varda's love of beaches as their inspiration to realize a peaceful, airy experience for our visitors.

The success of any project depends on the cooperation of many. I'd especially like to thank the exhibition's project manager, Cindy Ha, who—with humor and patience— kept track of schedules, budgets, and deliverables; Martha Polk, who edited the in-gallery texts quickly and carefully; registrar Bernie Sale, who assured the safety of works during shipping and installation; the expert conservation team, led by Sophie Hunter; and former colleagues Sherry Huang and Vanessa McKenzie, who were instrumental in developing the exhibition design and graphics.

Watching an exhibition come to life in a three-dimensional space is thrilling. Having the freedom to make adjustments during installation is invaluable, as no plan on paper will ever reflect the reality of a gallery in every detail. To everyone involved in preparing and installing the exhibition, thank you for your flexibility, creative problem-solving, and sense of fun. Another big shout-out to our A/V and Media Production teams for making the triptych montage look and sound so good.

The three-screen projection is surrounded by works that speak to the evolution and essence of Varda's artistry. This eclectic selection provides insight into Varda's approach and production: how she found expression through diverse artforms and was inspired by those around her, even as she retained something undeniably personal in her own output. My sincere gratitude goes to the lenders, including Ciné-Tamaris and the Academy's Margaret Herrick Library. *Merci beaucoup* to Varda's family: her daughter, Rosalie Varda; her son, Mathieu Demy; and her daughter-in-law, Joséphine Wister Faure. Their partnership, generous support, and desire to share Varda's work with the public made this exhibition possible. For fostering this relationship, I thank Margaret Herrick Library Director Matt Severson and Vice President of Curatorial Affairs Doris Berger. Thank you also to the entire Ciné-Tamaris team, especially Shérine El Sayed Taih, for their invaluable assistance.

Lastly, I'd like to thank Julia Welter for sharing her profound knowledge of and deep admiration for Agnès Varda with me.

Jessica Niebel
Exhibitions Curator

Installation view of *Director's Inspiration: Agnès Varda*, November 3, 2022– January 5, 2025, at the Academy Museum of Motion Pictures, Los Angeles

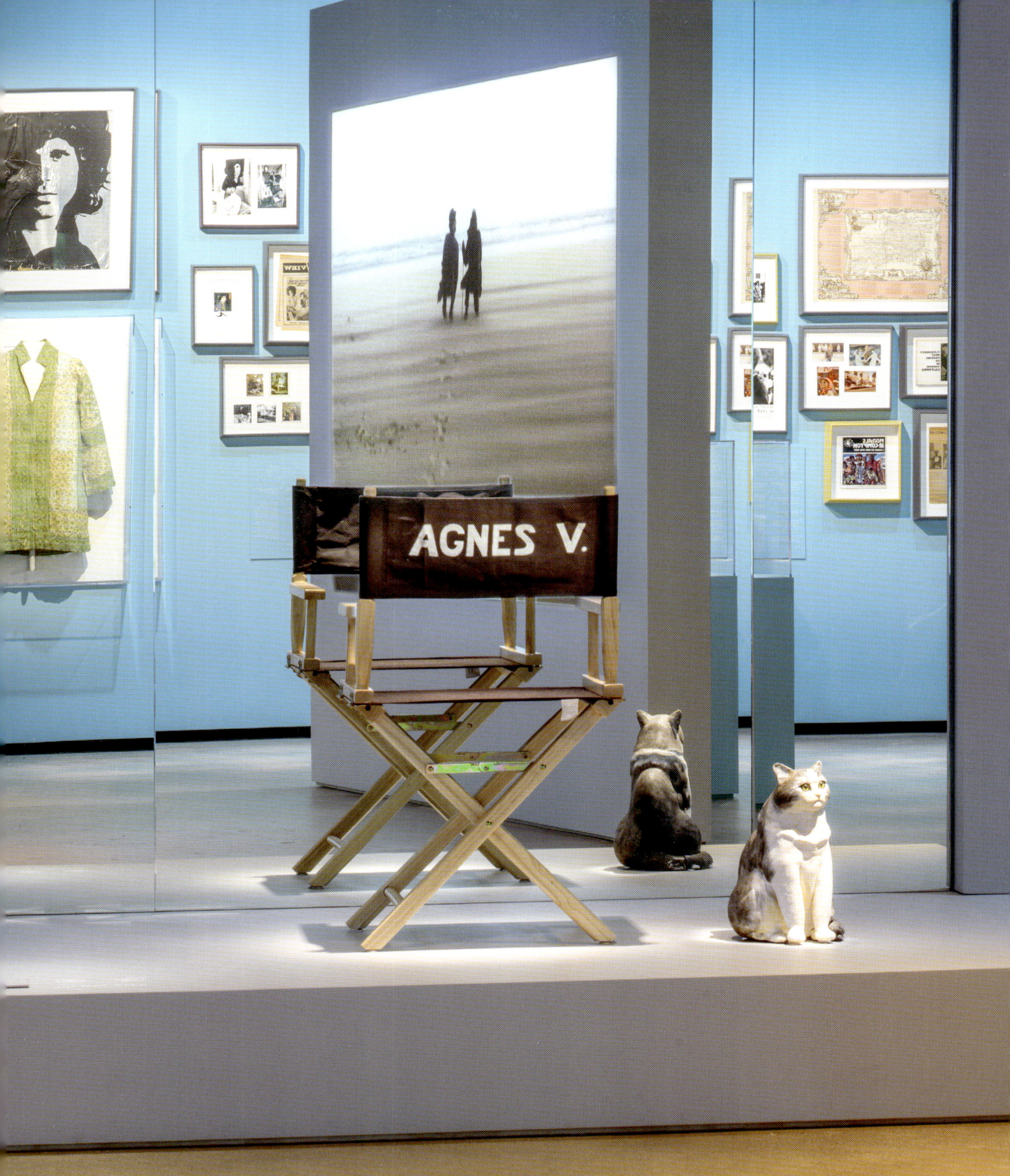

AGNES V.

ACKNOWLEDGMENTS

Agnès Varda was a true vanguard. It is impossible to overstate her place in the history of cinema, but it was Varda as public figure too—with her unwavering belief in herself, her unlimited curiosity, and her compassion for all sentient beings (with an affinity for animals and those on the margins)—that pulled people to her like a centrifugal force. It was a dream come true to know her during her final years, and it is my hope that this volume stands as a testament to her many talents and enduring legacy. *Viva Varda!*

I am deeply indebted to Varda's children, Rosalie Varda and Mathieu Demy, for their friendship, hospitality, and collaboration throughout this project. Rosalie oversees the day-to-day operations of Ciné-Tamaris and allowed us unprecedented access to the Varda and Demy archives, in addition to providing invaluable guidance during the creative development of the exhibition and book. A big thanks also to the Ciné-Tamaris team, especially Stanislas Biessy, Shérine El Sayed Taih, Jules Martin, Elvire Dolgorouky, and Eric Leprêtre.

I am grateful to Academy Chief Executive Officer Bill Kramer for his unwavering support. Executive Vice President of the Margaret Herrick Library, Academy Film Archive, and SciTech Council Randy Haberkamp offered encouragement and guidance to the library team's work on this two-year project, which included travel, digitization, and preservation. Academy Museum Director and President Jacqueline Stewart shared her great knowledge of and passion for Varda's accomplishments; her commitment to the project extended to Turner Classic Movies, where she brought me on as cohost for an evening celebrating five of Varda's films. Thank you also to Academy Museum Vice President of Curatorial Affairs Doris Berger, former Assistant Curator Ana Santiago, Exhibitions Curator Jessica Niebel, and Research Assistant Manouchka Kelly Labouba. Ana, who originally developed the exhibition that was seamlessly carried through by Jessica, combined her love and deep understanding of Varda's work with a brilliant aesthetic and nuanced sensibility that was a guiding influence on the work that followed.

A special acknowledgment to the talented staff of the Margaret Herrick Library, especially Associate Director of Core Collections Files Russ Butner, Associate Director of Graphic Arts Collections Anne Coco, Associate Director of Library Conservation Dawn Jaros, Associate Director of Authority Control and Credits Lucia Schultz, Associate Director of Special Collections and Photograph Archive Warren Sherk, Associate Director of Technical Services Lea Whittington, and Associate Director of Reference and Public Services Elizabeth Youle, who provided incalculable support. Sincere gratitude also to Senior Library Operations Manager Andrea Livingston and a few other members of my team who helped in various capacities big and small: Jacob Beal, Jeanie Braun, Elizabeth Cathcart, Jon Cross, Charles Cruz, John Damer, Laura Darlington, Alan Duignan, Allison Francis, Ben Friday, Phillip Garcia, Christina Ha, Megan Harinski, Louise Hilton, Laura Lee McKay, and Barbara Weiss.

I am indebted to Director of Publications Stacey Allan, who was a remarkable collaborator, and I'm grateful for her guidance and support throughout the development of this book. Thank you to her incredible team, Senior Editor Chelsea Bingham and Publications Coordinator Lars Eckstrom. Major kudos to designers Adam Michaels and Carina Huynh of IN.FO-CO for their exquisite work. Thank you also to Nikki Bazar for her careful editing and to Dianne Woo for her meticulous proofreading. I want to extend a sincere thanks to the wonderful Lisa Blok-Linson, Gwen Deglise Moore, and

Joséphine Wister Faure for sitting down with me to share their experiences with Varda. I am also incredibly grateful to this book's many talented contributors: Sasha Archibald, Jane Birkin, Sandrine Bonnaire, Manohla Dargis, Peter Debruge, Mathieu Demy, Julia Fabry, JR, Lynne Littman, Didier Rouget, Martin Scorsese, Rosalie Varda, Viva, and Chloé Zhao.

Thank you to my family and friends, especially my mom and dad, Diane and Bob Severson, and my aunt and uncle, Eileen and Richard Lloyd, who have supported my movie love from a very young age. Thanks also to Sherry, Shannon, Ryan, Denise, Larry (and the entire Lavoie-Corcoran family), Mark, Julia, Channing, Zoe, Michael R., Harmony, Doug, Troy, Bret, Sharōn, Dave, Ben, Beth, Mitch, Alex, Peter, Matheus, and Daniel, and my teachers Forrest J Ackerman, Genni Klein, Jim Stratton, Thyrza Goodeve, and Manohla Dargis. All of you have had immeasurable impact on my life and this book.

Finally, thank you to my husband, Paul Lavoie, who traveled with me to rue Daguerre multiple times over the course of this book's evolution. Like me, he became an honorary member of the Varda-Demy clan, and he has been stalwart in his support of this project from the very beginning.

Matt Severson
Director, Margaret Herrick Library

Shared grave of Agnès Varda and Jacques Demy at Montparnasse Cemetery, Paris, 2019

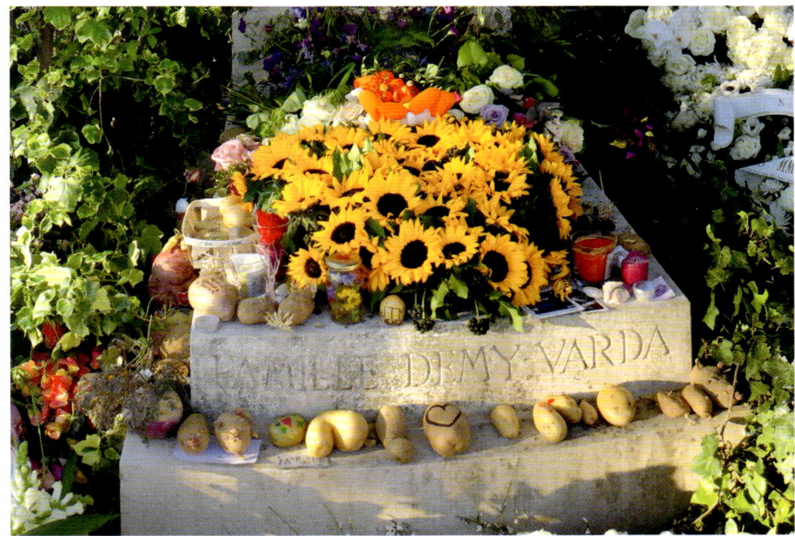

AGNÈS V.
PAR MATT S.
Matt Severson

Today, Agnès Varda's place as one of the most innovative and transformative artists of her generation seems firmly cemented. However, for many of her 65 years as a filmmaker she was treated as a footnote in film histories or not acknowledged whatsoever, perpetually relegated to the shadows of the male directors of the Nouvelle Vague. To see how Varda was awarded and celebrated toward the end of her remarkable life might easily lead one to think that Varda, who was often referred to as either "Mother" or "Grandmother" of the French New Wave, was long ensconced alongside her contemporaries, including Jean-Luc Godard, François Truffaut, Claude Chabrol, Eric Rohmer, Alain Resnais, and her late husband, Jacques Demy. The reality was that Varda, even with brief moments of critical and box-office success, had to fight tenaciously to get her films made. It was the result of her indefatigable creative spirit that she was lecturing, working on new art installations, and making films right up to the end.

I first met Varda in 2017 when, as an Academy representative, I escorted her and her family through the weekend events leading up to the annual Governors Awards ceremony. She was to receive an Honorary Academy Award for her trailblazing career, and it would be the first time the award was presented to a female filmmaker. When we met on the evening of her rehearsal for the awards ceremony, she was focused on her acceptance speech. While she appreciated that three remarkable women—the director Kimberly Peirce and actors Jessica Chastain and Angelina Jolie—would be giving speeches in her honor, Varda wryly observed there were no men introducing her. "Are there no men who love me?" she exclaimed incredulously. It was David Rubin, an Academy Governor at the time, who suggested, "Agnès, why don't you incorporate this into your speech?" She did, and it ended up being one of the ceremony's highlights. When she posed the question from the podium, many of Hollywood's biggest male stars and directors, including Steven Spielberg and Tom Hanks, leaped to their feet or raised their hands up in the air, attesting to their enthusiastic, collective admiration for the vanguard filmmaker.

Varda and I engaged in small talk, discussing filmmakers we admired, such as Robert Bresson, John Cassavetes, and Carlos Reygadas. I was struck by her intensity and felt, on some level, I was being quizzed not only about these filmmakers but also about my knowledge of her films. Luckily, she seemed satisfied with my answers. The night of the ceremony, with her family and friends in attendance—many of whom had flown in from France—I brought a copy of Michael Childers's portrait of Jacques, made from the Academy Library's collections. I told her, "Since everyone else is here to celebrate your achievement, I thought Jacques should be here too." Varda was moved (she claimed she had never seen that portrait before) and kept the photo at her table throughout the ceremony. It was the beginning of our brief friendship, which included letters, phone

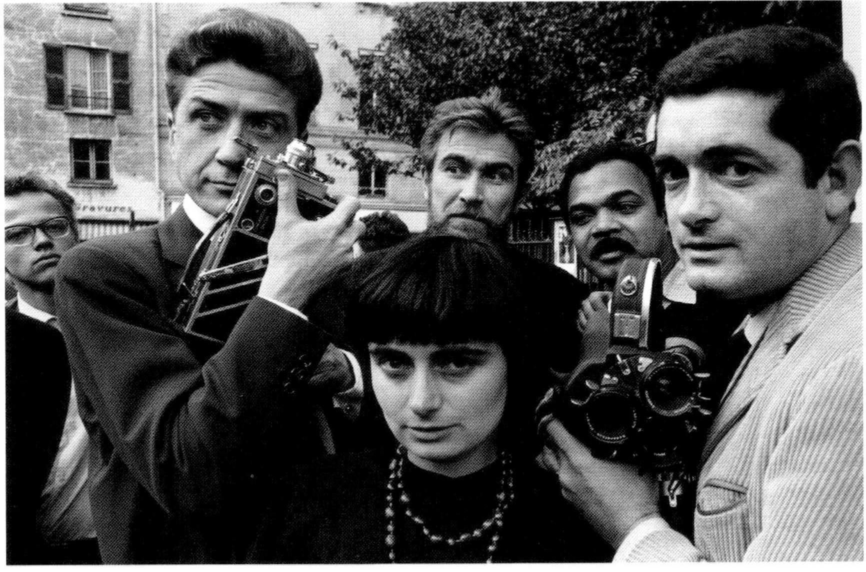

Foreground, from left: Alain Resnais, Agnès Varda, and Jacques Demy, Paris, 1965, photographed by William Klein

calls, her return visit to Los Angeles when *Faces Places* (2017) received a nomination for Best Documentary Feature, and my first visit to her home on rue Daguerre; I was accompanied on that trip by my friend the film critic Peter Debruge, whose thoughtful essay on Varda introduces this volume.

As others have reported, a friendship with Agnès wasn't a traditional friendship; rather, you were pulled into her orbit, often to help her or her friends, or to assist on her films or on other projects. I was honored to experience a wee bit of that Varda tradition. My first assignment came a couple of days before the 2018 Oscars: "I need to see *Ladybird*! I'm having lunch with Greta Gerwig on Monday." I obliged and drove a DVD to her son's house on the east side of town the next morning. Over coffee, we reviewed the pre-Oscars movie ads in the *New York Times*. "Explain *Dunkirk* to me!" she demanded, her finger pressing into the advertisement for the film. I tried my best, but she was a harsh critic and wasn't a fan of war films in general.

* * *

I was thrilled when the Academy Museum team asked me to collaborate with them on their preliminary work for the *Director's Inspiration* exhibition devoted to Agnès Varda and later to be the editor of this volume. Our work began during the pandemic closure and included a research trip to the Parisian beehive otherwise known as the Ciné-Tamaris archives on rue Daguerre, in Varda's former home and studio, in 2021. Ciné-Tamaris (originally Tamaris Films) is the production and distribution company Varda created when she made *La Pointe Courte* (1955), and it is today owned and operated by her daughter, Rosalie Varda. In addition to managing and distributing the films of Varda and Demy, Rosalie and her team have done an extraordinary job of organizing all

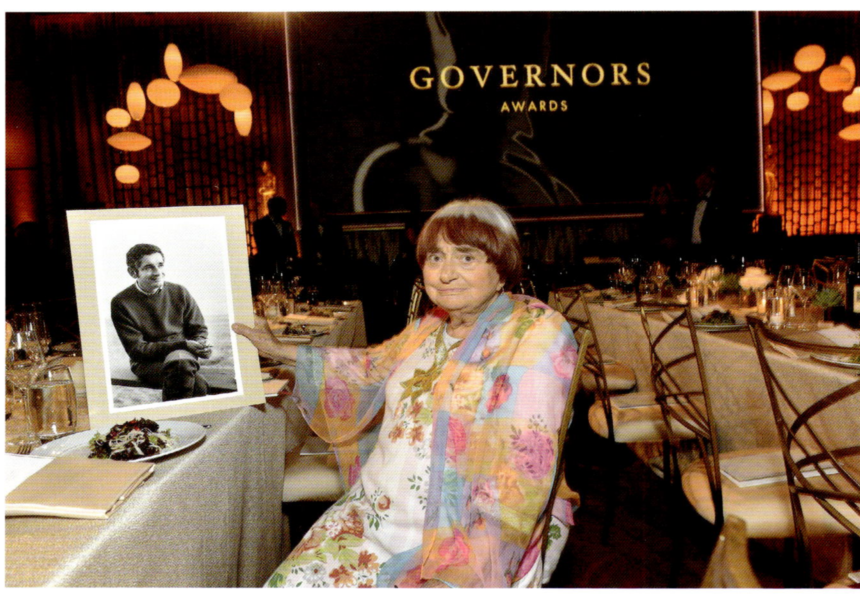

Varda holding a portrait of Demy at the Academy of Motion Picture Arts and Sciences' Governors Awards ceremony, 2017

the various papers and ephemera relating to her parents' work. Sorting through the Varda and Demy archives provided a rare opportunity to examine the process by which these singular filmmakers approached their art.

Both the exhibition and this book are arranged in three sections that mirror Varda's three lives as a photographer, filmmaker, and visual artist. Varda's first profession emerged after the war as a result of her passion for art: courses at the École du Louvre, where she had initially planned to become a curator, and evening classes at the Vaugirard School of Photography. Her skill with a Rolleiflex camera led to a 10-year stint as the official photographer for the Théâtre National Populaire (TNP). During that time, she wrote a "tentative scenario" that ultimately became her first film, which prefigured the French New Wave and propelled her second life as a filmmaker; this practice spanned more than six decades and encompassed a uniquely personal and boundary-pushing body of work. In 2003, the curator Hans Ulrich Obrist invited Varda to participate in the Venice

Biennale, and thus began her third life, creating installations for galleries and museums around the world, all while still taking photographs and making films. By the end of her life, these creative strands were all actively engaged. As Varda describes it in the visual history interview toward the end of this book, "When I began work as a photographer, I didn't know then I'd become a filmmaker. When I was a filmmaker, I didn't know that I'd dare to become an artist and put on exhibitions. This means that none of this was planned. I've tried to listen to what comes naturally, whatever enters my mind in my desire to create, and to follow those inspirations."

As we examined the contents of the Ciné-Tamaris archives, it was striking to see the abundant notebooks containing diagrams, storyboards, and drawings (often with pictures or postcards attached), along with handwritten script pages and newspaper clippings that were folded into her research. One could see how Varda's methodologies and writing style changed over the years. In the beginning, with her debut film, *La Pointe Courte*, her penmanship is neat and tiny; her notebooks are meticulously organized and laid out, with small drawings representing her film frames worked out in advance. She also created proof sheets by cutting out small (2¼ × 2¼ inches) images and arranging them on colored construction paper, carefully numbering and organizing them on each page. This precise and tidy writing style continues through the mid-1960s, with *Le Bonheur* (1965), and seems to evolve to a looser, free-flowing style after Varda and Demy moved to Los Angeles in 1967. Varda considered Los Angeles a second home and made films here in both the 1960s and 1980s. Sasha Archibald's essay in this volume provides a rich biographical and historical context for these key films in the Varda filmography.

In one area of the archives' many rooms, there are shelves of bound binders with negatives and contact sheets for each of their films, through Varda's *The Gleaners and I* (2000). I was enchanted by Varda's photographs taken on the sets of Demy's films, dating roughly from *Lola* (1961) to *Donkey Skin* (1970). And I was further delighted to discover in the binders for those films exceptional portraits of Anouk Aimée, Catherine Deneuve, Jeanne Moreau, and Delphine Seyrig, all credited to Varda. Her naturalistic approach to capturing these iconic actors, combined with her innate skill for striking compositions, underscores the essential connection between photography and cinema in Varda's art: for her, they are intrinsically linked.

The photographs from Varda's first life as a still photographer—a selection of which appears in this book—get their own separate building across the street, located inside a courtyard. Housed therein are large flat files containing exhibition prints of the pictures she took while working for the TNP and portraits of artists and filmmakers such as

Catherine Deneuve during production of *The Umbrellas of Cherbourg* (1964), photographed by Varda

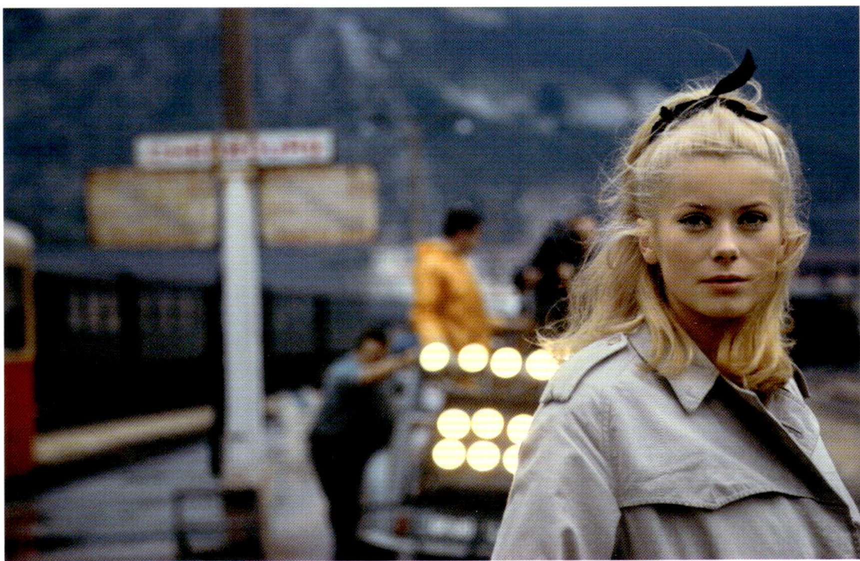

Brassaï, Alexander Calder, Salvador Dalí, Federico Fellini, and Luchino Visconti. One of her most beguiling is a portrait of the Hungarian artist Pierre Székely posing next to a curiosity cabinet, circa 1956, with his young daughter Anne-Maria. There are photos that Varda took around the world, including China, Italy, Portugal, and the United States. There are also exhibition prints of Varda's "autoportraits," including three that form a triptych of sorts from various stages of her life: a photomontage-mosaic she created in 1949 at the age of 20, a 1960 self-portrait in profile in front of a painting by Gentile Bellini, and an image of her face reflected in a myriad of mirrors from 2009.

The last of these self-portraits, *Autoportrait morcelé*, is included in the section of this book representing Varda's third career as a visual artist, which she embarked on in her 70s. The selection of memorable installations includes the Venice Biennale piece *Patatutopia (Spudotopia)*, comprising a video triptych featuring heart-shaped potatoes in various stages of decay, 1,500 pounds of the starchy vegetable on the floor, and Varda herself in costume as a large spud. Also featured is her series of Cinema Shacks, structures incorporating strips of celluloid from reels of her films, cleverly stretched over metal frameworks to create translucent walls of color and shadow. Varda took to this late career with great fervor, and the two- and three-dimensional art she created during this nearly 20-year period is often very personal in nature, returning to familiar subjects such as beaches, potatoes, cinema, widowhood, and her beloved cats. There is also an exuberance to these pieces. You feel her joy in activating this new creative side of herself.

Throughout her life, Varda refused to be pigeonholed: she was a master at reinvention and contradiction. To regard her solely as a filmmaker without considering her work as a photographer or, later, as a visual artist is to misunderstand the rich complexity of her career. To view her as "a little old lady, plump and talkative," as she describes herself in *The Beaches of Agnès* (2008), would be to disregard her fierce intelligence, seemingly limitless well of creativity, and feisty presence on and off film sets ("she was a tougher film director than any man I ever worked with," Warhol superstar Viva recounts in her contribution to this volume). And even though she aligned herself with women, feminism, and progressive causes, she rejected ever being categorized strictly as a feminist filmmaker.

These facets and contradictions are explored in the personal reflections in this book from some of her closest collaborators and ardent admirers. One vision that emerges repeatedly is of her as an indomitable life force, someone wholly committed to her vision and her art. Even though Varda had woven the subject of her own mortality into her art for a number of years, it was still a shock when this life force ended

Varda in her "Dame Patate" (Mrs. Potato) suit at the Paul Valery Museum in Sète, France, 2011. Costume: Joséphine Wister Faure

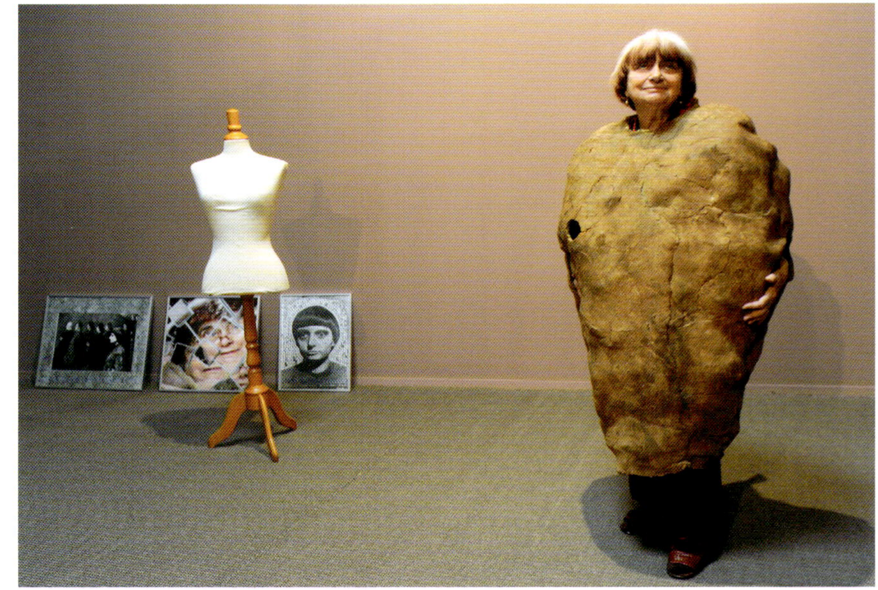

on March 29, 2019. Her funeral, held at Montparnasse Cemetery—where the street posts were mischievously painted by one of her grandsons in a two-color tribute to her hairstyle—was an unforgettable experience. Hundreds gathered to pay their respects. Varda's son, Mathieu Demy, told the story behind his mother's potato costume to the rapt, star-studded audience, grateful to laugh. At the end of the ceremony, musicians Matthieu Chedid and Yarol Poupaud performed a raucous extended version of the Doors' "L.A. Woman" as the attendees placed flowers and potatoes at Jacques and Agnès's shared grave. It's worth noting the Varda-like contradictions of this ceremony at the most stately of Parisian cemeteries with rock-and-roll soaring from its center, a fitting tribute to a woman who lived her life defiantly and passionately, on her own terms.

During our visit with the Ciné-Tamaris team in 2021, Rosalie showed us a handmade scrapbook Varda created for Jacques for Christmas around the time he made *Bay of Angels* (1963), including photos from the set of the film as well as old postcards, notes, and images. It's a small book that is essentially a multipage collage, a visual love letter to Demy. When I saw it, I thought, *"That's* what I want this book to be like." *Director's Inspiration: Agnès Varda* has been a dream project for me, and I'm grateful to everyone involved with its production. I hope the reader can sense our admiration for its subject and that the textures, images, and words help create a unique mosaic of this extraordinary artist: a visual love letter to Agnès Varda.

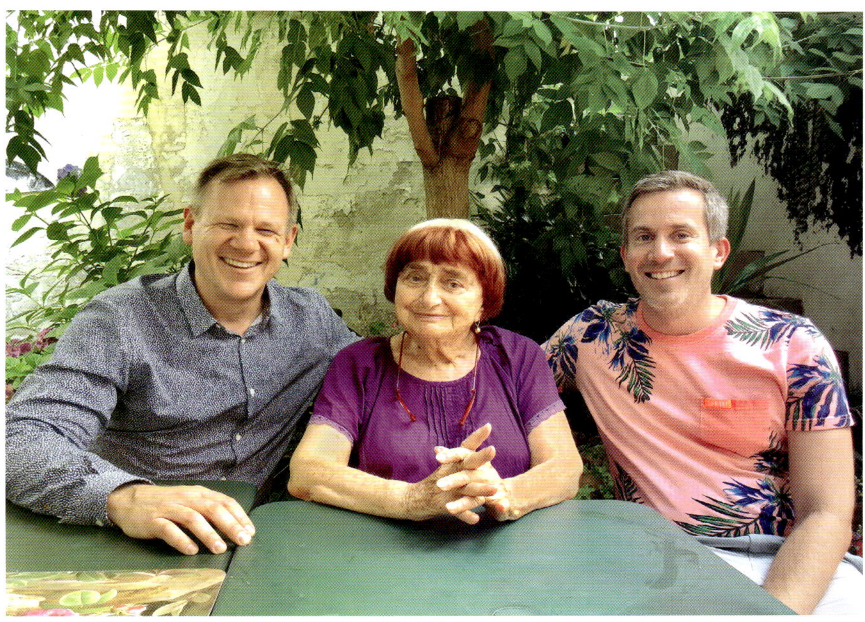

From left: Matt Severson, Varda, and Peter Debruge at Varda's home on rue Daguerre, Paris, 2018

NAVIGATING THE UNIVERSE OF AGNÈS VARDA

Peter Debruge

Filmmaker. Photographer. Feminist. Visual artist. Pioneer of the French New Wave. Oscar honoree. Working mom. Wife of the director Jacques Demy. Personal friend of Jean-Luc Godard, Jane Birkin, and Jim Morrison. Cat lover. Free spirit. Any of these labels could be used to describe Agnès Varda. Taken individually, none quite encapsulates this incredible woman's identity. In America, where Varda's films were relatively difficult to find until recently, her reputation remains even trickier to pin down: she's beloved by cinephiles but still largely unknown to the general public.

So, where to begin with a woman who was touted as a prodigy at age 26 and managed to remain quite radical in her approach toward every medium she touched through her 90th year? Do you start with her debut, *La Pointe Courte* (1955), a film that many historians now recognize as the first ripple of the French New Wave? Or is it better to work backward from the lively, career-spanning master class *Varda by Agnès*, which she presented at the Berlinale just weeks before her death, in 2019? With Varda, who loved beaches and constructed much of her art around them, the ideal approach is just to dive in and discover the sheer pleasure of seeing the world through her lens. One needn't be intimidated: Varda was one of the most approachable and unpretentious artists on the planet.

The most important and unique of her films is also the most unassuming: *The Gleaners and I* (2000). In this intimate, intricate, and formally inventive essay film, Varda likens herself to those who descend after the harvest or as the market packs up to collect the still-usable treasures left behind. She implies that her own method of filmmaking was not so different, amassing bits and bobs in her travels. The film features several of Varda's signature themes and techniques. It recenters those whom society considers outsiders or otherwise invisible, including artists, nonconformists, and the poor. "I never made films about the bourgeoisie, about heads of industry, bankers," Varda once explained. "I'm attracted by people who are out of place, people without power. I find them very interesting because by filming them, you give them…not power, but the dignity of inventing their own words."[1]

Varda and her subjects often break the fourth wall, gazing straight into the camera and directly into the audience's eyes. *The Gleaners and I* muses on the impact of time, with Varda embracing new technology even as she mourns disappearing customs, the unreliability of memory, and the onset of old age. Instead of paying homage to other movies, as so many directors do, Varda's references are often artistic or literary, explicitly identified, for example, in the scene where she salvages a reproduction of Jean-François Millet's painting *The Gleaners* (1857). Perhaps most importantly,

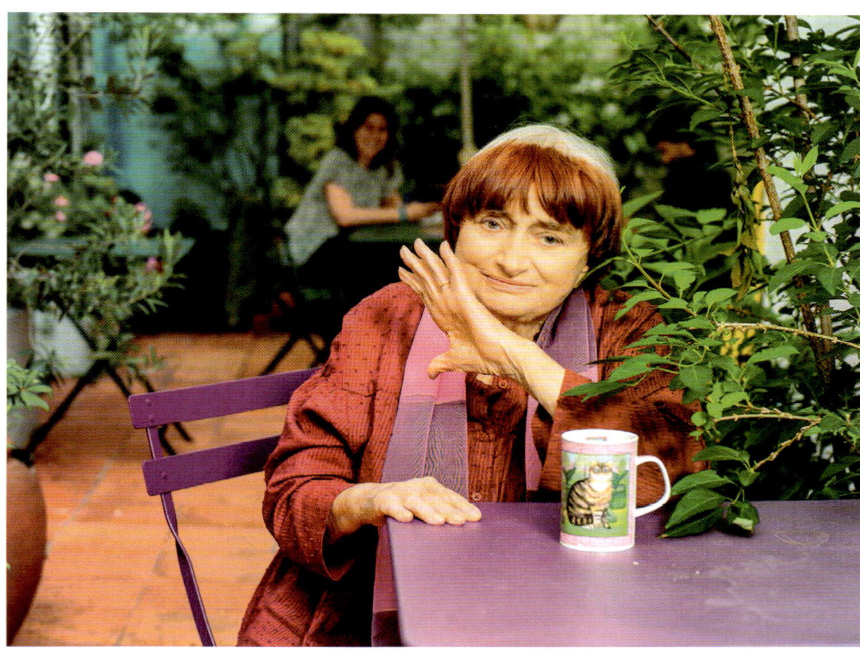

Agnès Varda at her home on rue Daguerre, Paris, 2018

the film displays her willingness to bring whimsy to her work, no matter how serious the subject, as in the scene where she films her outstretched hand "collecting" 18-wheelers on the autoroute, the way a child might. "I'd like to capture them. To hold on to what's passing by?" she asks via voice-over. "No, just for fun." Coming from a then-septuagenarian filmmaker, that capacity for play sets Varda apart.

From 1951 until her death, Varda lived in a modest house on rue Daguerre in Paris. It was impossible to miss. She decorated the white facade with giant purple polka dots and later painted it pink with a mauve-striped door and accents. When Varda moved in, the building was abandoned, lacking heat or proper plumbing, but she transformed it into something cozy and personal, as she so often did with her art. In time, she filled the space with trinkets and kids and cats. Varda loved cats. They feature in nearly all her films, with no fewer than 15 appearing in *La Pointe Courte* alone.

In later years, Varda expanded, operating her Ciné-Tamaris production company from the building next door and an abandoned shop across the street (the same street whose colorful characters she chronicles in the 1975 documentary *Daguerréotypes*). She'd sit in the front room editing her latest project but would stop for tea when admirers dropped by. Instead of being annoyed by such interruptions, she welcomed them. In Varda's view, sharing—that is, discussing audiences' personal reactions to her work—was the key reason to have made the films in the first place.[2] That sensibility distinguishes Varda from the vast majority of directors for whom making movies is so often a one-way act of transmission: they design their films so that audiences of all cultures and generations experience the story more or less the same. By contrast, for Varda each project resembled that proverbial message in a bottle. She sent them out

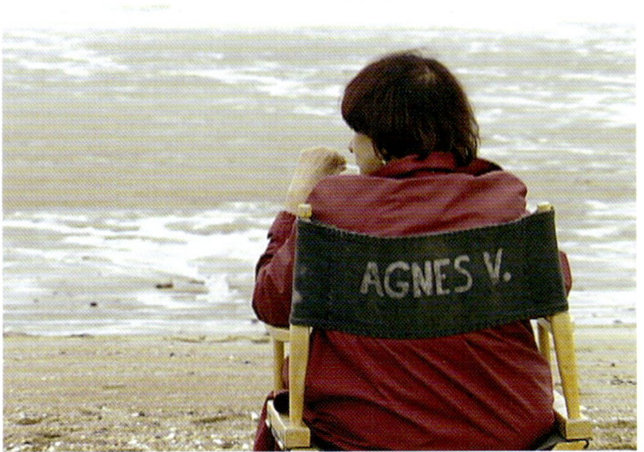

Varda in *The Beaches of Agnès* (2008)

into the world, hoping they might be read and interpreted differently by whoever received them. Perhaps that's why so many of her films feel like conversations with an old friend—albeit one who isn't afraid to challenge or contradict you should your ideas veer too far off-base.

Perhaps the ideal entry point for audiences unfamiliar with the woman and her oeuvre is another self-reflexive memory film, *The Beaches of Agnès* (2008). Varda appears on camera throughout, describing herself as "a little old lady, pleasantly plump and talkative." More than just modesty, this was strategy. By presenting herself as an innocuous old granny, Varda lures audiences into a kind of instant familiarity. But don't be fooled. Beneath the slightly kooky exterior was a serious artist, a trailblazer who never lost her sense of youthful rebellion, creative curiosity, and playful independence. Consider her hairstyle: a bowl cut, bleached white on top, fringed in rich burgundy dye. Fashionable Parisians, like New Yorkers, consider black the chicest of all colors, whereas Varda nearly always wore purple. No wonder one of her grandkids dubbed her "Mamita punk."[3]

Those same qualities are present in all of her work, from the 1962 classic *Cléo from 5 to 7*, in which a young Parisian singer (played by Corinne Marchand) awaits a possible cancer diagnosis, to *Vagabond* (1985), a quasi-documentary portrait of a fictional female hitchhiker (Sandrine Bonnaire, surrounded mostly by nonprofessional actors) that works backward from her death, observing the impact she made on the people she encountered along her route. Varda described *Vagabond* as "a puzzle, with not all of the pieces present," challenging the idea that we could ever truly know this woman who said no to society.[4]

These subjects may sound heavy, but Varda's treatment seldom was. She loved words and images alike, embracing both linguistic and visual puns. Even within a film as serious as *Vagabond*, there's room for wordplay: in one scene, Bonnaire's character accepts money offered in charity, calling the gift "du blé pour du pain" (dough for bread). In Varda's poetic and personal 16-minute short, *L'Opéra-Mouffe* (1958), subtitled "A Notebook Filmed by a Pregnant Woman in 1958," she cut from the swollen belly of a pregnant woman to a close-up of a ripe pumpkin being cleaved in two—a startling juxtaposition on par with the shock-cut in Luis Buñuel's *Un Chien Andalou* (1929), when a razor appears to slice through a woman's eye.

Born in Ixelles (a suburb of Brussels, Belgium) to a French mother and Greek refugee father in 1928, Varda was forced to flee with her family to the South of France when the Germans invaded in May 1940. Varda reinvented herself multiple times over the span of 90 years, starting at age 18, when she legally changed her first name from Arlette to Agnès. "I didn't like it because I don't like names with 'ette'—you know, it looks like a little girl's name," she has said.[5] That same year, Varda bought a train ticket to Marseille and passage by ship to Corsica without telling anyone. She was young, independent, and ready to conquer the world.

The world, it turned out, was constantly underestimating Agnès. After studying art history at the École du Louvre, she began her career as a photographer, a woman in a largely male field. Spotting her at a special session arranged for press, the director of Paris's Théâtre Hébertot called on Varda and teased: "And you, it's for *La Semaine de Suzette*?"—the equivalent of dismissing her as a correspondent for the teen magazine *Tiger Beat*.[6] Luckily, Varda had an instinct for image making. In 1951 she landed a job as official photographer for the Théâtre National Populaire (TNP), where she made friends with actors and intellectuals such as Jean Vilar and Gérard Philipe who introduced her to communist ideas and an egalitarian work ethic. Years later, when the film critic Richard Roud dubbed the arty, avant-garde subset of young French auteurs who lived and worked on the south side of Paris the "Left Bank Group," Varda embraced the term.[7] She identified "left" in geography and politics alike.

In French, the word for "director" varies, depending on whether the subject is male or female: *réalisateur* for men, *réalisatrice* for women. With Varda, people often added the word *petite* to her name—as in "la petite Varda" or "petite réalisatrice"—with a sense of affection that bordered on condescending.

Library card issued to Arlette Varda, 1948

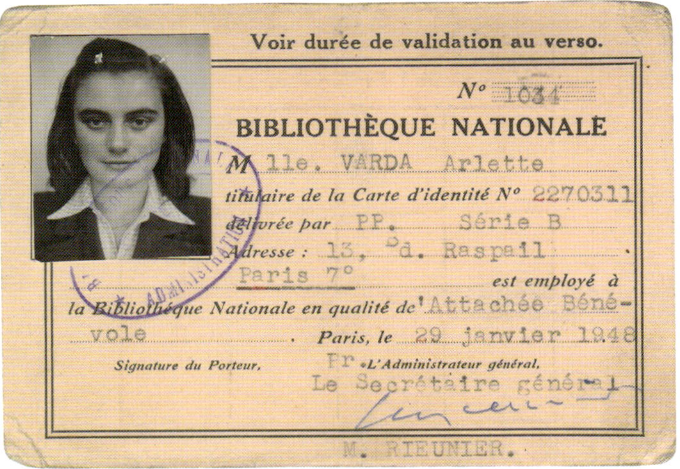

It is true that, standing just shy of 5 feet tall, Varda was smaller than most of the men in her field, a detail that's part and parcel of her cultural importance. Varda's gender and stature meant she could be a relatively nonthreatening and inconspicuous presence when filming documentaries. That helped in 1968, when she shot footage of Black Panther protests in Oakland, California. "I was this little woman with a 16mm camera," she recalls in the film *Varda by Agnès*. "I'd say, 'French television,' and they'd let me in while they were training."

Three decades earlier, when she first picked up a film camera to make *La Pointe Courte*, precious few *réalisatrices* had come before to show that such a thing might be possible. Alice Guy-Blaché and Germaine Dulac had worked as directors during the silent era, but they were exceptions. Filmmaking was seen as a man's profession, and in the exclusive French studio system of the time, to become a director meant paying one's dues: you started at the bottom and worked your way up the ladder. But not Varda. Naivete worked to her advantage. Longtime friend Martin Scorsese compared *La Pointe Courte*—which braids the story of a young couple deciding whether to call it quits with scenes of everyday struggle among the local fishermen—to the Italian neorealist tradition seen in films such as Roberto Rossellini's *Rome, Open City* (1945) and *Paisan* (1946).[8] While a stylistic affinity certainly exists, especially in her use of nonactors, Varda wasn't looking to Rossellini or his peers; she'd seen fewer than 10 movies before deciding to make one of her own, which meant she had few preconceived notions of what a feature ought to be.

In fact, Varda's inspiration was largely literary. *La Pointe Courte* was set in the poor fishing district of Sète, the coastal Mediterranean town where she had grown up on a houseboat during the war. Varda structured the film around a formal conceit that had impressed her in William Faulkner's *The Wild Palms* (1939), a novel in which two separate stories are told in alternating chapters, intertwined but never merging. "I loved the arts," Varda wrote of her mindset at the time. "I didn't necessarily love all of Picasso, nor all of Bram van Velde, and to be frank, I was incapable of reading Joyce's *Ulysses*. But his way of writing, the collages of Dos Passos, the freedom of tone of Cendrars, and the interiority of Virginia Woolf didn't seem to have an equivalent in the few films I'd heard about."[9] Varda's background may have been photography, but she wrote out a detailed script, complete with the shots and framing she envisioned.

She did not, however, have the first clue about how to edit the footage, and for this she reached out to Alain Resnais, who would go on to make *Hiroshima mon amour* (1959) and *Last Year at Marienbad* (1961). The entire project was financed with a modest loan from her parents and a resourceful idea borrowed from the TNP: instead of paying her crew, she offered them shares in the film. She proposed the same arrangement to Resnais, who declined at first but was eventually won over by Varda's determination. As Telluride Film Festival cofounder Tom Luddy put it during a 2019 tribute to Varda, "You can't say no to Agnès."[10]

Resnais and Varda hit it off. They would eventually become romantically involved, but in this early period, as friends and artistic collaborators, the pair simply inspired each other. Resnais was astonished by how few films Varda had seen and sent her to the Cinémathèque Française to catch up on the classics. She, in turn, showed him that there was no obstacle to making movies. Years later, Resnais affirmed, "Agnès Varda and Jean-Pierre Melville were the first ones to say, in effect, 'No, one does not need formal training to make a film.'"[11] For an entire generation of cinephiles and film critics—including Godard, François Truffaut, Claude Chabrol, and others writing for *Cahiers du Cinéma* at the time—Varda's and Melville's examples gave them license to follow suit.[12]

"When I was 32, they called me the 'grandmother of the New Wave,'" Varda once told the *Village Voice*, clearly amused that the nickname had been applied to her at such a young age.[13] Still, while Godard may have been just two years her junior, Varda got there first, putting into practice ideas that seemed merely theoretical in the pages of *Cahiers*: Alexandre Astruc had made the case for the *caméra-stylo* (camera-pen), while André Bazin floated the so-called auteur theory, arguing for a fresh way of seeing directors as the "authors" of their work. Varda even coined a word for her unique approach to film style: *cinécriture* (cinematic writing), by which she meant "the cutting, the movements, the points-of-view, the rhythm of filming and of editing have been felt and determined like the choices of a writer."[14]

La Pointe Courte was greeted with a tentative kind of respect—the American trade paper *Variety* misspelled the film's title, observing, "Main aspect of this film is that it was made for $20,000 by a 25-year-old girl"—and did not immediately open doors to other filmmaking opportunities.[15] "Obviously people in the movie business said it was a UFO, extraordinary but unreleasable," Varda later recalled.[16] In fact, for the next six decades Varda had to fight for nearly every project, including her Oscar-nominated 2017 documentary *Faces Places*, which she and fellow visual artist JR were able to fund via crowdsourcing. "I'm a perfect cultural gadget," Varda once said. "They have me in all libraries and cinémathèques. I'll be unforgotten. But they don't want me to make films."[17] Throughout the 1950s, Varda continued to work primarily as a photographer, but she accepted a couple of commissioned assignments for the French Tourism Office that gave her a chance to

practice filmmaking. While pregnant with her daughter, Rosalie, in 1958, she made *L'Opéra-Mouffe*. In it she looks at a street full of drunk, dispossessed faces and wonders how their mothers would feel to see them like this. Will her unborn child turn out like them?

That short got Varda invited to the Festival de Courts Métrages in Tours, where she met her future husband, Jacques Demy. The pair would go on to become what tabloids call a power couple: Demy directed extravagant, popular fantasies and won the Palme d'Or at Cannes for *The Umbrellas of Cherbourg* in 1964, two years after Varda premiered *Cléo from 5 to 7* there. But they did not interfere in each other's work, and their creative impulses were quite different, beautifully fused in the film *Jacquot de Nantes* (1991)—Demy's memoirs, as interpreted by Varda, when he was dying of AIDS and too weak to direct. "What I've been trying to do all along," she told the film critic

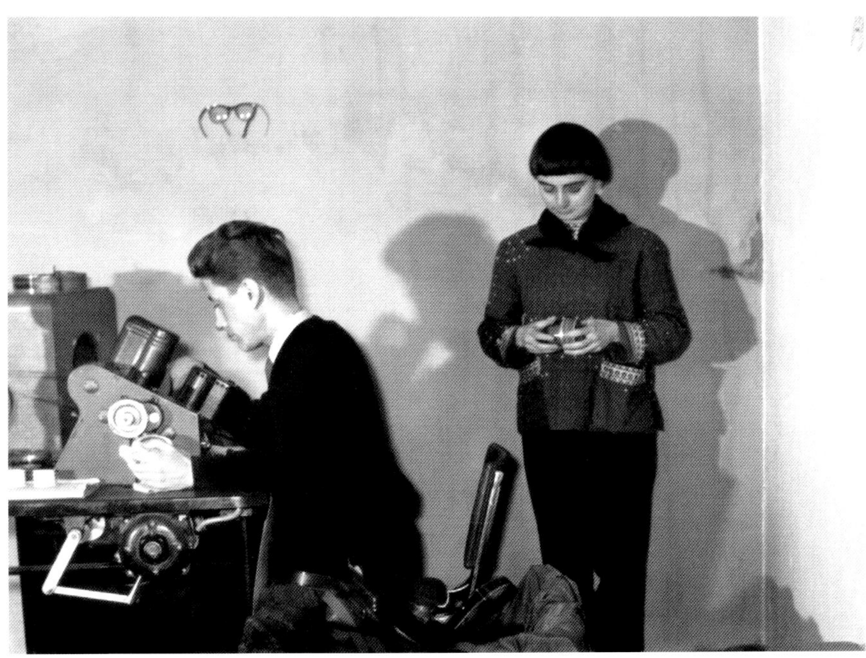

Alain Resnais and Varda editing *La Pointe Courte* (1955) on a Moritone flatbed

Melissa Anderson, "is to bridge the border of these two genres, documentary and fiction," as in the unscripted scene where she captured a street performer swallowing frogs in *Cléo*. The goal: "to put into fictional films the *texture* of documentary."[18]

For seven decades, as both photographer and filmmaker, Varda turned her camera on the marginalized and overlooked, focusing on aspects of humanity that other filmmakers ignored, like memory and motherhood, aging and abortion. "I like to film and get the best out of normal people," she said.[19] "Jacques, however bittersweet his own feelings about life, wanted to make films with music, feelings, and fake happy endings—let's put it that way. He loved some Hollywood films very strongly, including one that I hated, *Sound of Music* [1965]. I hate it so deeply that I said, 'If you love that film then we should break. How could you love a stupid, bullshit film like this, with that stupid baby-sitter who wishes to marry the father? I mean, is it interesting to see someone wash the pants of 11 children to get a man?' Please!"[20]

Demy and Varda split for more complicated reasons later on, but during their three decades together the couple inspired and supported each other. In 1960, seeing opportunity in the success of Truffaut's *The 400 Blows* (1959), the French producer Georges de Beauregard took a gamble, giving their friend Godard a chance to make a low-budget film in black and white. After *Breathless* (1960) became a hit, Beauregard asked Godard to recommend another young talent capable of doing the same. He named Demy, and thus *Lola* (1961) was made. When the producer next asked Demy to suggest someone else, he put forth Varda's name— and so *Cléo* came to be. It wasn't the feature Varda had intended to do next. A few years earlier, she'd been developing a high-concept color movie called *Le Mélangite*, a film in which her main character would have split

into five different versions of himself, each played by a different actor. She wanted to shoot in Venice with *L'Avventura* (1960) star Monica Vitti, but she could not secure funding. *Cléo* was a clever pivot, since it could be made cheaply on the streets of Paris.

According to Rosalie Varda, Demy had long dreamed of receiving a call from Hollywood. Finally, in 1967, after the international success of *The Umbrellas of Cherbourg*, Columbia Pictures invited him to Los Angeles to direct a film, the first of two times the family relocated to Los Angeles. Demy wound up making *Model Shop* (1969), a spirit sequel to *Lola*. The studio also expressed interest in working with Agnès, who didn't speak a word of English but taught herself by watching a dubbed version of *Cléo*. It was the Summer of Love, and she pitched a film called *Peace and Love* to Columbia but wound up walking away when the studio declined to give her director's cut. Many of that unrealized film's ideas found their way into *Lions Love (...and Lies)* (1969). Varda would have liked to make bigger films but instead succeeded in maintaining the creative freedom she craved by scaling her ambitions accordingly. When it comes to women and other marginalized filmmakers, the unproduced projects often say more than those that ultimately get made.[21]

"There's a difference between Hollywood films and mine," she told the *Los Angeles Times* in 1978. "Hollywood is doing them because they will make money. Mine will make money, too, but that is not my motivation. My pleasure is to show women in their totality—their joys, problems, potentials. And above all, the unique rhythms by which they live their lives."[22] Today, the film industry is making a concerted effort to give women a voice. But Varda didn't wait for permission to create, which made her a hero to many. Nor did she worry about the rules and conventions of the male-driven movies around her.

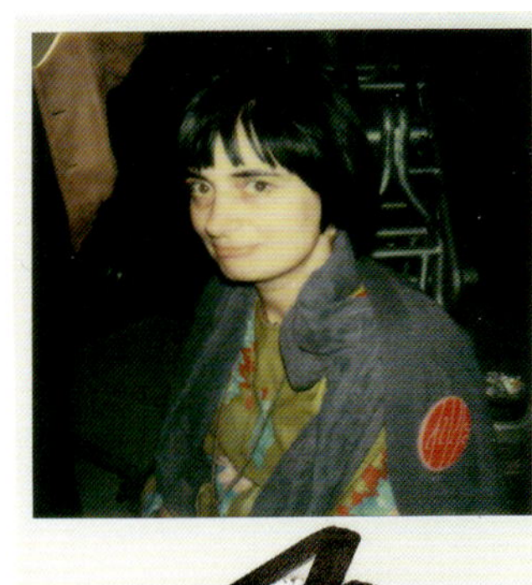

Photo of Varda taken and signed by Andy Warhol, 1973. According to Rosalie Varda, this was made at Cinecittà studios in Rome during the production of Warhol's *Flesh for Frankenstein* (1973).

Early in her acting career, Madonna wanted to do an American remake of *Cléo from 5 to 7*. On another occasion, Andy Warhol told Varda the original was a "divine movie" and convinced Factory superstar Viva that it would be a good idea to make a film with its creator. According to Varda, "He called Viva and introduced me as someone who had taken two months to shoot *Cléo from 5 to 7* and two months to edit it, whereas he would have shot between 5 and 7 o'clock and wouldn't have edited it."[23]

Viva agreed to appear in Varda's Los Angeles–based *Lions Love*, along with the underground filmmaker Shirley Clarke and the cowriters of *Hair* (1967), James Rado and Gerome Ragni. Warhol put the film on the cover of the first issue of *Interview* magazine in 1969. Varda was no hippie, but she was fascinated by their lifestyle. She clicked more with other outsider artists, making friends with Dennis Hopper, Monte Hellman, and Jim Morrison, among others.

A few years later, in Paris, Varda was the first person Morrison's girlfriend called when the singer died unexpectedly at age 27.[24] The Jim Morrison Varda knew was a sensitive artist with a poetic soul. He'd fallen out with his strict naval officer father, whose disapproval distressed him. When Varda got the call, she wasn't concerned with the cause of death but did her best to honor Morrison's wishes and dealt with the authorities herself. That meant bypassing an autopsy and arranging for him to be discreetly buried at Père Lachaise Cemetery, keeping the press and his conservative parents away from the funeral. Then, as at the end of her own life, Varda wasn't worried about rules.

Her second stint in Los Angeles, from 1980 to 1981, proved far trickier than the first. Varda and Demy were no longer together. He was coming to terms with his sexuality and trying to make a roller-skating fairy tale (tentatively titled *Skatarella* or *Cinderolla*), and she had followed so their

son, Mathieu, could see both of his parents.[25] It was during this time that Varda made her most personal film to date, *Documenteur* (1981), about a single mom raising her son alone in Venice Beach, California. It's a heartbreaking film, deeply felt and far more honest than the eponymous play on words suggests; in French, *menteur* means "liar." Varda gave it the subtitle "An Emotion Picture."

In 1988, at the age of 60, Varda finally put herself in the title of one of her films, *Jane B. par Agnès V.*, a postmodern portrait of the actor-singer Jane Birkin. In fact, Varda had been putting herself into her movies all along. From as far back as *L'Opéra-Mouffe*, her handwriting appears in the credits for many of her films, and throughout her filmography you can see her face reflected in mirrors and hear her voice, speaking either to her subjects or directly to the audience. Varda wasn't afraid to appear on camera; she was a diminutive but charismatic presence and made breaking the fourth wall seem perfectly natural. Long before documentaries became the widely celebrated 21st-century form they are now, Varda innovated the so-called essay film, of which *The Gleaners and I* was her most groundbreaking example.

During the last two decades of her career, this became Varda's working method: she embraced spontaneity in the act of recording the world—collecting what she could, like mutant potatoes from the reject pile, which to

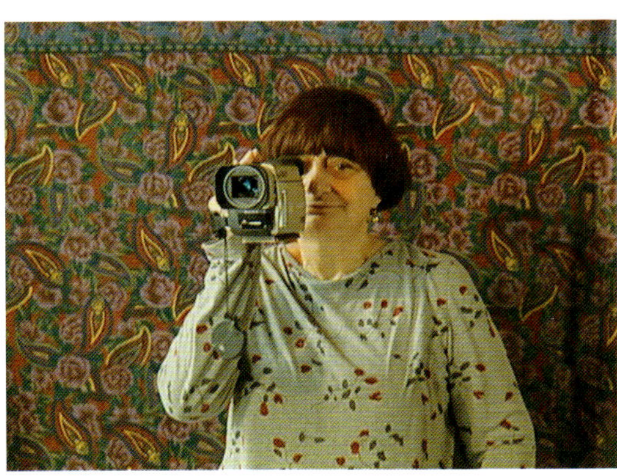

Varda in *The Gleaners and I* (2000)

25

Varda's eye suggested heart-shaped lucky charms—then spent ages shaping the material in the editing room. To audiences, Varda's later features often feel like inviting handmade collages or a crafty sort of audiovisual scrapbook, but that familiar, faux casual approach disguises just how sophisticated their construction truly is. Rosalie, who now oversees the Demy and Varda estates, says it was her mother's belief that viewers "should not see the work."[26] Ironically, making the associations Varda wanted the audience to experience look spontaneous, as if they were happening entirely in spectators' heads, took enormous effort to pull off.

Early in her career, Varda, the former art student, had looked to the experimentation she saw happening in literature to inspire her cinema. By the mid-1980s, when she made *Vagabond*, she had found a new way of working, steered by emotion and intuition. Here Varda found herself envious of the way painters work: "I saw them paint, stop, step back, take some distance and look things over before going back to work. For five to ten years, my method has been to improvise freely around a well-prepared structure, but I lack the time."[27]

In the making of *Gleaners*, Varda used a digital camera, which allowed her to easily pick up missing shots. The apparatus was light enough that she could film her own hands, which she did, examining the effects of aging on her skin—another subject that rarely arises in commercial cinema but which she confronted head-on. In her final movies, one finds Varda contemplating her own mortality, much as Cléo had all those years ago on a summer afternoon in Paris. She visits graves and revisits old friends; in *Faces Places*, Godard famously refuses to answer the door.

This, too, fits the pattern. Much of Varda's work circles back to earlier projects—not so much recycling the past as reexamining

it through fresh eyes. These include the 1983 short film *Ulysse*, in which she seeks out two models she'd photographed nearly three decades earlier; a short documentary called *The Young Girls Turn 25* (1993), in which she blends behind-the-scenes footage she'd taken on the set of Demy's *The Young Girls of Rochefort* (1967) with interviews of Catherine Deneuve and residents of Rochefort who fondly remember the production a quarter century later; *The World of Jacques Demy* (1995), a feature-length tribute to her late husband; and her hourlong follow-up *The Gleaners and I: Two Years Later* (2002). Toward the end of her life, Varda turned her attention to visual art, creating video installations and physical objects. One of these— a shack made of celluloid, in which she repurposed prints of her films *Le Bonheur* (1965) and *The Creatures* (1966) and turned them into the skylights and walls of a translucent structure—splendidly illustrates how her films were never meant to stay fixed in people's minds but could become whatever our imaginations wanted them to be.

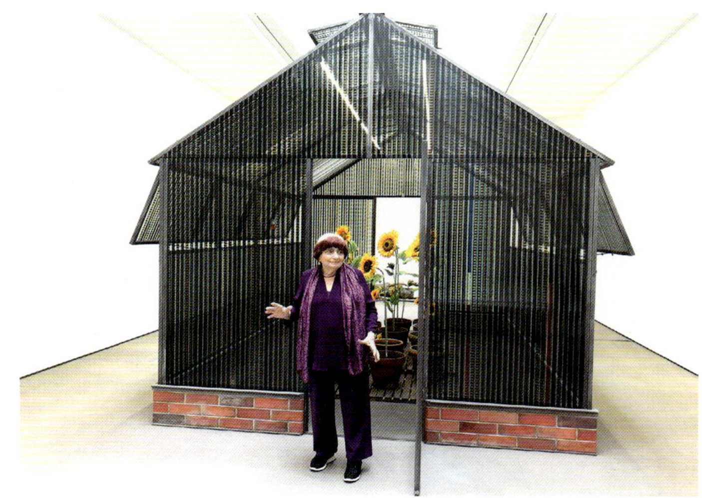

Varda at the opening of her exhibition *Une cabane de cinema, la serre du Bonheur* (A cinema hut, the greenhouse of happiness) at Galerie Nathalie Obadia, Paris, 2018

Notes

1 Giovanni Marchini Camia, "Interview with Agnès Varda," *Fireflies* 5 (2017): 88.

2 I first met Agnès Varda at a screening of the director Maïwenn's film *Polisse* at the 2011 Cannes Film Festival. She invited me to stop by her atelier on rue Daguerre the next time I was in Paris, which of course I did. Then, and in the years to come, she was receptive to hearing my thoughts but not shy about debating them when she saw fit.

3 Owen Myers, "Agnès Varda's Last Interview: 'I Fought for Radical Cinema All My Life,'" *The Guardian*, March 29, 2019, https://www.theguardian.com/film/2019/mar/29/agnes-varda-last-interview-i-fought-for-radical-cinema-all-my-life.

4 Rob Edelman, "Travelling a Different Route: An Interview with Agnès Varda," *Cineaste* 15, no. 1 (1986): 20.

5 Myers, "Agnès Varda's Last Interview."

6 Agnès Varda, *Varda par Agnès* (Paris: Cahiers du Cinéma, 1994), 38. This and all subsequent translations are mine.

7. Richard Roud, "The Left Bank: Marker, Varda, Resnais," *Sight and Sound* 32, no. 1 (Winter 1962/1963): 24–26.

8 "Telluride Film Festival 2019" supplement, disc 1, *The Complete Films of Agnès Varda* (New York: Criterion Collection, 2020), Blu-ray.

9 Varda, *Varda par Agnès*, 38.

10 "Telluride Film Festival 2019" supplement. Luddy should know. In 1967 he introduced Varda to the artist Jean Varda, a long-lost relative of hers living on a houseboat in Sausalito, California. Agnès was immediately inspired by the encounter and wanted to go back right away to film this reunion, relying on Luddy to find her a local crew. Two days later, they were shooting what would become *Uncle Yanco* (1968).

11 Peter Cowie, *Revolution! The Explosion of World Cinema in the 60s* (London: Faber and Faber, 2006), 29.

12 Melville started to make films outside the system in the late 1940s, converting an abandoned factory on rue Jenner into his own independent studio in 1955, the same year Varda made *La Pointe Courte*.

13 Steven Drachman, "A Simple Life," *Village Voice*, June 29, 1993, 58.

14 Varda, *Varda par Agnès*, 14.

15 Gene Moskowitz, "Capsule Foreign Film Reviews: *La Pointe Courtel* [*sic*]," *Variety*, July 11, 1956, 10.

16 Cowie, *Revolution!*, 30.

17 Barbara Quart, "Agnès Varda: A Conversation," *Film Quarterly* 40, no. 2 (Winter 1986–87): 10.

18 Melissa Anderson, "The Modest Gesture of the Filmmaker: An Interview with Agnès Varda," *Cineaste* 26, no. 4 (Fall 2001): 27.

19 Simon Hattenstone, "Spot the Genius: Agnès Varda on Ageing, the Nouvelle Vague and Waiting for Godard," *The Guardian: G2*, September 21, 2018, 9.

20 Drachman, "A Simple Life," 58.

21 In 1965, three years before France's younger generation took to the streets in protest, Varda shot test scenes with Gérard Depardieu about these young rebels. The film, *A Christmas Carol*, would have been the actor's first feature. Years later, inspired by a news report of an unarmed (and unclothed) man shot and killed by Los Angeles police, she wrote *Maria and the Naked Man*.

22 Joan Owens, "Varda—At Ease in Her Own Contradictions," *Los Angeles Times*, August 6, 1978, 28.

23 Varda, *Varda par Agnès*, 34.

24 Agnès Varda, conversation with the author, March 6, 2018.

25 Varda, *Varda par Agnès*, 216.

26 Rosalie Varda, conversation with the author, August 21, 2022.

27 Françoise Audé, "Conversation avec Agnès Varda," *Positif* 325 (March 1988): 2–3.

FIRST LIFE:
PHOTOGRAPHER

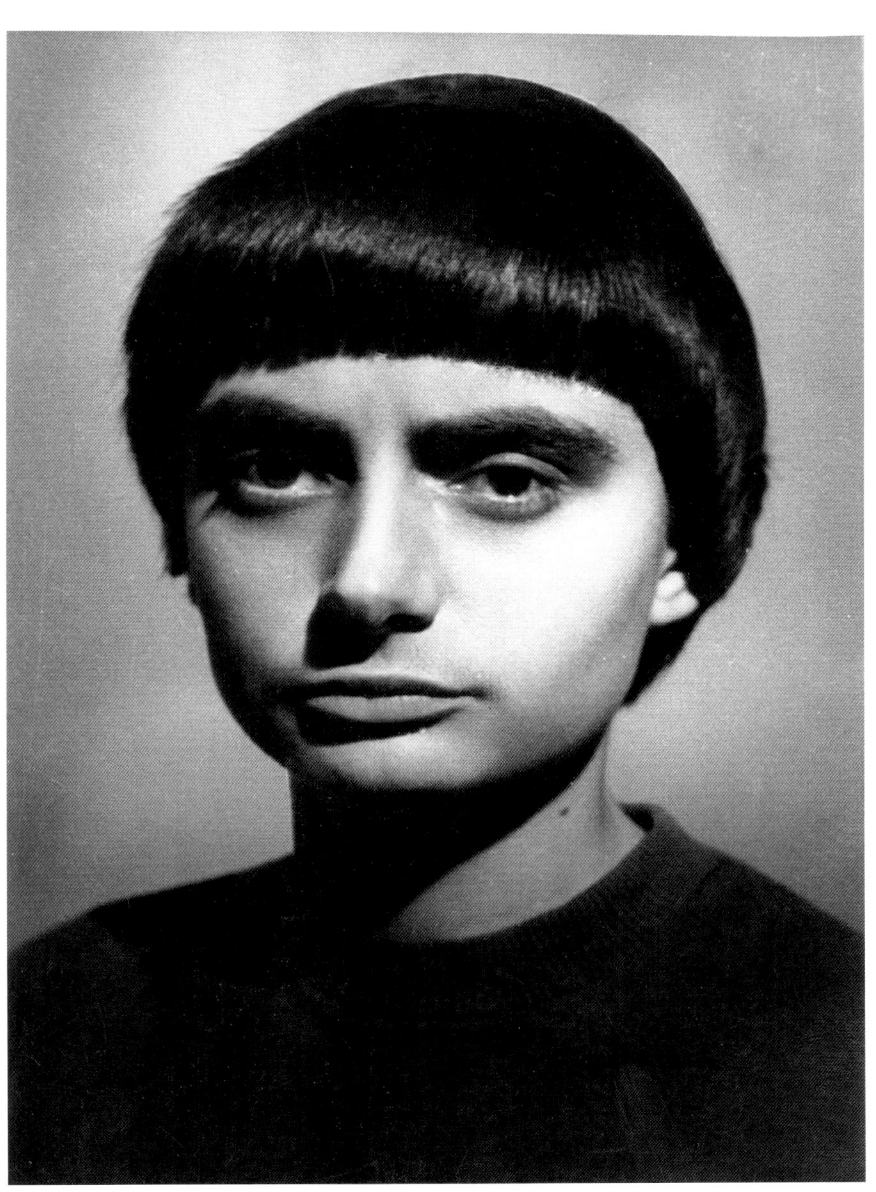

Autoportrait, 1949

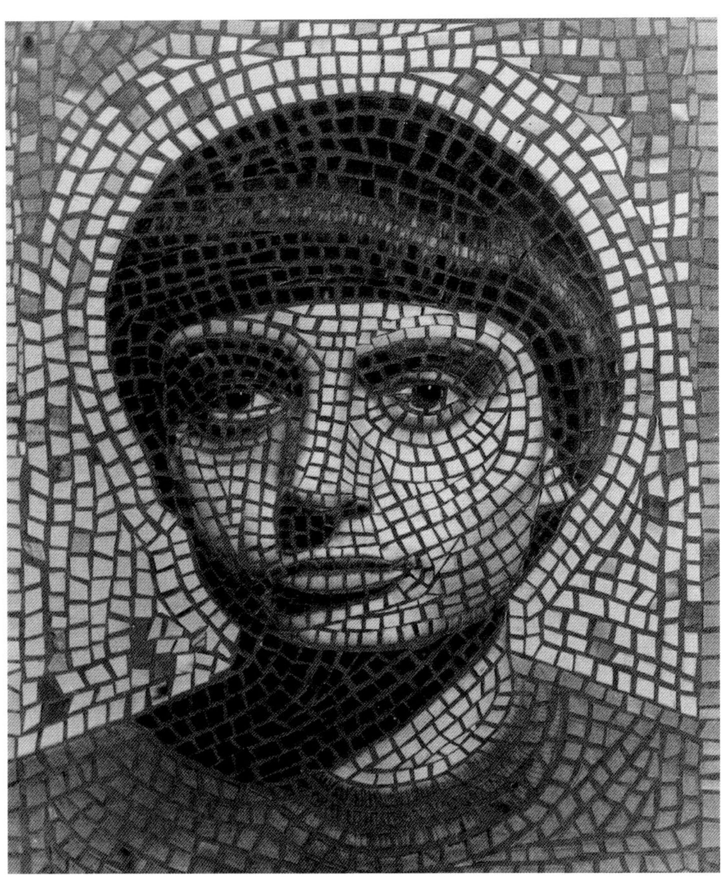

—

I studied to be a museum curator at the Louvre for four years. Suddenly I thought I would be spending my life in a little town, filing things. Maybe there would be four or ten good paintings; the rest are in Leningrad and New York, as we all know. So, I changed my mind and became a still photographer.

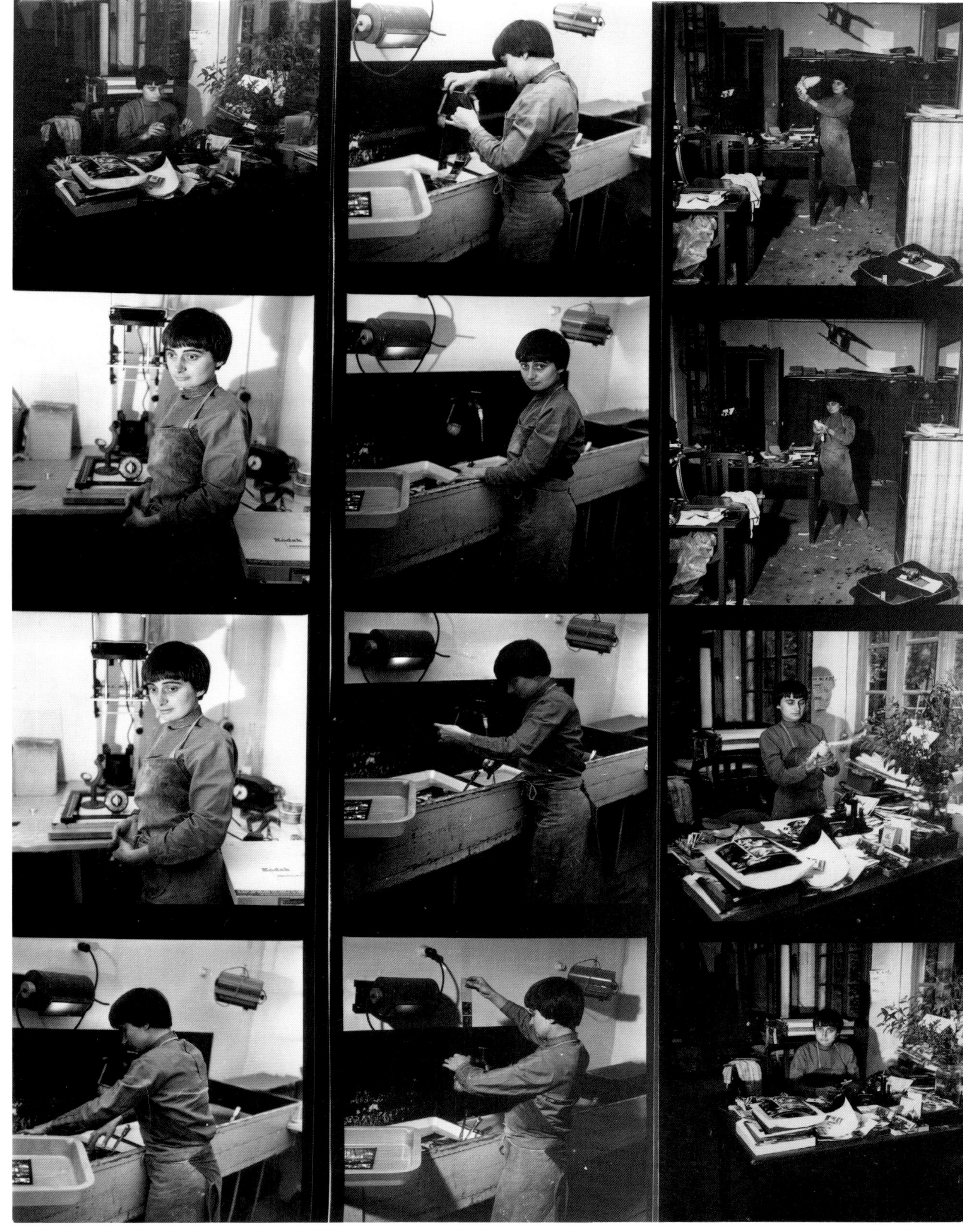

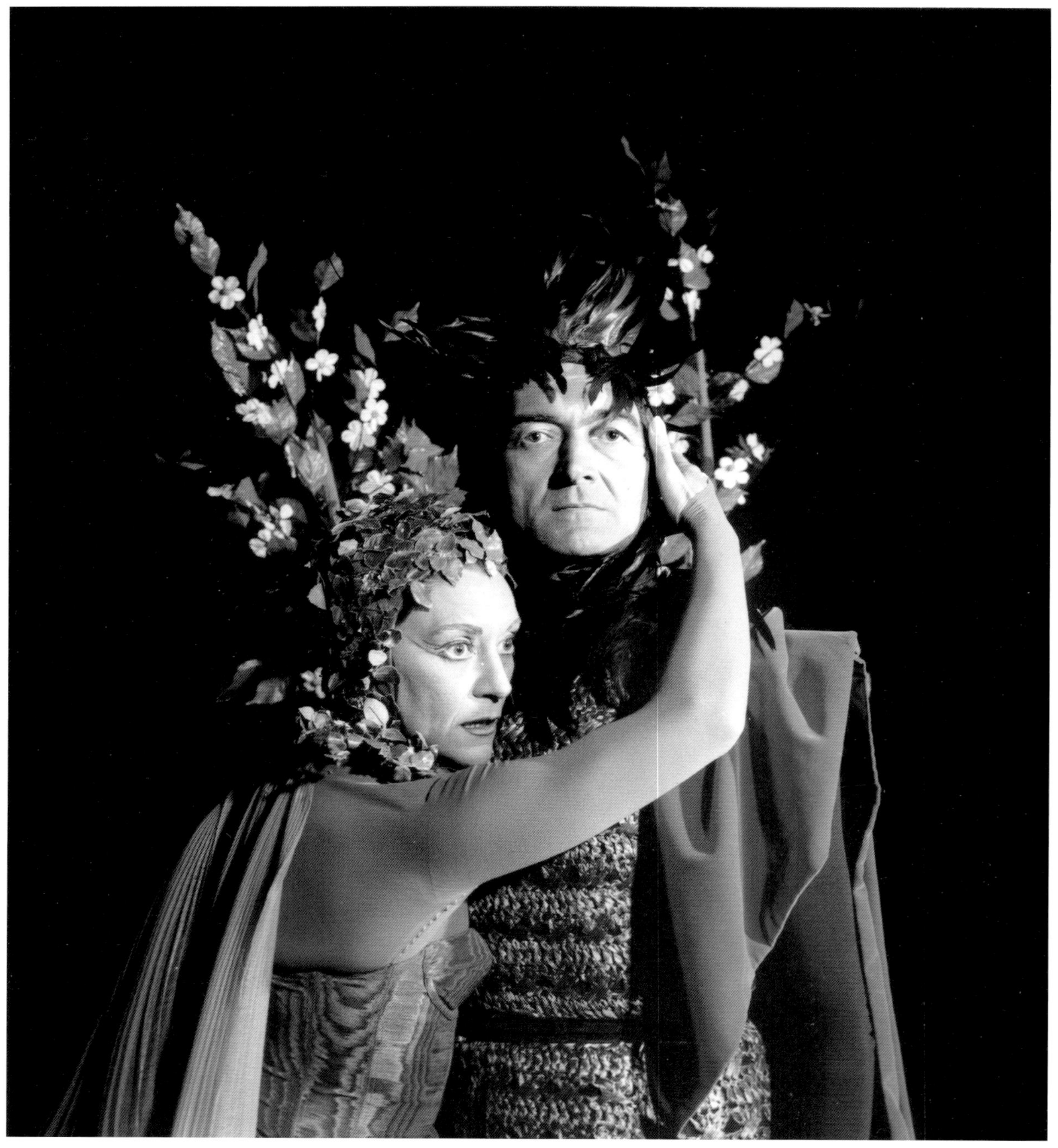

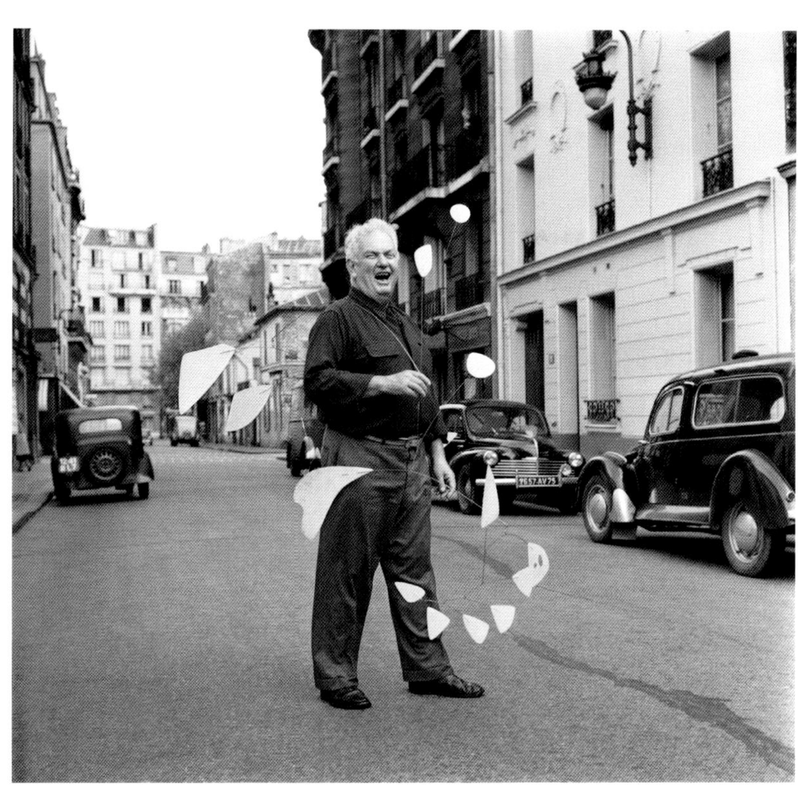

Varda worked as official photographer for the Théâtre National Populaire from 1950 to 1961. She also took freelance magazine assignments, photographing artists and filmmakers such as Salvador Dalí, Federico Fellini, and Luchino Visconti.

Opposite: *Maria Casarès and Jean Vilar in* A Midsummer Night's Dream, *Festival d'Avignon*, 1959

Above: *Alexander Calder with* 21 White Sheets (1953)*, Paris*, 1954

Right: *Salvador Dali in Port-Llegat*, 1955

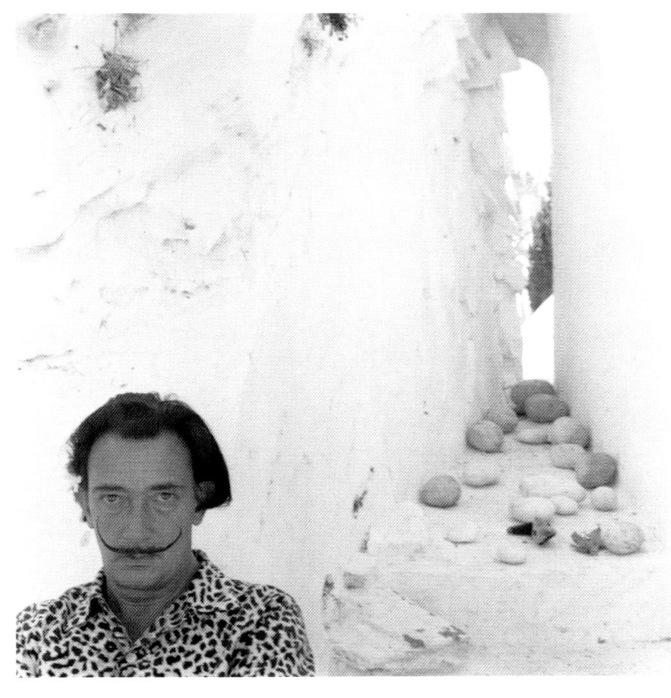

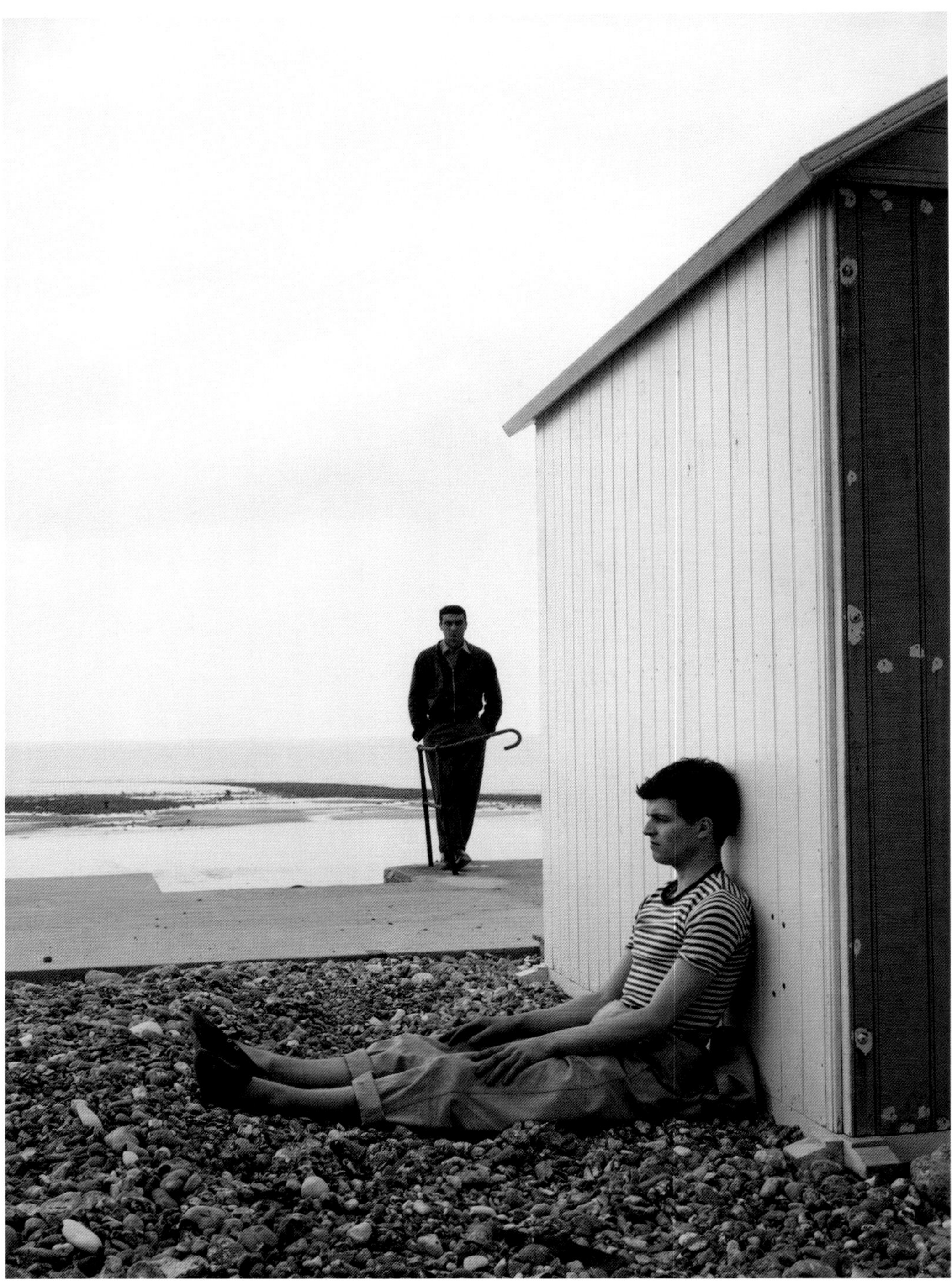

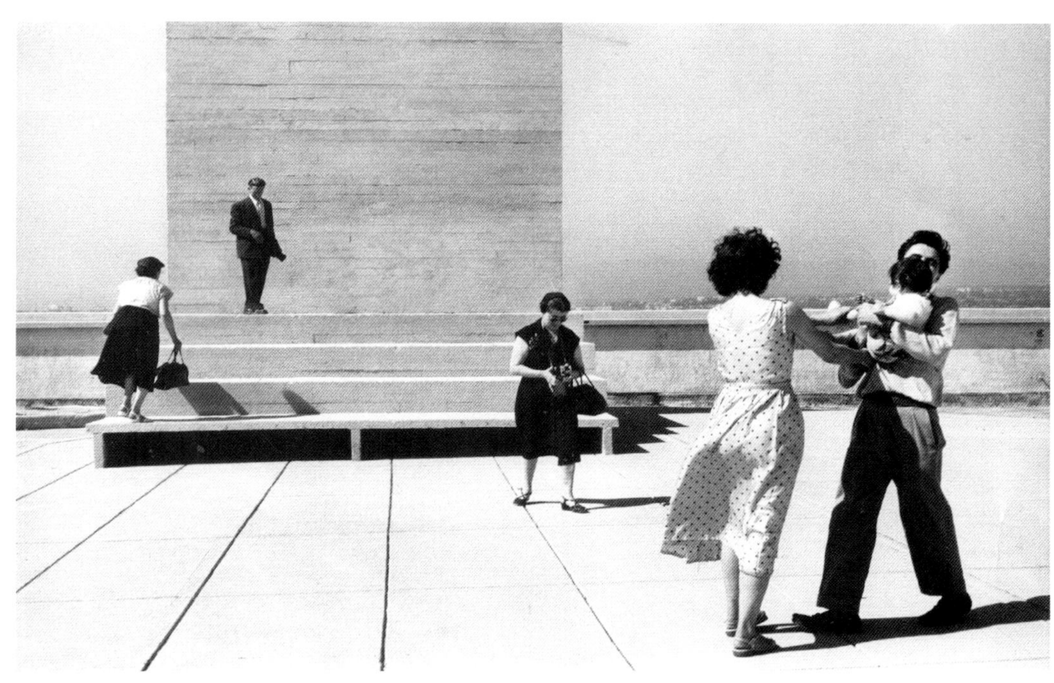

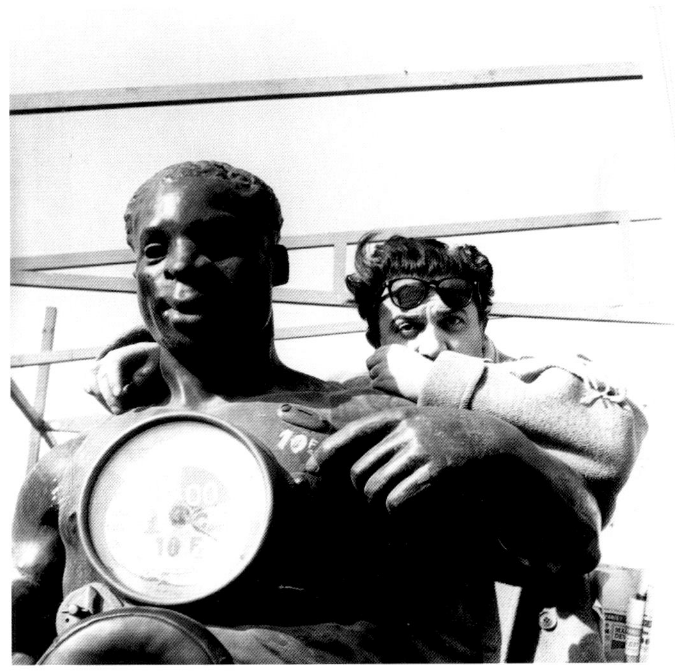

Opposite: *Guy Bourdin*, 1954. Varda would later use this photo for a seaside installation piece cocreated with JR and documented in *Faces Places* (2017). In an interview for that film's release, she explains, "I was extremely moved by how the meaning of the photo was transformed, of what it briefly became. Then in came the tide and washed it all away."

Above: *La terasse du Corbusier à Marseille*, 1956

Right: *Federico Fellini, Paris*, 1956

When I began work as a photographer, I didn't know then I'd become a filmmaker.

Ulysse, 1954. This haunting photograph would become the subject of a short essay film by Varda in 1982. She recalls: "Ulysse is the name of the little boy at the center of the photograph I took in 1954, on a beach in Normandy. Twenty-eight years later, I explored this image, my memories, and those of the people who posed for it. What is an image? And what is a film about an image?"

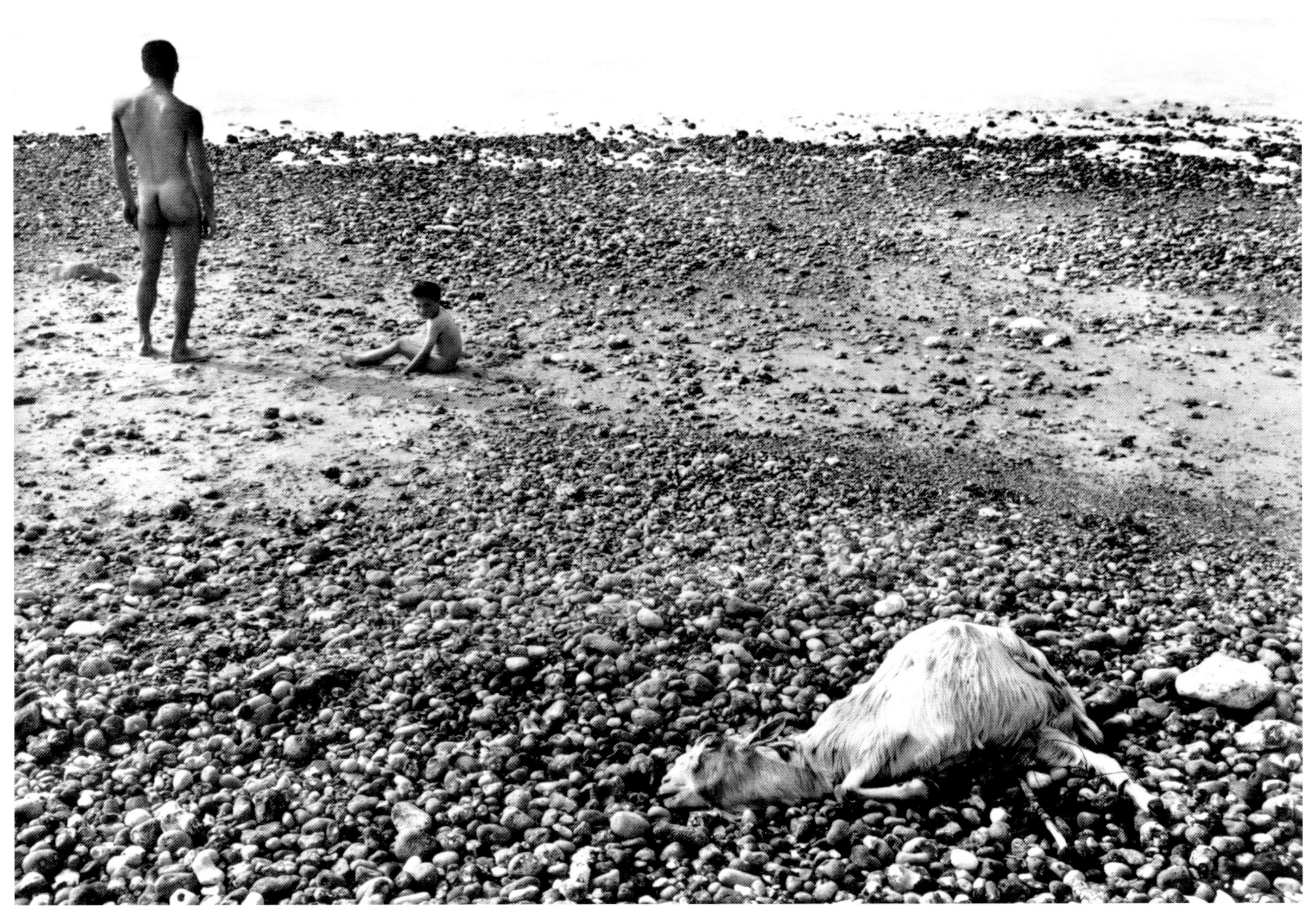

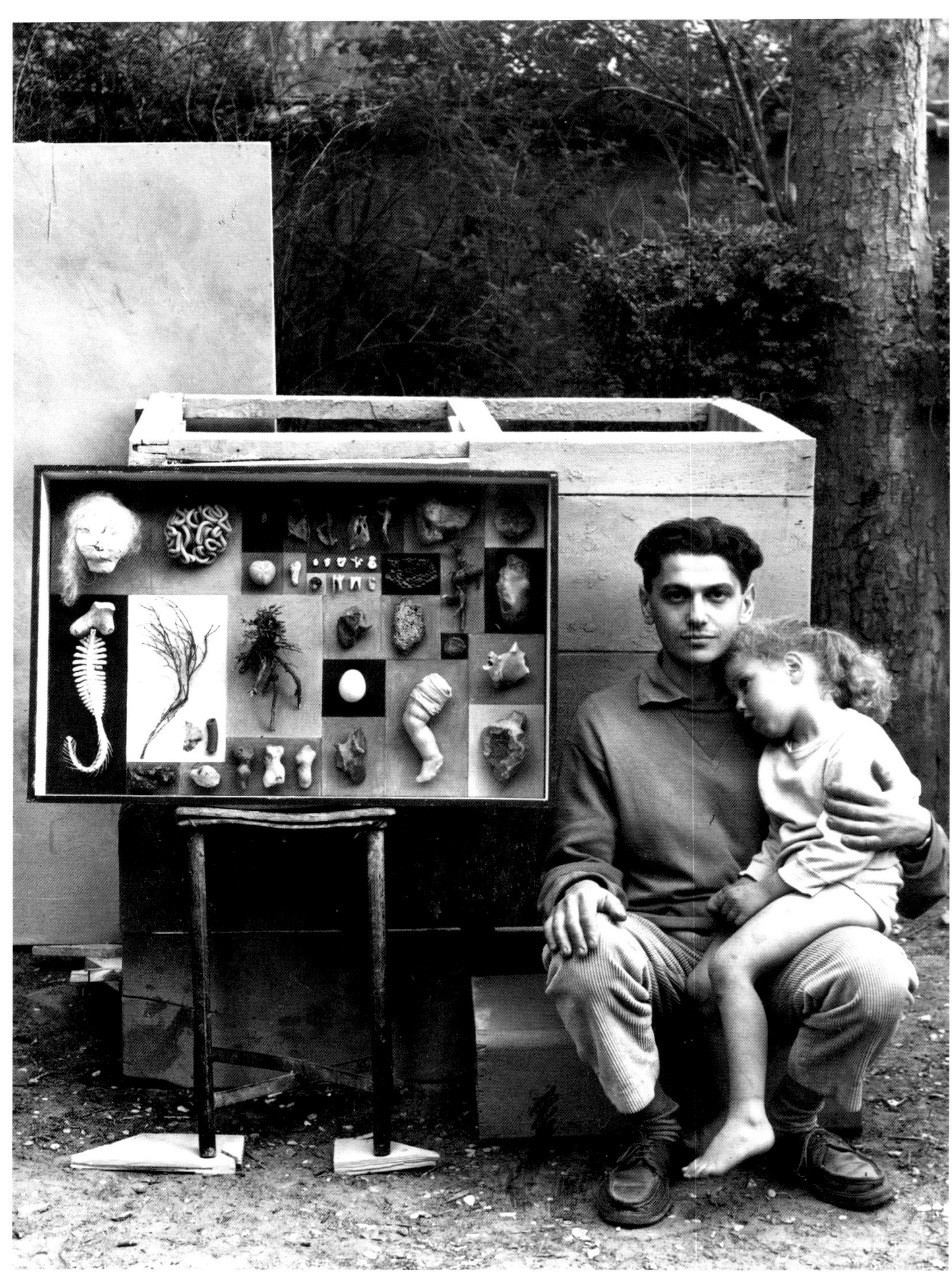

Pierre Székely, Anne-Maria Székely and La Table des Matières, ca. 1956

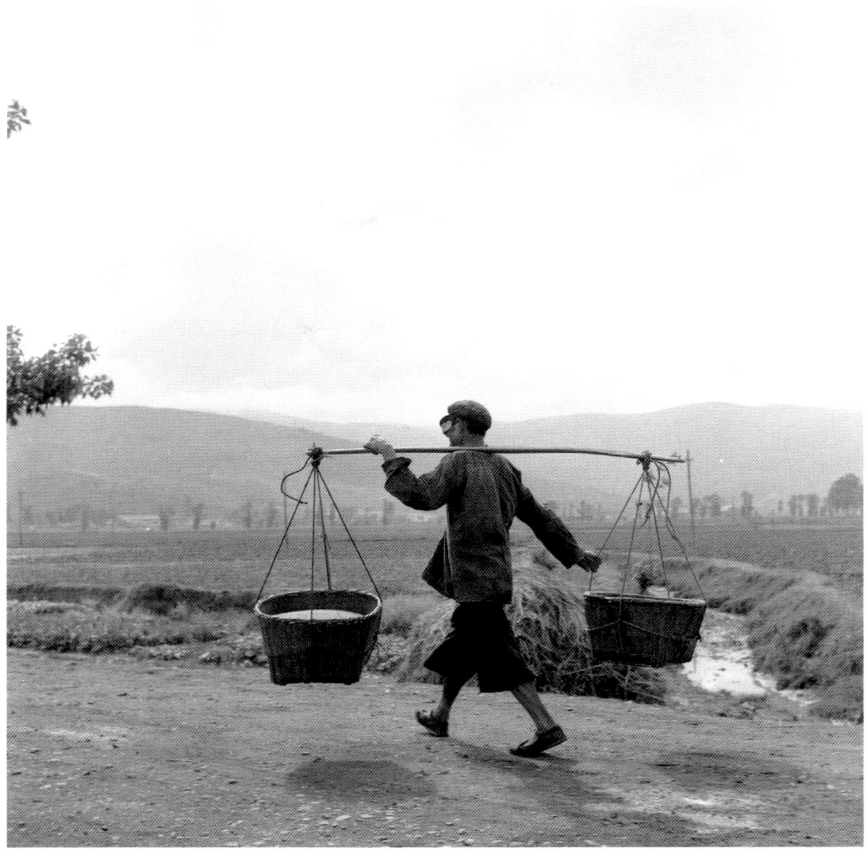

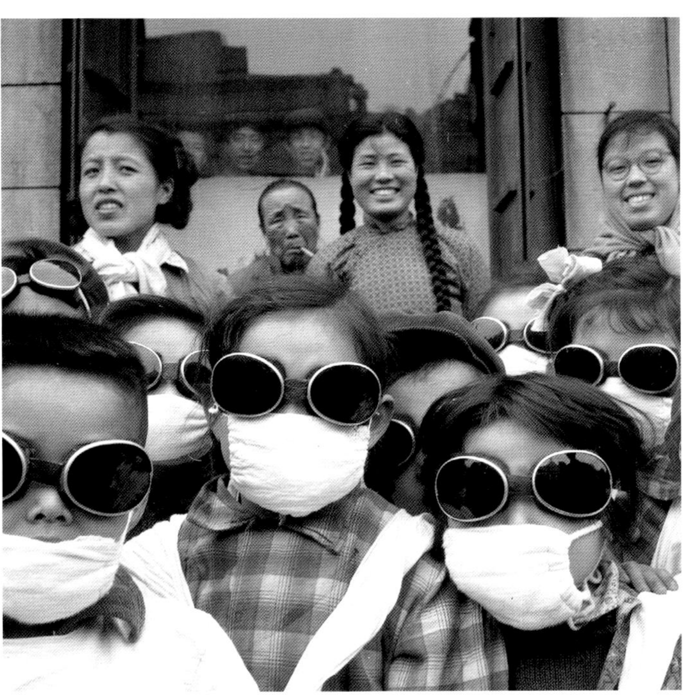

For two months in 1957, Varda traveled throughout China with a delegation of French dignitaries. "There were millions of bikes and little children as beautiful as little cats," she would later recall. "In our chaotic world full of disasters, hate and suffering, it helps me to believe that cultural exchange is good for everyone. Art is a wind we need to feel blow."

Above: *The Water Porter, China*, 1957

Left: *China, Schoolgirls wearing face masks (to protect them from the sand from the Gobi Desert)*, 1957

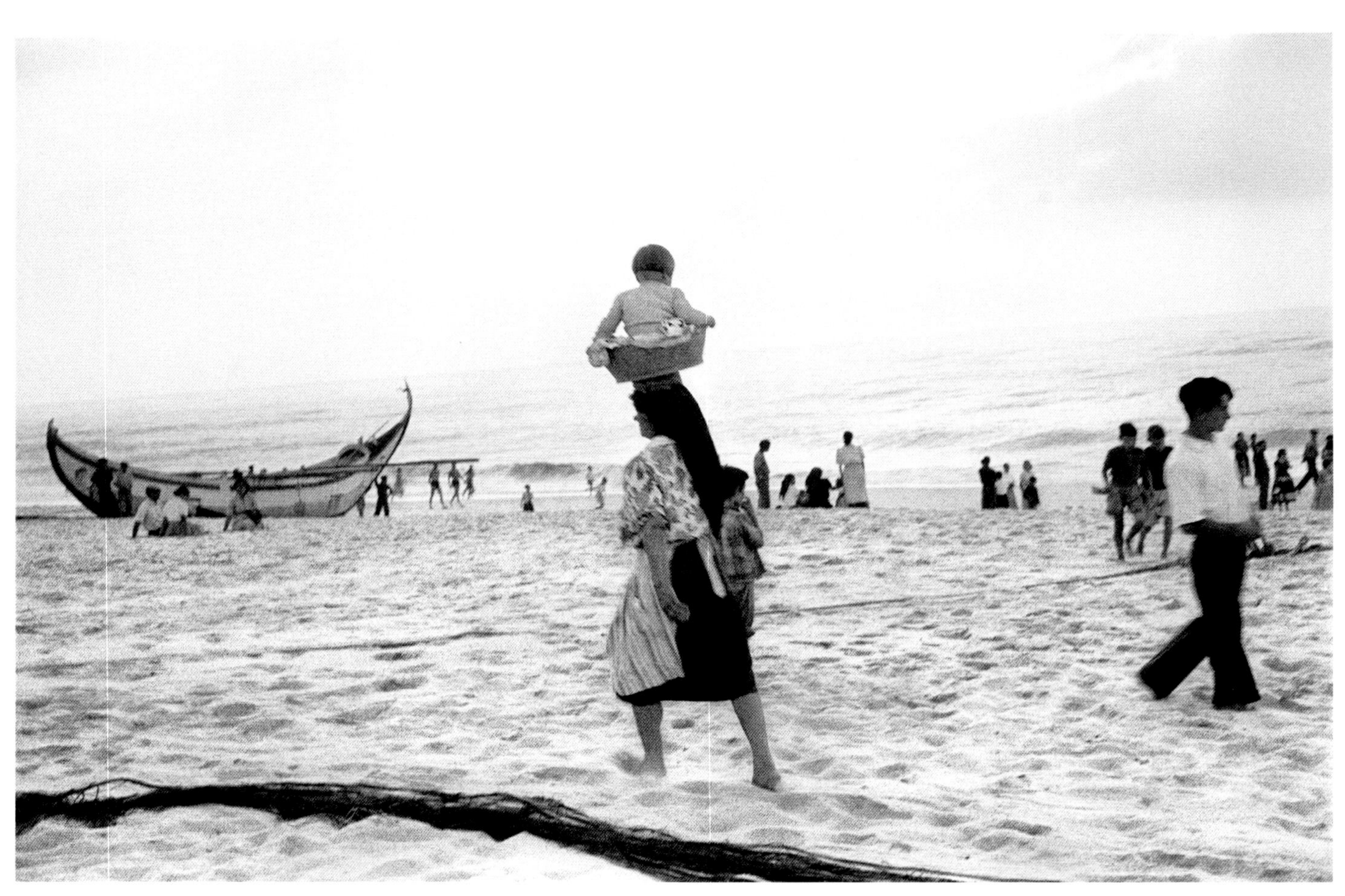

Above: *Nazaré, Portugal,*
1956

Opposite: *Sophia Loren
au Portugal, Povoa de
Varzim*, 1956

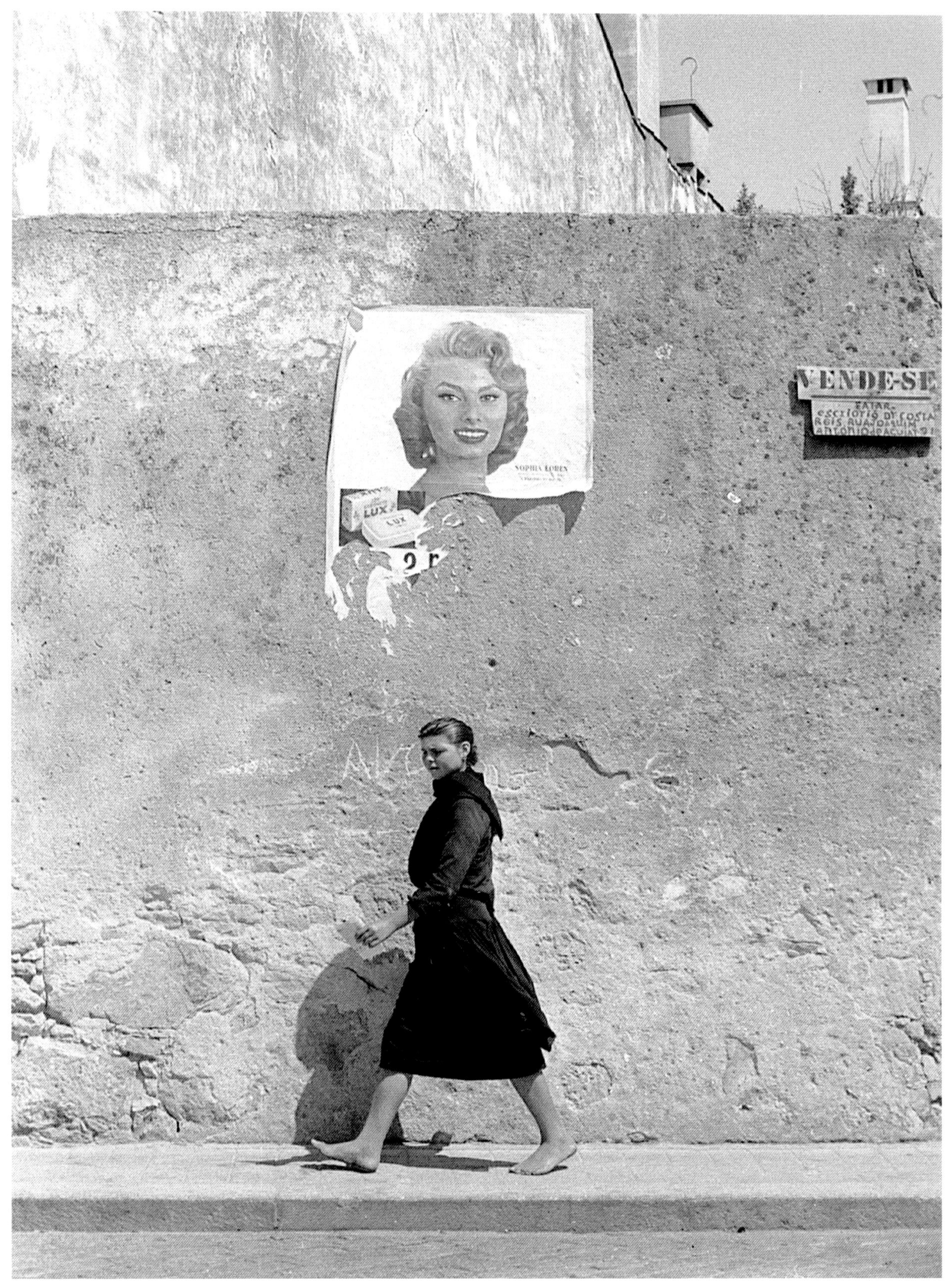
SOPHIA LOREN
LUX
VENDE-SE

Varda and her family moved to Los Angeles in 1967. "[In California] we had peace and love, we had flower children, we had love-ins and sit-ins and huge free concerts. What we found was a real desire for brotherhood that was magnificent, that wasn't just about making demands."

This page and opposite: *Love-in, Griffith Park, Los Angeles*, 1968

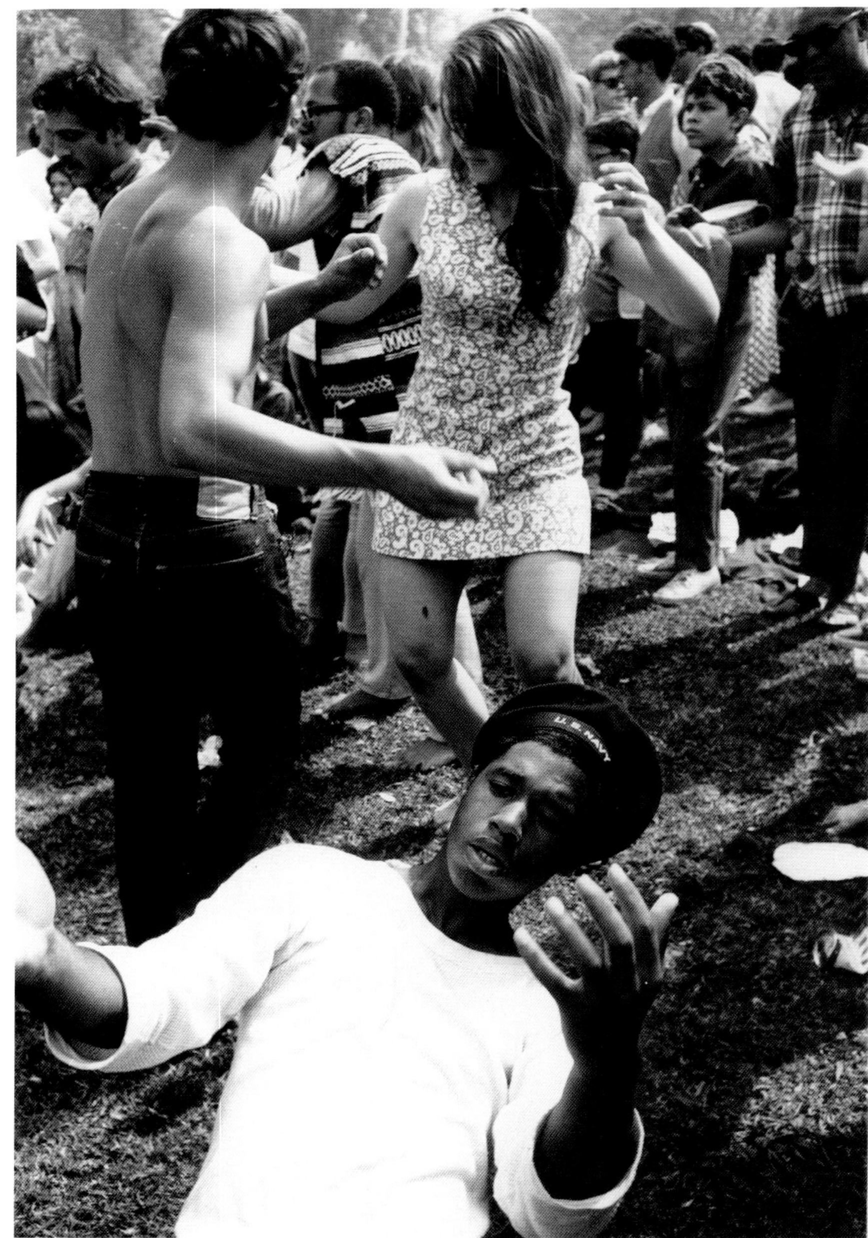

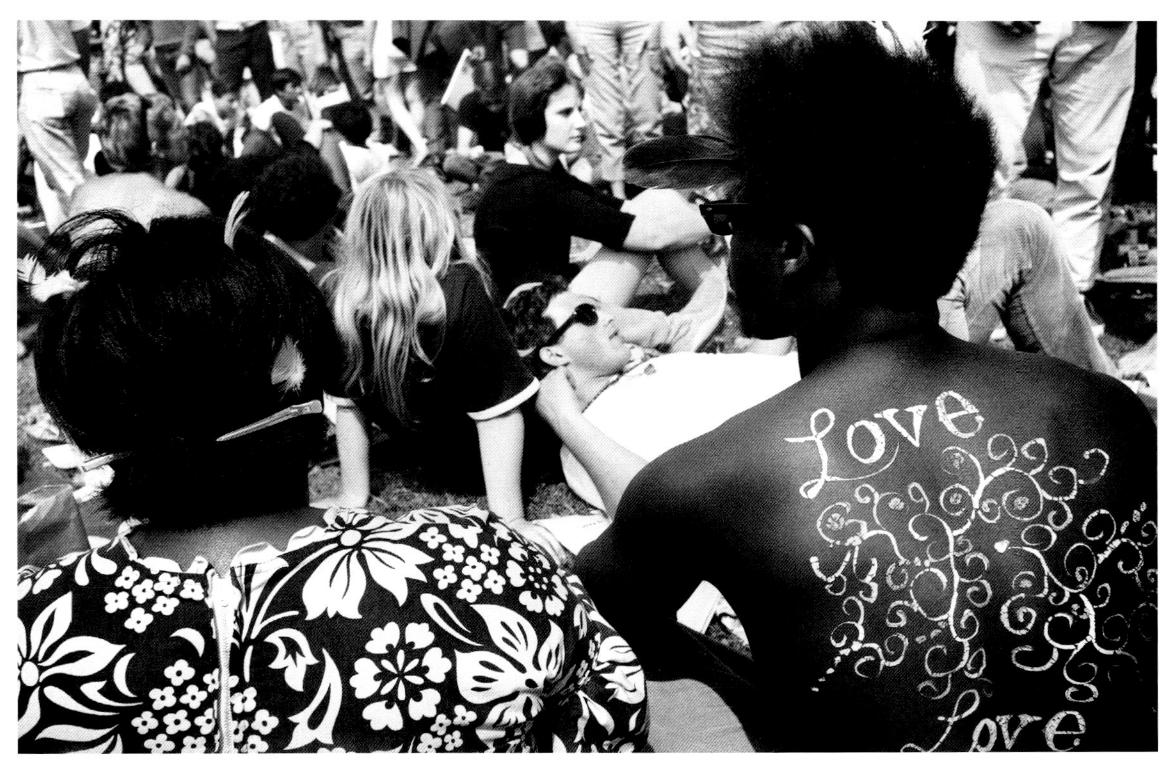

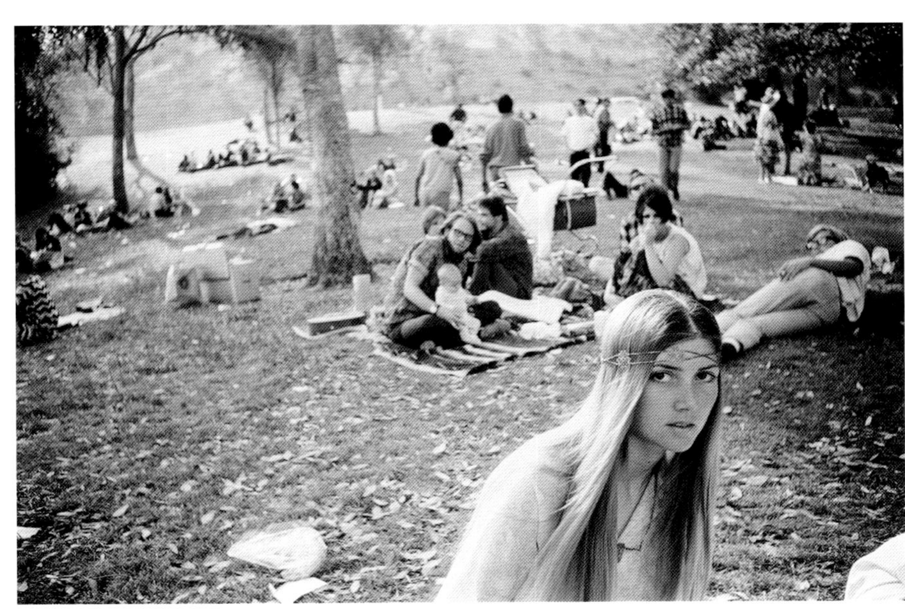

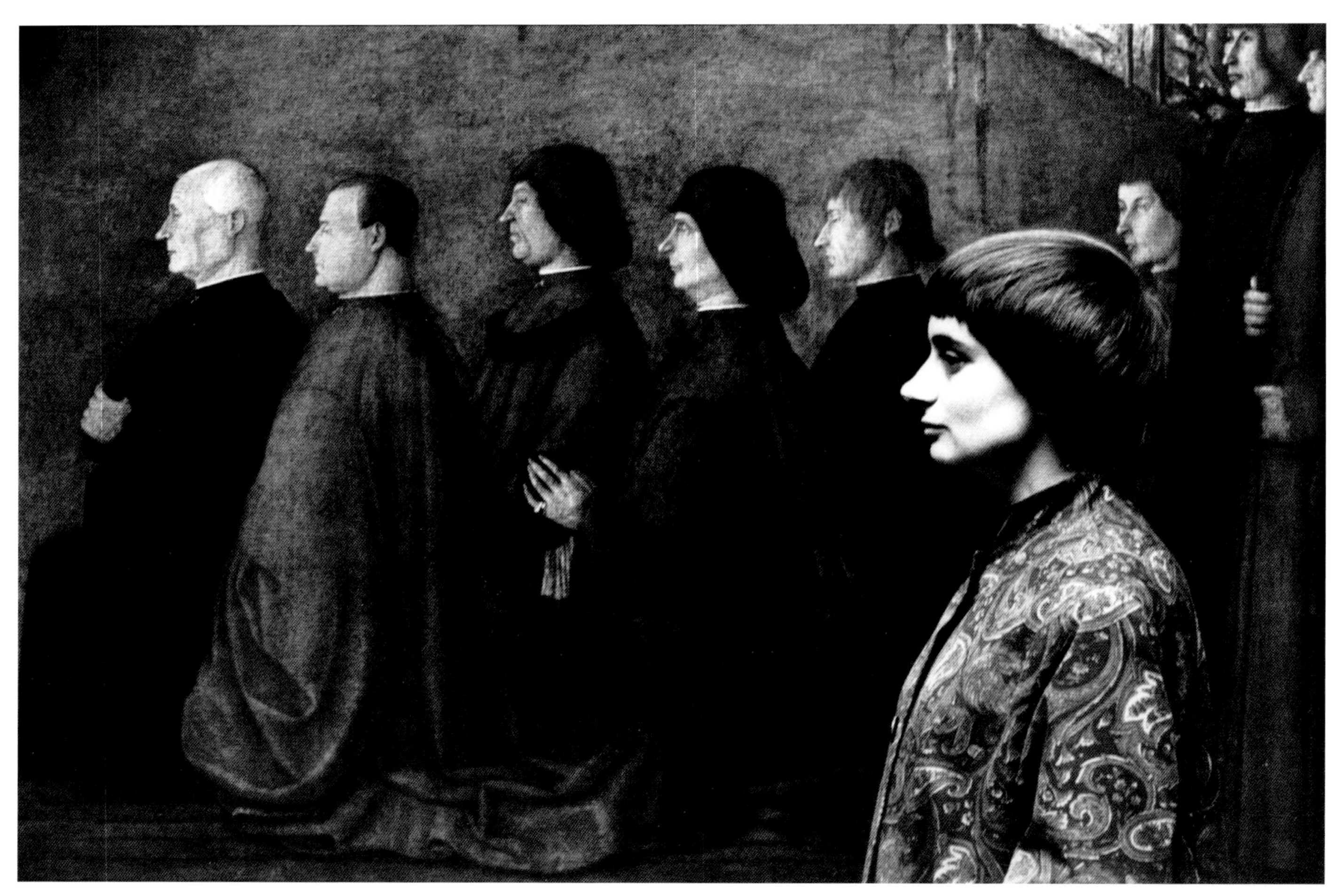

Photography has never
stopped teaching me how
to make films.

Above: *Self Portrait in front of Gentile Bellini*, 1960

Opposite, top: *Salt (Sel)*, 1951

Opposite, bottom: *The Siesta (La Sieste), Sète*, 1956

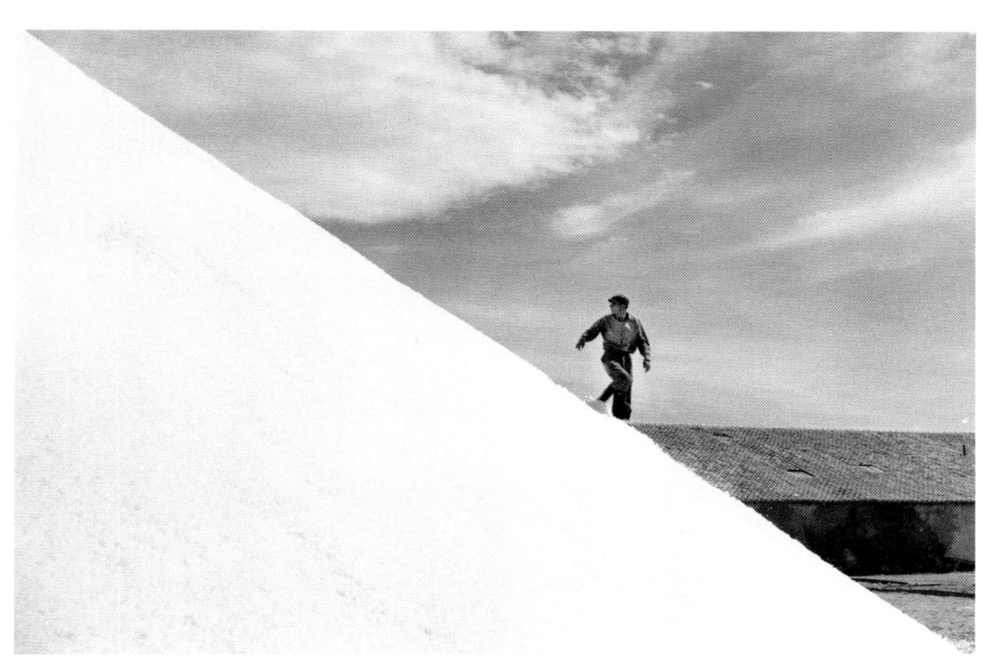

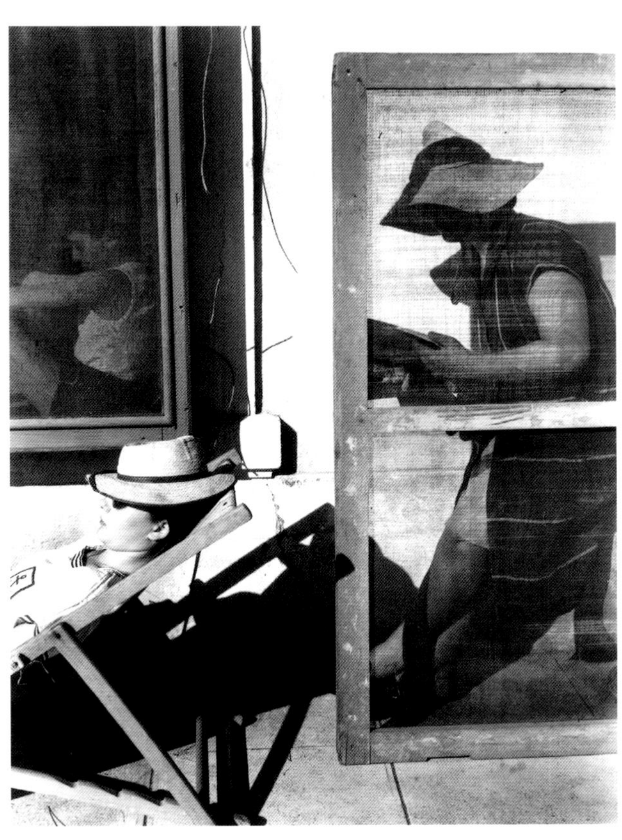

SECOND LIFE: FILMMAKER

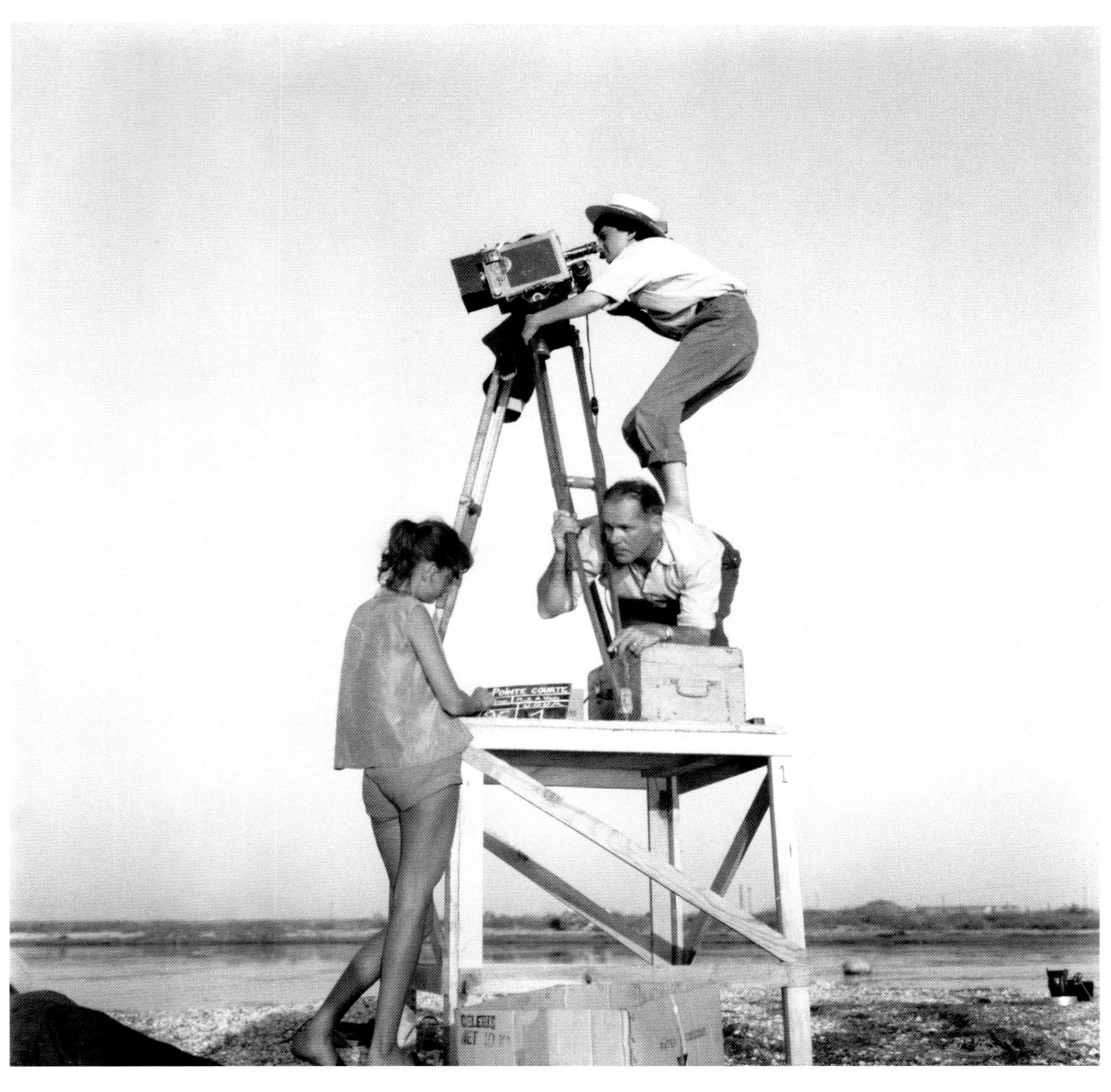

Varda (with camera)
filming *La Pointe Courte*
in 1954

I knew nothing, so I was not afraid. If I had known the masterpieces I had seen later, I would not have started. I would not have dared.

I thought that pictures plus words, that was cinema. It was only later that I discovered it was something else.

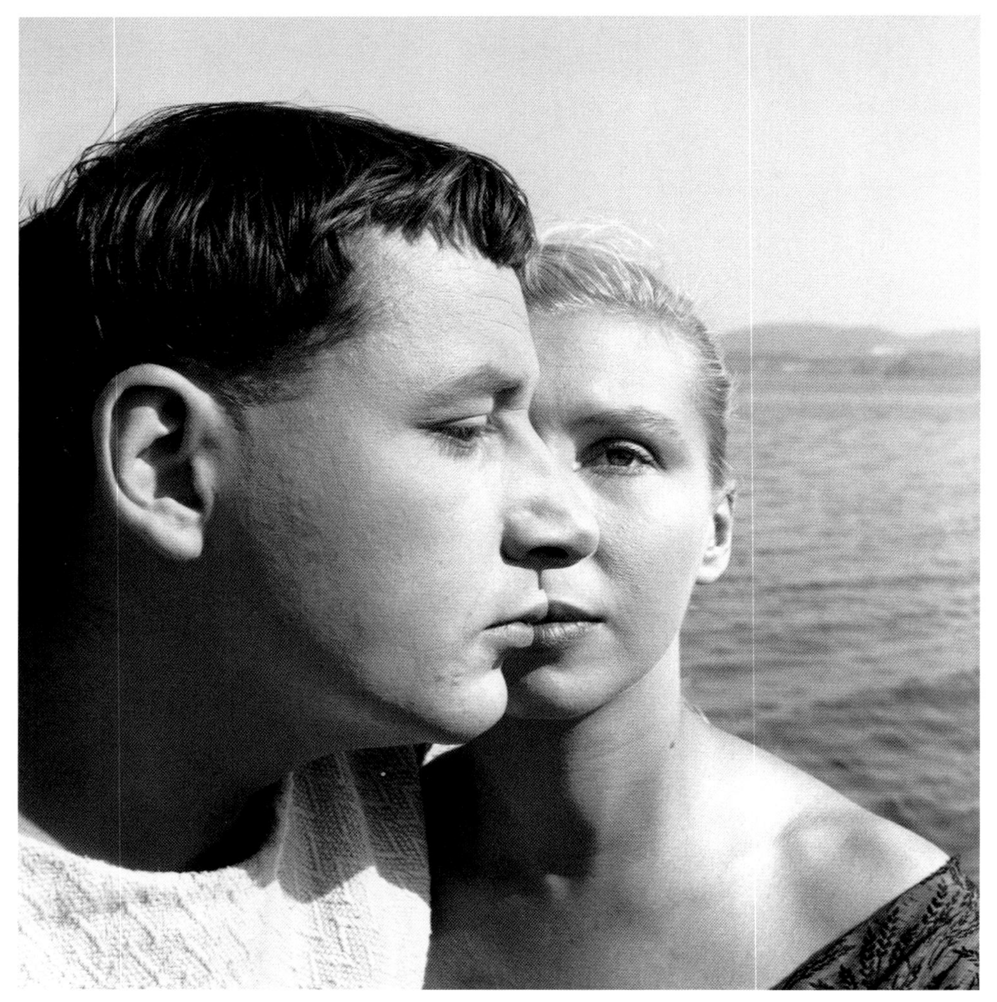

La Pointe Courte (1955) tells the story of a young couple in a small French fishing village trying to save their deteriorating marriage.

Left: Philippe Noiret and Silvia Monfort during production of *La Pointe Courte*, photographed by Varda

Opposite: Scenes from *La Pointe Courte*

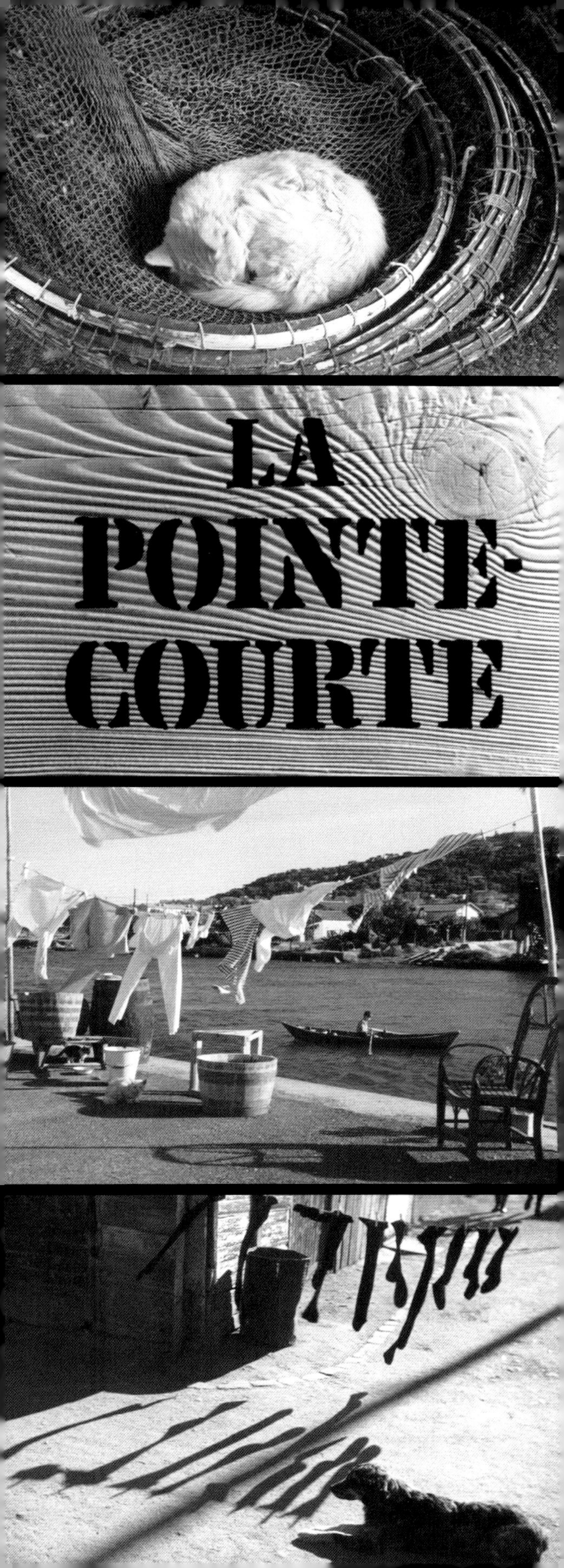
LA
POINTE-
COURTE

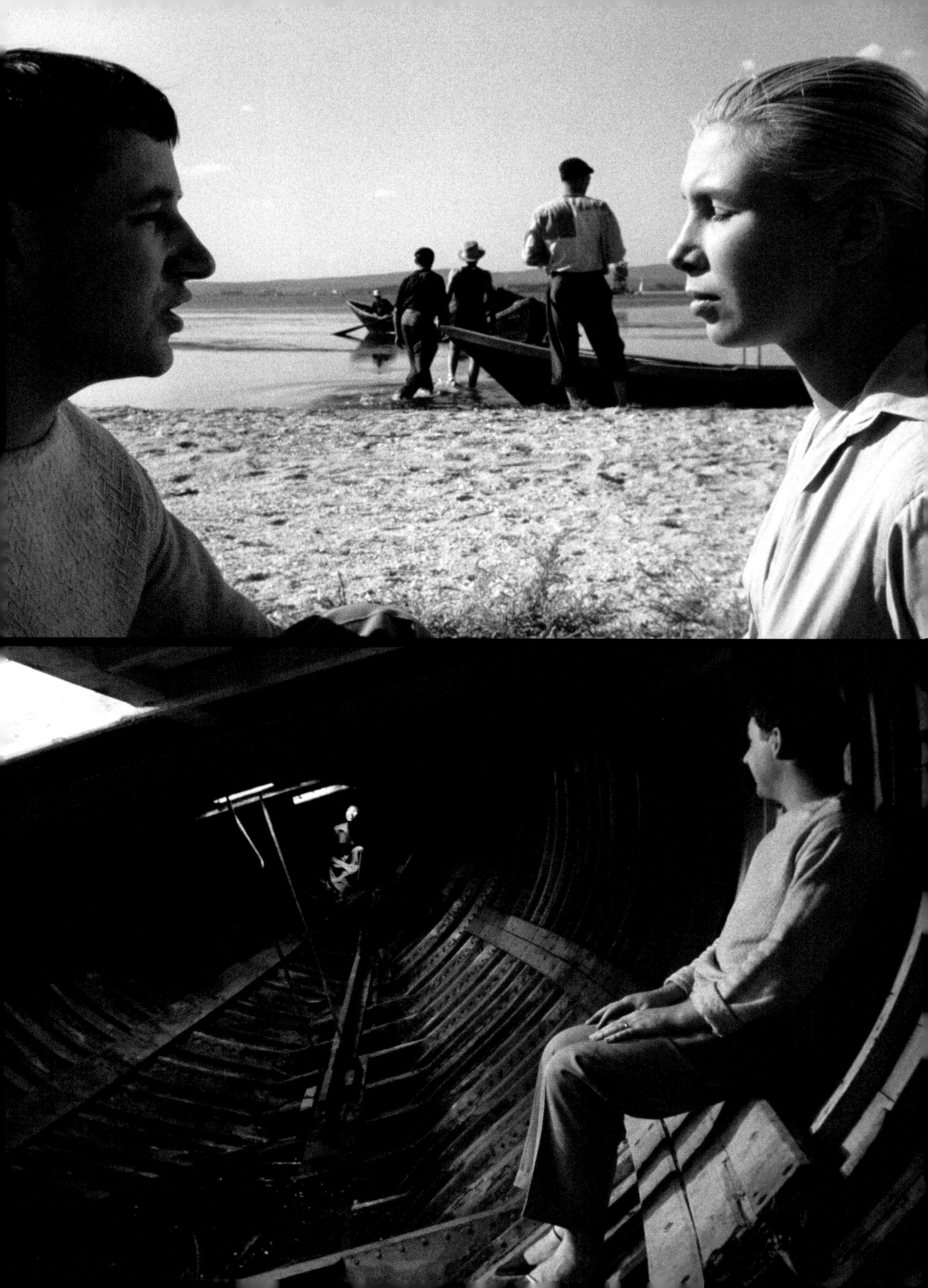

passe pour s'avancer jusqu'aux bois
de charpente.

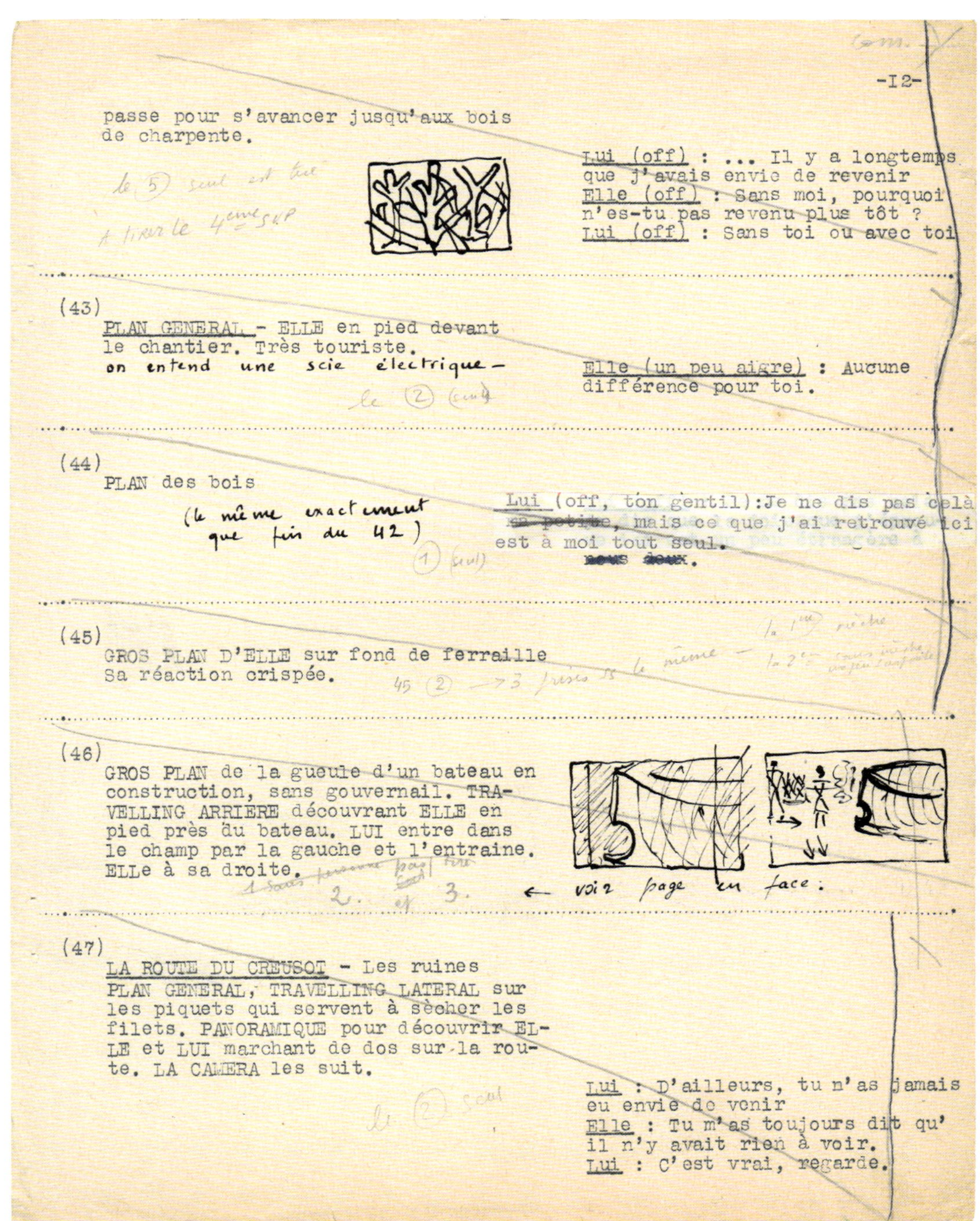

Lui (off) : ... Il y a longtemps
que j'avais envie de revenir
Elle (off) : Sans moi, pourquoi
n'es-tu pas revenu plus tôt ?
Lui (off) : Sans toi ou avec toi

- -

(43)

PLAN GENERAL - ELLE en pied devant
le chantier. Très touriste.

Elle (un peu aigre) : Aucune
différence pour toi.

- -

(44)

PLAN des bois

Lui (off, ton gentil):Je ne dis pas celà
~~en petite~~, mais ce que j'ai retrouvé ici
est à moi tout seul.
~~NOUS deux.~~

- -

(45)

GROS PLAN D'ELLE sur fond de ferraille
Sa réaction crispée.

- -

(46)

GROS PLAN de la gueule d'un bateau en
construction, sans gouvernail. TRA-
VELLING ARRIERE découvrant ELLE en
pied près du bateau. LUI entre dans
le champ par la gauche et l'entraine.
ELLE à sa droite.

- -

(47)

LA ROUTE DU CREUSOT - Les ruines
PLAN GENERAL, TRAVELLING LATERAL sur
les piquets qui servent à sècher les
filets. PANORAMIQUE pour découvrir EL-
LE et LUI marchant de dos sur la route. LA CAMERA les suit.

Lui : D'ailleurs, tu n'as jamais
eu envie de venir
Elle : Tu m'as toujours dit qu'
il n'y avait rien à voir.
Lui : C'est vrai, regarde.

Opposite: Scenes from
La Pointe Courte

Right: Page from Varda's
production notebook for
La Pointe Courte

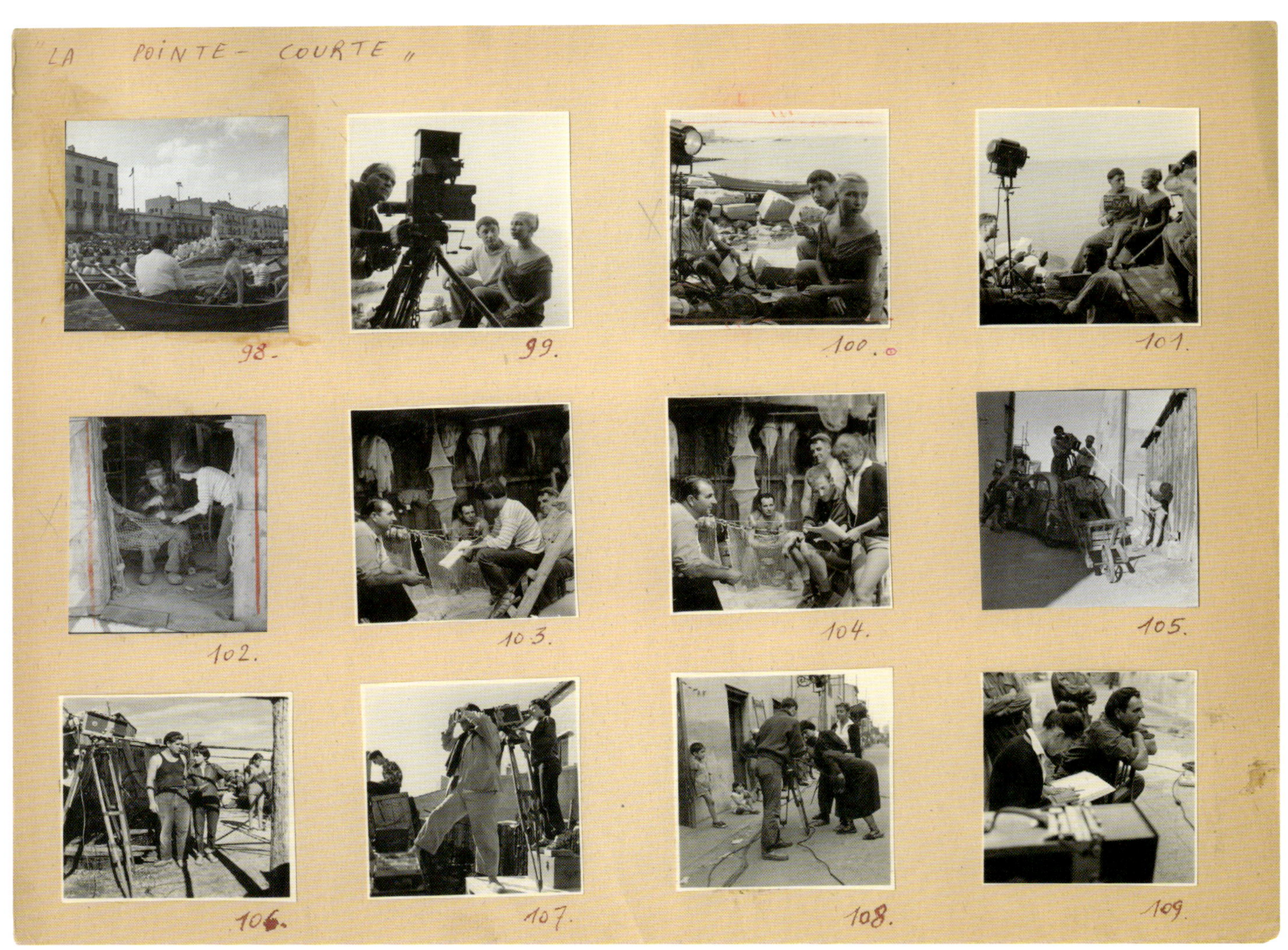

The scouting images helped me to imagine the film. They started moving in my head. I was preparing as a photographer to become a filmmaker.

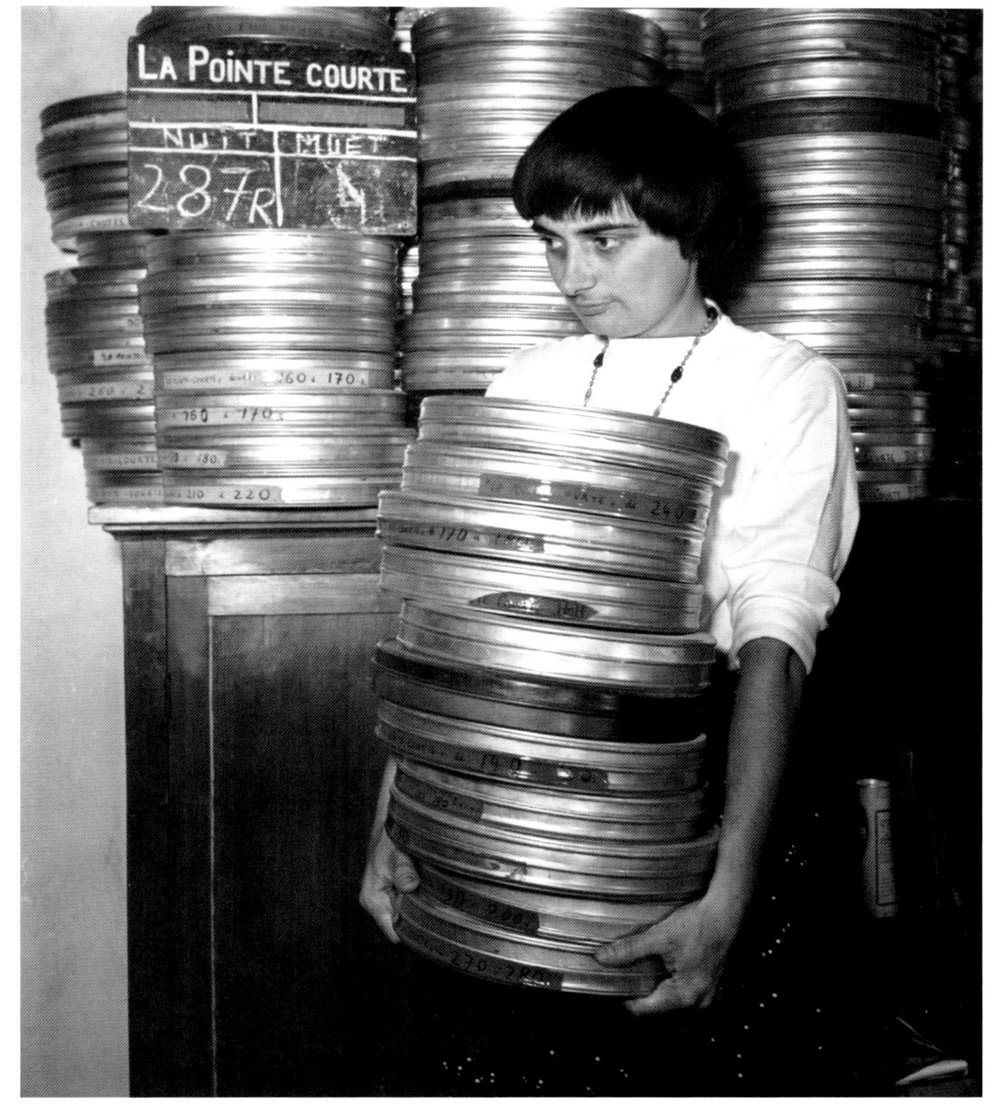

Opposite: Varda's
handmade proof sheet
of production images
from *La Pointe Courte*

Right: Varda, ca. 1955

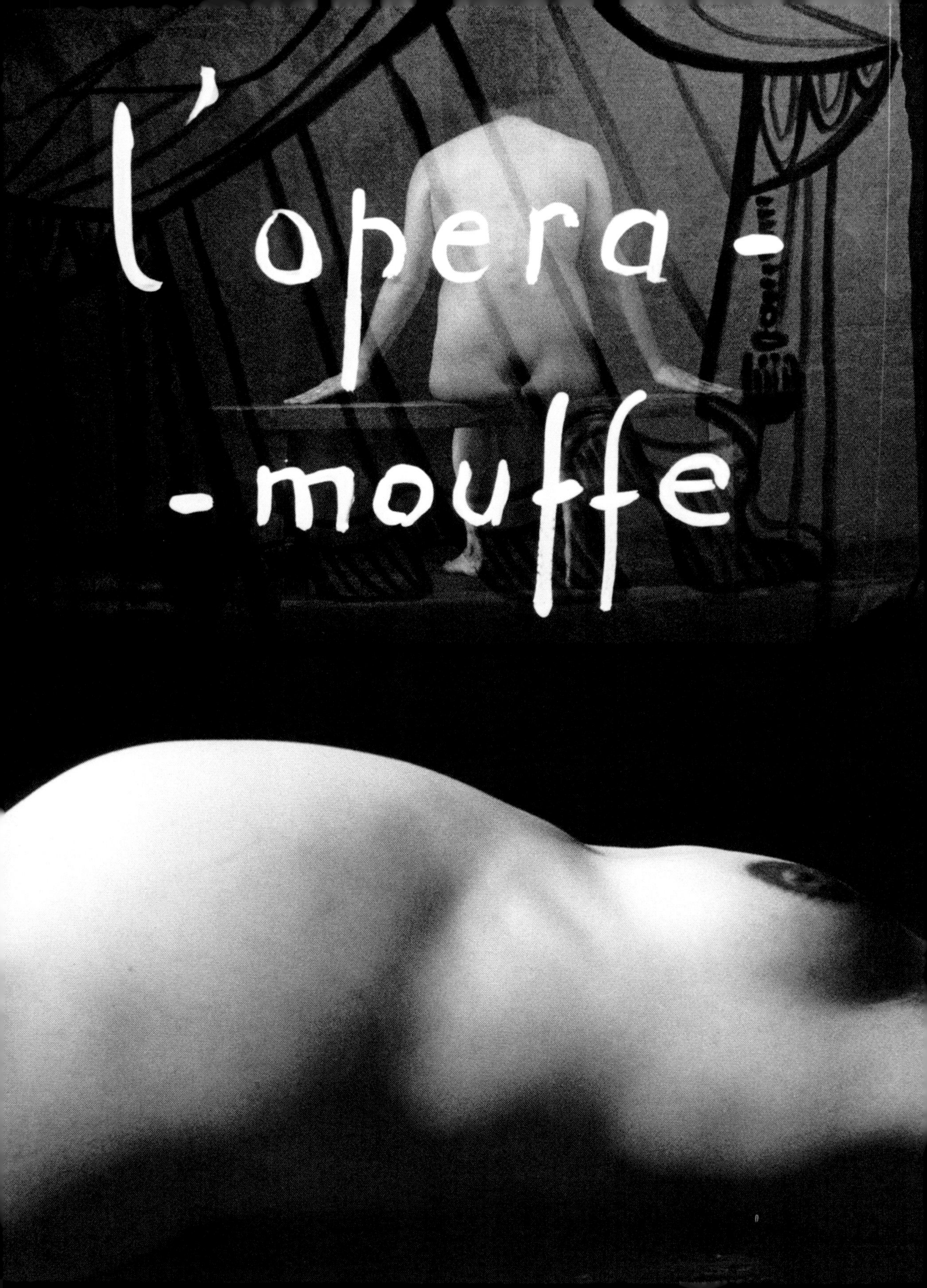

l'opera -
-mouffe

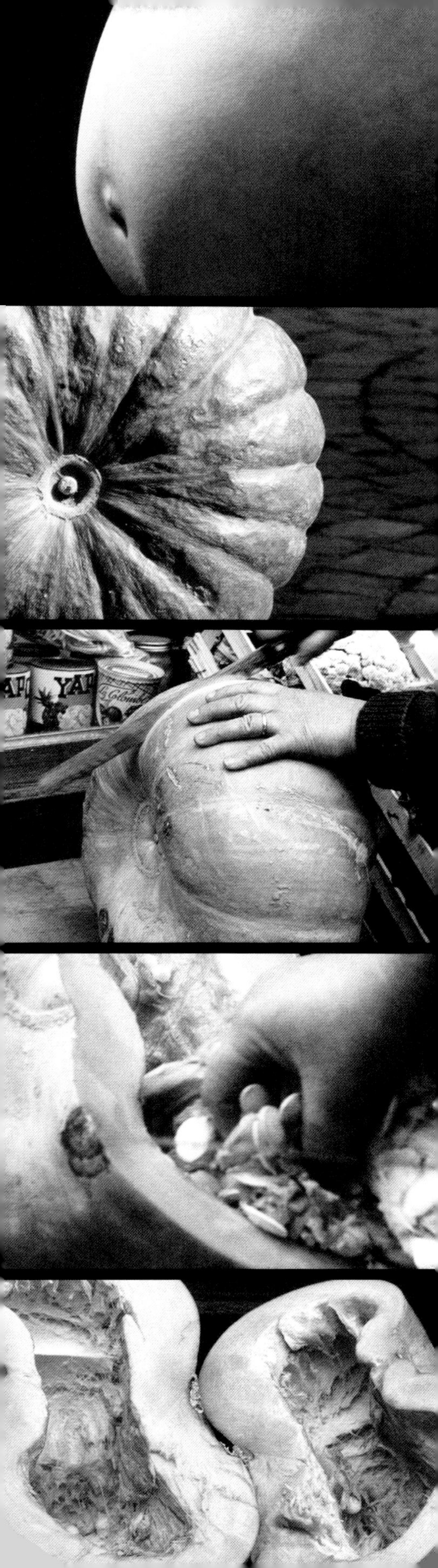

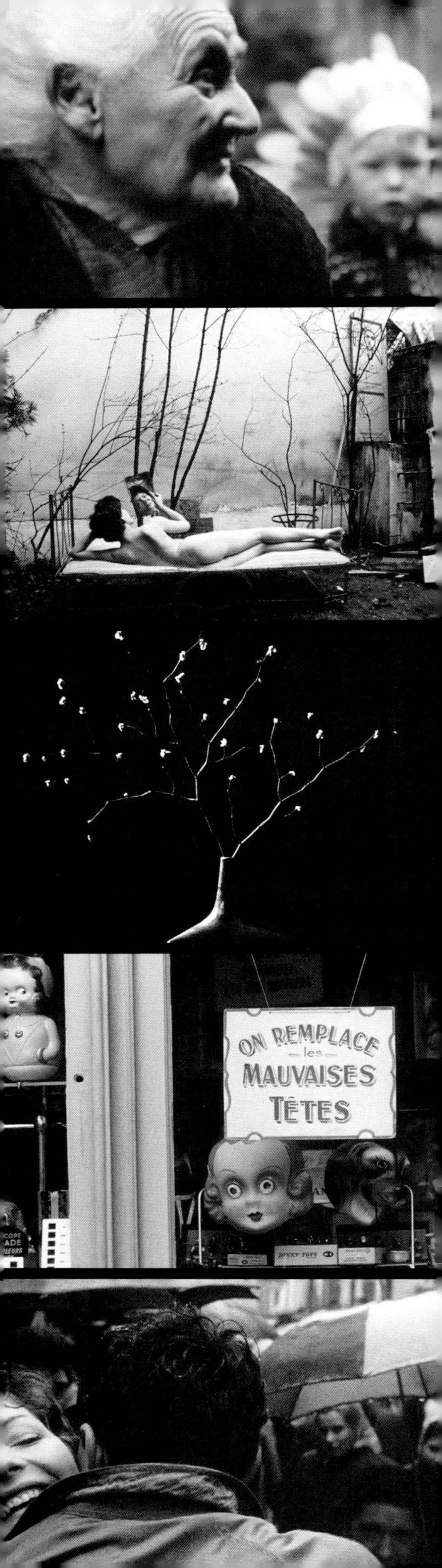

ON REMPLACE
les
MAUVAISES
TÊTES

—

I enjoyed capturing in the middle of Mouffetard markets the confusion between a stomach heavy with child and one of food. And so many contradictions! A pregnant woman watches the waves of people, especially older people, on a steep incline and she thinks: "They were all newborns once; someone sprinkled fresh talcum powder on them and then kissed their little behinds."

"I shot *L'Opéra-Mouffe* in 1958 when I was pregnant," Varda explained. "The film is not my diary, but the diary of a pregnant woman in the context of a social documentary."

Opposite and previous spread: Scenes from *L'Opéra-Mouffe* (1958)

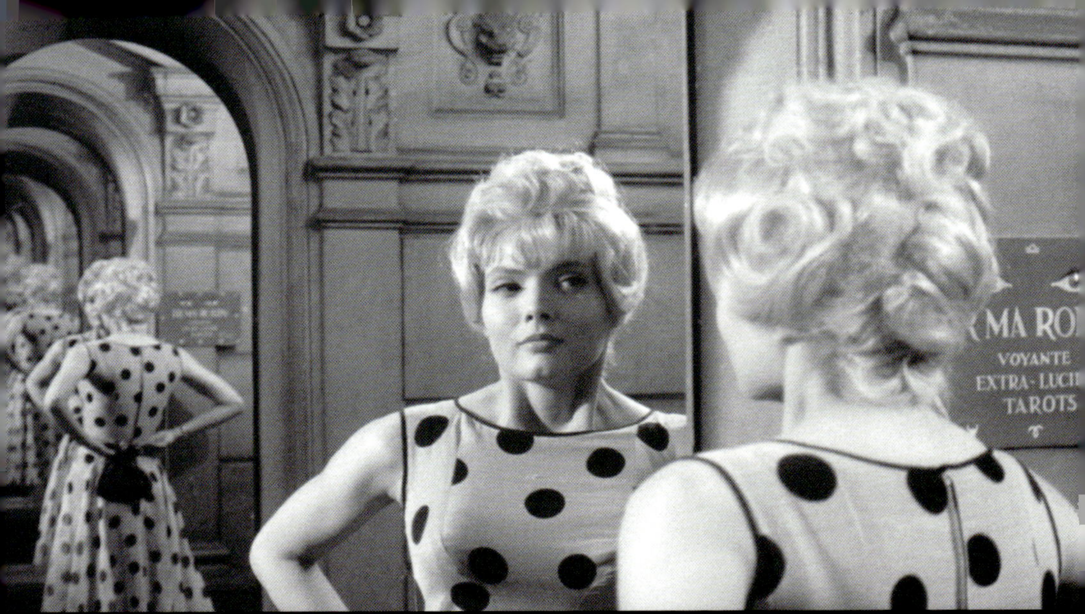

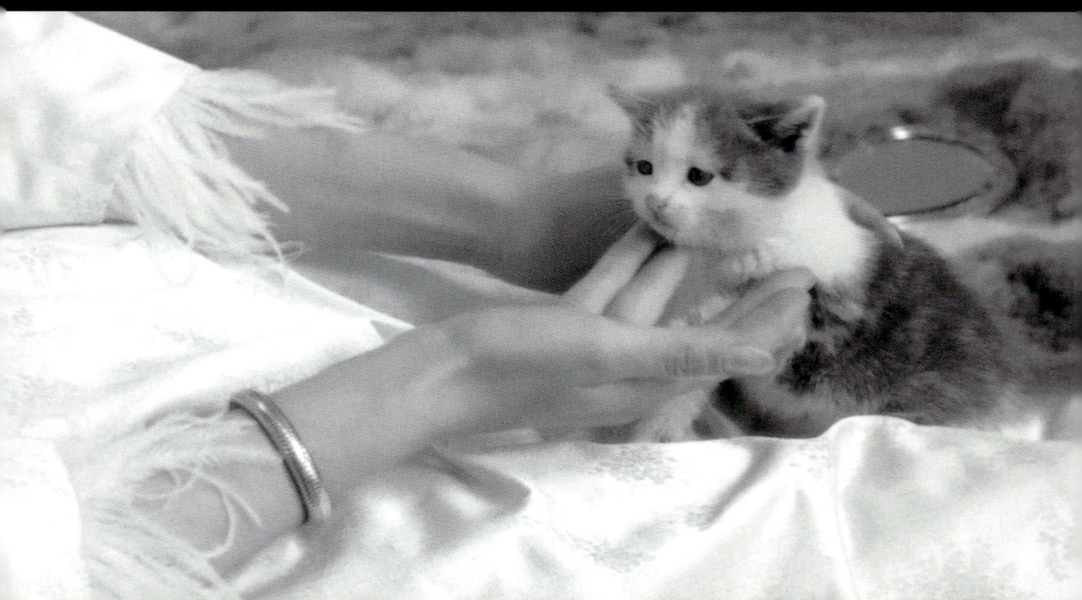
MA RO
VOYANTE
EXTRA-LUCIE
TAROTS
CLÉO 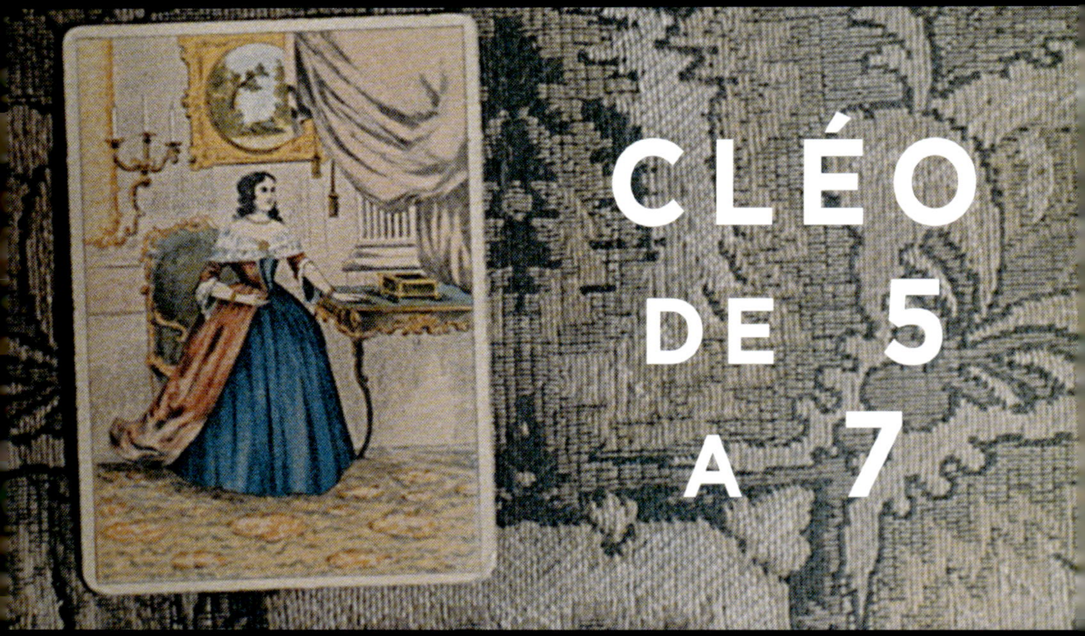
DE 5
A 7

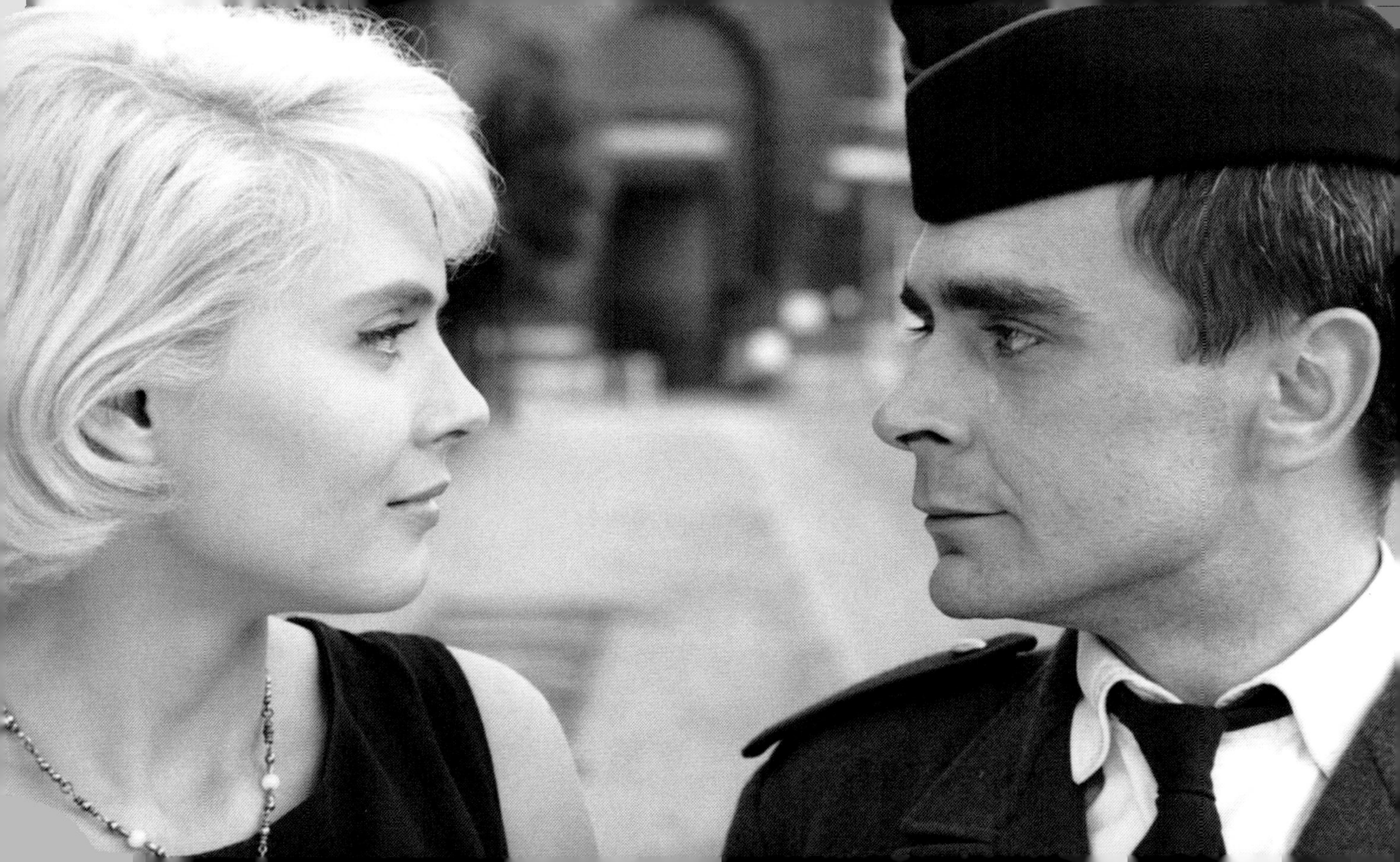

Corinne Marchand plays Cléo, a young pop singer nervously awaiting cancer test results. The film employs objective time—Varda's clever use of clocks marks the protagonist's two-hour journey—as well as subjective time, which is felt to move quickly or slowly according to one's emotional state.

Previous spread: Scenes from *Cléo from 5 to 7* (1962) featuring Corinne Marchand and Antoine Bourseiller

Below: Corinne Marchand during production, photographed by Varda

Cléo is the type of person for whom the thought of death is so surprising that it completely undoes her. She's led to question her entire existence, the musicians, Angèle, her lover, and even her profession as a singer.

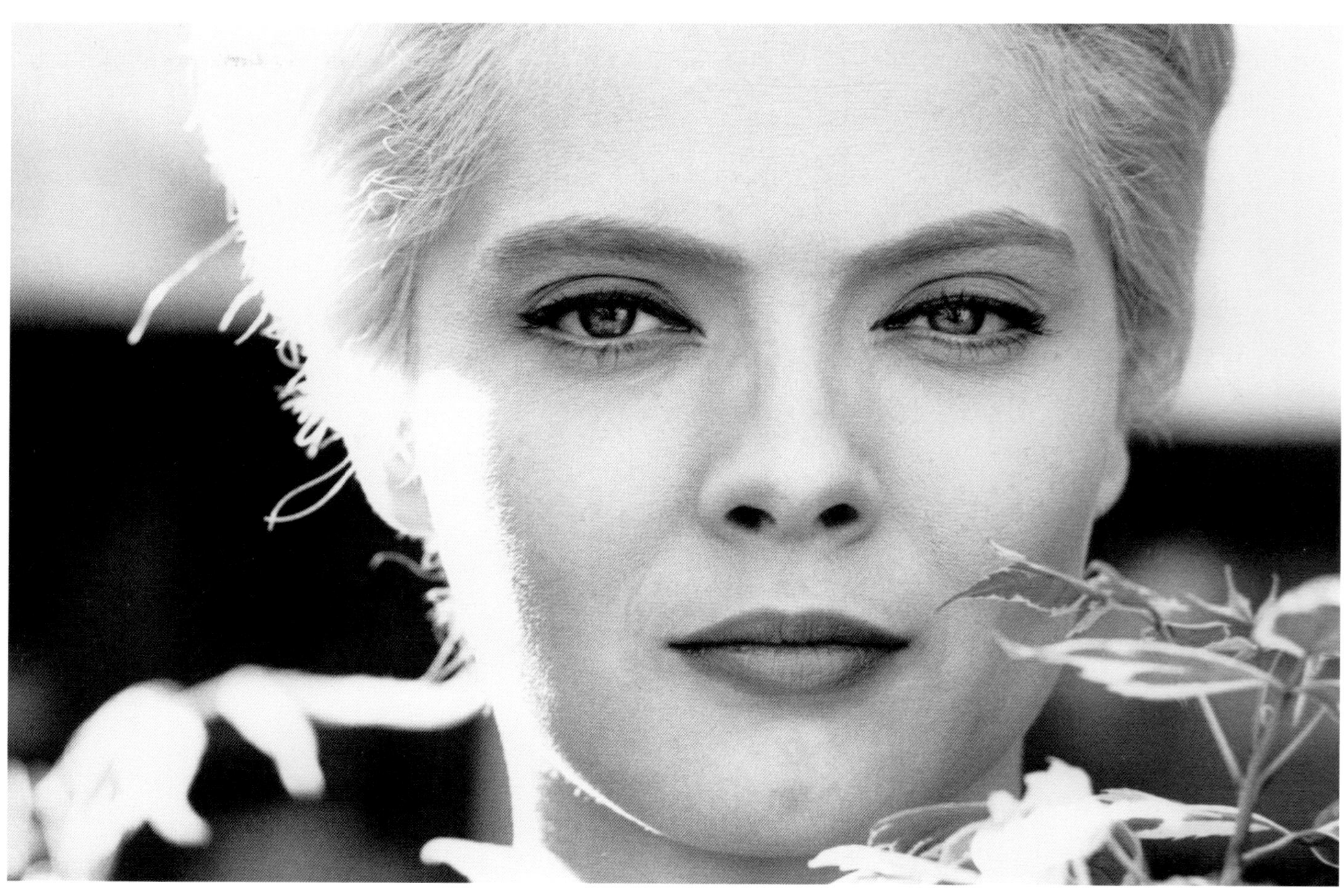

MARTIN SCORSESE

Agnès and I became friends in the early 1970s and stayed friends. She would get in touch with me, or I'd get in touch with her, or—and this happened quite frequently—she would just show up. I would be on set, in the middle of a shoot; I'd turn around and there was Agnès. She never had an ulterior motive. It wasn't "let's make a film" or "produce this or that." She just wanted to talk.

I remember, once, she came to my editing room—this was when we were finishing up *Gangs of New York*. She was in New York for the restoration of Jacques's *The Young Girls of Rochefort*. I asked if she wanted me to present the film. She said, "No, no, I just want you to come and see it." No favor, just come. This was very touching to me that she would seek me out as a fellow filmmaker and a friend. I always made time for Agnès.

I guess I wanted her approval. She was my friend, but she was also one of the gods of cinema, right at the heart of the French New Wave from the start. Agnès seemed to like my movies—I was never quite sure. I'm still not quite sure. She would sort of gently scold me at times.

Once she said, "You know, I like your movies, but what about mine?" I said, "I love *Cléo from 5 to 7*." I think I mentioned *Le Bonheur* too. She said, "Old! Those are *old* ones!" So, we started talking about *Vagabond*, which I find quite hard to watch but really admire, an absolutely uncompromising film from beginning to end. *Uncle Yanco* is also a thing of beauty, shot by Dave Myers, a great cameraman and a lovely human being. Agnès loved him and so did I.

The pictures that had the deepest and most lasting effect on me were *Cléo* and *Le Bonheur*. I saw *Cléo* on its first release. In Truffaut's and Godard's films, women were often the main characters. In Bergman's films as well. But *Cléo* was different. The point of view was different. It's difficult to put into words. Was it a feminine point of view? I'm not sure. But it was different. I was too young to fully appreciate everything that was going on with the character, but I found myself *concerned* for her in a way that was different from other movies. And there was this lightness to it, a true lyricism, that was unlike anything else being made at the time. Maybe I could call it a lyricism generated from within.

I was very young when I saw the film, and it got me thinking about women in a totally different way. It was genuinely enlightening. And then *Le Bonheur* came as a kind of shock. The *color* shocked me. The point of view shocked me. The idea of a man who genuinely loved two women at the same time shocked me as well. And it stood in stark contrast to other films made around the same time, tragic romances that were completely decorative, like feature-length shampoo commercials.

Agnès broke all the forms of what a film should be. When I think of making a film, my mind goes right to feature length, the old theatrical experience. But Agnès never stuck to that. She made films of all shapes and sizes as she was moved to. It wasn't just that she had trouble getting features made; I think the muse took her in different directions. And she never stopped. She was a direct inspiration to me in that sense. All the documentaries I made—that impulse, which became a practice, really comes from Agnès's example and our conversations and friendship. The freedom to do films of any length, slip and slide in time, and break down narrative and the barriers between fiction and nonfiction; that comes from Agnès.

The last time Agnès came to my house, she was with her daughter, Rosalie. We sat down and started talking about our ailments, her eye problems, my eye problems. She was 88 at the time, and she said, "Memories are going—lots of memories are gone. But it's all right. I think of them as butterflies flying away. And it makes me lighter." That's her. That's Agnès.

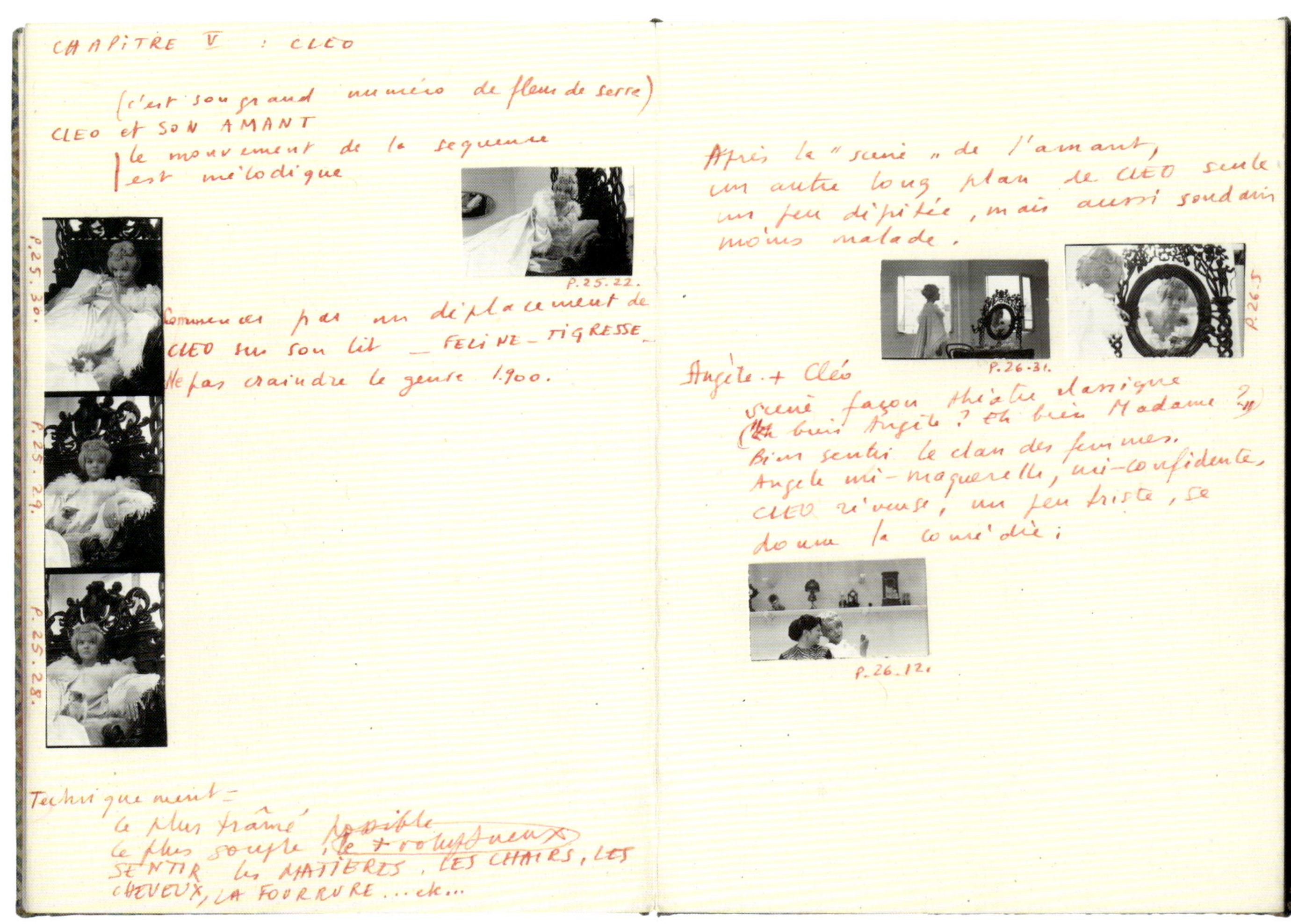

Above: Pages from Varda's production notebook for *Cléo from 5 to 7*

Opposite: Varda's handmade contact sheet of production images

She's a very beautiful girl but surrounds herself in every situation with screens: superstition, coquettishness, exaggerated femininity.

Corinne Marchand.
+ Cléo de 5 à 7. (Référence)

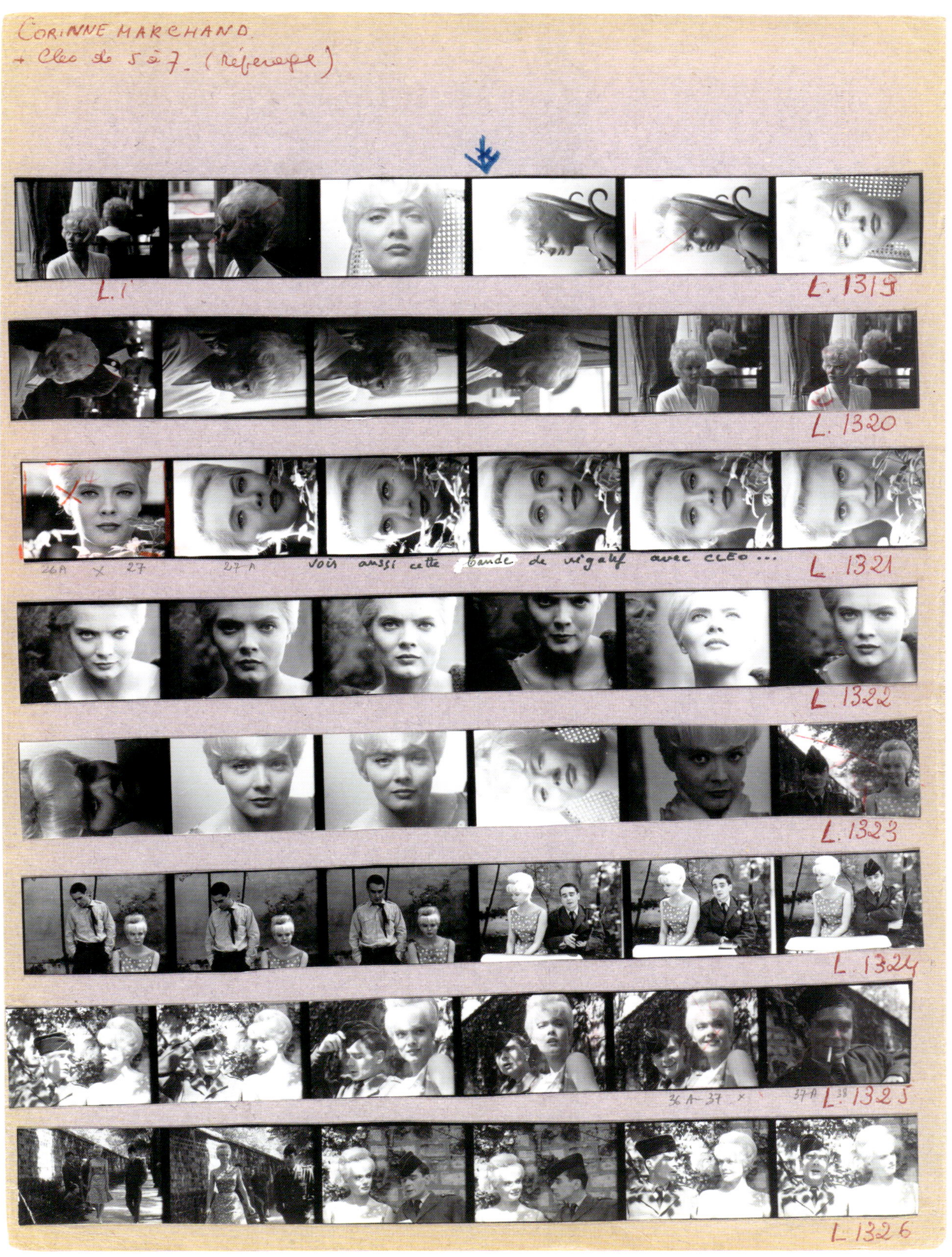
L. 1'   L. 1319
                                         L. 1320
26A   X   27   27 A   Voir aussi cette bande de régalef avec CLÉO...   L. 1321
                                         L. 1322
                                         L. 1323
                                         L. 1324
                              36 A - 37   X   37 A   L. 1325
                                         L. 1326

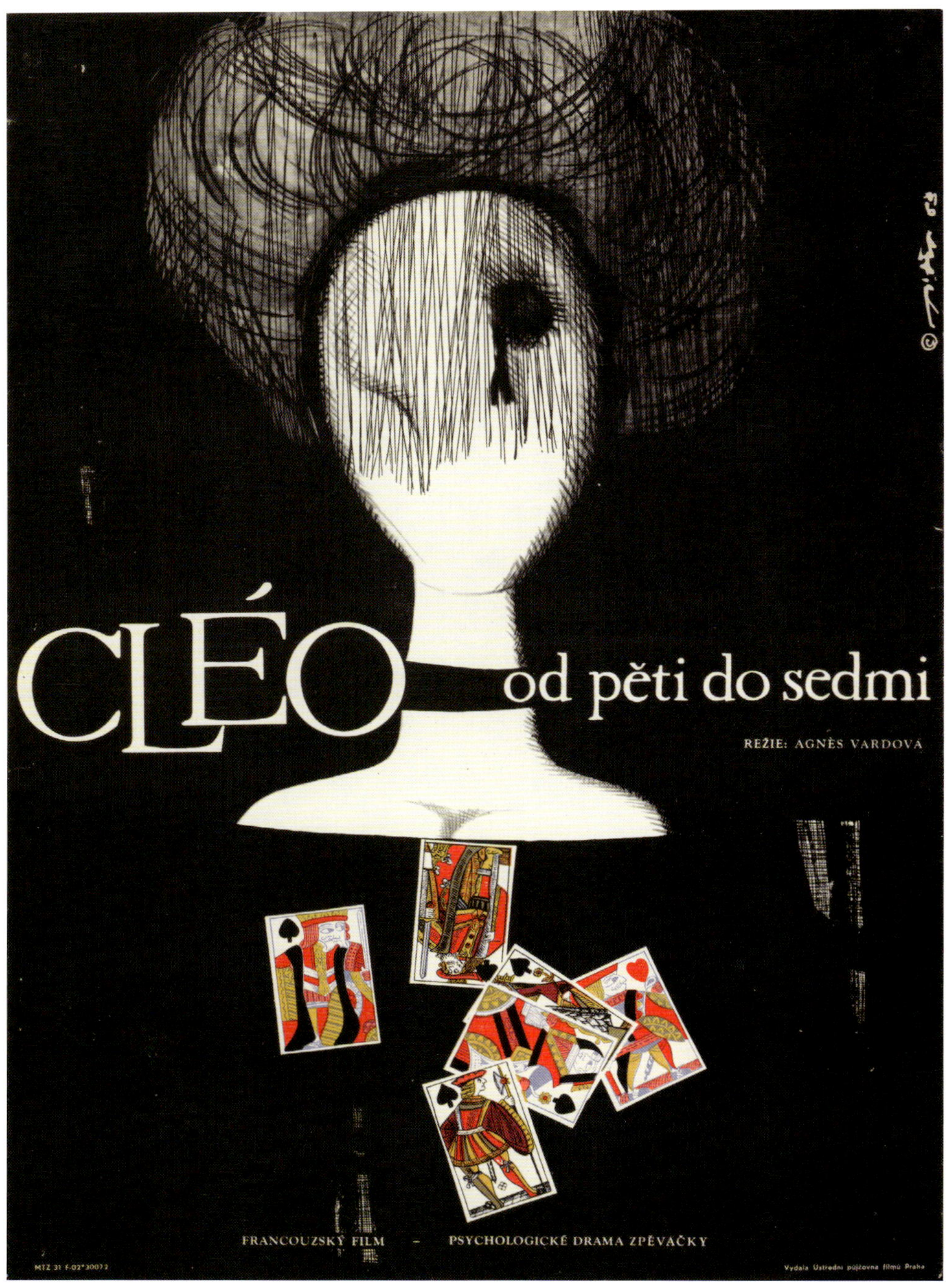

CLÉO
od pěti do sedmi
REŽIE: AGNÈS VARDOVÁ
FRANCOUZSKÝ FILM — PSYCHOLOGICKÉ DRAMA ZPĚVAČKY
MTŽ 31 F-02*30072
Vydala Ústřední půjčovna filmů Praha

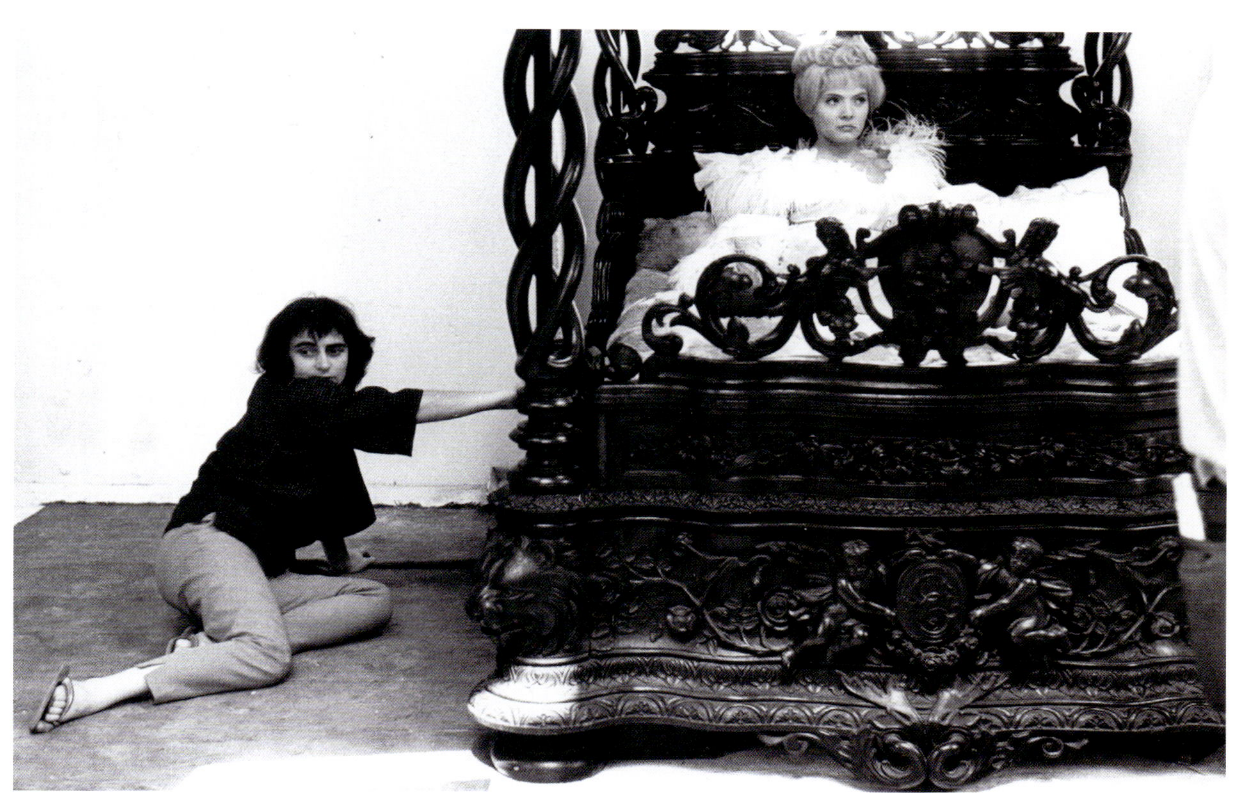

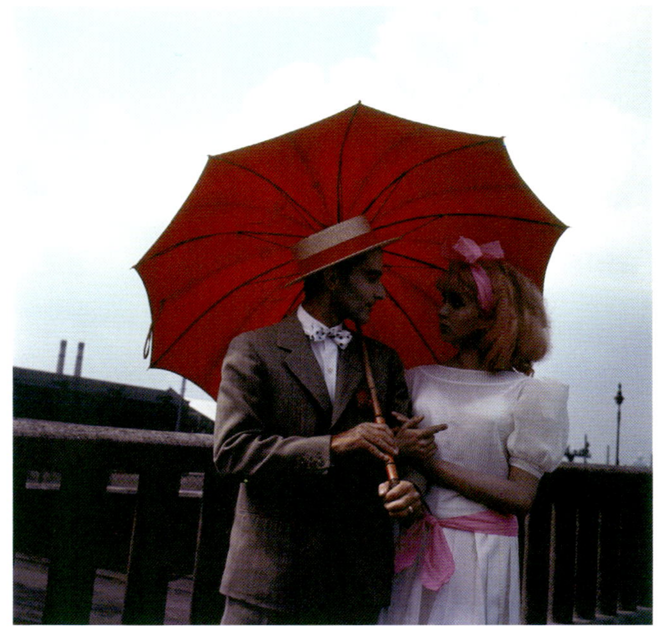

Opposite: Czechoslo-vakian theatrical poster for *Cléo from 5 to 7*. Illustration: Jaroslav Fiser

Above: Varda (left) and Corinne Marchand during production of *Cléo from 5 to 7*

Right: Jean-Luc Godard and Anna Karina on set, photographed by Varda. Godard and Karina appear in the silent film-within-a-film that Raoul (Raymond Cauchetier) shows to Cléo.

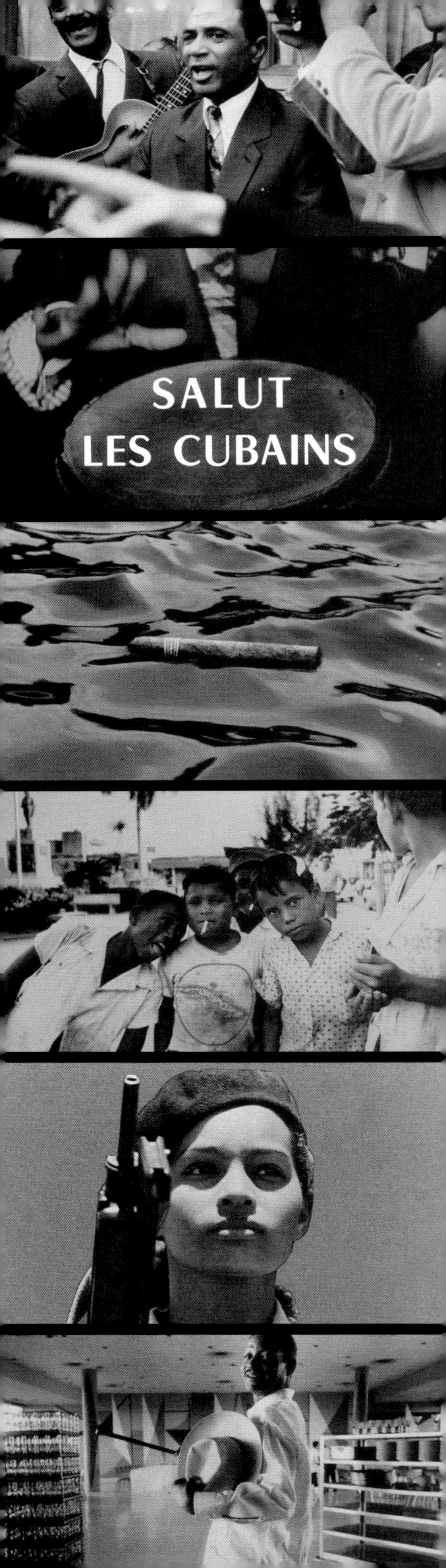
SALUT
LES CUBAINS

The Cuban Film Institute invited Varda to visit Cuba in 1963, four years after the revolution. Her resulting film *Salut les Cubains* (1963) celebrates the Cuban people, a 30-minute montage composed entirely of still photographs taken during her trip.

Opposite: Scenes from *Salut les Cubains*

This page: Photographs from Varda's 1963 trip to Cuba. She photographed the Cuban revolutionary leader Fidel Castro (right) with "wings of stone," as she would later describe it in *Varda by Agnès* (2019).

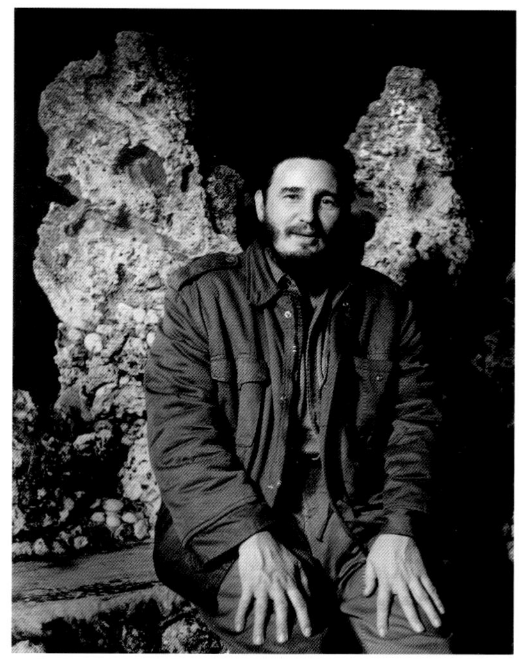

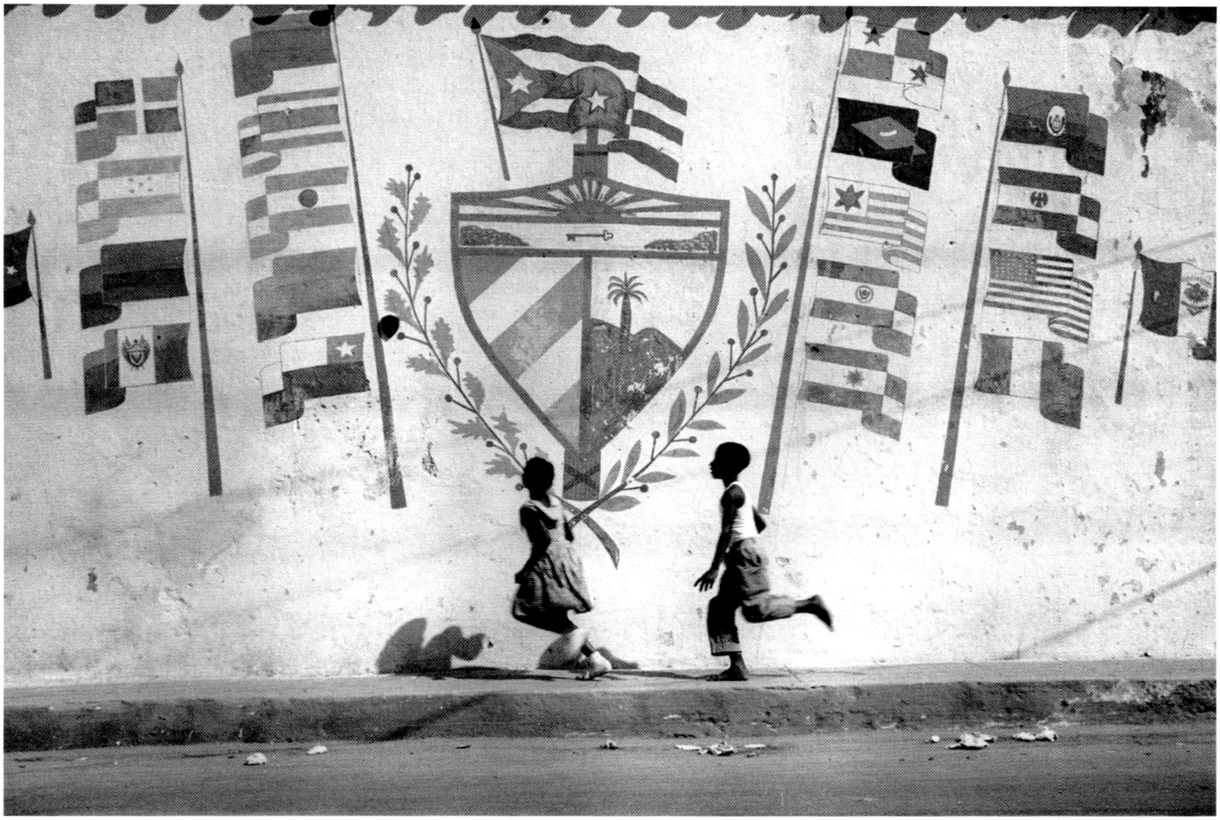

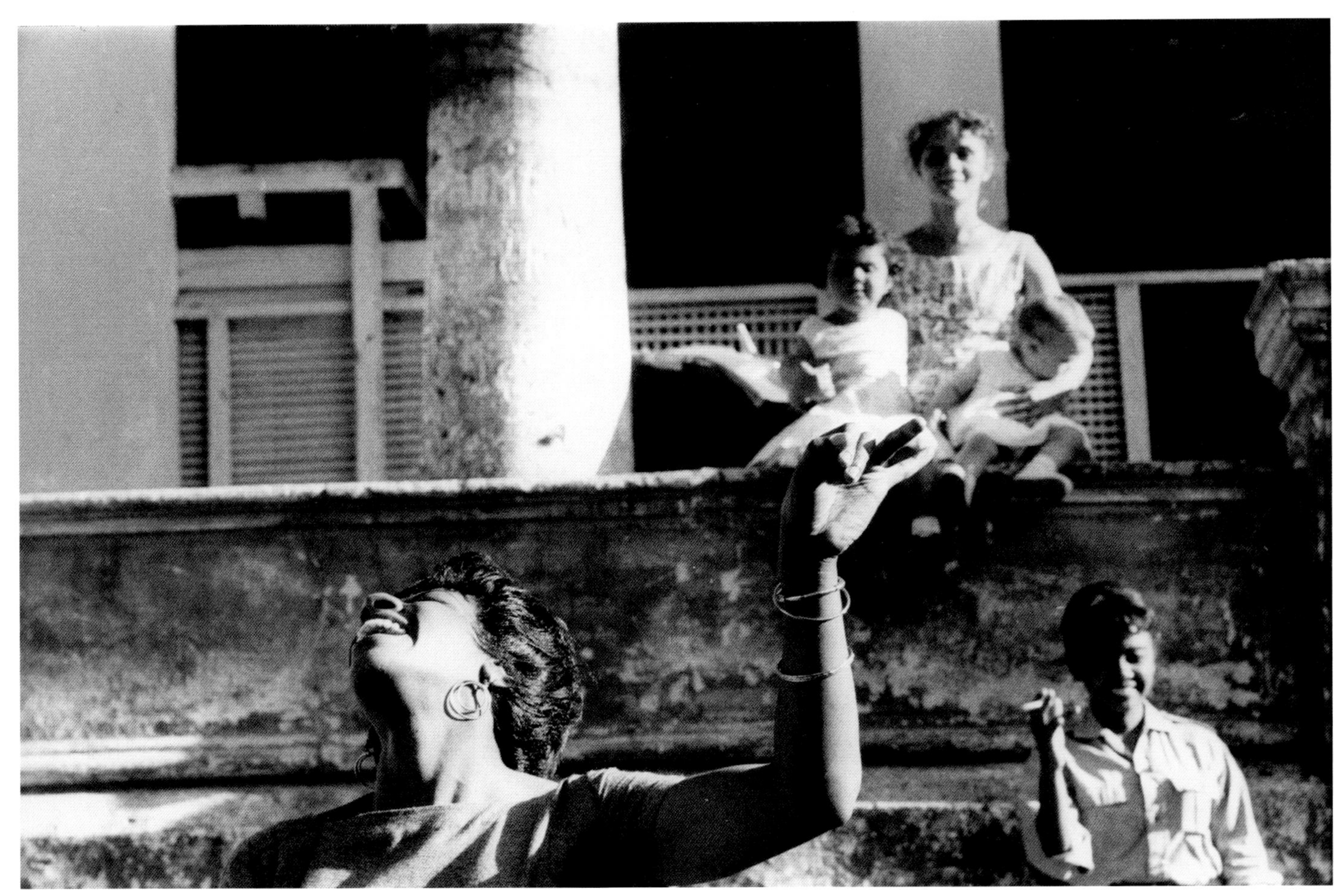

I brought back over four thousand photos and spent six months editing about 1,500 of them, but it was worth it: in Cuba they say that it has the *sapor* (flavor) of a Cuban film.

Varda would often describe *Salut les Cubains* as "socialism and cha-cha-cha."

Above: Members of the Cuban Institute of Cinematographic Art and Industry, photographed by Varda

Opposite: Scenes from *Salut les Cubains*

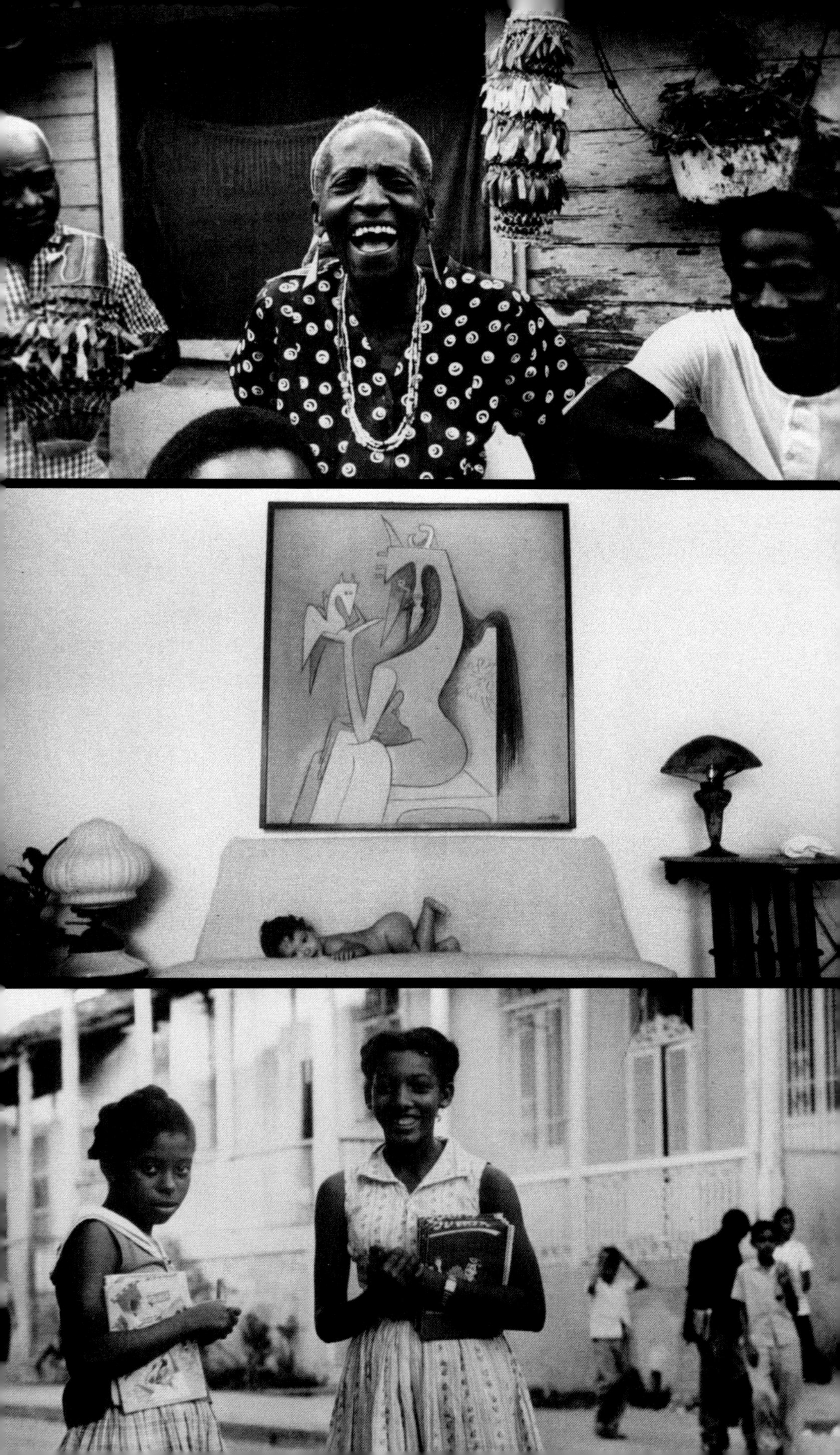

MANOHLA DARGIS

Soon after I first met Agnès Varda, I drove her to the Hollywood police station. It was 2009, and we were supposed to be at a dinner for the Los Angeles opening of her documentary *The Beaches of Agnès*, a lyrical ramble through her life. At that point, Varda had been making movies for more than a half century, a milestone that then seemed to me as impossible as her death in 2019 at 90 seems to me now.

Varda showed up late for the dinner, hurrying into the restaurant in a state of agitation. While at a Starbucks, her bag had been stolen—wallet, passport, *tout*. Her greatest concern was the digital video camera that had the images she'd shot earlier that day of her friend Sharon Stone. Dazed that Stone and Varda occupied the same corner of the universe, I got it together and took her to the police station, where she filled out a report and murmured doubts about the young desk officer.

We returned to the restaurant for our dinner, the first of many encounters that we had over the next decade, sometimes for a leisurely meal or at a festival where invariably she was being honored. The last time I saw her was in May 2018 at her house on the Left Bank in Paris, an area that became part of her identity. Varda was routinely called the mother or grandmother or godmother of the French New Wave and often grouped with its Left Bank flank, alongside her friends Chris Marker and Alain Resnais. She wasn't always comfortable with the maternal moniker, though she later embraced it—and why not? She had shown the way.

A longtime feminist, she was acutely sensitive to oppression, and many of her movies center on women. [...] Among her most unsettling films is *Le Bonheur*, a shocking, pitiless evisceration of the romantic vision of heterosexual marriage in which women are fundamentally disposable and replaceable. *Le Bonheur* was criticized, including by those who wanted Varda to wag her finger at patriarchy and female oppression, doing the audience's work for it. But hers is not a cinema of the obvious. One sustaining pleasure of her films is that they don't neatly fit into boxes, including feminist ones, even while being unmistakably feminist. She wasn't creating ideals or role models but specific women in specific places (villages, streets, beaches) who are navigating a world in which the very definitions of women, of the feminine and femininity, are in upheaval.

This wasn't necessarily what the industry was interested in, and sometimes Varda directed short movies "to keep alive in my own research," as she once put it. The latter-life acclaim and honors were overdue and welcome—she clearly enjoyed being feted—but she didn't always have institutional and critical support. In the early 1980s, she spoke about being omitted from history books and special issues of *Cahiers du Cinéma* dedicated to French cinema. "I was just plain forgotten," she said. She kept going even if, as she admitted in 1986, with each film she had "to fight like a tiger." [...]

For a few years, my friend Joan Dupont and I would have an annual lunch with Varda at her home, eating and talking while periodically visited by one of her cats. She was predictably funny and warm and brilliant but also sharp and strong and willful. During our last lunch together, Varda said she was tired. But she was as voluble as ever and filled with plans. She reminisced about her mother, who loved art, and her father, who didn't, and spoke about growing old. "Never complain, never explain," she said. The next week, Varda was off to the Cannes Film Festival, where she presented a restoration of her 1977 film *One Sings, the Other Doesn't*. She joined Ava DuVernay and Cate Blanchett on the red carpet to protest gender inequality at the festival. It was gratifying and deeply moving to see her among all these other women, though I wondered how many understood what Varda—through her example, her will, and her art—had done to pave the way for them.

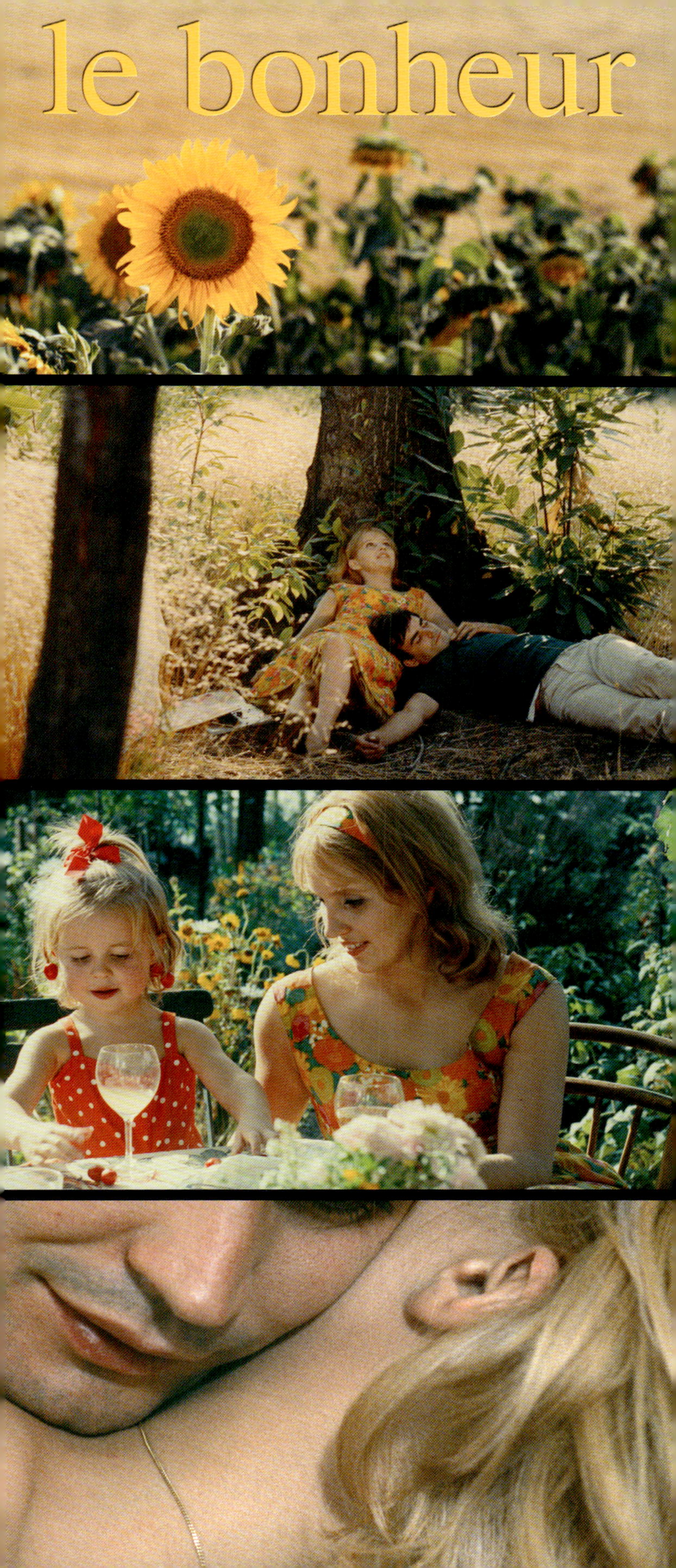

le bonheur

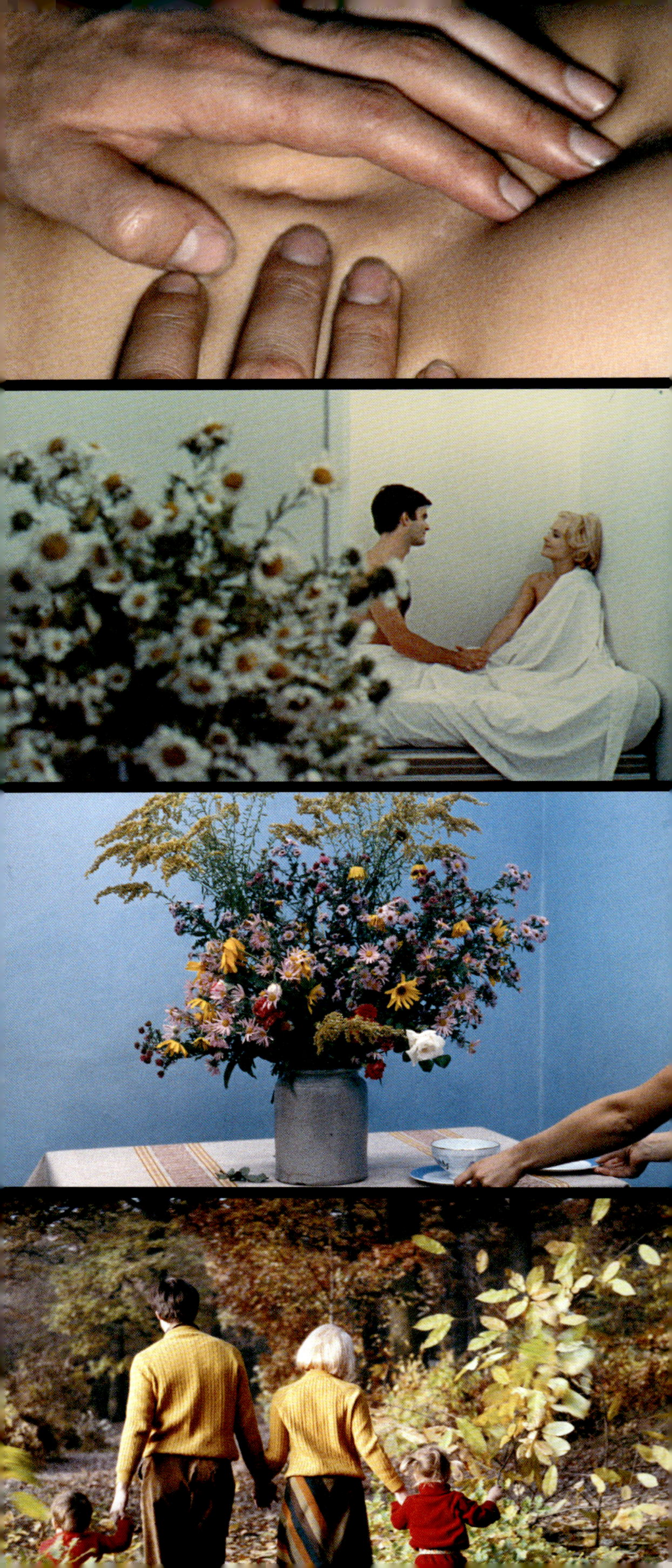

[*Le Bonheur* is] a film about how everyone is unique but replaceable in our society. It's like a beautiful fruit with a worm inside.

François and his wife, Thérèse, live a happy, contented life, enjoying weekends in the countryside with their children. All seems ideal until François meets Émilie, an attractive single woman who works at the local post office, and he begins an affair. Varda wrote the script in three days. "I was asking myself, and it's still a valid question: Is desire natural?"

Opposite and previous page: Scenes from *Le Bonheur* (1965)

Right: Varda during production of *Le Bonheur*

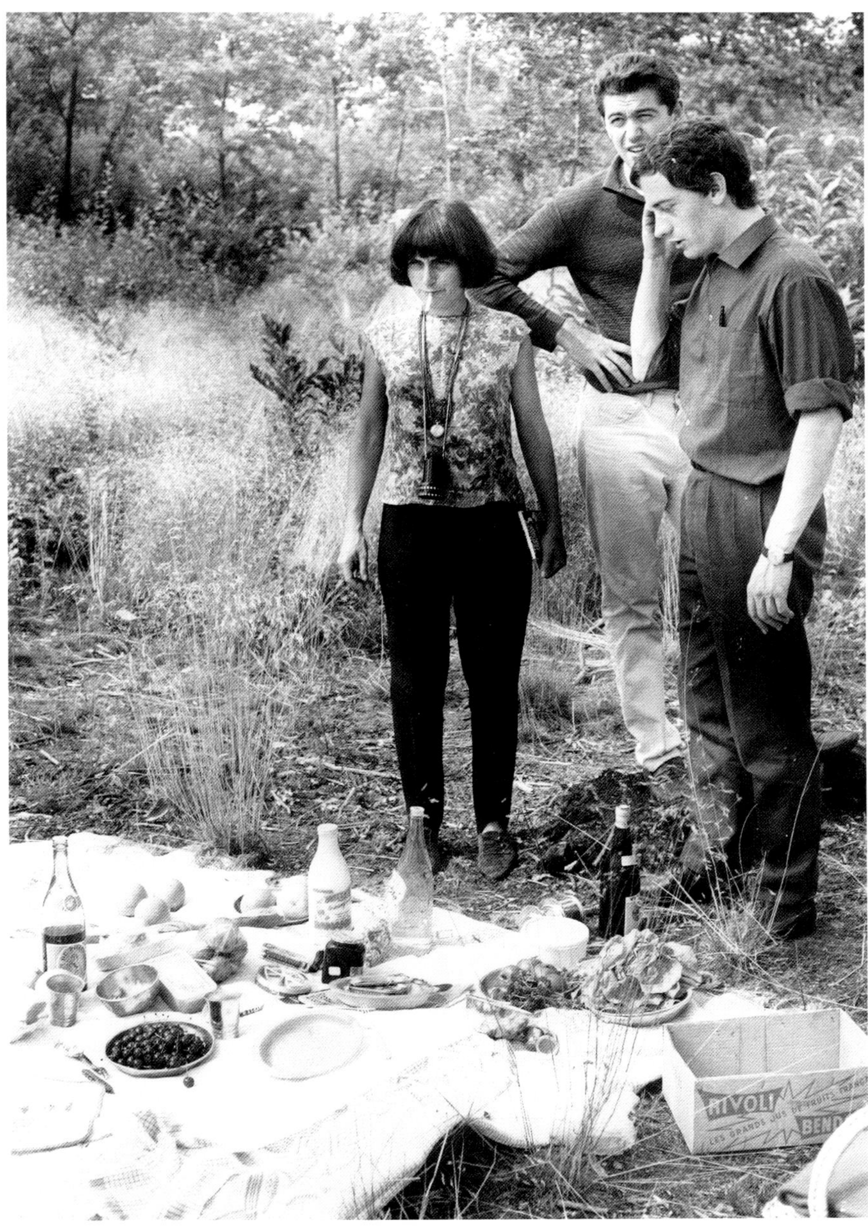

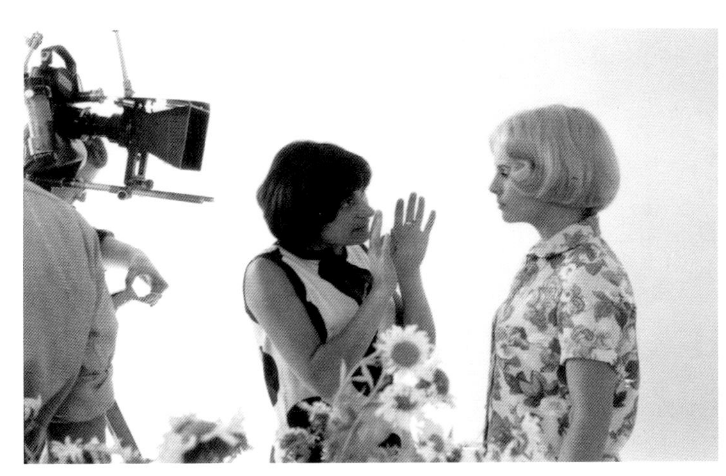

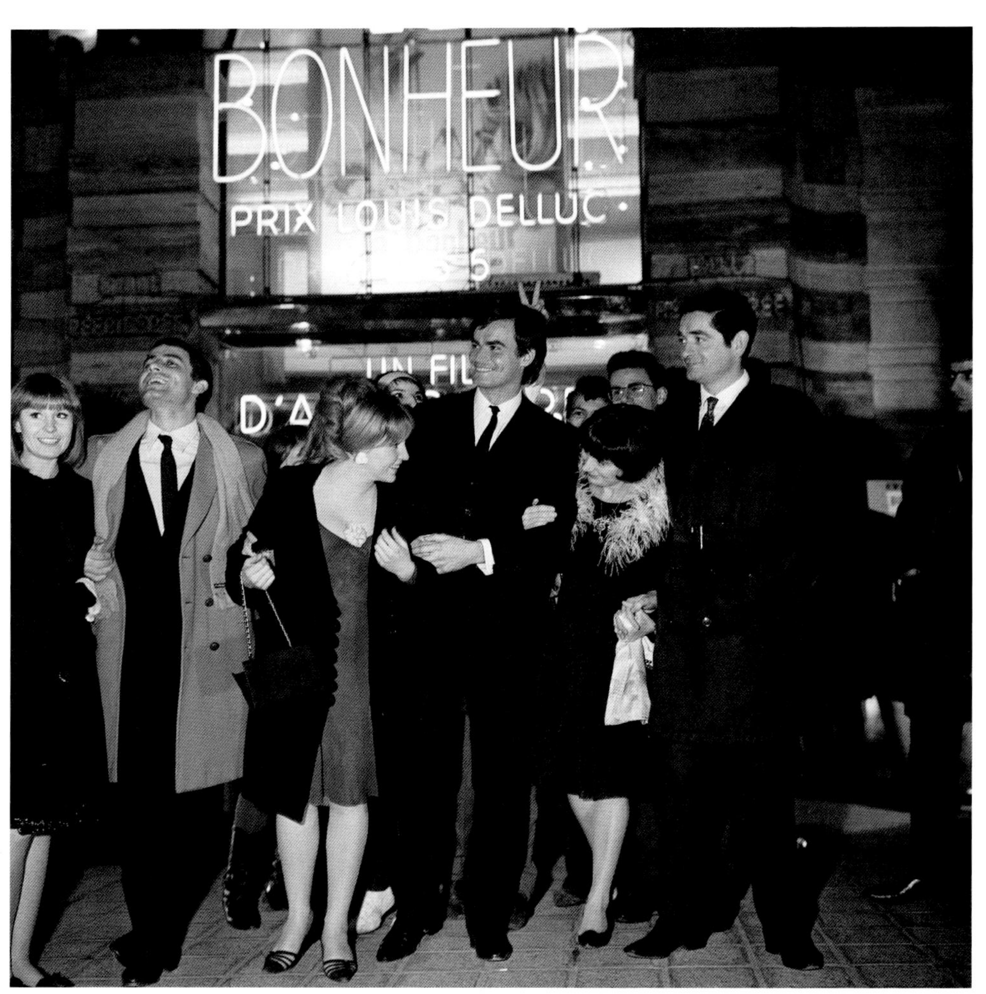

Above: Varda and Marie-France Boyer during production of *Le Bonheur*

Left: Varda and Jacques Demy (right) with Claire and Jean-Claude Drouot (center) and an unidentified couple at the premiere of *Le Bonheur* in Paris, February 23, 1965

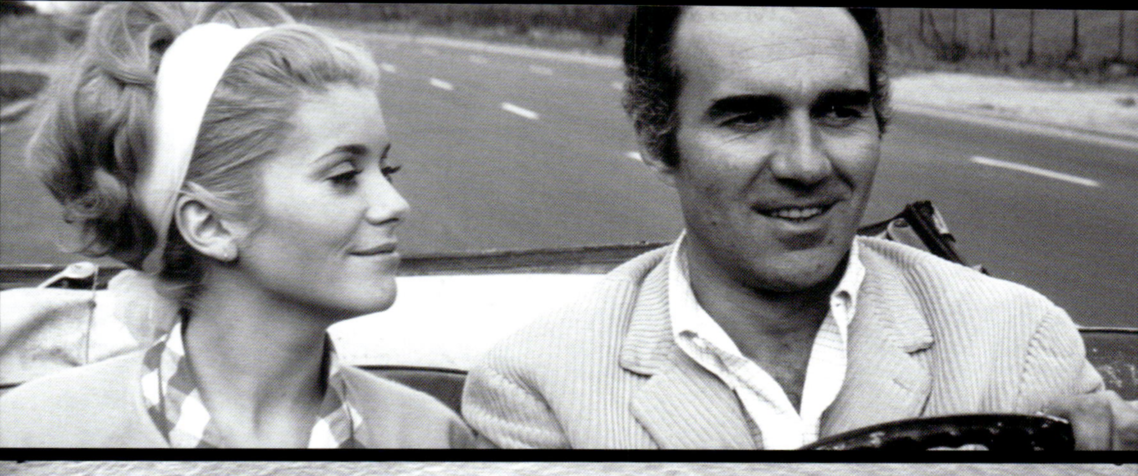

LES CREATURES

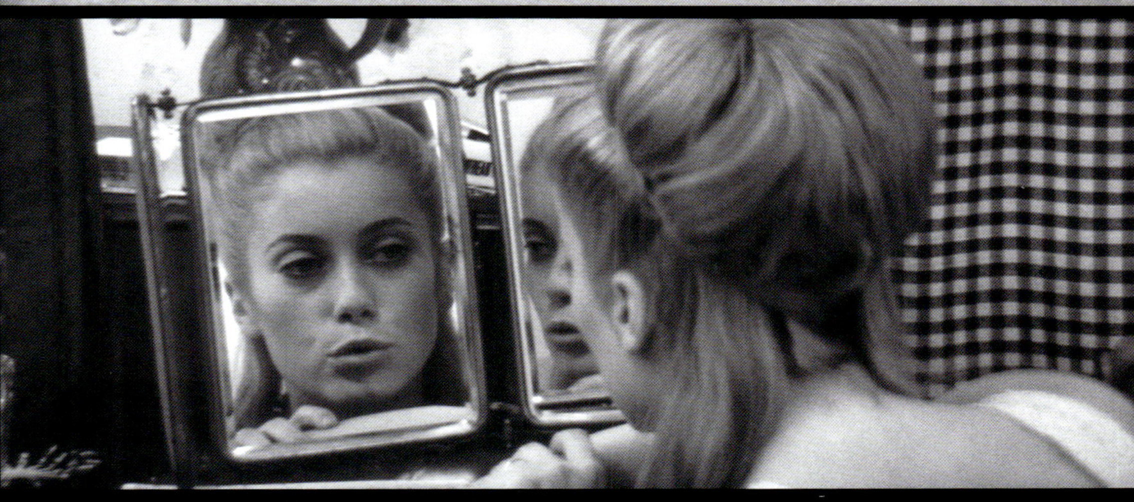

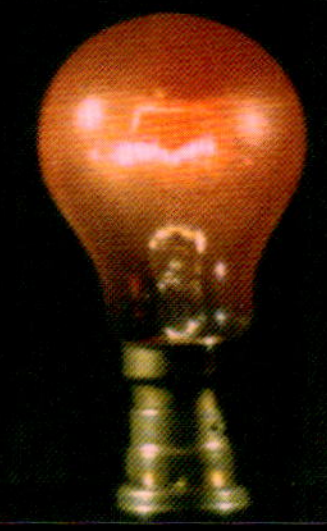

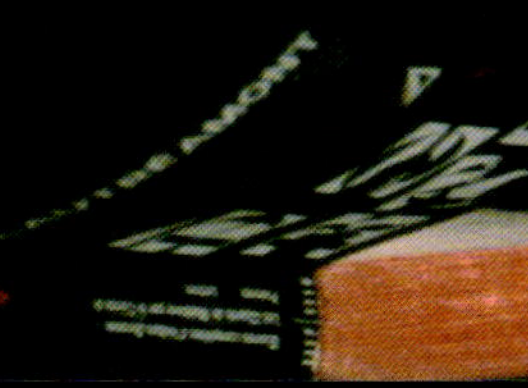

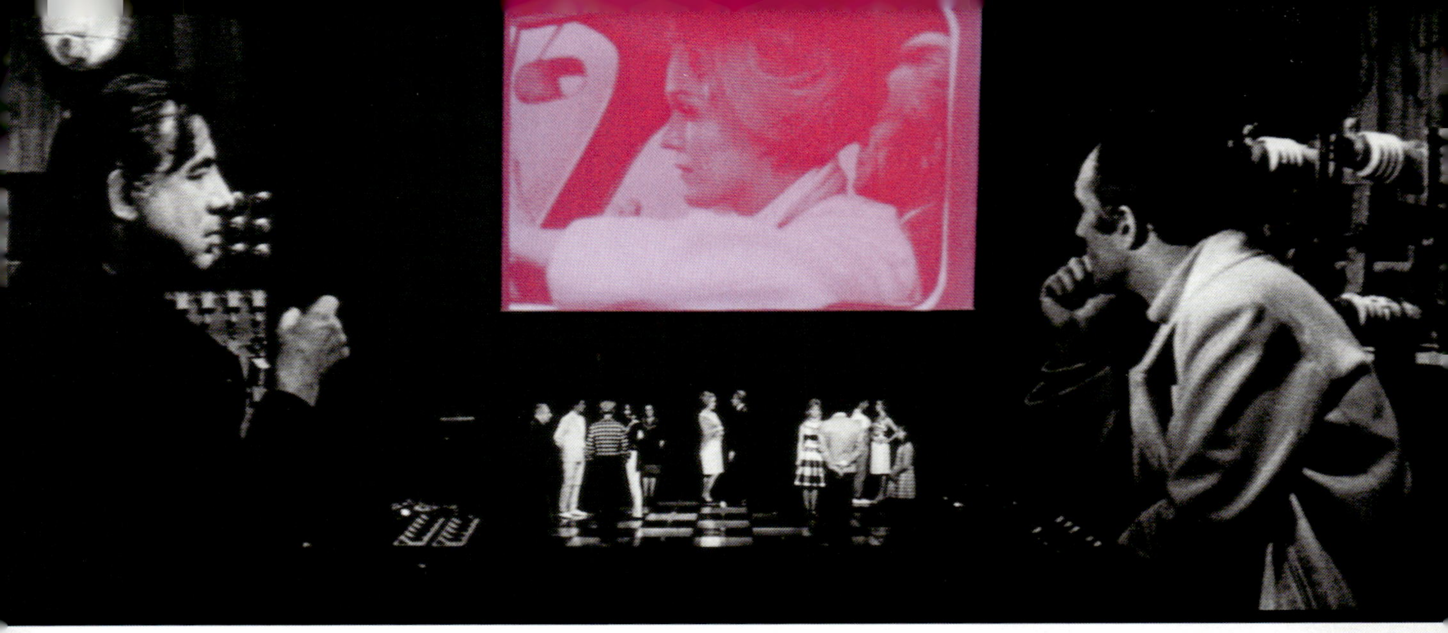

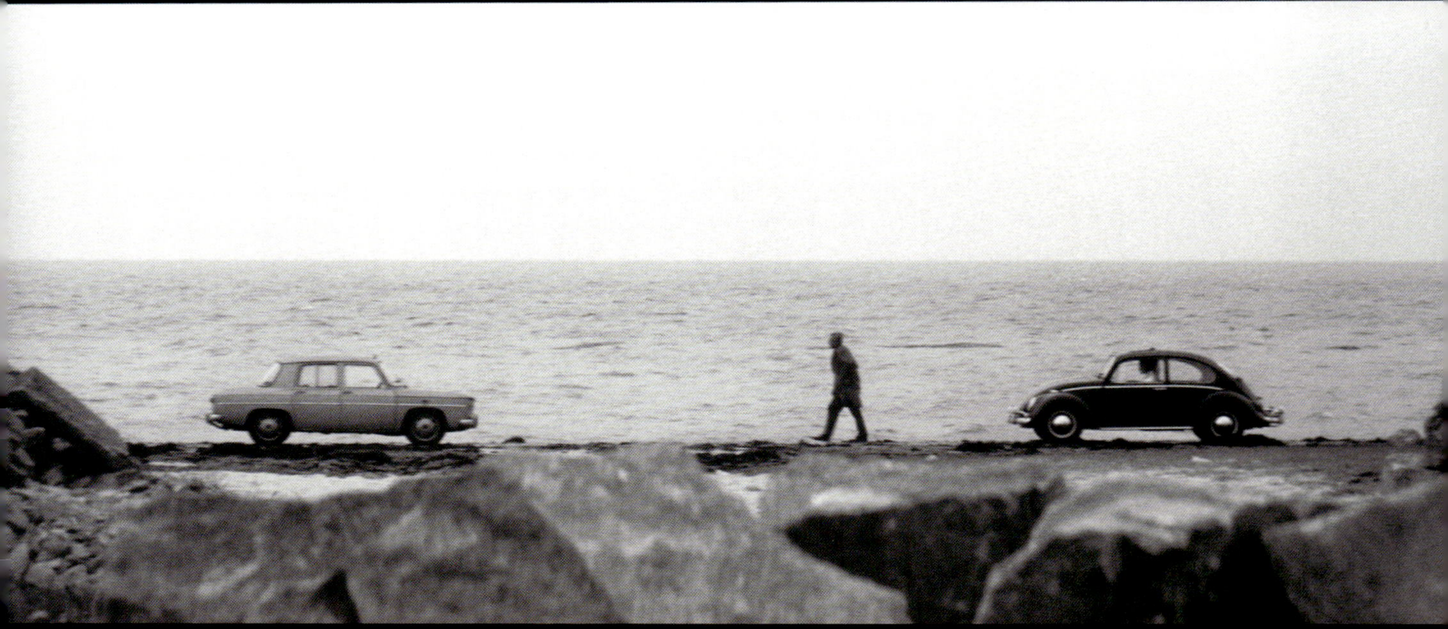

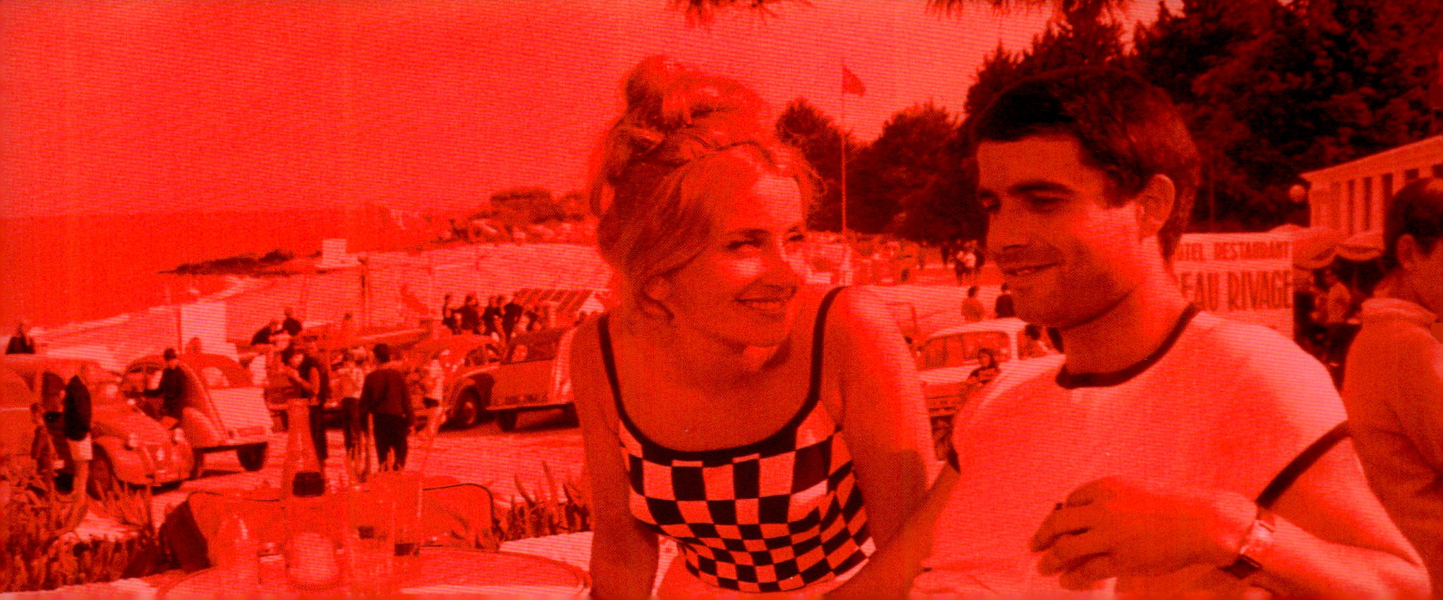

—

[*Les Creatures*] was written during a winter in Noirmoutier where we had decided to stay for a few months. I thought of a couple like that, living in a castle in a secluded place by the sea. I made Mylène a mute and Edgar, who tries to write, a taciturn character.... And I was daydreaming.

Les Creatures (1966) is a fantastical, pre-multiverse era examination of the marriage between a science fiction author and his wife. After a car accident, Edgar wanders and writes, looking for inspiration for his next novel, and Mylène loses the ability to speak. Varda begins to dissolve the barriers between reality and fiction, experimenting with color, genre, and a widescreen canvas.

Opposite and previous page: Scenes from *Les Creatures*

Right: Michel Piccoli and Catherine Deneuve during production

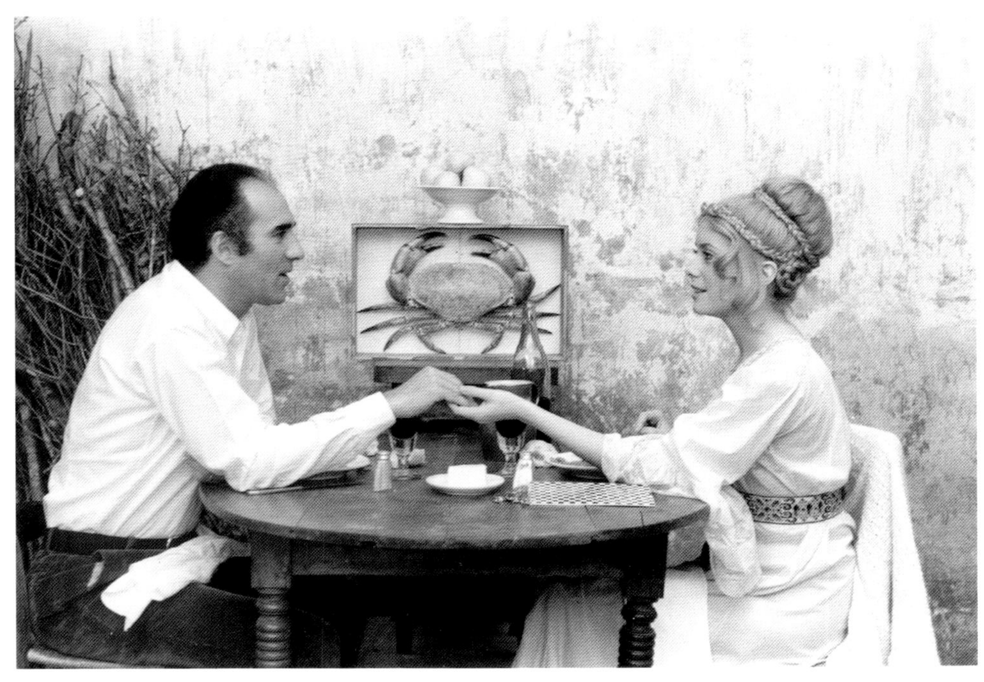

I made a short film about my uncle Yanco, this father of my dreams that I discovered very late on. He was fabulous and tender. He spoke eloquently of the colors in his paintings and said, "Between the desire and the painting there is a little bitterness, a passing shadow." I found that very touching. There's no light without shadow, and the shadows are very beautiful.

Varda traveled to Sausalito, California, to meet a Greek immigrant relative previously unknown to her. The artist Jean Varda, known as Yanco, lives on a boat and enjoys a hippie lifestyle. The filmmaker's exuberance at finding this bohemian uncle within her family provides the foundation for a colorful time capsule of 1960s counterculture.

Right: Pin worn by Varda in *Uncle Yanco* (1967)

Opposite: Scenes from *Uncle Yanco*

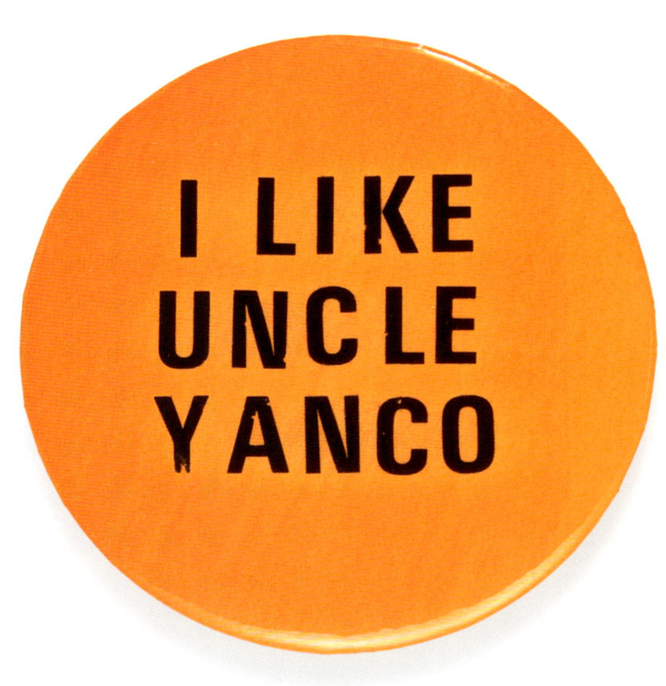

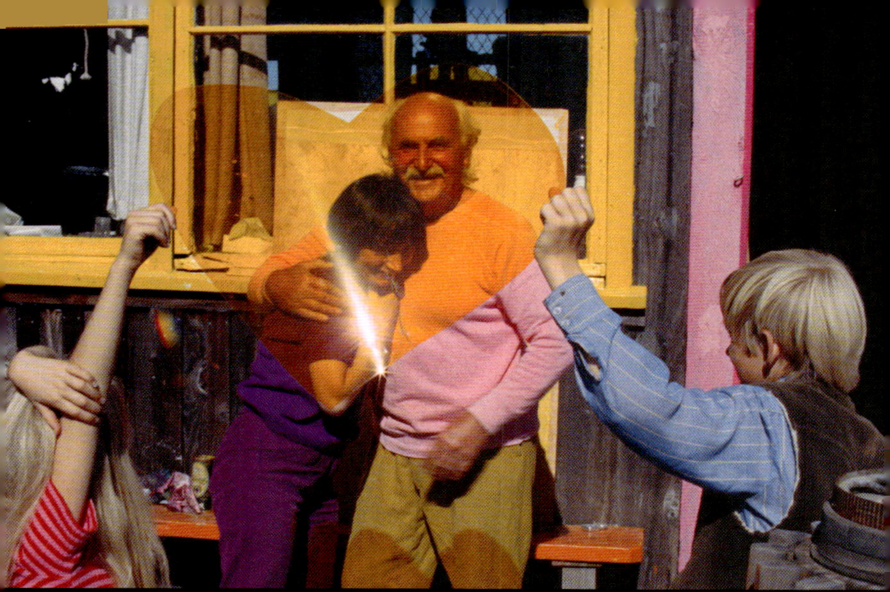

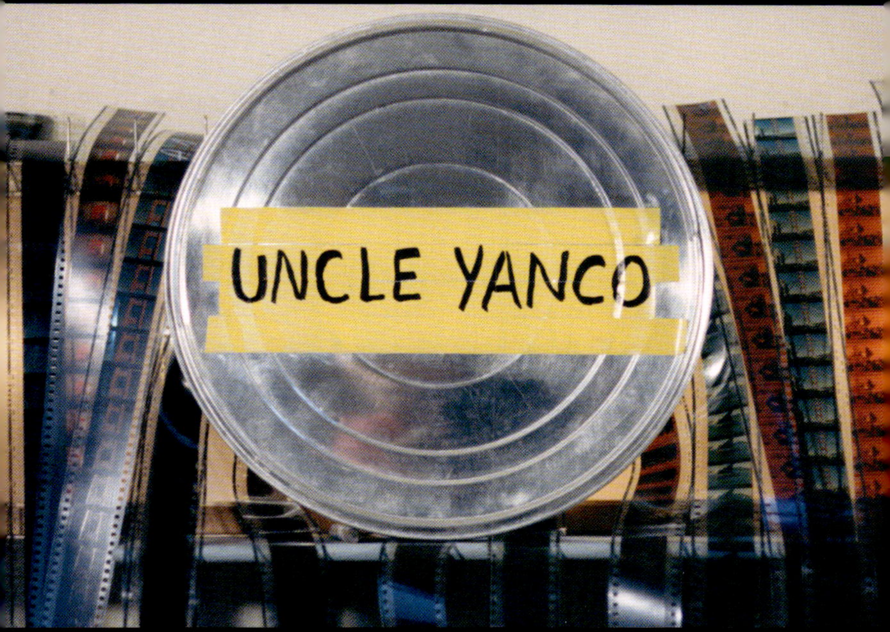

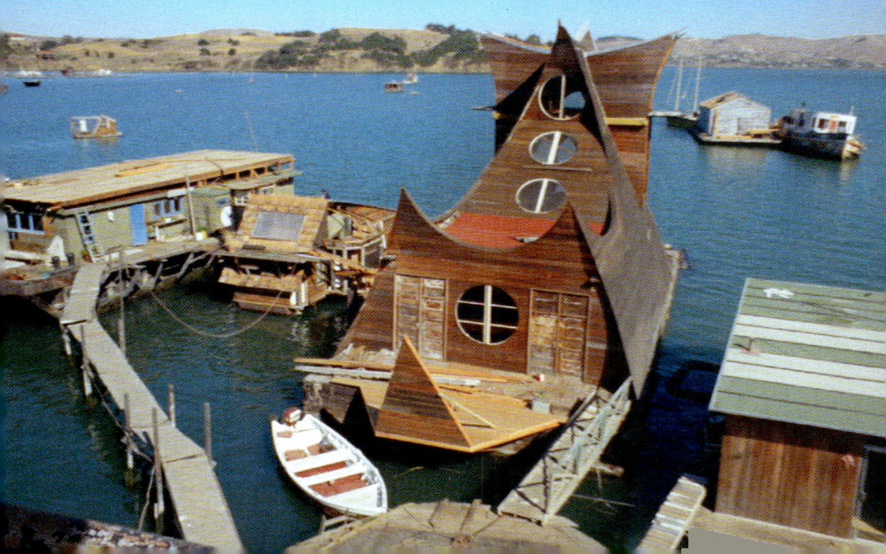
UNCLE YANCO

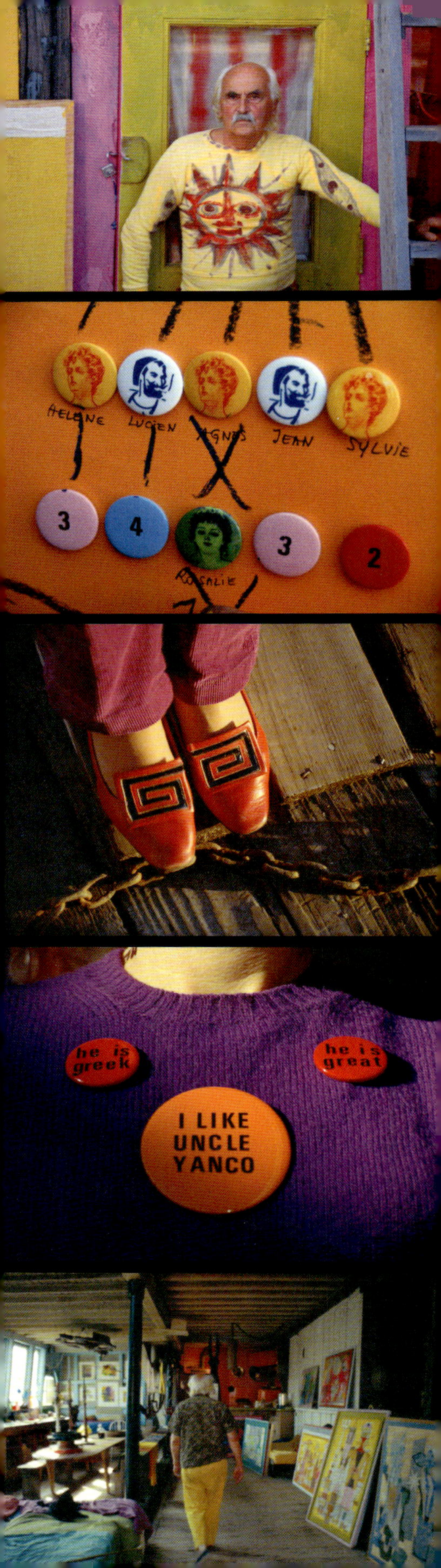
HELENE LUCIEN AGNES JEAN SYLVIE
3 4 3 2
ROSALIE
he is greek
he is great
I LIKE UNCLE YANCO

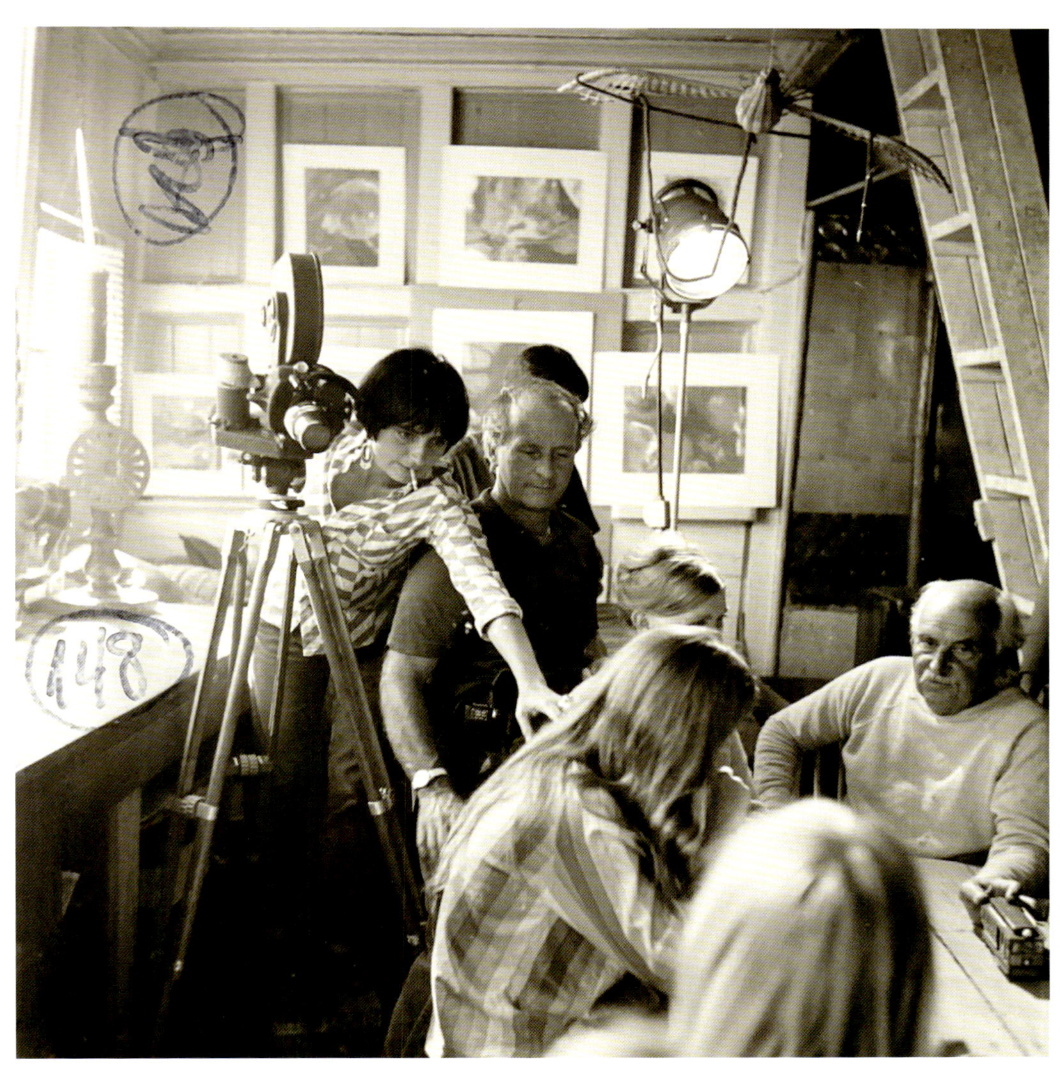

Opposite and overleaf:
Scenes from *Uncle Yanco*

Above: Varda, Jean Varda
(seated, far right), and
crew during production of
Uncle Yanco

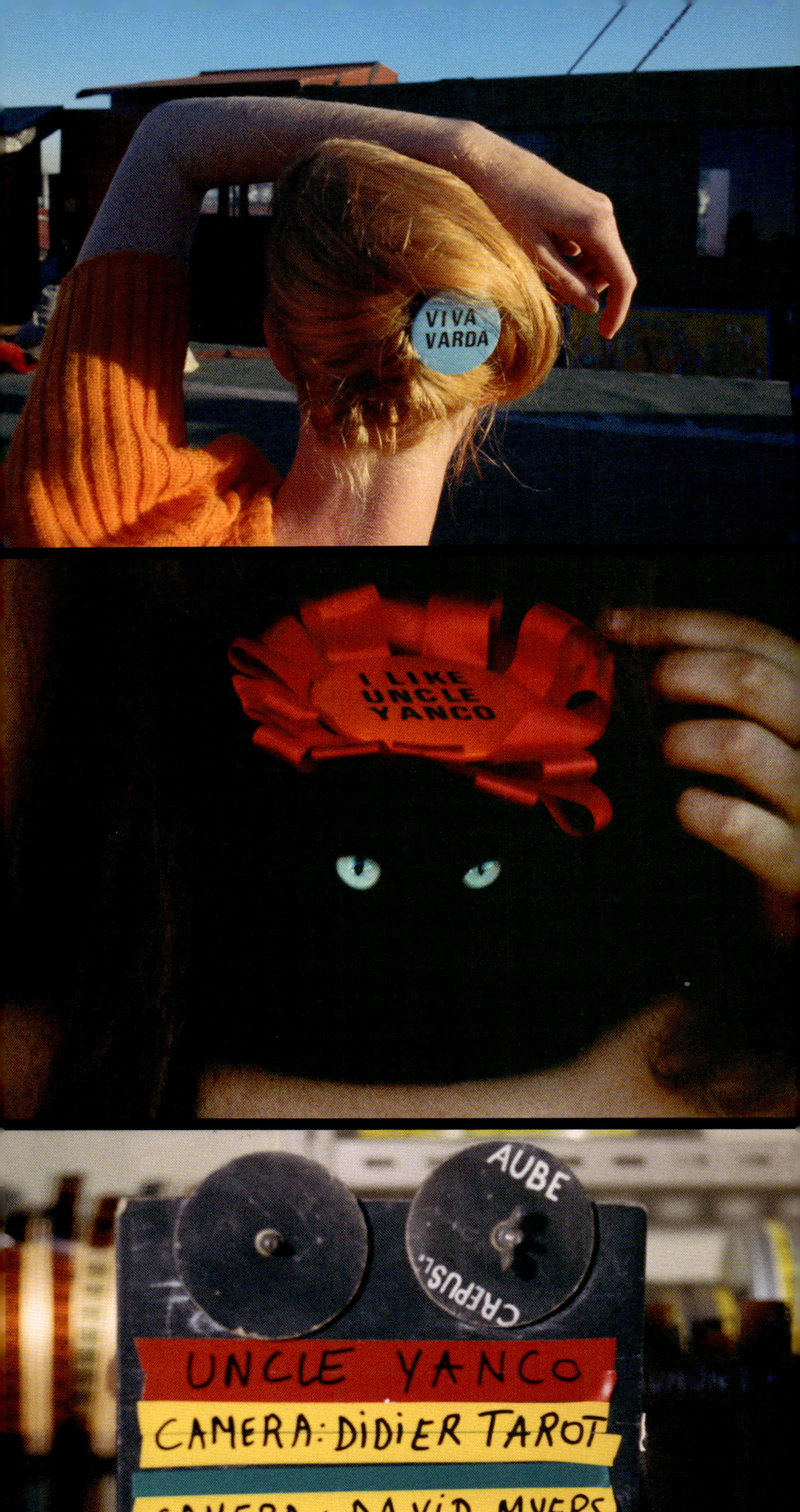
VIVA VARDA
I LIKE UNCLE YANCO
AUBE
CRÉPUSᵉ
UNCLE YANCO
CAMERA: DIDIER TAROT
CAMERA: DAVID MYERS

When I came to America I was on the defensive because of the politics, which I hate…. But on the other hand, I found something I didn't expect—a huge part of the population that is radical and living it too.

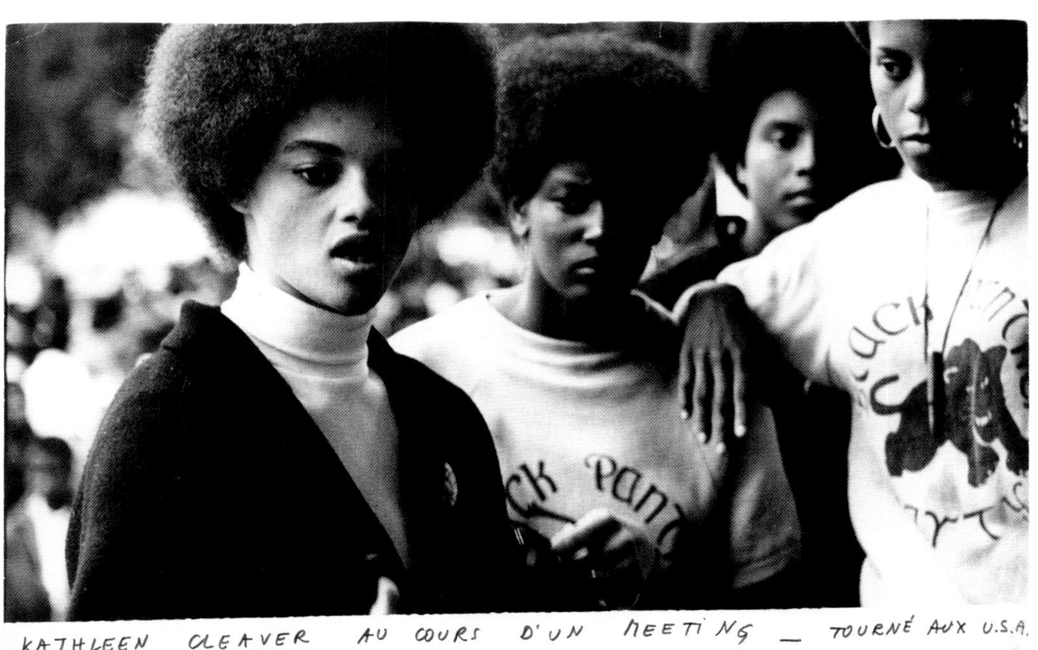

Back to the courthouse!

The trial of Black Panther leader Huey Newton will be over in two weeks or less.

Already, it is evident that the state has a very shaky case against Newton, as revealed by the contradictory testimony of the three star prosecution witnesses:

---- a policeman wounded by a police bullet on the morning of Oct. 28, who never saw a gun in Huey Newton's hands, who shot at Huey as he grappled with another policeman, and who had subsequent memory lapses.
---- a melodramatic black bus driver whose vivid description of Huey gunning down a cop contradicted both his earlier statements to the police and the testimony of the wounded police officer.
---- a third key witness, for the prosecution, Dell Ross, a black man who was supposedly kipnapped at gunpoint and "forced" to drive Huey to the hospital - refused to testify, pleading the fifth amendment.

In fact, many observers believe that if this were not a political and racial case, Newton would be acquitted, or would never have been brought to trial.

But Newton is a political prisoner, he is a leader of a black group that is beginning to seriously challenge the power structure and the police.

This is why we have raised the demand to "Free Huey." This is why Newton faces a possible conviction, and this is why we must demonstrate our support for Huey on Monday at the Courthouse.

This weekend will be the last major demonstration of support begore the end of the trial. It is very important for us to be there now!

    DEMONSTRATION: MONDAY, AUGUST 26   9:30-12 noon
       (carpools will leave from Haste & Telegraph)

    RALLY: SUNDAY, AUGUST 25   BOBBY HUTTON MEMORIAL PARK
                       (formerly De Fremery Park)
            18th & Adeline   1 pm
            Bar-B-Que Dinner $1.00
        SPEAKERS: STOKELEY CARMICHAEL, BOBBY SEALE, ELDRIDGE
          CLEAVER, JACK WEINBERG, and others

    (The NEWTON-SEALE Campaign (Newton for Congress, Seale for Assembly) will be kicked-off Sunday. Campaign workers are urgently needed. To volunteer, call Peace & Freedom - 549-0690, or the Black Panther Office - 654-2003)

ayn— Probably the best opportunity to get what was lost last time, as well as STOKELEY, it — Call me if you want to EKN IT — Tom

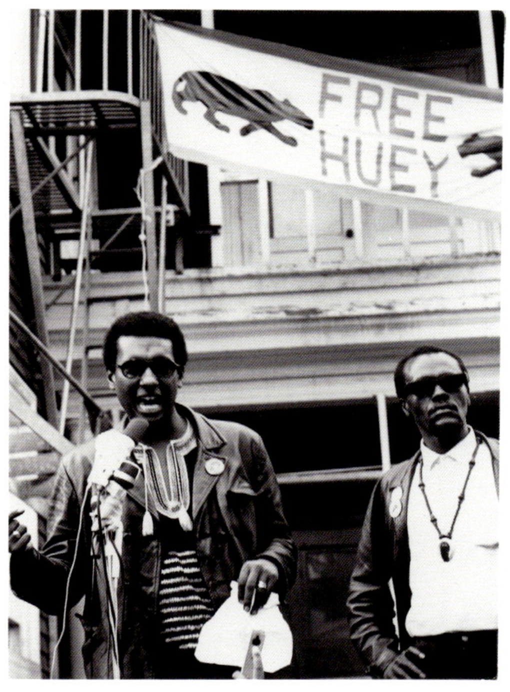

"Every Saturday, I would fly from Los Angeles to Oakland," Varda recalled in 2015 of her efforts to film the Black Panther protests. "With the help of Tom Luddy and a few others, I would take my 16mm camera and record what I could every Sunday for three or four weeks. I needed to get the speeches because I wanted to have what their message was clearly, so I could understand."

Above left: Black Panther Party protest flyer with handwritten note from Luddy

Above right: Stokely Carmichael speaking at a "Free Huey" rally in 1968, photographed by Varda

Opposite: Scenes from *Black Panthers*

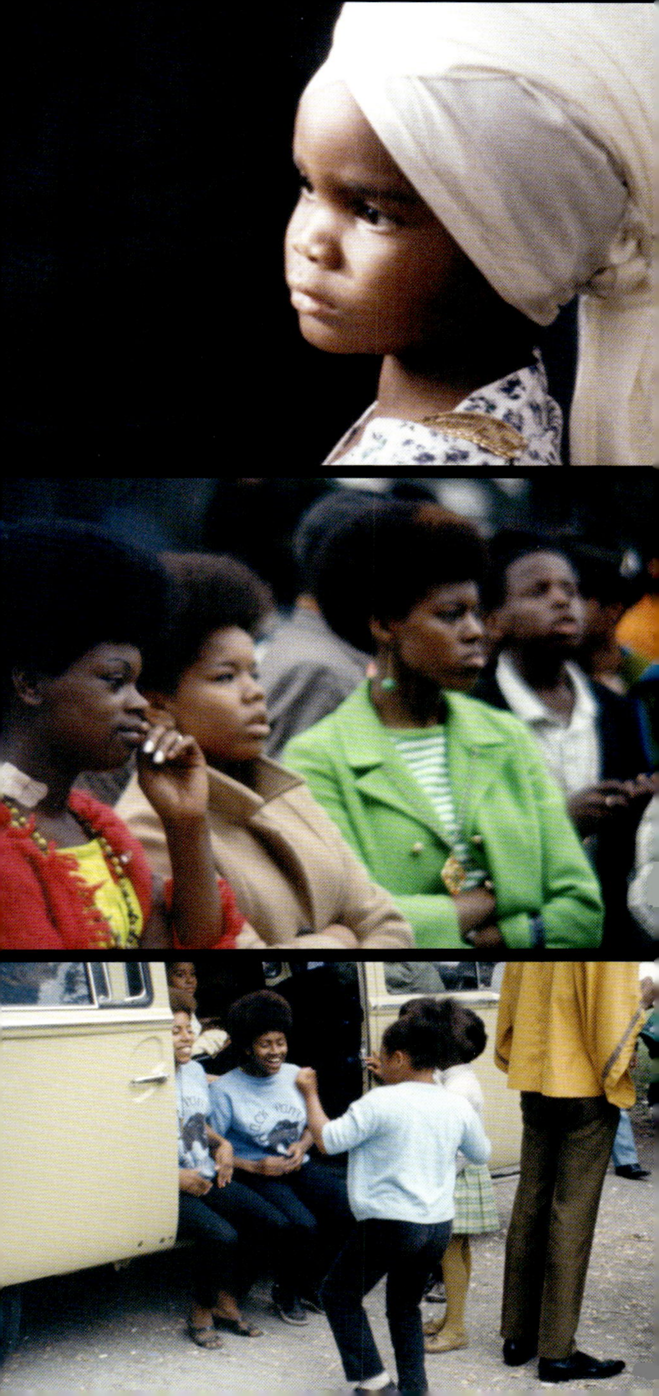

BLACK PANTHERS
reportage réalisé par
AGNES VARDA
PAUL ARATOW   PADDY MONK
EVE CRANE   DAVID MYERS
MICHEL HUGO   PAUL OPPENHEIM
PIERRE LENOIR   JOHN SCHOFILL
TOM LUDDY   PASCAL THOMAS

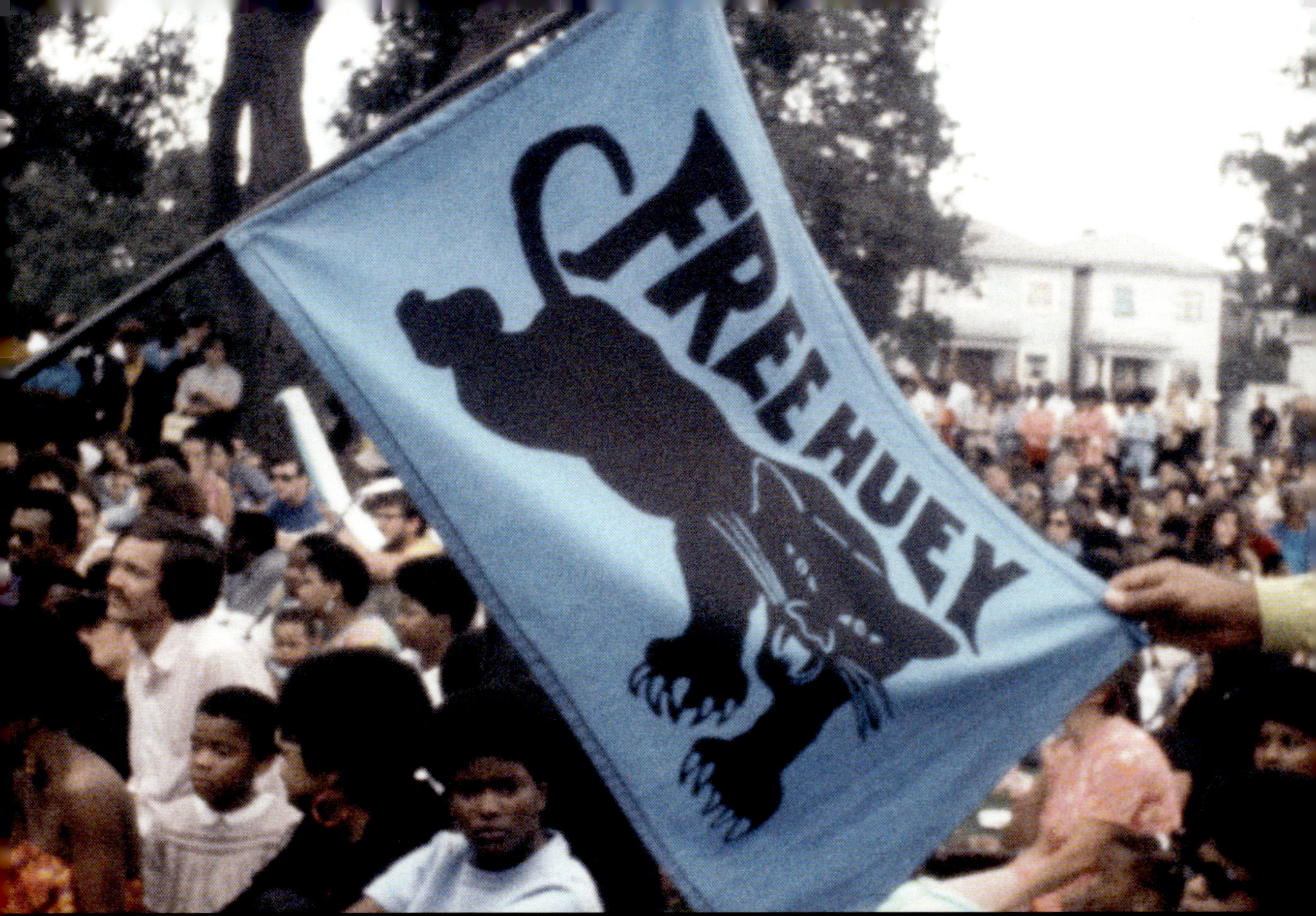

FREE HUEY

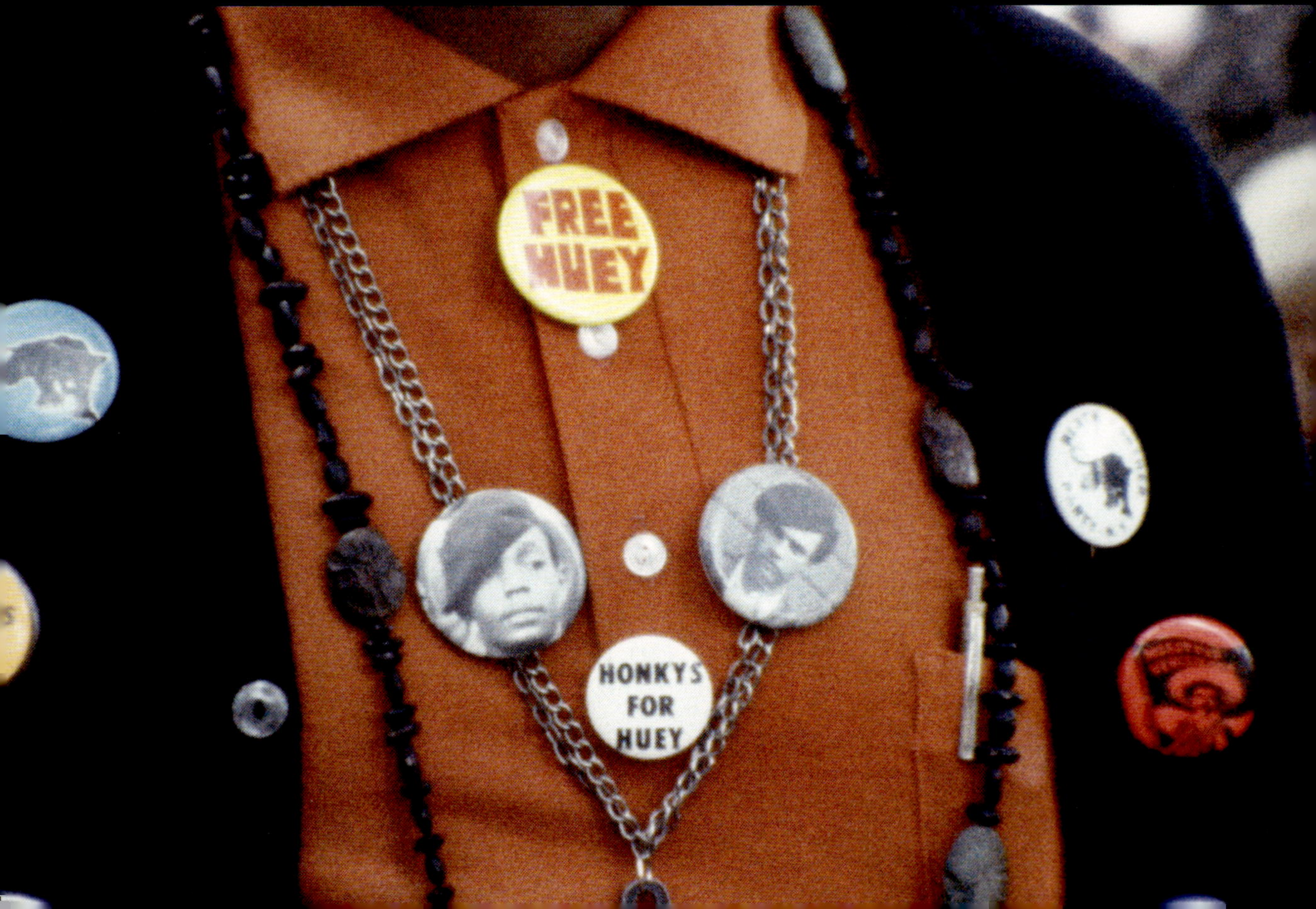

FREE HUEY
HONKYS FOR HUEY

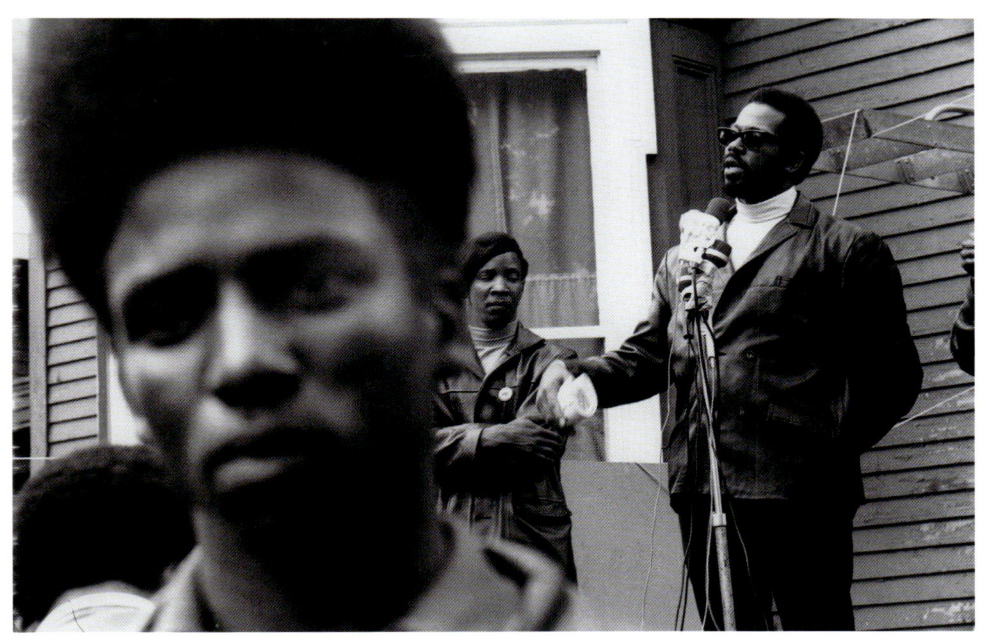

I, Huey P. Newton, Minister of Defense for the Black Panther Party,
agree to a filmed interview, conducted by Pascal Thomas and Tom Luddy
on August 1 1968, and give permission for that filmed interview to be
included in a film produced and directed by Agnes Varda on the subject
of the Black Panther Party and Free Huey Campaign.

Opposite and overleaf:
Scenes from *Black Panthers*

Above: Eldridge Cleaver
speaking at a "Free Huey"
rally in 1968, photographed
by Varda

Right: Release form signed
by Huey P. Newton

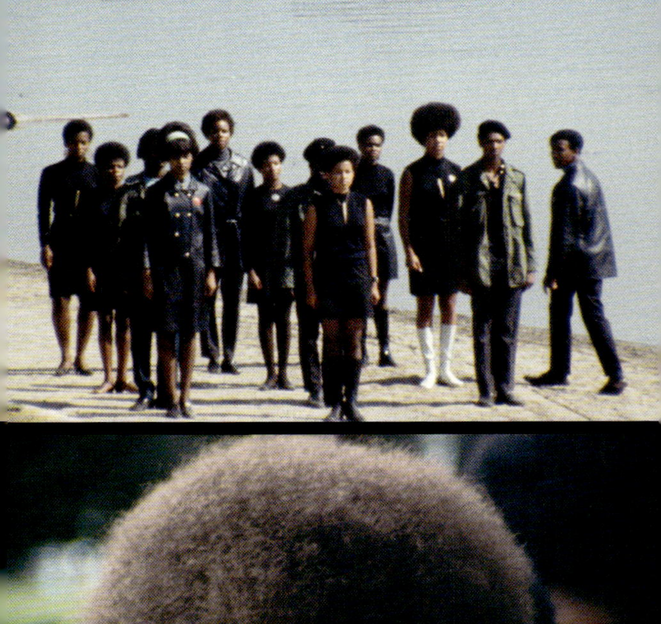

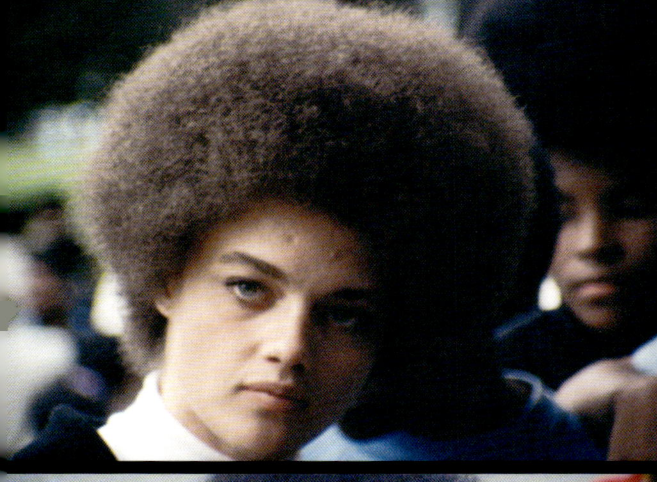

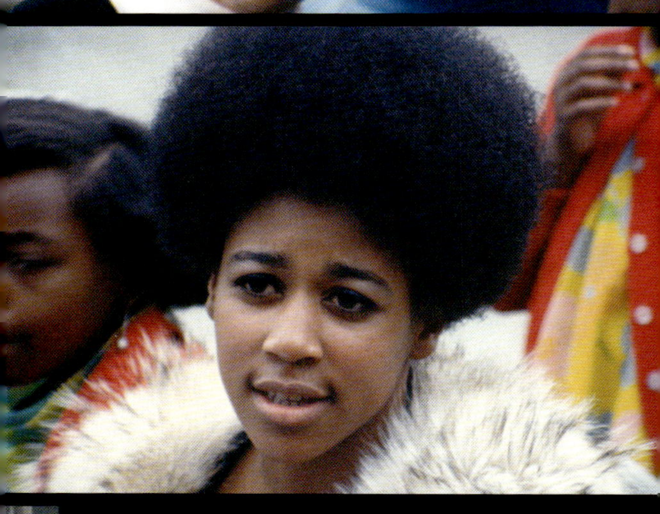

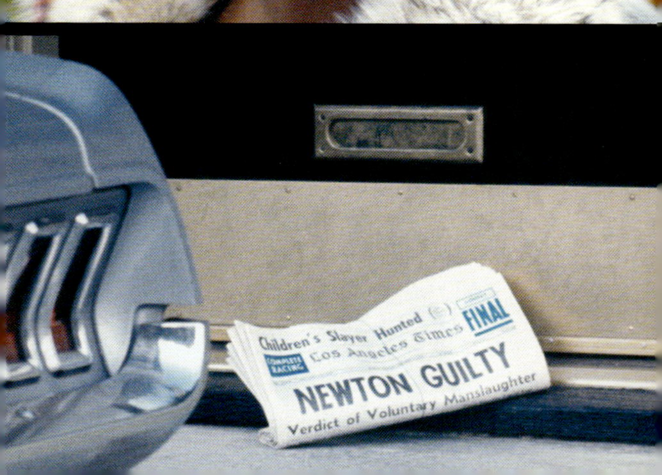
Children's Slayer Hunted
Los Angeles Times
FINAL
NEWTON GUILTY
Verdict of Voluntary Manslaughter

LYNNE LITTMAN

When *Le Bonheur* had its US premiere at the New York Film Festival in 1966, I was in love and living with a French photographer. We'd seen the film together sometime before that, and I remember not approving of its premise that everyone is replaceable—that each love you have, no matter how wonderful or tragic, can be replaced by another. My photographer went off to the festival one night and miraculously brought Agnès Varda back to our railroad flat on 82nd Street for dinner. She immediately made herself at home, took over the cooking, and took over the evening. We were thrilled. She never left my life after that. The photographer did, but Agnès didn't.

Back then I was an associate producer at National Educational Television, which later became PBS. I knew my way around film crews and production, and this had made an impression on Agnès, who called the apartment a few months later, quite sure I'd remember who she was. With no introduction and few details, she asked if I wanted to come to Los Angeles and be her *assistante*. I packed my bags.

By the time I arrived, Agnès had shot most of her Black Panthers documentary and was embarking on a new film, *Lions Love*. She lived in a lovely little house in Beverly Hills with her husband, Jacques Demy; daughter Rosalie; and Monique, their French Moroccan maid. I felt like I had walked into *Le Bonheur*. She put me up in her garage, called "La Villa Princesse," which she had named for their dog, Princesse. I shared the space with Shirley Clarke, the amazing filmmaker who would stand in for the character of Agnès in the new film. I always thought it would have been fascinating to film these two dark-haired originals together, since they often disagreed!

My work for Agnès was nothing like anything I'd done in the documentary field. I'd never been anywhere near a scripted film with actors. I could hardly drive, but she rented me a white Chevy Corvair convertible, and I drove. Agnès always assumed you'd fulfill her expectations no matter what was asked. And as far as I know, we all did. We filmed in a beautiful house on St. Ives Drive, above the Sunset Strip. I was moved in to guard the cameras at night while Viva and her boyfriend were living in the bedroom next door. I cooked for the crew, checked the costumes, and took script notes while the actors roamed around half-naked with television footage of Bobby Kennedy's death playing as background to their scenes. Agnès's view of America was one of innocence and corruption, which she captured simultaneously in this living room.

Coming from still photography, she had extensive knowledge of lenses and lighting. She used every inch of that house and its natural light. Her technical skills allowed her to be in charge while remaining creative—rare for most directors. She could have done everyone's job on the set. Her whole approach to filmmaking was original and unique. She truly was a gleaner, a *glaneuse* who made use of everything and everyone she came into contact with.

There's never been anything in my life comparable to working with her, which is why she has remained an inspiration to me.

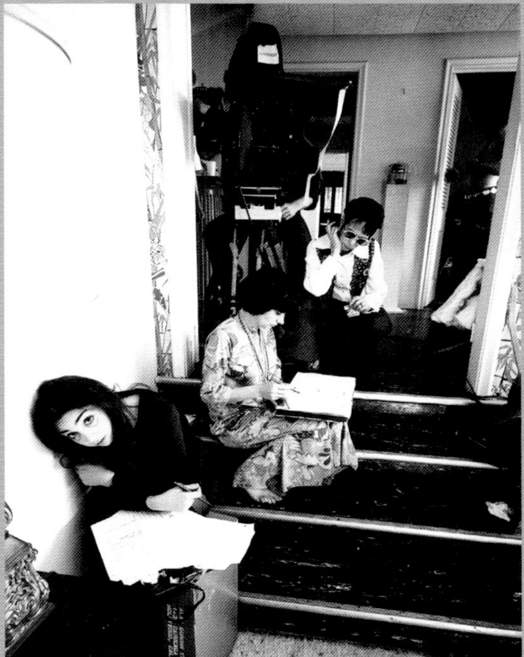

From left: Lynne Littman, Varda, and Shirley Clarke during production of *Lions Love (...and Lies)* (1969)

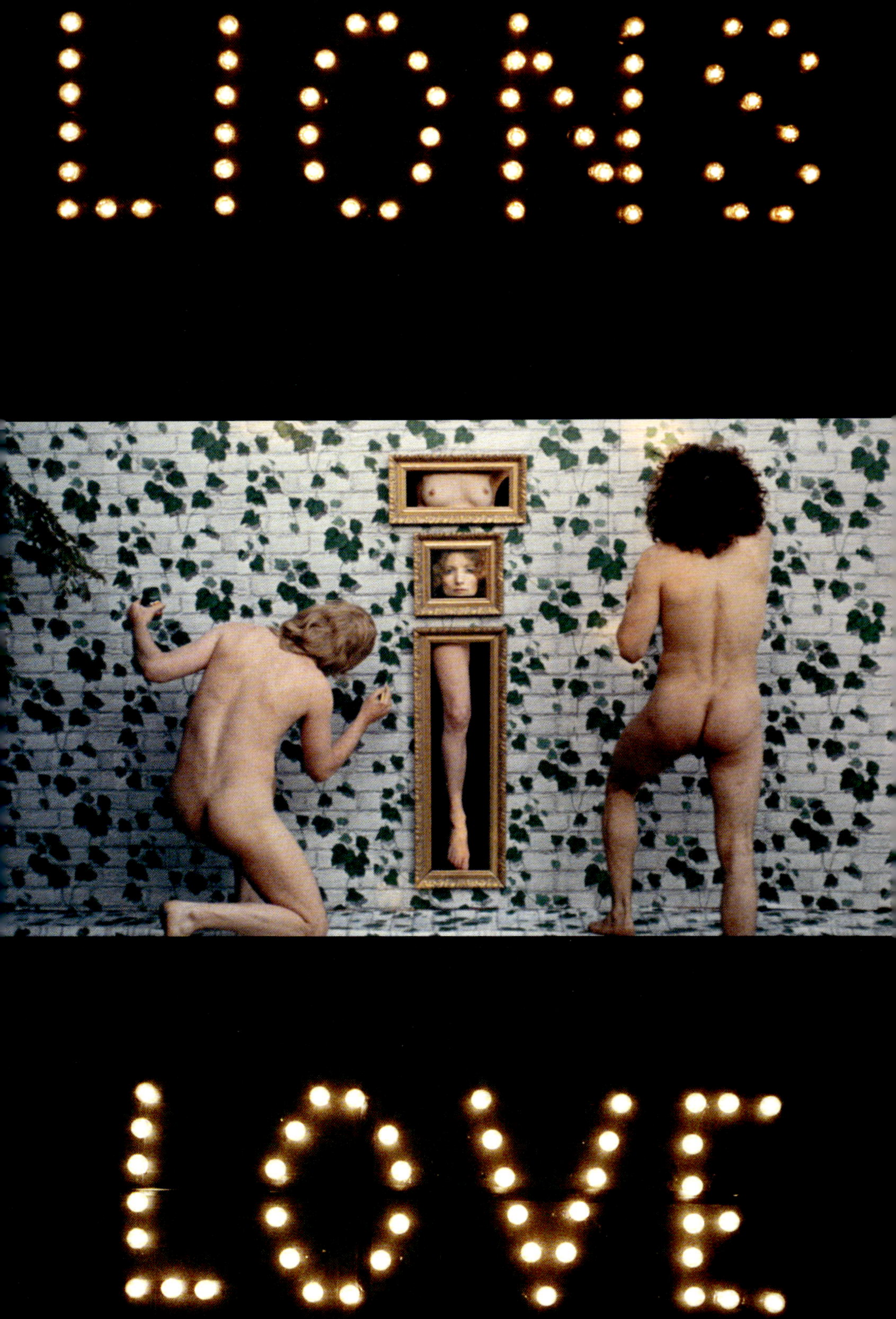

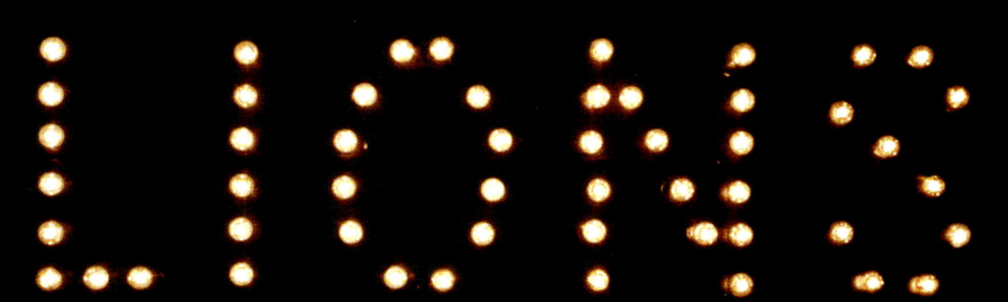
LIONS

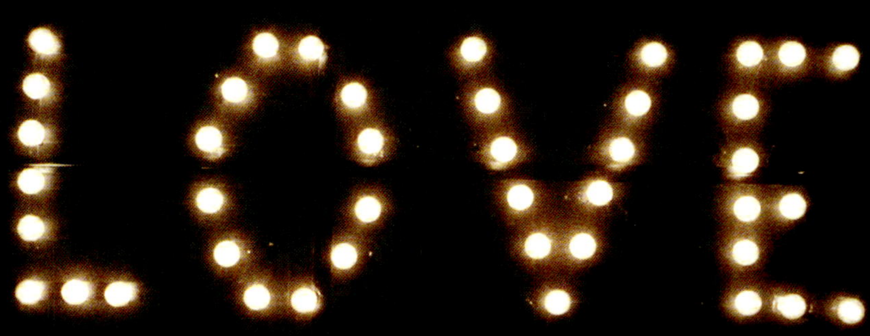
I LOVE

It's not really that I wanted to make a film about youth, but I [was] interested in exploring the problem of the relationship between form and content and in seeing how and why the problems of young people have taken on such importance.

Varda's wild meta movie *Lions Love (…and Lies)* presents a different side of California: Hollywood. Three actors—Viva, Jim, and Gerry, a ménage à trois—live in a house in the Hollywood Hills. Accompanied by their houseguest from New York, the director Shirley Clarke (playing herself), they watch real-life events of the summer of 1968, such as the assassination of Robert F. Kennedy, unfold on television.

Opposite: Scenes from *Lions Love (…and Lies)*

Right: Newspaper ad for *Lions Love (…and Lies)*

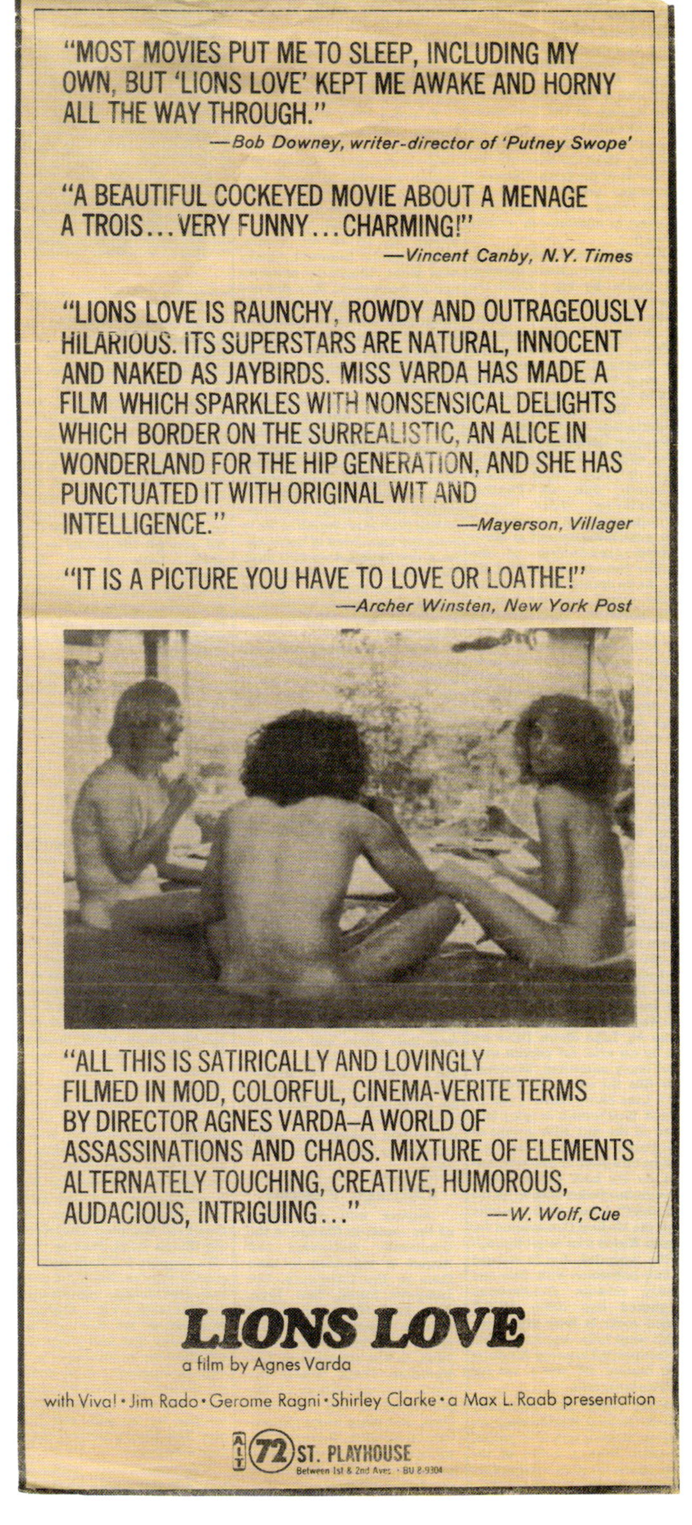

The film's subject is stars, films, free love, freedom of editing, California trees, television, the end of youth, plastic flowers, political heroes, swimming pools, red glasses, rental properties in Hollywood, coffee, and who has to get up first to make it.

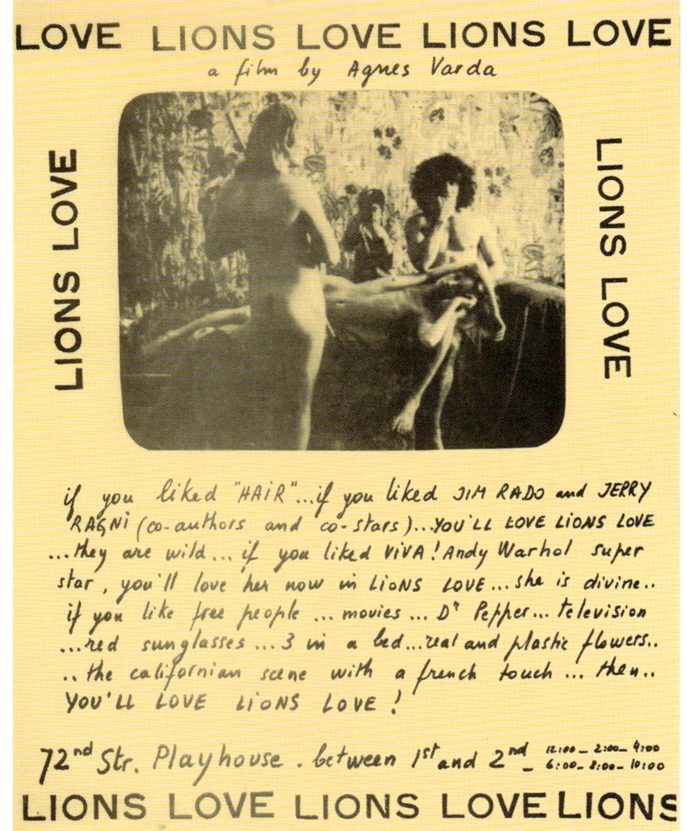

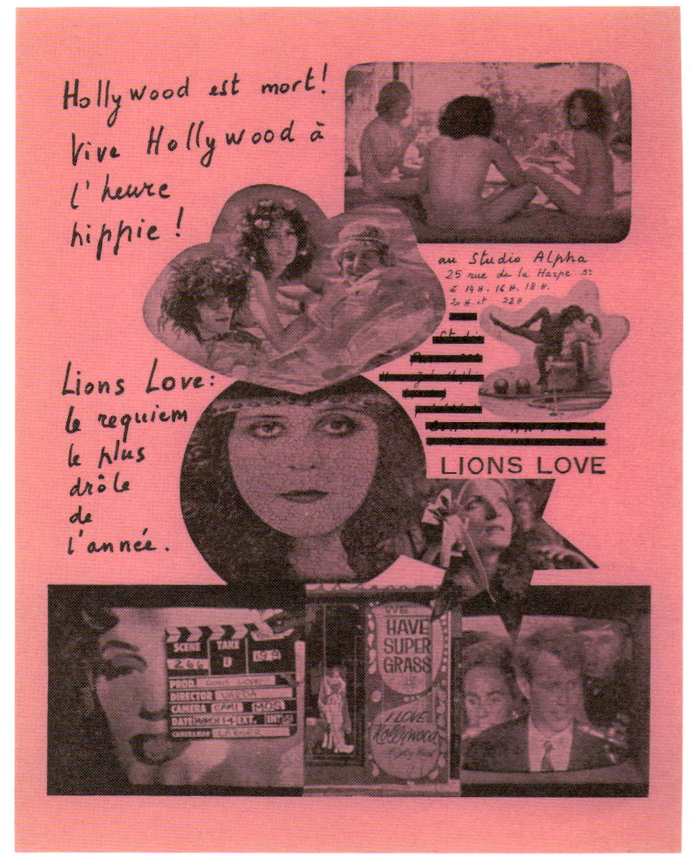

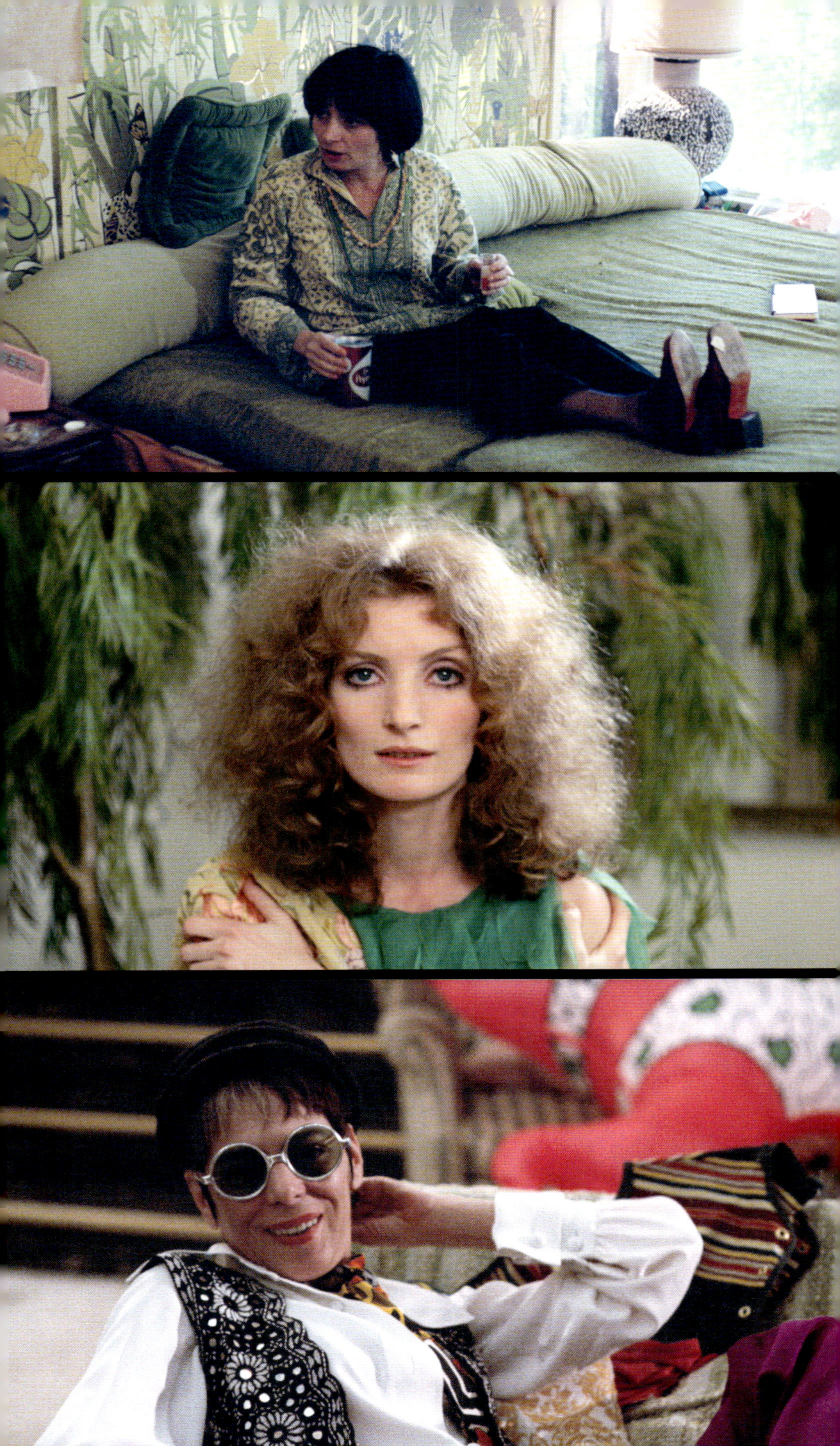

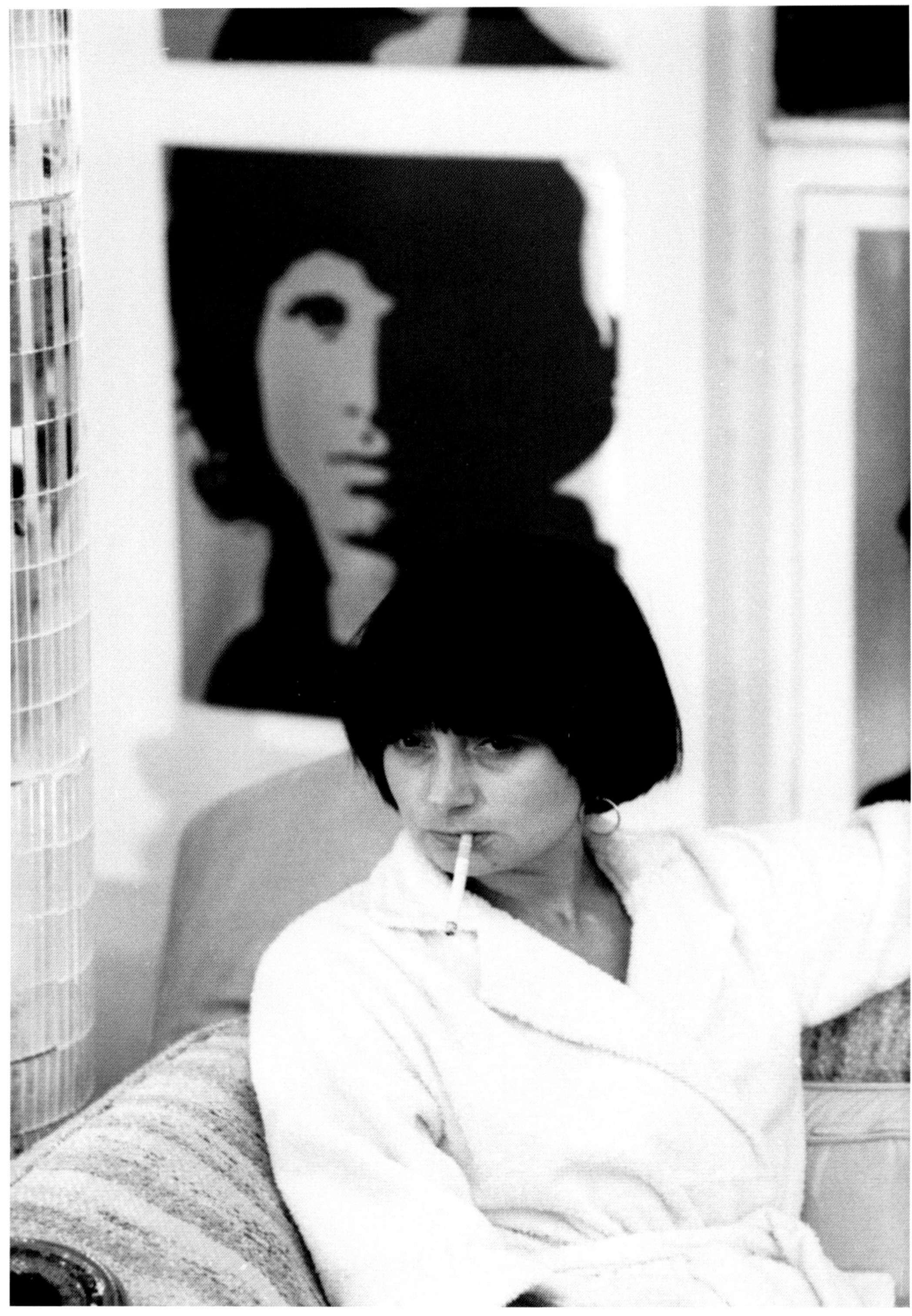

Varda had initially wanted Jim Morrison to play one of the male leads in *Lions Love (...and Lies)*. Though he declined, Morrison visited the set and can be seen briefly in the film's opening scene as part of the audience watching the theater performance of "The Beard."

Left: Varda during production of *Lions Love (...and Lies)*

Opposite: Varda and Viva on set

VIVA

I was introduced to Agnès Varda by the first love of my life. He was a photographer twice my age—I was 22 or 23 at the time—and he was obsessed with European film. The very minute *Cléo from 5 to 7* came out, he dragged me to see it. I remember being on the edge of my seat, worrying that she would end up with cancer. And I was kind of puzzled because I'd never seen any film like it before.

Years later, when Agnès approached me about *Lions Love (...and Lies)*, I was married to a Frenchman who told me I shouldn't meet with her. But he had also discouraged me from meeting with Fellini about *Satyricon*, saying, "Fellini is so unhip, nobody likes him anymore." So, I didn't meet with Fellini. Can you believe it? My sister Mary Beth said, "You aren't going to listen to him *again*, are you? Don't be ridiculous. Go see Agnès."

By then I had done a number of films with Andy Warhol. Andy gave no direction other than he would sometimes say, "Do that over again." And it turned out that he only ever said that when he had run out of film on the previous take. Working with Agnès was completely different. She was a total workaholic. Rough, domineering, and to the point. No frills, no humor. There was no comparison between them. She was a tougher film director than any man I ever worked with.

Agnès didn't ask us for our opinions about anything, really. She was very business-like. Now and then she'd say, "Do you want to improvise this or that?" I think she did that in the scene where we are drinking coffee and looking out the window, for example. But it was basically all scripted. It doesn't seem to be, but it was.

The atmosphere on that shoot was pretty chaotic and tense. Gerome Ragni was constantly whispering about cameras every-where. He would say, "Agnès is filming us in the bathroom while we pee!" I mean, he was so paranoid! I don't even know if he was smoking pot. Some people think Ragni, James Rado, and I really were a threesome, but I had never met them before. I'm surprised how many people believe it was all real, everything happening in the film, and that Agnès was just documenting it.

The film ends with close-up shots of the three of us. When Agnès shot mine, I said at the end, "I'm not going to talk. I'm just going to breathe." I guess I was sick of talking. So, it's a three-and-a-half-minute shot, mostly wordless, that ends the film; it's beautiful.

Agnès really was a great filmmaker, one of the best. Considering who she had to work with, me and those two crazies, she did a pretty good job! I think she did capture the vibe of the time. She's also one of my daughter [the actress] Gaby Hoffmann's favorite directors. We both loved *The Gleaners and I*.

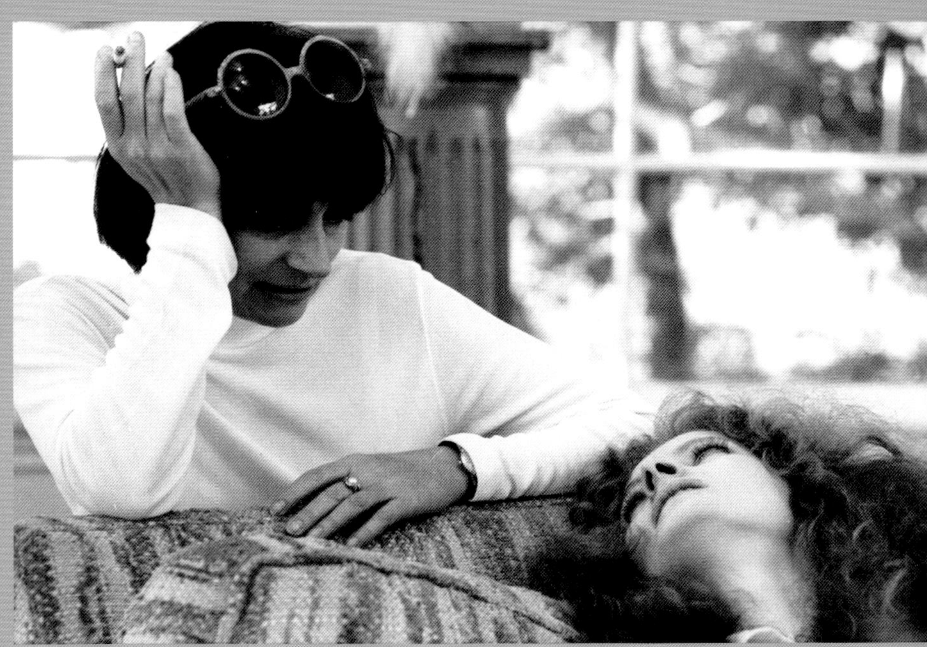

I set out from this idea... that most women are stuck at home. And I attached myself to my hearth. I imagined a new umbilical cord.

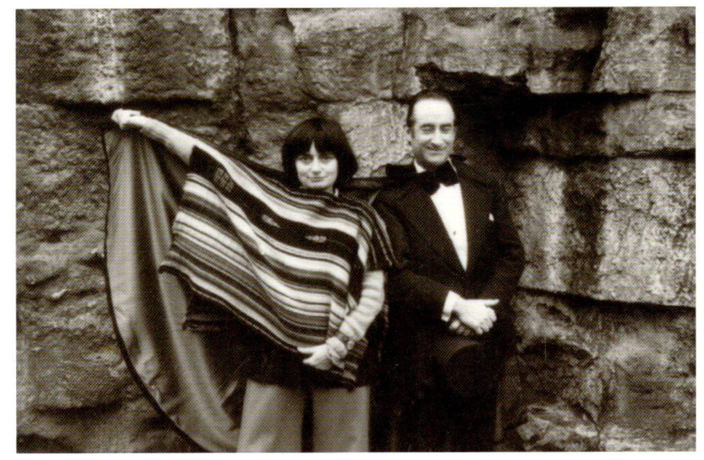

Varda received an offer to direct a film for German television in the early 1970s, when she was raising her young son, Mathieu. Since she couldn't travel far, she made a documentary on the shopkeepers in her rue Daguerre neighborhood.

Above: Varda and Robert François as Mystag the Magician during production of *Daguerréotypes* (1975)

Right: French poster for *Daguerréotypes*

Opposite: Scenes from *Daguerréotypes*

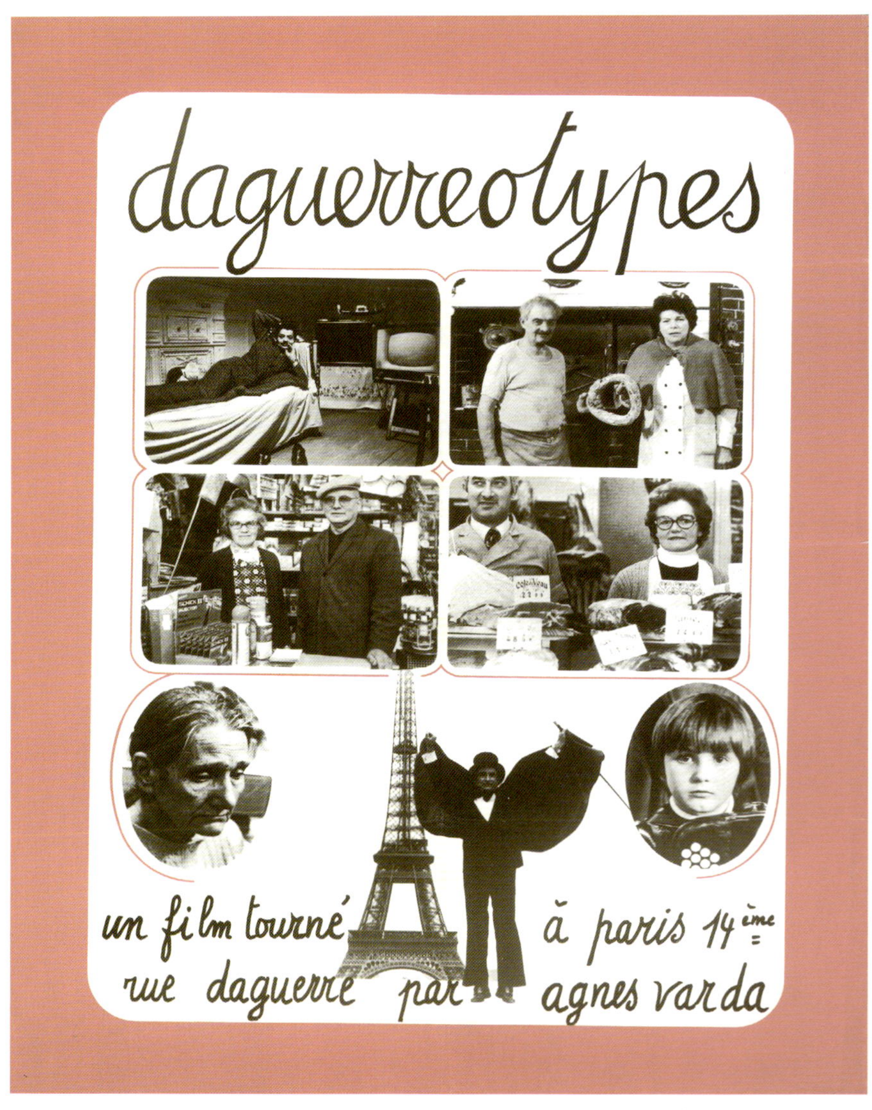

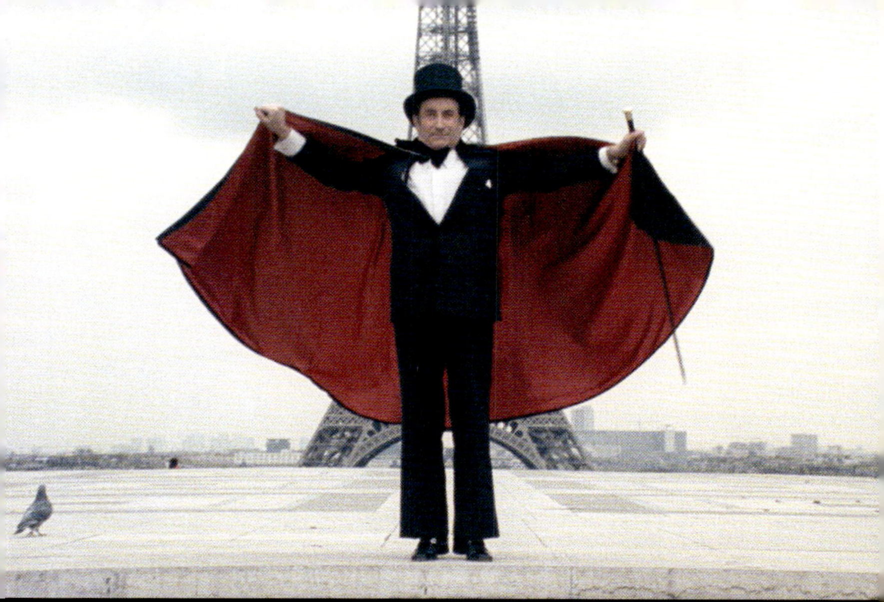

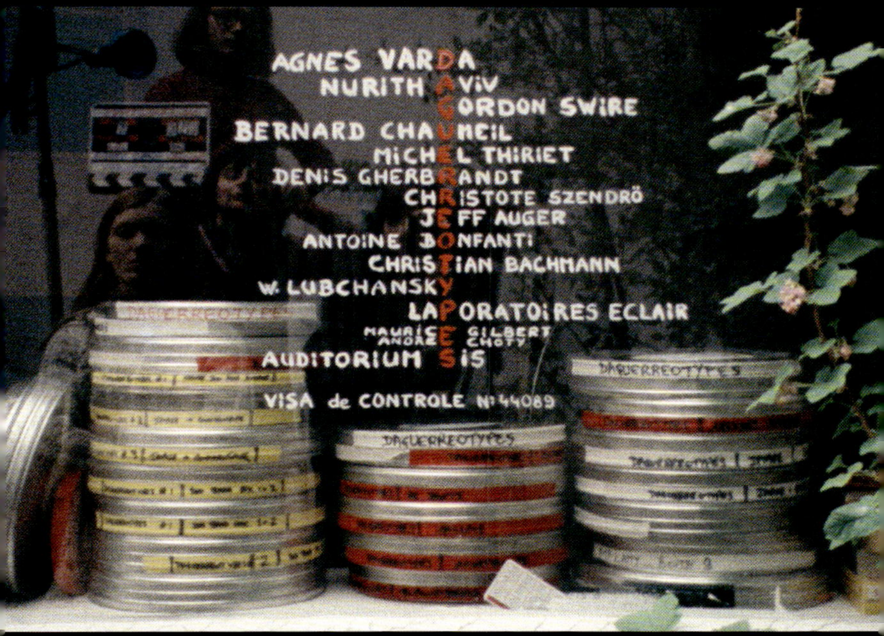

AGNES VARDA
NURITH AVIV
GORDON SWIRE
BERNARD CHAUMEIL
MICHEL THIRIET
DENIS GHERBRANDT
CHRISTOTE SZENDRÖ
JEFF AUGER
ANTOINE BONFANTI
CHRISTIAN BACHMANN
W. LUBCHANSKY
LAPORATOIRES ECLAIR
MAURICE GILBERT ANDRÉ CHOTY
AUDITORIUM SIS
VISA de CONTROLE N°44089
DAGUERREOTYPES
DAGUERREOTYPES

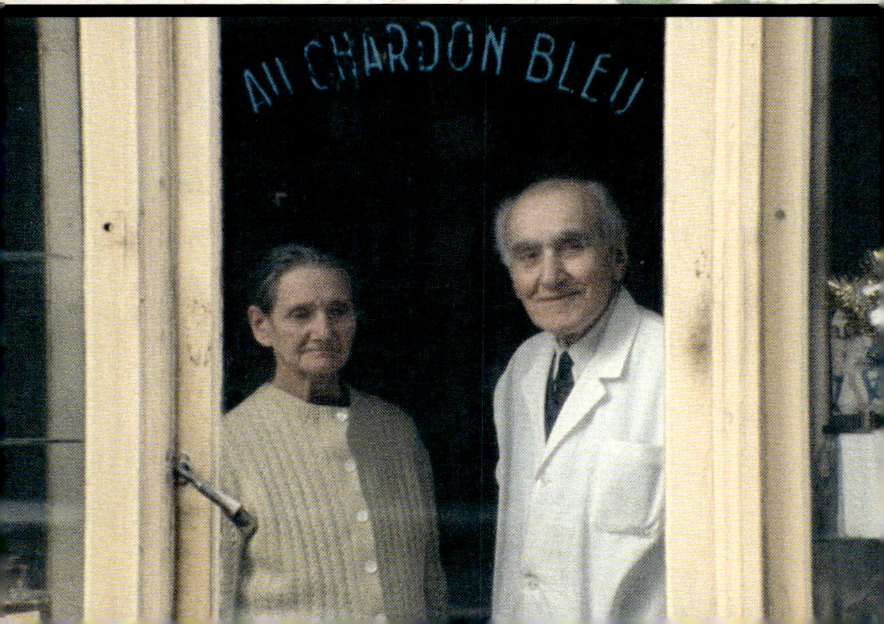
AU CHARDON BLEU

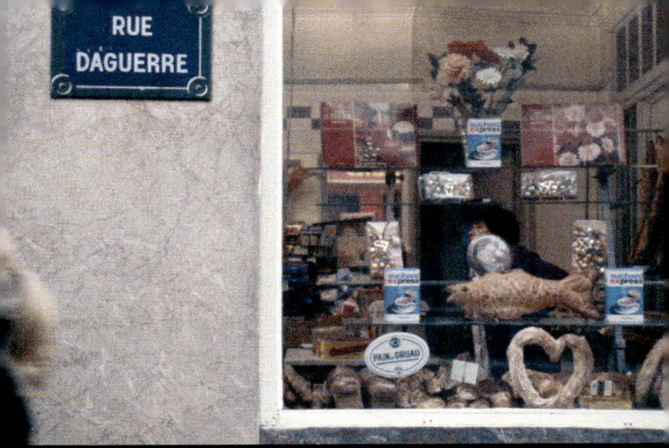

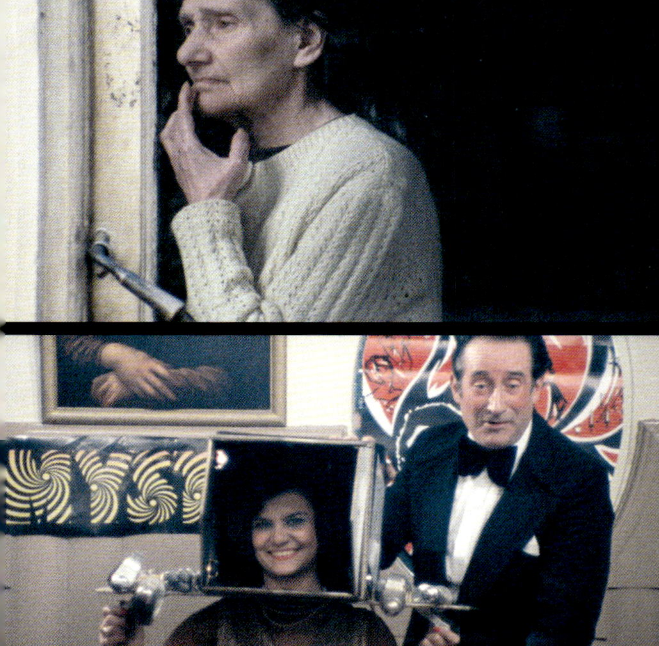
RUE
DAGUERRE
PAIN de GRUAU

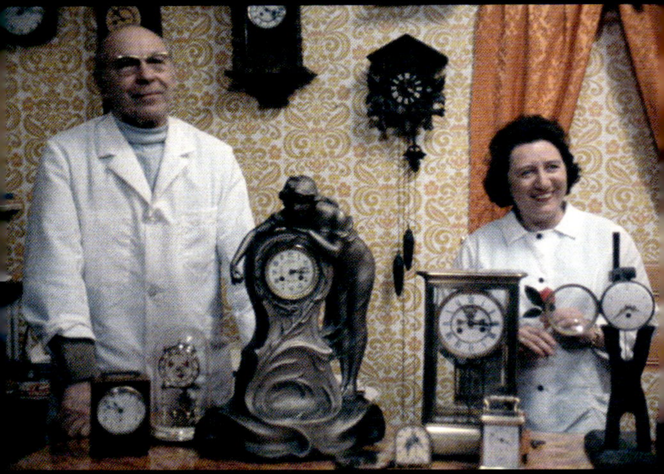

—

I had a special 80-meter electric cable attached to the electric box in my house. I decided I would allow myself that much space to shoot *Daguerréotypes*. I could go no further than the end of my cable.

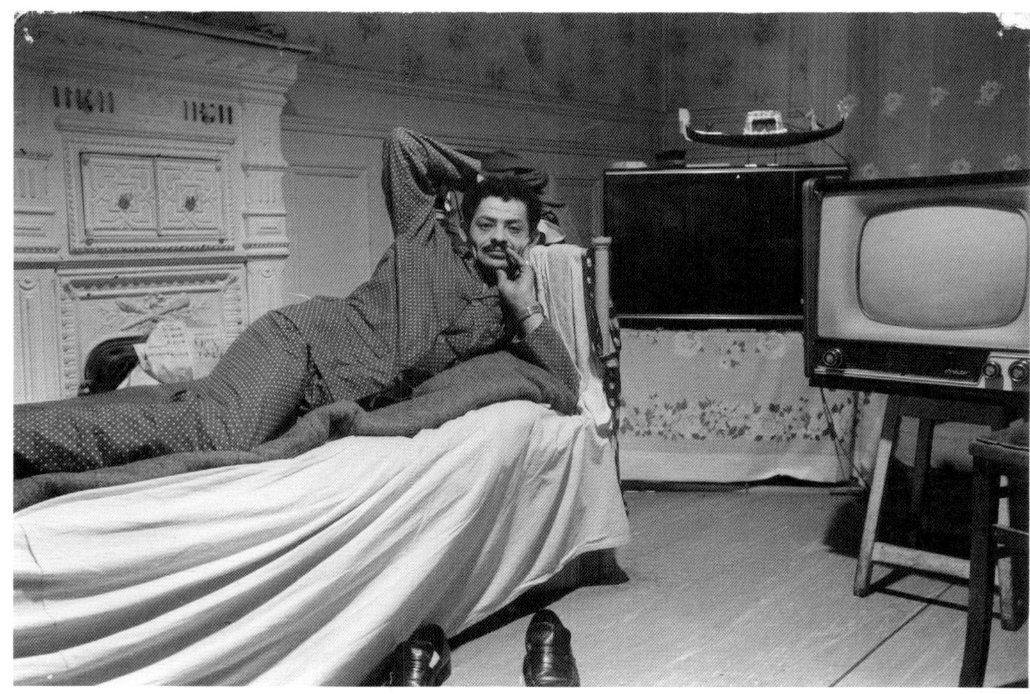

Opposite: Scenes from *Daguerréotypes*

Right: Promotional card for *Daguerréotypes* featuring shopkeeper Boukraa Mustapha, photographed by Varda

One Sings, the Other Doesn't
is not only a musical, but it
sings of the solidarity among
women. For me, it's a very
important film because it tells
of a 10-year battle.

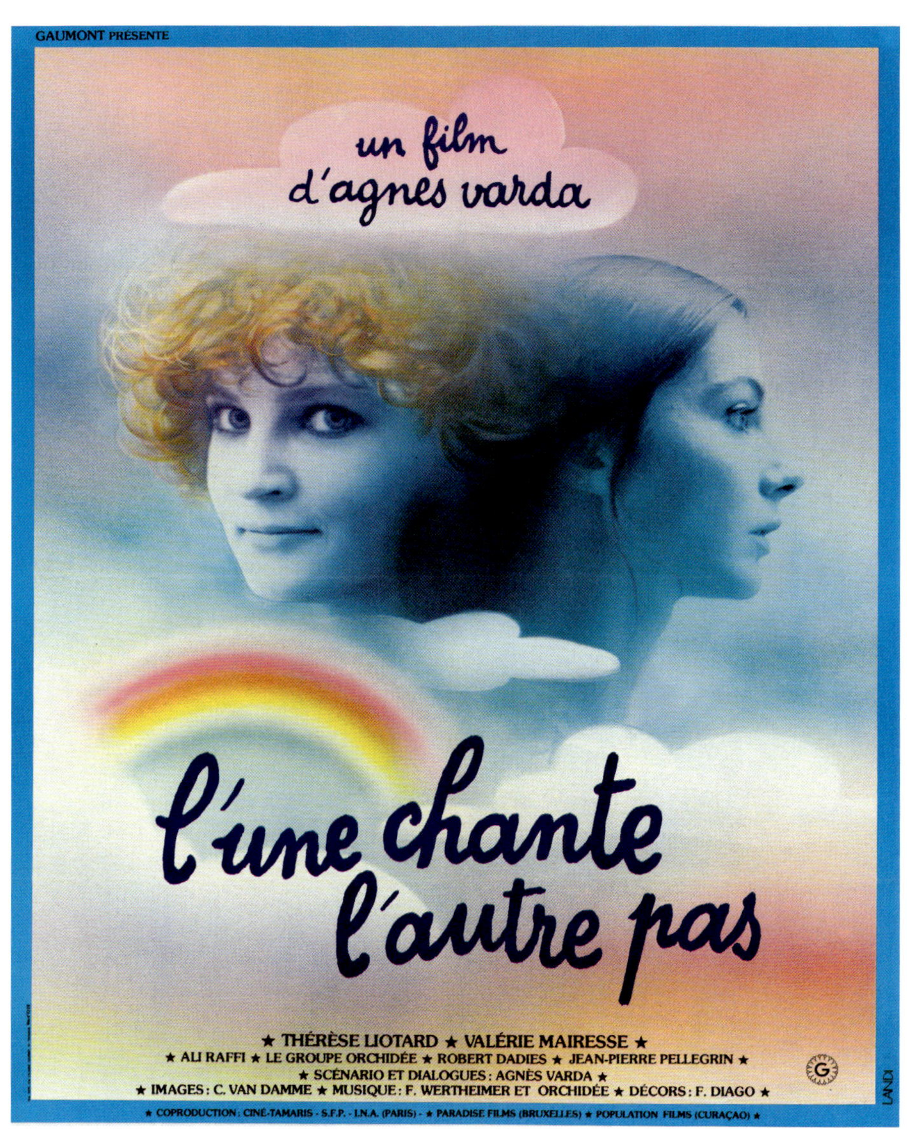

One Sings, the Other Doesn't (1977) charts the 15-year friendship of Pomme, an aspiring singer, and Suzanne, a single mother, who meet in the early 1960s. The quasi-musical intertwines their personal journeys of self-discovery with the women's liberation movement and the fight to legalize abortion. Varda says she "wanted to testify to the profound friendship among women."

Left: French poster for *One Sings, the Other Doesn't* (1977), with portraits by Varda

Opposite: Scenes from *One Sings, the Other Doesn't*

l'une chante l'autre pas

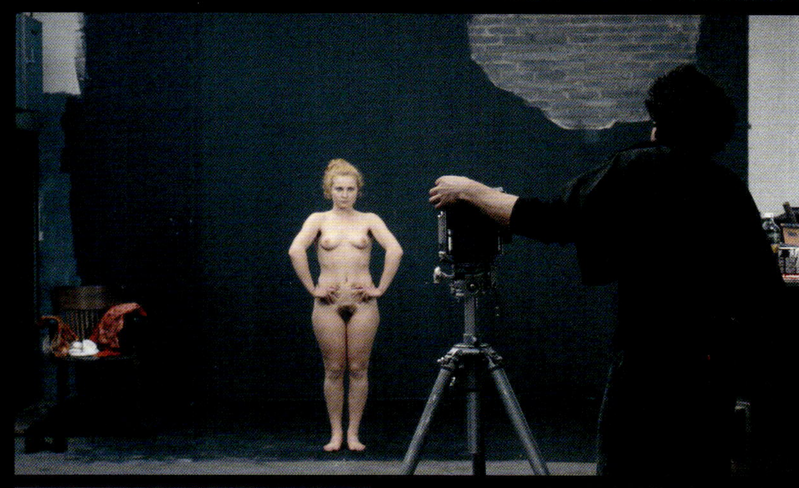

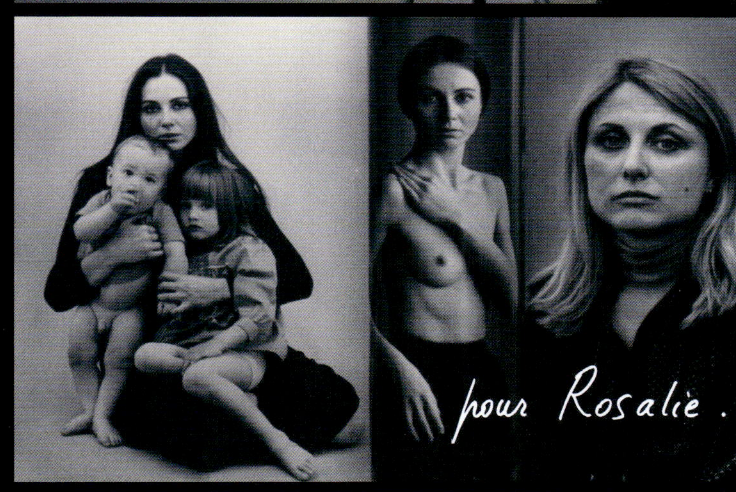

pour Rosalie ...

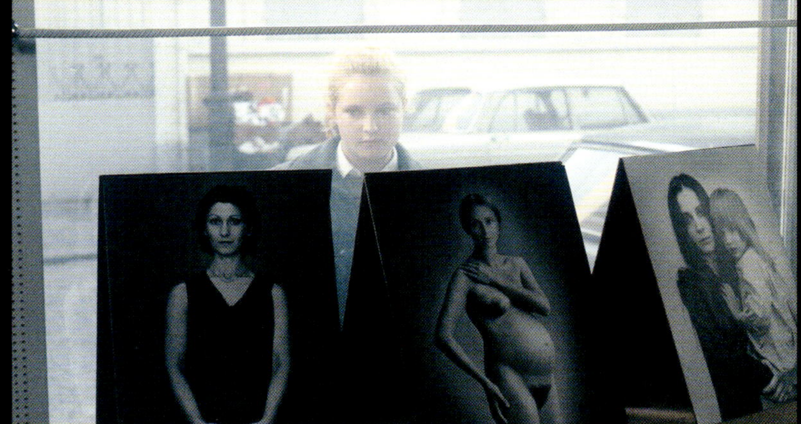

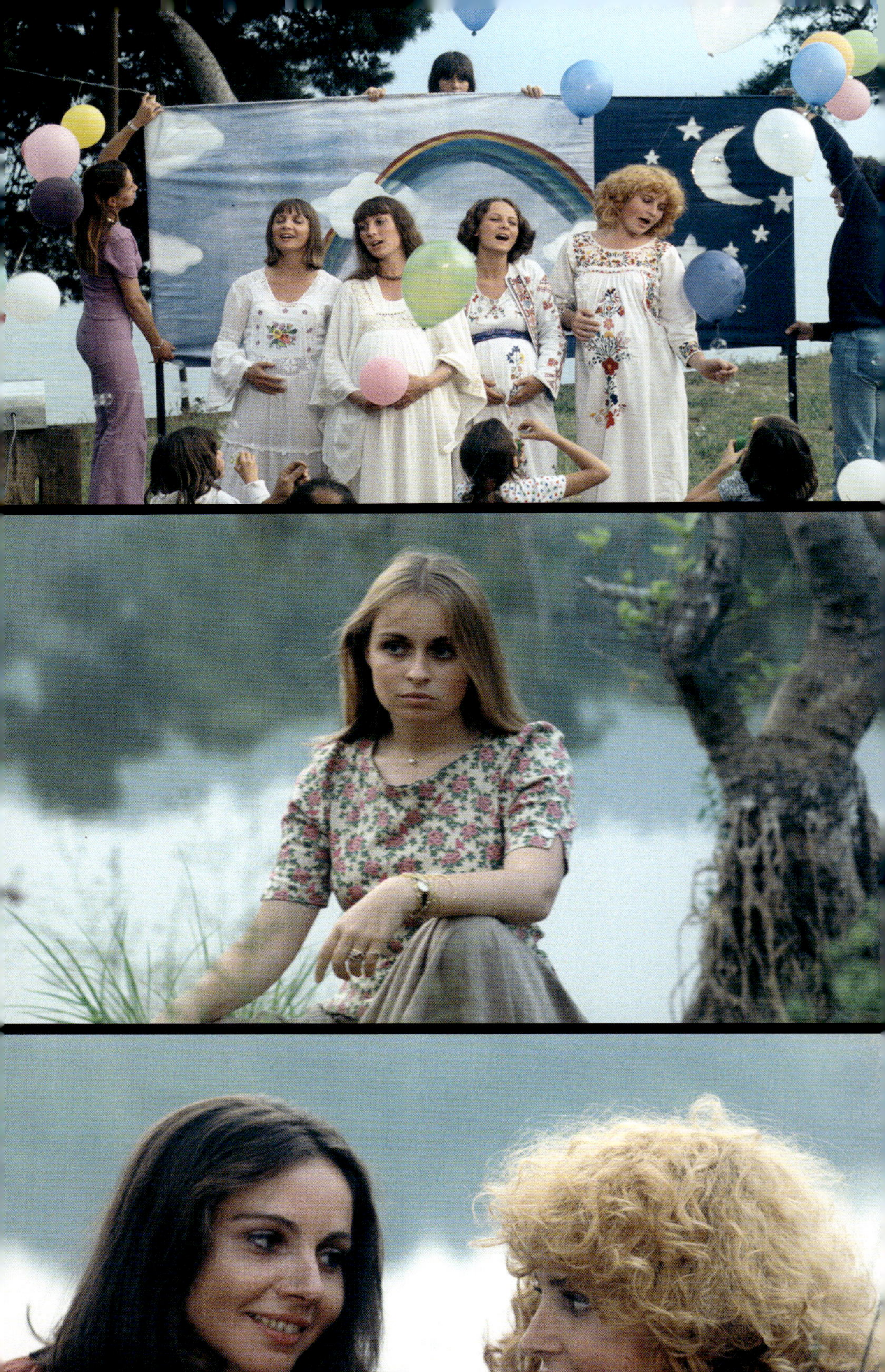

There are always stories about virile male friendships, Brando and Nicholson, Newman and Redford, and so on, but not about friendship between women.

Varda dedicated the film to her then 18-year-old daughter, Rosalie, who appears in the closing scene as Suzanne's daughter. Varda's son, Mathieu, also appears as Zorro.

Opposite: Scenes from *One Sings, the Other Doesn't* featuring Rosalie Varda (middle) and Thérèse Liotard and Valerie Mairesse (bottom)

Below left: Flyer designed by Varda

Below right: Varda and crew during production

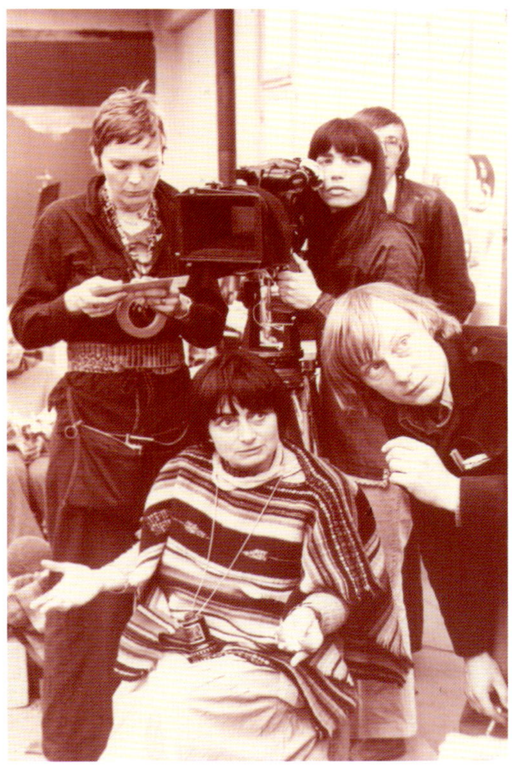

ROSALIE VARDA

I spent my early childhood in France. In 1967, Jacques signed a contract with Columbia Pictures—a lifelong dream for him—and we moved to Los Angeles, settling down in a nice little Beverly Hills house with a pool. Agnès had already directed *La Pointe Courte*, *Cléo from 5 to 7*, *Le Bonheur*, and some short films. They were the young, successful couple of the Nouvelle Vague in Los Angeles, and Hollywood wanted to know their filmmaking recipe.

It was a special time, maybe the only time America was so open minded. Coming from Paris, it was a shock. My parents arrived and found the Vietnam War protests, nonstop television, Robert Kennedy's assassination, Jack in the Box, big cars, the Pacific Ocean, the beach, and, most of all, the hippies' peace-and-love atmosphere, music, "space cake," and love-ins. It was an extraordinary new world in front of them. I think they developed a crush on Los Angeles that they felt all their lives, even after they returned to France. Many European filmmakers went to Hollywood—Michelangelo Antonioni, Miloš Forman, Roman Polanski, Jean-Luc Godard—but none had that same strong relationship with the City of Angels. Even François Truffaut, who loved America, didn't make a film here.

Agnès quickly made two short films, *Uncle Yanco* and *Black Panthers*, and then the crazy feature *Lions Love (...and Lies)*—a fictional documentary starring Warhol muse Viva, Gerome Rado and James Ragni of the hippie rock musical *Hair*, and Agnès's near-double the filmmaker Shirley Clarke. It was funny for me to visit after school and see these adults pretending to be in a threesome, with the set full of marijuana smoke. Agnès kept up her energy to finish the film, but I remember she was totally exhausted.

She came back in the 1980s and made *Mur Murs* and *Documenteur*, which are like yin and yang. *Mur Murs* is the light, and *Documenteur* is the darkness. *Documenteur* is a beautiful film, intense. She was separated from Jacques then, and it was a very sad time in her life. Artists are smart—they only give you what they want you to know. *Documenteur* is the only time Agnès opened the door to show what she usually would hold back.

For me it was a difficult film to watch. At the first screening in Cannes, I had to leave because I was crying so much. It took years before I could see it again. I found it so powerful, how she could talk about what it feels like when somebody doesn't love you anymore. Some people don't understand this film, but it's one Agnès loved. I think of it as her only truly autobiographical film, because in *The Beaches of Agnès*, where she tells her story, she controlled everything. *Documenteur* is the only film where she didn't control it. Her sadness and her creativity were in control.

I started to work with Agnès in 2006 and never left her side, producing her films and art exhibitions until she left us in 2019. I don't have a favorite film because it changes over time. However, for my 18th birthday she made a film—*One Sings, the Other Doesn't*—about feminism and the right to legal abortion, subjects very important to her. It tells the story of two women who are different but share a passion for life and the desire to be free. And she dedicated this film to me. Today I think about what an incredible gift that was.

When I present this film to young audiences, I tell them, "This is about the freedom of your bodies, minds, and hearts. Agnès taught me I could do whatever I wanted in life: have a career or not, be a mother or not, be in love or not, do the cooking or not. You also have the right to decide." This film helps them see the history of what we've been through as women. It is even more important now as we see those rights taken away in countries where abortion had been legal. I think if Agnès saw this happening today, she would be furious and sad.

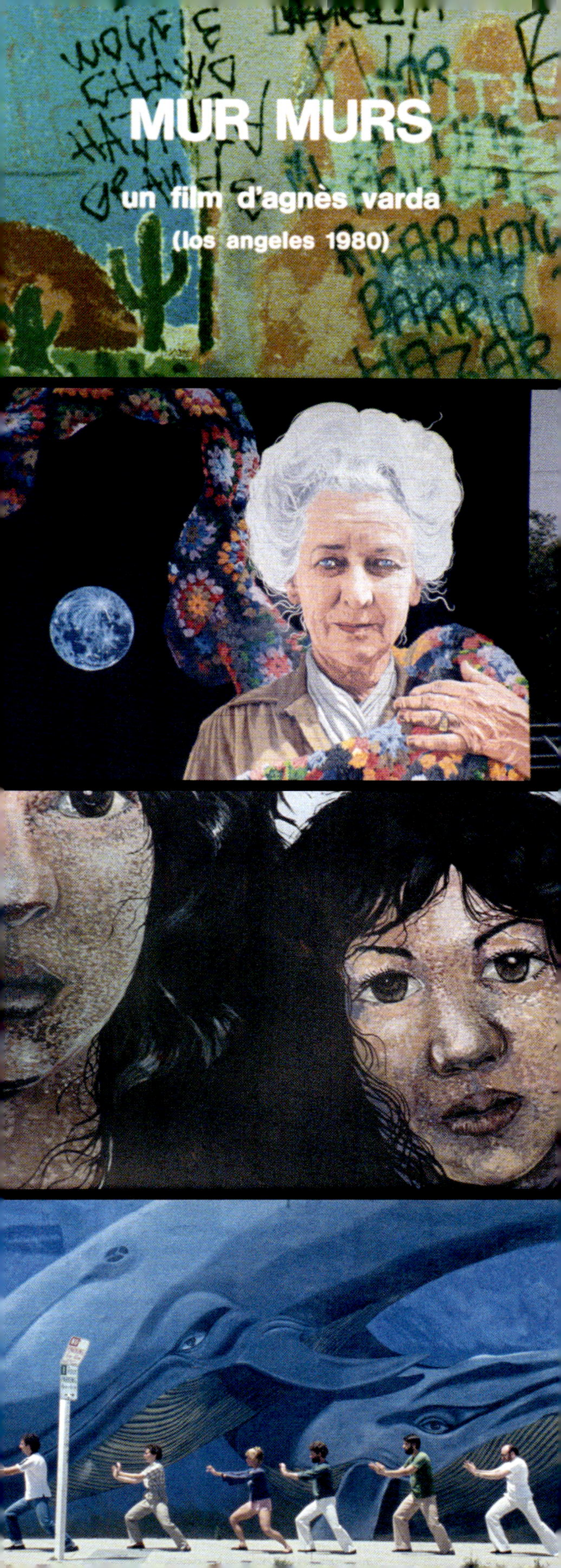

MUR MURS
un film d'agnès varda
(los angeles 1980)

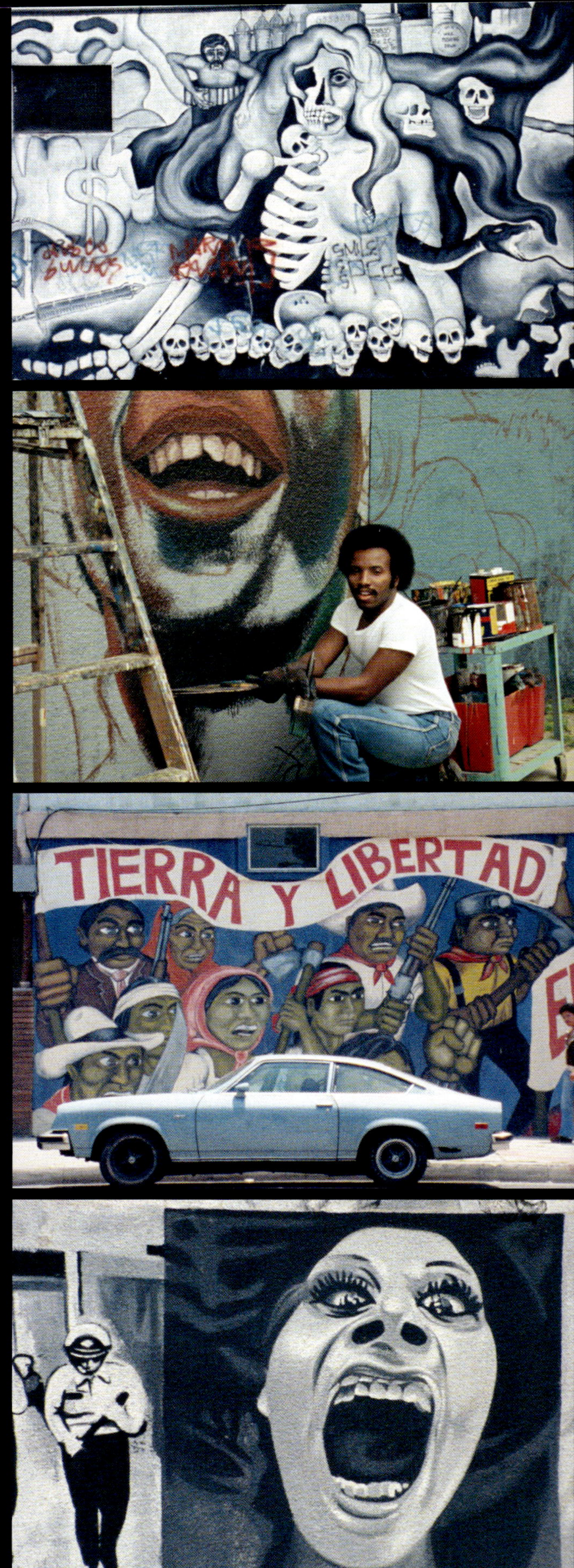

TIERRA Y LIBERTAD

Documentary is like popular art, handmade toys or street singers. You have to stand outside in the streets. So do the muralists. They don't work for galleries or museums. They are in the streets; their fans are people who pass by.

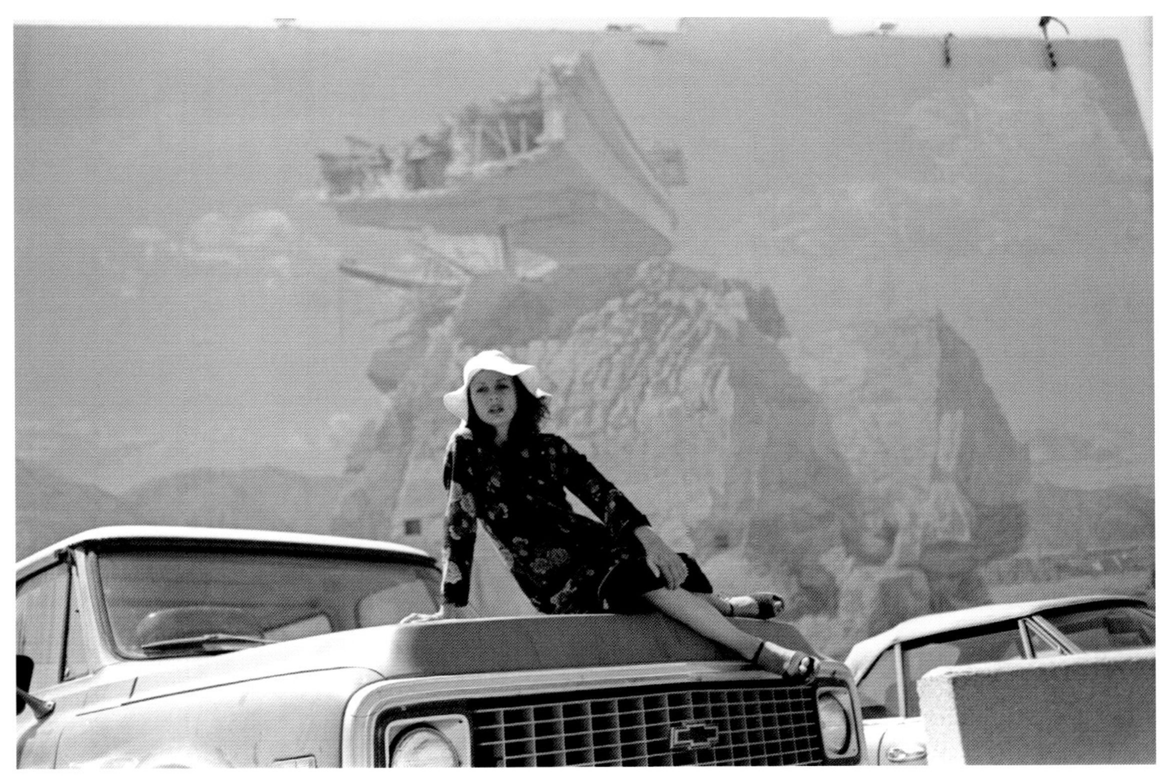

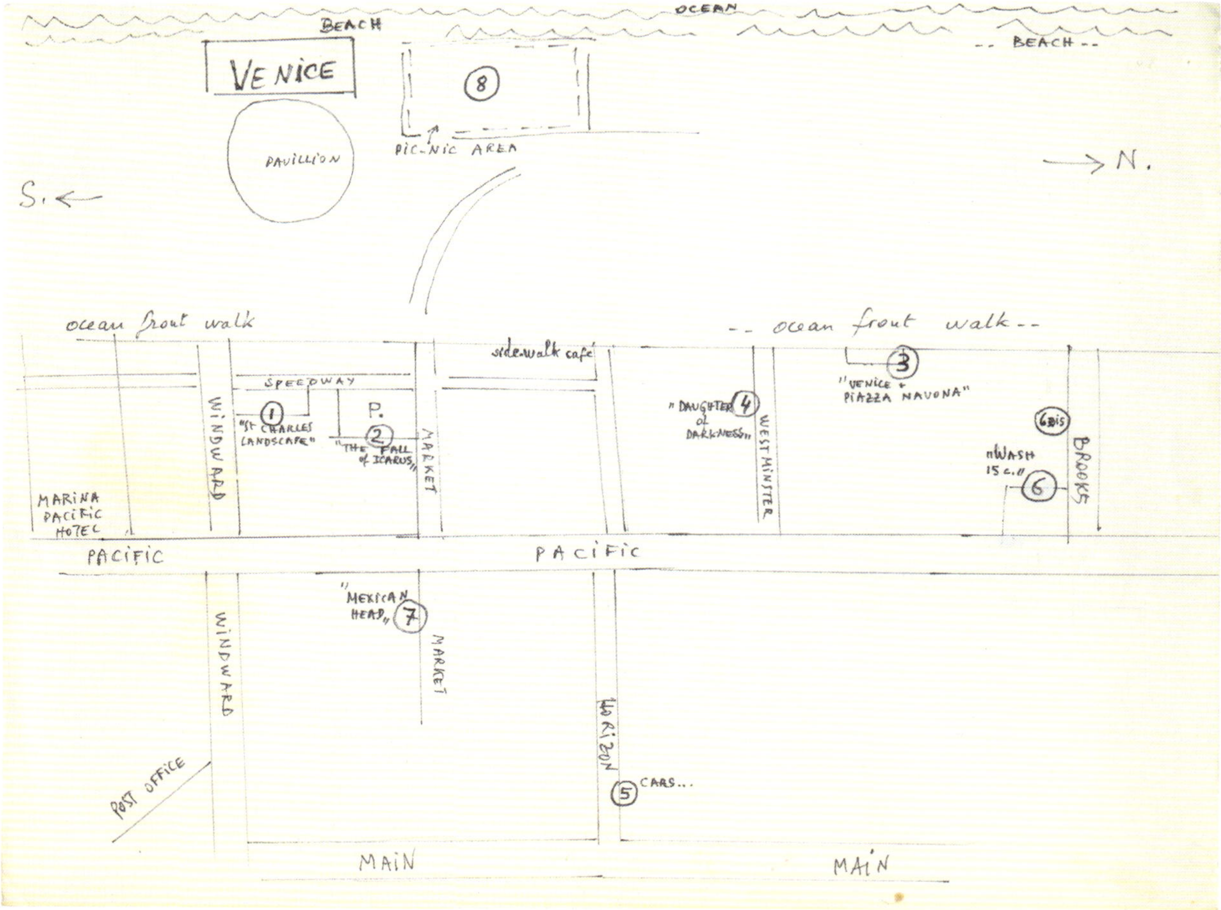

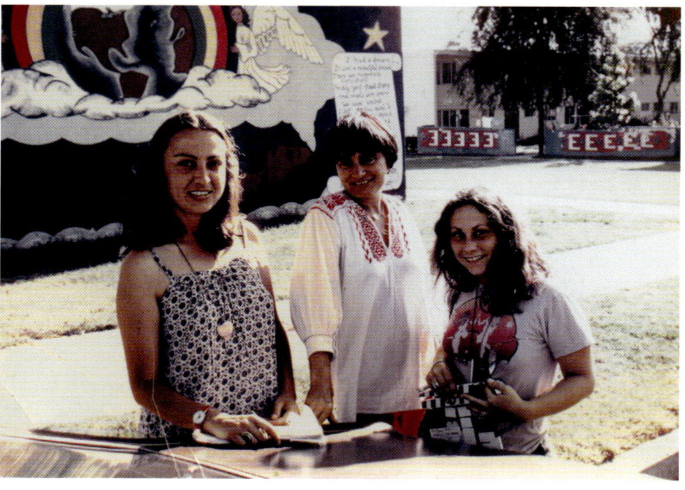

Above: Hand-drawn map of Venice Beach and the mural locations featured in *Mur Murs*

Left: Sabine Mamou, Varda (center), and production assistant Lisa Blok-Linson

Opposite, from left: Production photographs from *Mur Murs* showing *The Bride and Groom* (1976) by Kent Twitchell and a roller skater at the Venice Pavilion

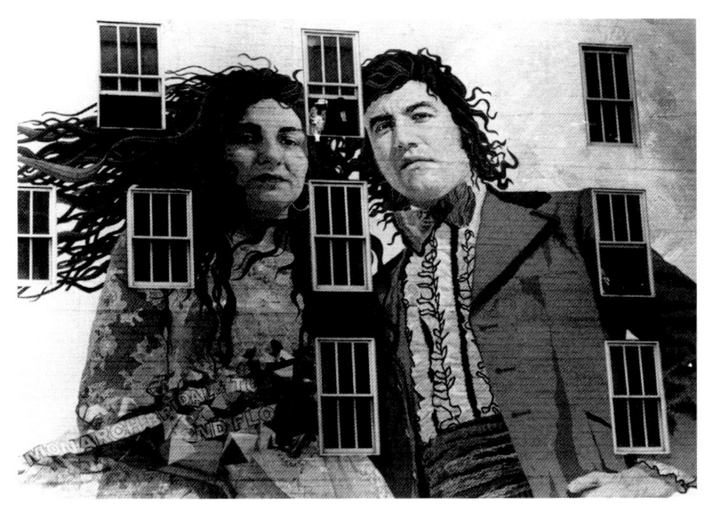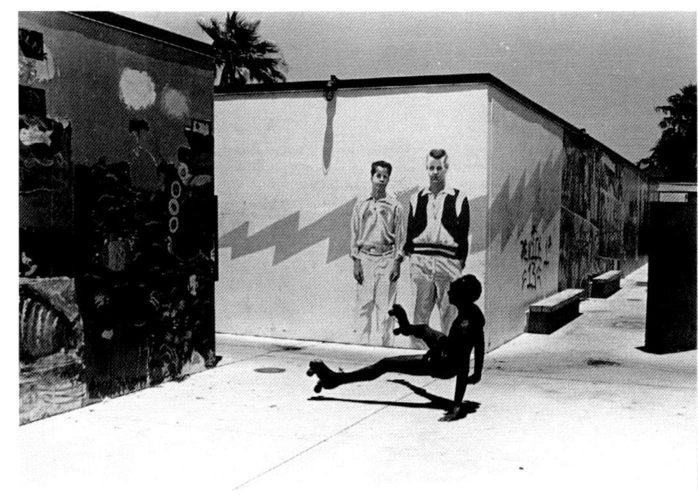

[Murals] represent very well
a city in which nothing lasts.
You notice a shop and two
months later it has disappeared.
People move; shops move.
People buy something and then
throw it away.

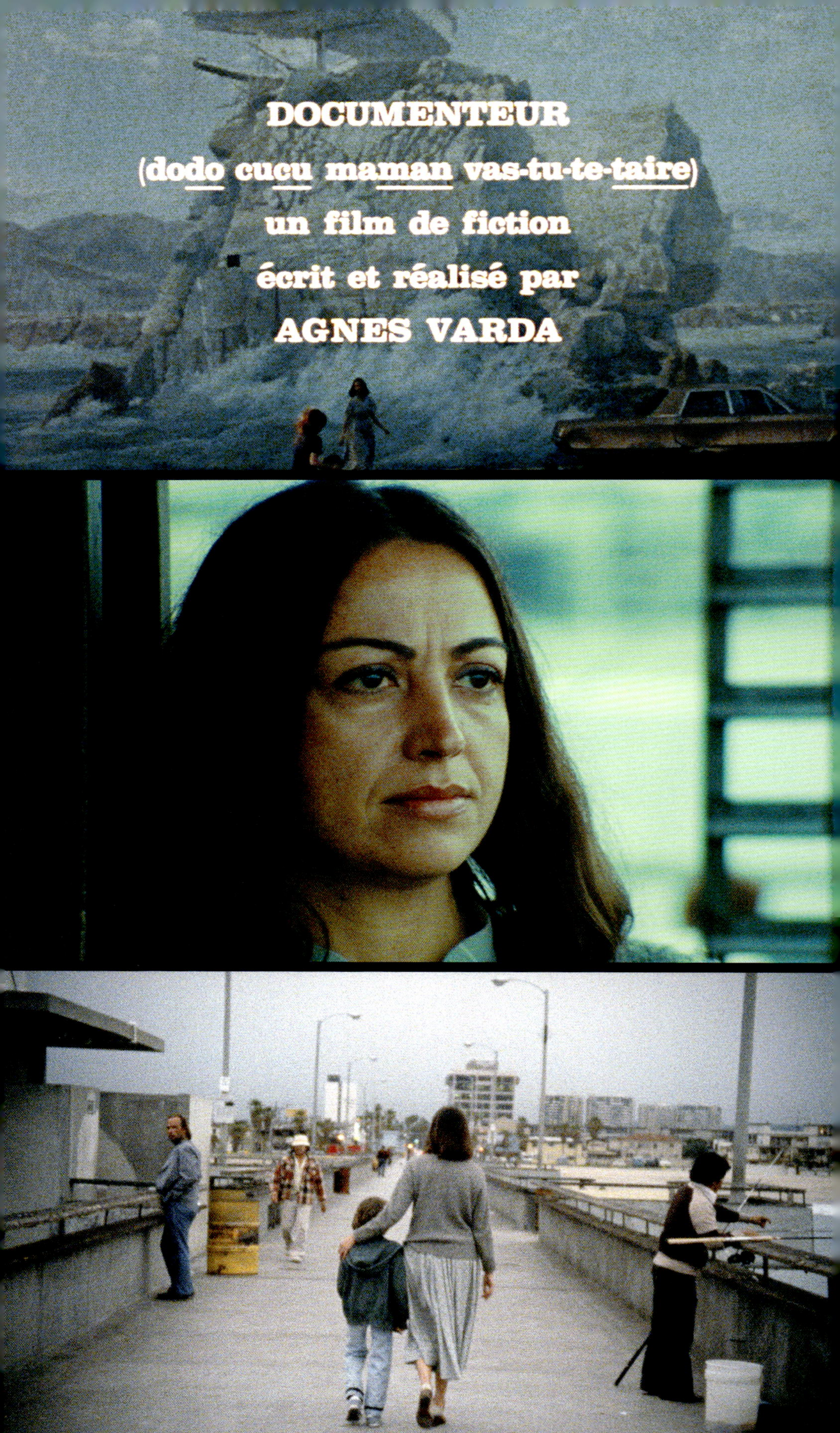

DOCUMENTEUR
(dodo cucu maman vas-tu-te-taire)
un film de fiction
écrit et réalisé par
AGNES VARDA

[Documenteur is] the shadow of _Mur Murs_. It's an idea I've had for a long time: to do a series of films on the same subject, the way painters do sketches, drawings of watercolors.

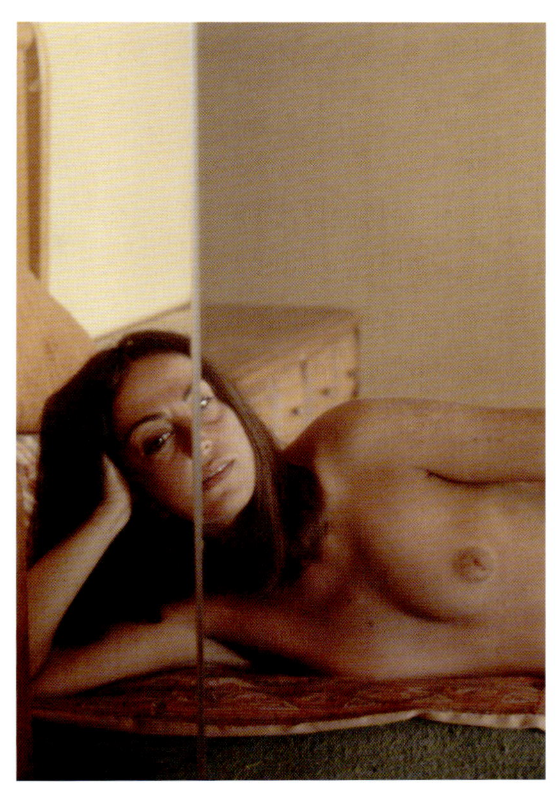

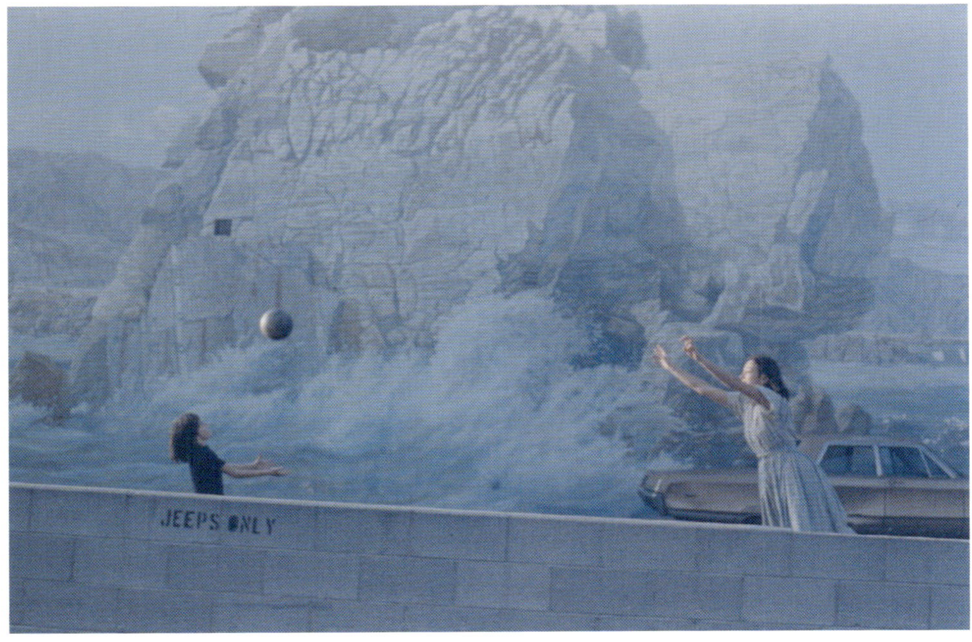

In _Documenteur_ (1981), a Frenchwoman living in Venice, California, with her young son attempts to put her life back together after a breakup. This melancholy film is perhaps Varda's most personal: its story mirrors her life at this time, and her son, Mathieu, plays the boy.

Opposite: Scenes from _Documenteur_

Above: Sabine Mamou during production, photographed by Varda

Left: Demy and Mamou in _Documenteur_. This opening scene connects the film to _Mur Murs_, which ends with Varda tossing a ball to Mathieu in front of the same mural.

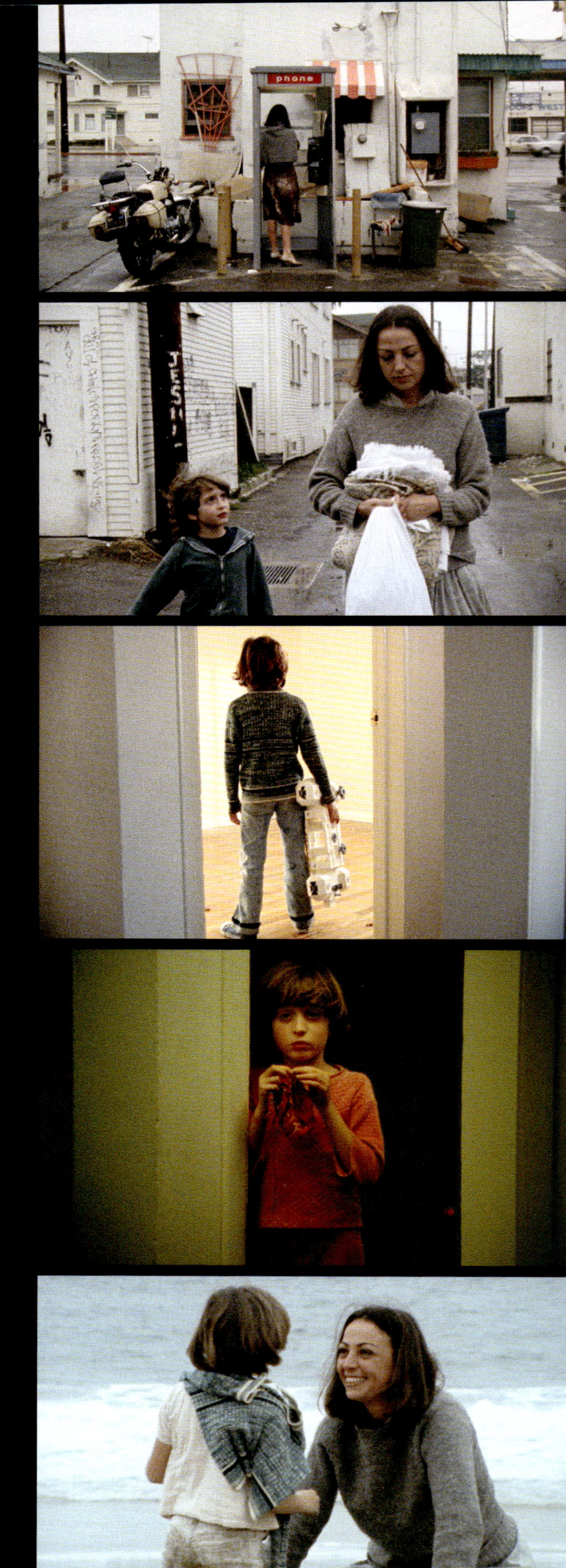

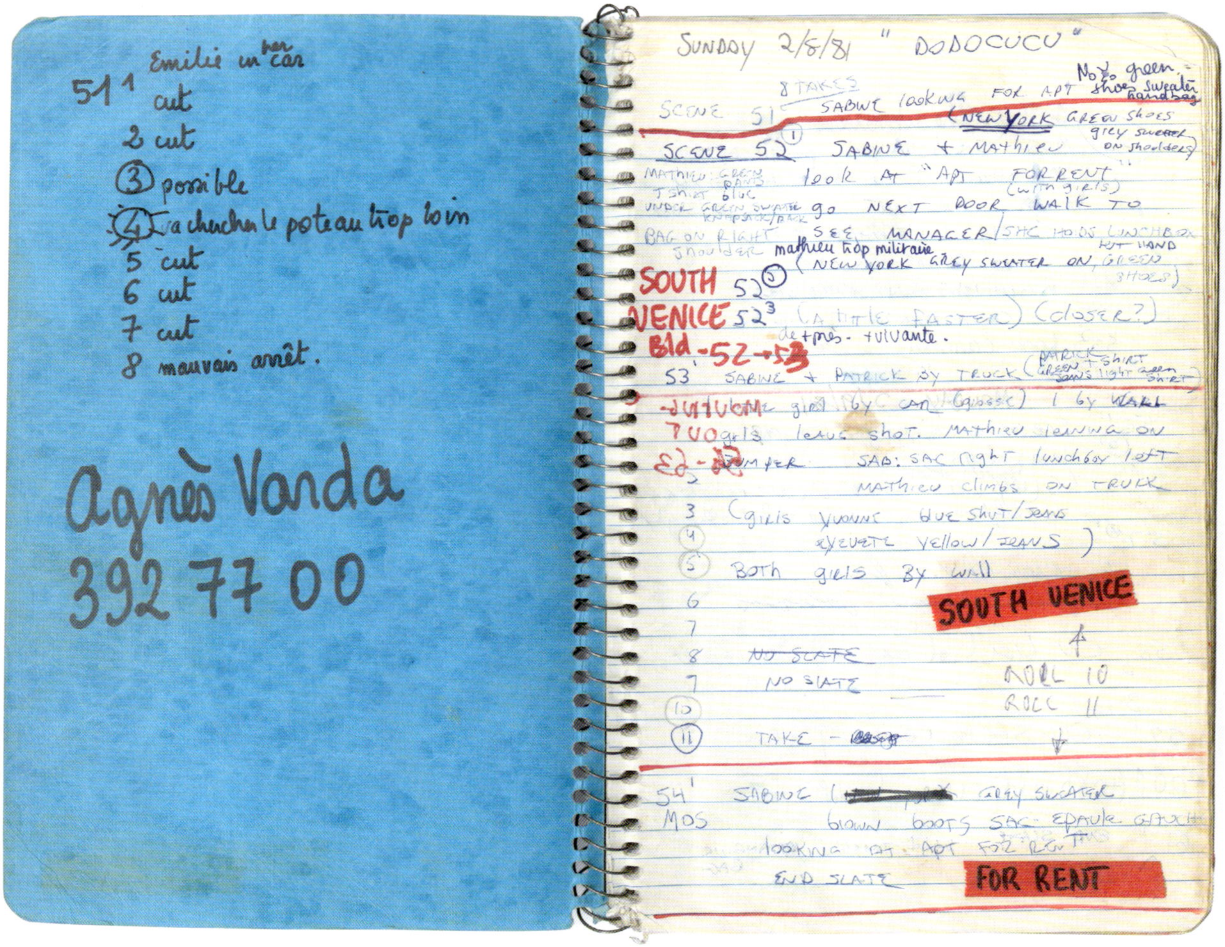

Émilie in her car
51¹ cut
2 cut
③ possible
④ va chercher le poteau trop loin
5 cut
6 cut
7 cut
8 mauvais arrêt.

Agnès Varda
392 77 00

SUNDAY 2/8/81 " DODOCUCU "

8 TAKES
SCENE 51 SABINE looking FOR APT No green shoes sweater handbag
SCENE 52① SABINE + MATHIEU (NEW YORK GREEN SHOES grey sweater on shoulders)
MATHIEU GREEN PANTS Tshirt blue UNDER GREEN SWEATER KNAPSACK/BACK BAG ON RIGHT shoulder look AT "APT FOR RENT" (with girls) go NEXT DOOR WALK TO SEE MANAGER / SHE HOLDS LUNCHBOX HOT HAND
mathieu trop militaire (NEW YORK GREY SWEATER ON, GREEN SHOES)
SOUTH 52②
VENICE 52³ (A LITTLE FASTER) (closer?)
BLd -52→53 de +près - suivante.
53¹ SABINE + PATRICK BY TRUCK (PATRICK GREEN + SHIRT jeans light green shirt)
2 JULIENNE girl (by car) (assise) 1 by WALL
TWO girls leave shot. MATHIEU leaning on BUMPER SAB: SAC right lunchbox left
MATHIEU climbs ON TRUCK
3 (girls YVONNE blue shirt/ JEANS
④ GEUETTE yellow/ JEANS)
⑤ BOTH girls BY WALL
6
7
8 NO SLATE
9 NO SLATE ROLL 10
⑩ ROLL 11
⑪ TAKE -

54¹ SABINE (______) GREY SWEATER
MOS brown boots SAC EPAULE GAUCH looking AT APT FOR RENT
END SLATE FOR RENT

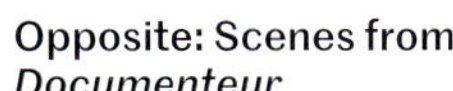

Opposite: Scenes from
Documenteur

Above: Varda's production
notebook for *Documenteur*

Right: Mamou and Varda
during production (1980)

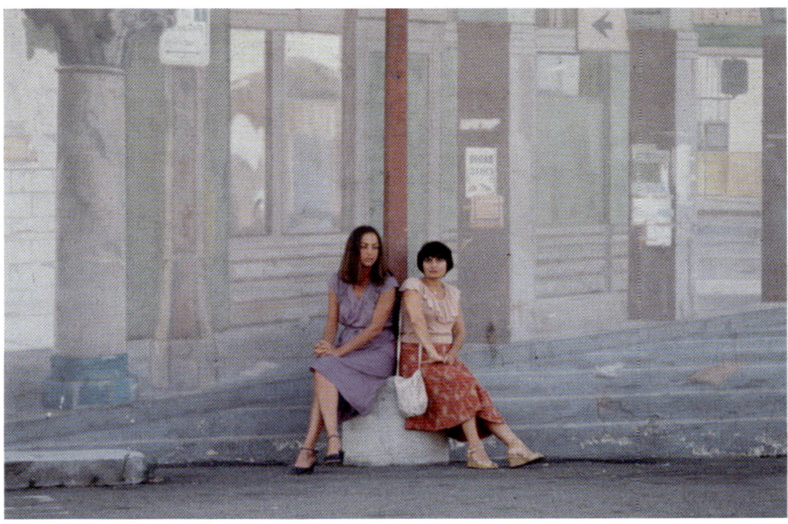

END OF THE END OF THE END: AGNÈS VARDA IN LOS ANGELES

Sasha Archibald

Denizens of high culture have long trea-
sured Hollywood as the butt of their jokes.
Hollywood is a reviled yet useful counter-
point—the distaste to taste, the crass to
high-mindedness, "the antipode to critical
intelligence."[1] Nonetheless, almost from
its inception, the film industry has scooped
talent from theater, literature, dance, and
visual arts, tapping the very sorts of cultural
workers that disdain it most. Enticed by
piles of money and sunshine postcards,
artists have arrived in Los Angeles in droves.
Often with misgivings and often against
their better judgment, and yet they arrived.
Few could afford to ignore Hollywood's
oily handshake.

The usual strategy for keeping a sense
of dignity while still cashing in on the spoils
of corporate film was to bite the hand that
wrote the paycheck. William Faulkner,
for instance, posed as a recalcitrant child,
swearing to his employer, MGM, that the
only movies he'd seen were newsreels and
Mickey Mouse cartoons. He famously
greeted Clark Gable at a party by inquiring,
"Mr. Gable, what do you do?" Some writers
tolerated Hollywood for decades, some
lasted only a few months, and some came
and went as their psyches permitted or
pocketbooks demanded. After years of
painful ambivalence and alcoholic binges,
Faulkner begged to be released from his
contract, citing emotional distress. The pay
was adequate, the arrangement flexible, his
colleagues pleasant—yet, he wrote, "I have
had about all of Hollywood I can stand.
I feel bad, depressed, [a] dreadful sense of
wasting time."[2] MGM eventually consented,
and Faulkner fled to Mississippi. He was
back, though, eight years later. He'd won
a Nobel Prize in the interim, but Hollywood
money talked.

The antipathy between Hollywood and
cultural elites began to erode in the 1960s,
due in part to the birth of the French New
Wave. Hollywood film flooded French

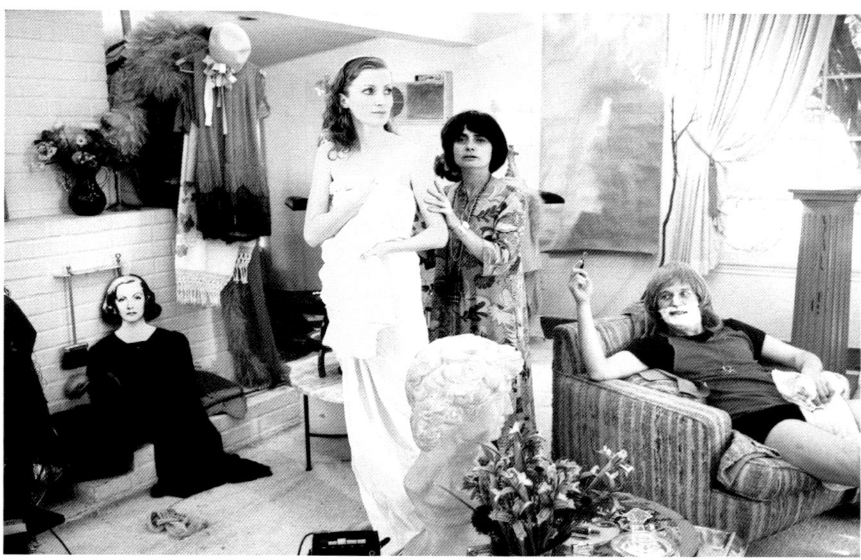

Agnès Varda (center) with
Viva (left center) and
James Rado on set of
Lions Love (...and Lies)
(1969)

theaters in the immediate postwar years:
38 American films were shown in France
during the first six months of 1946, and that
number jumped to 338 for the same period
in 1947. The deluge, which included such
classics as *Casablanca* (1942), *Citizen
Kane* (1941), and *The Wizard of Oz* (1939),
demanded a response. Forced to define
their position on American cinema, French
intellectuals chose nuanced critique rather
than blanket dismissal, singling out a few
Hollywood directors that deserved cultural
cachet. Charlie Chaplin, Alfred Hitchcock,
and Billy Wilder, for instance, were admired
by the editors of *Cahiers du Cinéma*, the
French film journal founded in 1951, while
a rival publication, *Positif*, touted the virtues
of John Huston and Orson Welles. These and
other film magazines legitimized cinema
with medium-specific discourse, while
ciné-clubs like Objectif 49 and Ciné-Club
du Quartier Latin analyzed films in detail,
ultimately dignifying film spectatorship
as something more than mindless leisure.
Hollywood saw its good fortune in this
Francophile turn. *Cahiers du Cinéma*

improbably became essential reading, and Fritz Lang and others began to pose for photographs clutching the latest issue.[3] Eventually, studio management joined the trend, counting French auteur filmmakers such as Agnès Varda and her husband, Jacques Demy, among their recruits.

Columbia approached Demy first, a logical choice. Despite his affiliation with the New Wave, Hollywood was Demy's stylistic touchstone. His films are riotous spectacles of color and song in the American musical tradition—films that pay homage, even as they deepen and complicate the genre. In fact, long before he arrived in California, it was said that Demy's films "smell[ed]" of Hollywood.[4] (By the same token, the work was also described as "fruity.")[5] Hollywood was also the only place where song-and-dance extravaganzas were amply funded. Georges de Beauregard, the French producer of many New Wave classics, liked Demy's ideas but balked at the price tag. When Demy approached him with the script for a filmic opera in which every line is sung and every backdrop wallpapered in an eye-popping pattern, Beauregard suggested it be shot in black and white, with no costumes and no music. Demy demurred and made his film instead with the producer Mag Bodard. *The Umbrellas of Cherbourg* (1964) went on to win the Palme d'Or at Cannes and receive five Academy Award nominations. With the film's international success, Demy's career moved three steps closer to California, and Columbia Pictures was soon in touch.

Varda later explained what anyone who knew Demy's work would have already understood—that the Hollywood deal was fait accompli: "When Jacques was 15 years old he wanted to get an American car. And he wanted to come to Hollywood to make a movie, and I followed."[6] In fact, Varda was not in the habit of following Demy. They had met at the Festival of Tours in 1958, two promising filmmakers at the start of their careers—Varda was in addition a single mother—and sustained a marriage generous enough to accommodate two singular visions. Neither partner, it seems, was martyred to the other's ambition. Yet, though Demy asked little of Varda in terms of wifely duties, having arrived in Los Angeles to begin work on what would become *Model Shop* (1969), he telephoned and requested her company for the months to come. She complied, and they rented a house in 1966.

Once the family was settled, the Columbia executive who brokered the contract with Demy, George Ayres, then pursued Varda, commissioning from her a manuscript about American hippies, *Peace and Love*. Columbia liked the script, but negotiations ended abruptly and the film was never made. Ayres (who also approached Andy Warhol) teases that Varda walked away because an executive pinched her cheek; Varda claims Columbia wouldn't promise her final cut, and signing on without it was unthinkable. The incident is a minor detail in Varda hagiography, yet it launched her extended engagement with Los Angeles, a relationship

Varda (right) with Jacques Demy and Anouk Aimée (foreground) during production of *Model Shop* (1969)

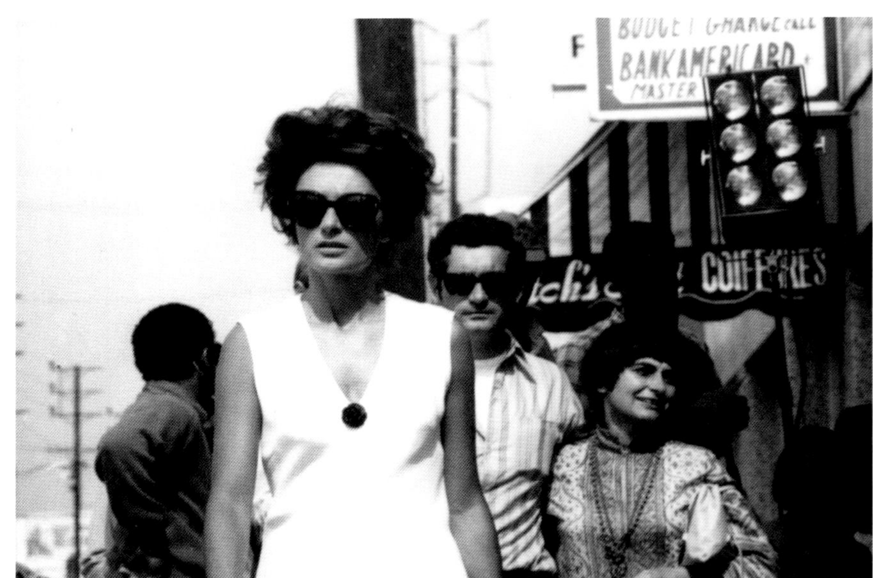

between city and filmmaker that would eventually include two sojourns and five films, all conceived, written, filmed, and edited in California. Of the five, two were shorts—*Uncle Yanco* (1967) and *Black Panthers* (1968)—shot, respectively, in Marin County and Oakland, while the three features, *Lions Love (...and Lies)* (1969), *Documenteur* (1981), and *Mur Murs* (1981), are Los Angeles films inside and out, indelibly marked by Varda's experience of the city.[7]

By the time of her first visit to Los Angeles in 1967, Varda was already an accomplished filmmaker, having directed four features in France, including the celebrated *Cléo from 5 to 7* (1962), a day in the life of a famous singer as she awaits the results of a life-or-death medical test. Her first film, *La Pointe Courte*, made in 1955, created even more of a stir, at least within a small and influential circle of burgeoning filmmakers. *La Pointe Courte* is now credited as heralding the arrival of a new movement in film and Varda's name inextricably attached to the moniker "Grandmother of the French New Wave." The compliment carries a whiff of condescension; the age difference between Varda and Jean-Luc Godard or François Truffaut is not a generation but less than five years. It is, however, to the point: *La Pointe Courte*'s innovative formal structure, use of natural light, and cast of nonprofessional actors predated the earliest work of any of Varda's contemporaries.

Initially at least, Varda influenced film as an outsider. When she made *La Pointe Courte*, she was entirely self-taught and a cinema naïf. "I seemed to be there by mistake," she later remembered of her first meeting with the New Wave cadre—Claude Chabrol, Eric Rohmer, Jacques Rivette, Truffaut, Godard, and others—"feeling small, ignorant, and the only woman."[8] Her miasma was unwarranted, as she was the only one of the group to have actually made

a film. Her would-be peers were critics and cinephiles first, filmmakers second, while Varda's background was in art history and her interest in literature. She wasn't watching films in her early 20s but attending classes by philosopher Gaston Bachelard at the Sorbonne and aspiring to be a museum curator, photographing children on the laps of Santa Claus and dancers for the Théâtre National Populaire. Her touchstone as a filmmaker was not Jean Renoir or Orson Welles, whom she claimed to have never heard of, but the formal strategy of Faulkner's *The Wild Palms* (1939), a novel told on two discordant tracks that she devoured, dissected, marveled at, and finally decided to try on film.

Like all travelers, Varda brought to Los Angeles a suitcase of assumptions and judgments. In the late 1960s, America in general—and California in particular—seemed to many foreign observers a cesspool of violence and imperialism. America's war in Vietnam, racist cops, and brutal attempts to contain civil unrest were international news. Los Angeles's reputation abroad was specifically haunted by the 1965 Watts uprising. American leftists found little redeeming in the violence, but in Paris, Guy Debord of the Situationist International circulated an essay describing the tragedy as a "rebellion against the commodity."[9] Varda may or may not have known Debord's work—more likely the former, since he had unfavorably reviewed her films—but she generally shared the politics of her milieu.[10] She was openly disgusted by American racism and, like many white European intellectuals (most famously Jean Genet), strongly identified with the Black Panthers. In fact, one of her major coups in California was a commission from French television to shoot a documentary short about the Black Panthers, including a coveted interview with Huey Newton in jail. Varda's depiction of the Panthers is unusually fair-minded, portraying protests in downtown Oakland as congenial family gatherings.[11] Her disgust with mainstream American culture is more transparently obvious in a 1969 discussion with *Newsweek* editor Jack Kroll, conducted at the New York Film Festival and later televised. Twice Kroll describes the filmic subjects in the first of Varda's Los Angeles films, *Lions Love (...and Lies)*, as "grotesque," and twice Varda recoils. Finally, brimming with disdain, she interrupts to tell Kroll his is a "racist position"—*racist* in this case summing up all variety of American stupidity.[12]

In fact, Varda's California films are devoted to "grotesque" characters, the marginalized and denigrated types that make of California a hypertrophic variation on America. Varda found in Los Angeles a city of seekers—explorers, refugees, and desperadoes who had pushed westward and westward again, compelled by nothing but dreams, finally arriving at the edge of a continent. The search that has no object resonated with Varda; she was, by her own admission, a gleaner for whom searching and living are coincident. The natural terminus of such a search—the beach—was where Varda felt most at home. The edge of the sea is both a symbol of dramatic finality and endless expansion, and what happens there is one of Varda's great themes.[13] How to live on a precipice? Having pushed westward until there is no more West, what sorts of searches remain?

Thom Andersen argues in his documentary *Los Angeles Plays Itself* (2003) that Hollywood is the pervasive source of mistruths about Los Angeles. Hollywood habitually maligns its home, making of Los Angeles a city that is salacious, trivial, corrupt, and disposable. Varda's first Los Angeles film radically reverses this pattern; *Lions Love (...and Lies)* represents Hollywood from the perspective of consummate outsiders. As Varda tells it, it is Hollywood, not Los Angeles, that is vain and morally bankrupt. The plot of the film undoubtedly references

Varda's own Hollywood experience. Filmmaker Shirley Clarke, playing herself as an avatar of Varda, is bid by the studios to make a movie, and the film opens with Clarke arriving in Los Angeles from New York to discuss the matter in person. During a series of meetings with white men in business suits, Clarke sits mutely as the men refer to her as "gal" (Varda herself was then 39), admit they haven't seen her previous films, and ultimately demand their right to make a profit, artistic integrity be damned. The chief Columbia executive, Max, appears to be played by Max Factor Jr., the president of the eponymous makeup line—an inside wink, no doubt, to the superficiality of the entire enterprise. (In a similarly witty aside, the film's dialogue confuses *decorator* with *director*.) After the doomed negotiations, Clarke tries to kill herself with sleeping pills. At this point in the film, she breaks character to protest. "I would never kill myself this way!" she complains. Varda insists, leaving her director's chair to irritably demonstrate.

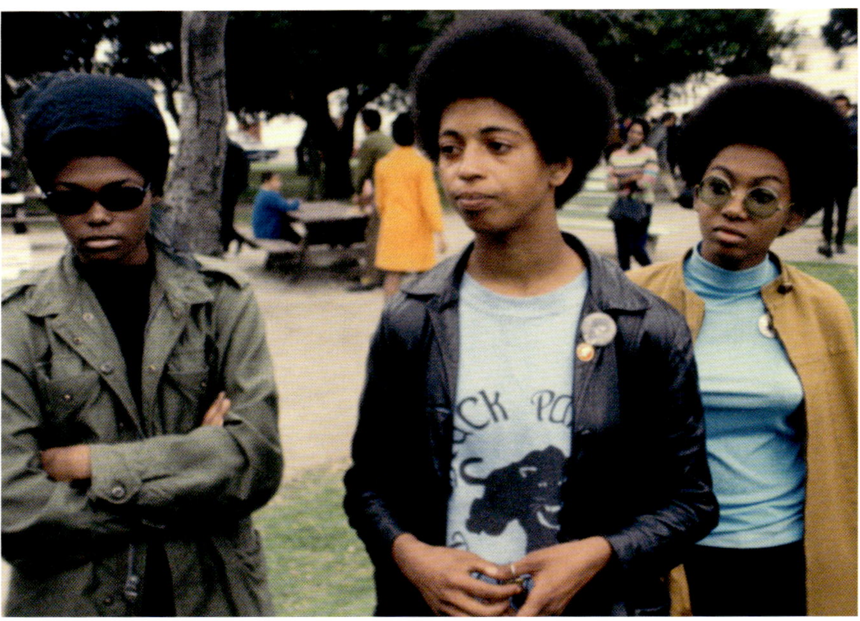

Scene from *Black Panthers* (1969)

The camera keeps rolling. It's a breach in film etiquette that denudes this film, or any other, of a definitive claim on reality, even as it exposes Hollywood's obsequious self-flattery. Only in the movies does a dead-end movie deal warrant suicide.

Clarke's crisis attempt takes place at her friends' tacky rental, the setting for most of the action in *Lions Love (...and Lies)*. The focus of the film is actually not Clarke's adventures in Hollywood but her bohemian Los Angeles hosts: the chaste ménage à trois of Viva—the haughty debauched intellectual of Warhol's *Blue Movie* aka *Fuck* (1969) and several other Warhol films—alongside Gerome Ragni and James Rado, creators and stars of the 1967 musical *Hair*. Naked and nuzzling, the three are languorous in their movements and arch in their speech, each sporting an unruly mane of hair. They play dress-up, read aloud, and lounge by the kidney-shaped pool, feigning vacuity. Varda initially seems interested in Viva, Ragni, and Rado's stylized identity performance, an act that moves seamlessly from stage to screen to living room and that Varda recognizes as forever undoing the distinction between real people and actors. But she doesn't hew closely to this theme—it's all rote at this point anyway—and instead indulges her fascination-repulsion with the detritus of American consumerism, particularly objects that seem like paragons of inauthenticity: wallpaper printed to look like trees, clothes printed to look like flags, plastic flowers, plastic fruit, French fries. (Indeed, Varda once described the movie as an "inventory.")[14] Clarke's welcome tour sums up the muddled relationship between artifice, reality, and Hollywood: "[Here is] a genuine plastic weeping willow," her hosts gesture. "There's a real one out there, but it belongs to Katharine Hepburn."

Varda's insouciance to Hollywood had scarcely diminished 13 years later, in 1980, when she was again approached by the studios to submit a script. Showing little concern for what was likely to be produced, she wrote a story based on a real Los Angeles event she'd read about in the Paris news-papers. A man was walking down the street naked at 5 a.m. He lived nearby, and his pregnant wife was home asleep. Strolling along the sidewalk, he encountered an LAPD police officer who shot and killed him. When the officer was questioned why, he simply said, according to Varda's telling of the story, "Because of his eyes."[15] Her script related the incident through the perspective of a French woman who happened to witness the murder from her window.

As Varda might have guessed, Hollywood refused to produce a film about police bru-tality. After the deal unraveled, Varda chose to remain in Los Angeles to independently produce two more features: *Documenteur*, about a single mother struggling to make a home, and *Mur Murs*, a documentary about murals and their creators. Varda conceived of the two films as twins and originally screened them together, though they were later separated when she decided each was stronger on its own.

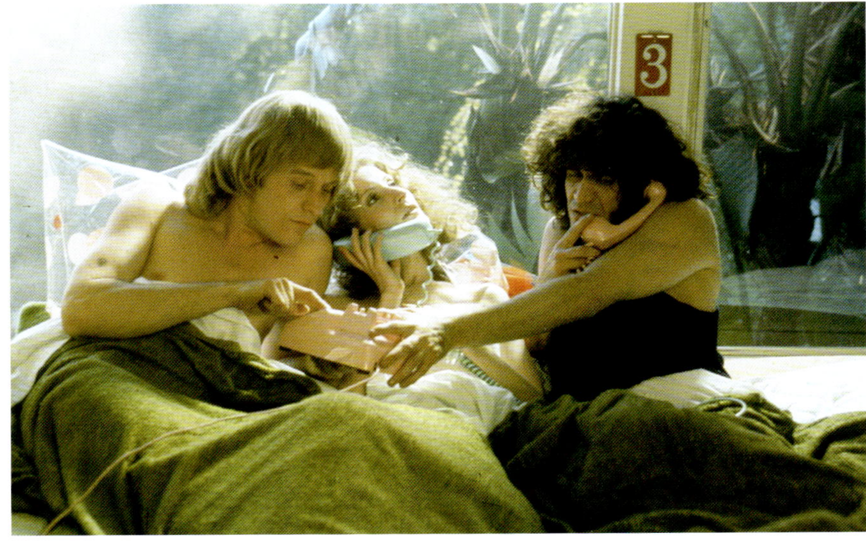

From left: Rado, Viva, and Gerome Ragni in *Lions Love (...and Lies)*

They are very different films. The charms of *Mur Murs* are straightforward—the verve of claiming a city wall, oddball artists and their motivations, murals long since disappeared—while *Documenteur* is often inscrutable. It's the latter film that Varda herself preferred; she described *Documenteur* as both her saddest film and her favorite. As the subtitle "An Emotion Picture" suggests, her subject is the vicissitudes of loss and resilience as refracted in the plight of Emilie, a mother, and Martin, her son, played, respectively, by Varda's editor Sabine Mamou and Varda's own son, eight-year-old Mathieu Demy. Emilie and Martin are striking out on their own, leaving behind the lover-father that completes their family. The separation has set mother and son adrift in a sea of melancholy.

Varda evokes Emilie's and Martin's despondency by sinking the film in wet shadows. Although *Documenteur* was shot entirely in Los Angeles, it is strewn with puddles and sweaters. The palm trees are familiar, but in *Documenteur* they forebodingly sway; the muted palate, status quo in Seattle or London, is in Los Angeles dystopic and unsettling. Varda spoke of trying through film to create smell—to suffuse the visual with so much texture as to solicit the olfactory.[16] The smell of *Documenteur* is unmistakably that of mildew, a rare stench in a town of arid winds. Varda seems to be poking around in a part of the city that has not been properly aired out.

As Emilie looks for housing, she and Martin encounter a city left to rot: dangling wires, peeling paint, toothless addicts. They visit a seedy Laundromat, stepping over a man passed out on the floor, and wash their clothes in machines covered with graffiti. Finding a run-down place to live, Emilie moves out from her friend's living room and begins to scavenge furniture off the street, despite Martin's protestations. Martin does not mention his father, but he does beg his

mother not to unpack their boxes and not to acquire furniture, and to let him sleep in her bed instead of his own. Martin's insistence on various trivialities elliptically suggests his sadness, which Varda refuses to poke or prod or fix, forcing the proverbial city of sunshine to countenance its melancholy. Emilie and Martin have just one conversation about grief. At a hamburger joint with fluorescent lights and vinyl swivel chairs, Martin tells his mother that he would cry a "King Kong cup of tears" if she died, or, he adds thoughtfully, if someone "put out his eyes." His talisman against pain is his mother, but his mother's talisman, he seems to understand, is her eyes.

Reprieve from depression and urban decay comes in the form of Emilie's fantasies about her former lover, the man she's just left. She daydreams about his naked body, sometimes as a feast for the eyes and sometimes tenderly coiled around her. Varda films these eroticisms deliberately, resting the camera on his penis or ear, until the anonymous lover becomes something more like textured landscape than corporeal form. (In all of Varda's sex scenes, she renders skin with the same enthrallment that she

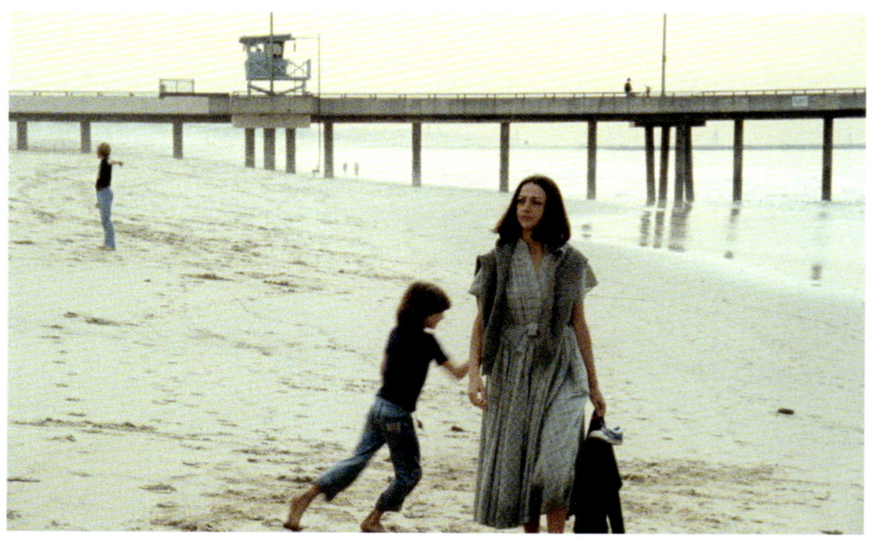

Sabine Mamou with Mathieu Demy in *Documenteur* (1981)

elsewhere films wood grain, rotten potatoes, and the aging spots on her hands.) Having eliminated warmth from the Los Angeles urban environment, *Documenteur* finds it instead in Emilie's erotic imagination.

Whereas *Documenteur* yields few explanations, *Mur Murs* incessantly pursues them.[17] A mural is never just a painted wall in *Mur Murs* but a picture with a story, the outside of a particular inside. Varda is not content with the adage that Los Angeles is a city of surfaces; at each stop on her tour of the city, she peels back a facade to reveal what lies beneath, creating in effect a Los Angeles travelogue turned inside out. At heart, *Mur Murs* is about people and why they make art; as is her habit, Varda coddles eccentricity. She lingers on the teenager who decided to paint murals while he was riding in the back of an ambulance after a gang shooting, and the artist who paints afghan blankets because they remind him of his grandmother, and because, he says, blankets last longer than cars. Given Varda's affection for kooks, the film is as amusing as it is beautiful: the juggler ex-soldier who works in "evangelistic Christian theater," the blond singer with sunburned cleavage whose portrait is painted on the side of her house, the born-again Christian who depicts the Holy Trinity as television actors. Varda takes special delight in murals that clash with the buildings they clothe. A Culver City DMV is dressed up with scenes of space travel, and a mural of happy pigs decorates the exterior walls of a Farmer John meat-packing plant in Vernon.[18] Varda asks the artist of *Pig Paradise*—an Austrian who has painted some 2,000 leaping, smiling pigs in 12 years of factory employment—if he likes to eat pork, and he replies that he does at breakfast.

The same mural that concludes *Mur Murs* opens *Documenteur*: L.A. Fine Arts Squad's *Isle of California*.[19] The massive painting depicts a broken concrete highway

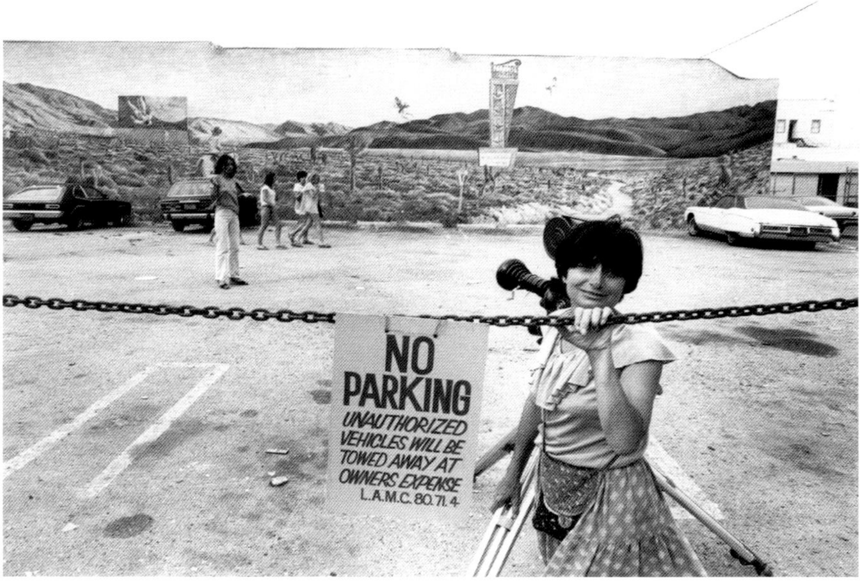

Varda during production of *Mur Murs* (1981)

precipitously perched on an island, dangling above a foamy ocean. Split from the mainland, Los Angeles is in ruins. Without the West, the edge of the West has become a nowhere. Varda once described *Documenteur* as a film about the "end of the end of the end," a phrase that also evokes the cataclysm to which this mural alludes, the specter of a catastrophe that will plunge Los Angeles into the sea.[20] The ocean reclaims and gifts land at will, such that the end of the end will at some point meet its end. In this respect and others, Varda's Los Angeles films insist on exposing the city's secret substratum—the geological precariousness, the outsider's take on Hollywood, the painful slivers of loss endemic to Angelenos' propensity for self-invention. If only Faulkner and others had seen Los Angeles as Varda did—as a city of seekers and misfits teetering on the edge of the world—they would not have hated it as they did. Of course, to find that Los Angeles, they would have had to leave Hollywood.

Notes

1 Mike Davis, *City of Quartz: Excavating the Future in Los Angeles* (London: Verso, 1990), 18.

2 Ian Hamilton, *Writers in Hollywood: 1915–1951* (New York: Harper & Row, 1990), 208.

3 Richard Neupert, *A History of the French New Wave Cinema* (Madison: University of Wisconsin Press, 2007), 30.

4 Ginette Billard, "Jacques Demy and His Other World," *Film Quarterly* 18, no. 1 (Autumn 1964): 27.

5 Cited in Amy Herzog, *Dreams of Difference, Songs of the Same: The Musical Moment in Film* (Minneapolis: University of Minnesota Press, 2010), 116.

6 Soren Agenoux, "Lions Love," *Interview* 1, no. 1 (November 1969).

7 *Lions Love (...and Lies)* was released in 1969 as *Lions Love*. Varda's working title was *Lions, Loves and Lies*, but she obliged her cast, who found the title "too long, too heavy, and too explicit" ("Lions Love," interview with Agnès Varda by Andre Cornand, *La Revue du Cinéma* [no. 247, February 1971], reprinted in *Agnès Varda: Interviews*, ed. T. Jefferson Kline [Jackson: University Press of Mississippi, 2014], 51). With the film's restoration and exhibition at the Los Angeles County Museum of Art (LACMA) in 2013, Varda reverted to a variation on her original preference. This essay follows LACMA in using the title *Lions Love (...and Lies)*.

8 Neupert, *A History of the French New Wave*, 63.

9 Guy Debord, "The Decline and Fall of the Spectacle-Commodity Economy," *Internationale Situationniste*, no. 10 (March 1966), reprinted in *Situationist International Anthology*, trans. and ed. Ken Knabb (Berkeley: Bureau of Public Secrets, 2006), 197.

10 For instance, with Alain Resnais, Jean-Luc Godard, Chris Marker, and others, Varda codirected *Far from Vietnam*, which opposed American involvement in the Vietnam War. She also spent part of 1963 in Cuba, filming sympathetic interviews with revolutionaries including Fidel Castro.

11 *Black Panthers* never aired. After May 1968, French TV was leery of screening anything that might reignite the protests. https://archive.org/embed/Black.Panthers_Agnes.Varda_1968

12 Susan Sontag and Agnès Varda, interview by Jack Kroll, *Camera Three*, CBS Television, October 12, 1969, https://www.youtube.com/watch?v=iX9mik2z29U

13 References to the sea are the most consistent of Varda's filmic motifs. In her bio-documentary, *The Beaches of Agnès* (2008), Varda uses the shoreline to suggest the oscillation between imagination and structure that typifies her work as an artist. "Because my father was Greek...I really need the sea," she told an interviewer in 1970. "I need the smell of it." (Gordon Gow, "The Underground River," *Films and Filming*, no. 16, March 1970, reprinted in Kline, *Agnès Varda: Interviews*, 41.)

14 Andre Cornand, "Lions Love," in Kline, *Agnès Varda: Interviews*, 50.

15 Barry Sabath, interview held at World Cinema lecture seminar, American Film Institute, Los Angeles, November 10, 2013.

16 Sabath, interview at World Cinema lecture. Varda credits this insight to the filmmaker Les Blank, who first screened his peon to garlic, *Garlic Is as Good as Ten Mothers* (1980), in a theater with garlic strung from the rafters. In depicting the homeless Mona in *Vagabond*, for instance, Varda's goal was that audiences recoil from Mona's stench: "Can I make people smell her bad smell?"

17 The making of these films followed the same trajectory. *Documenteur* was so psychologically difficult to tackle, Varda reports, that production fell prey to a series of mishaps that weren't entirely accidents. *Mur Murs* was a different sort of difficult—hundreds of hours of gregarious exploration, sometimes in neighborhoods that didn't welcome her curiosity.

18 As Thom Anderson points out in *Los Angeles Plays Itself* (2003), these murals are also featured in *Zabriskie Point* (Michelangelo Antonioni, 1970), *Carrie* (Brian De Palma, 1976), and *Angel City* (Jon Jost, 1977).

19 The mural is extremely faded but still exists at 1616 Butler Ave., south of Santa Monica Boulevard.

20 Barbara Quart and Agnès Varda, "Agnès Varda: A Conversation," *Film Quarterly* 40, no. 2 (Winter 1986–87): 9.

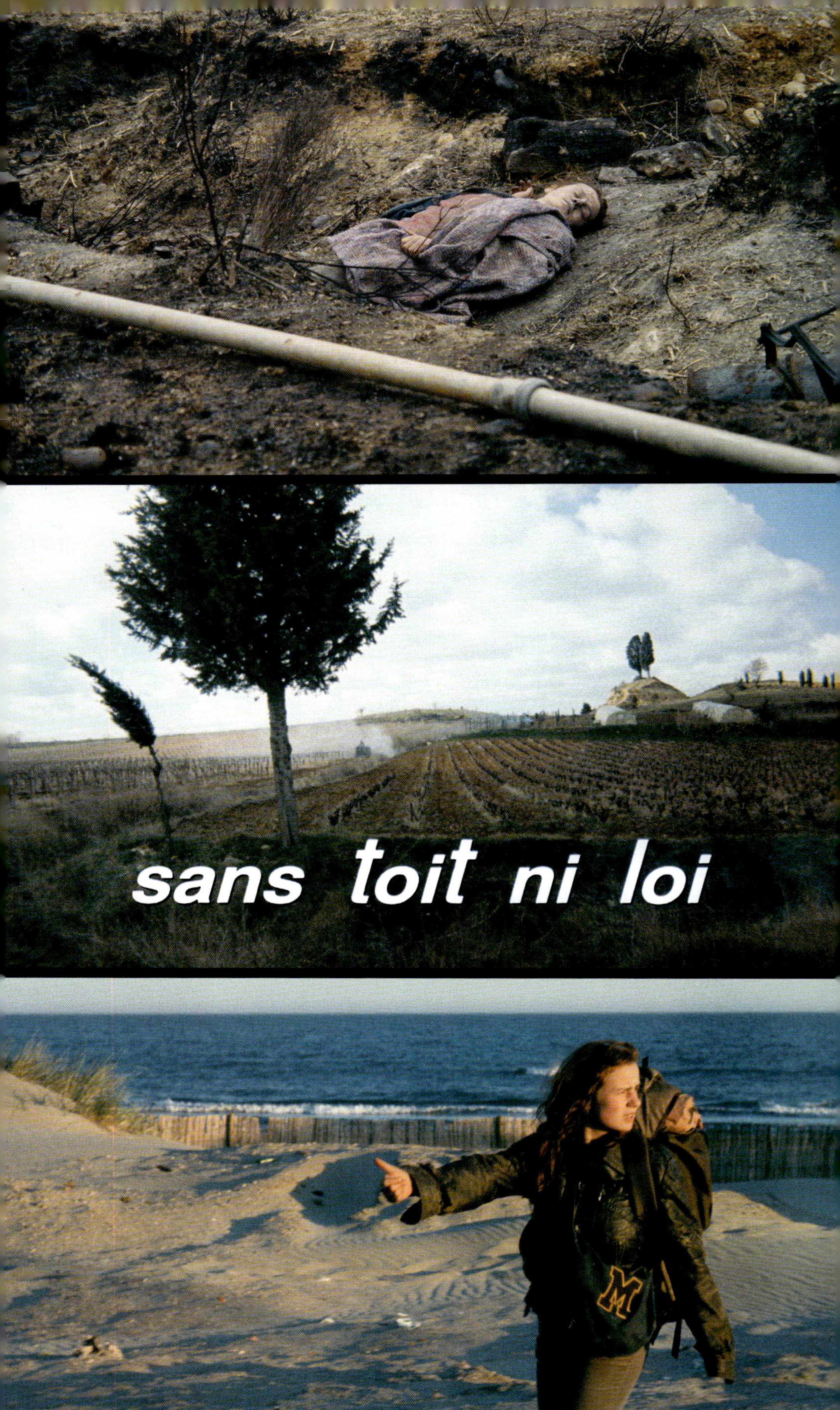

sans toit ni loi

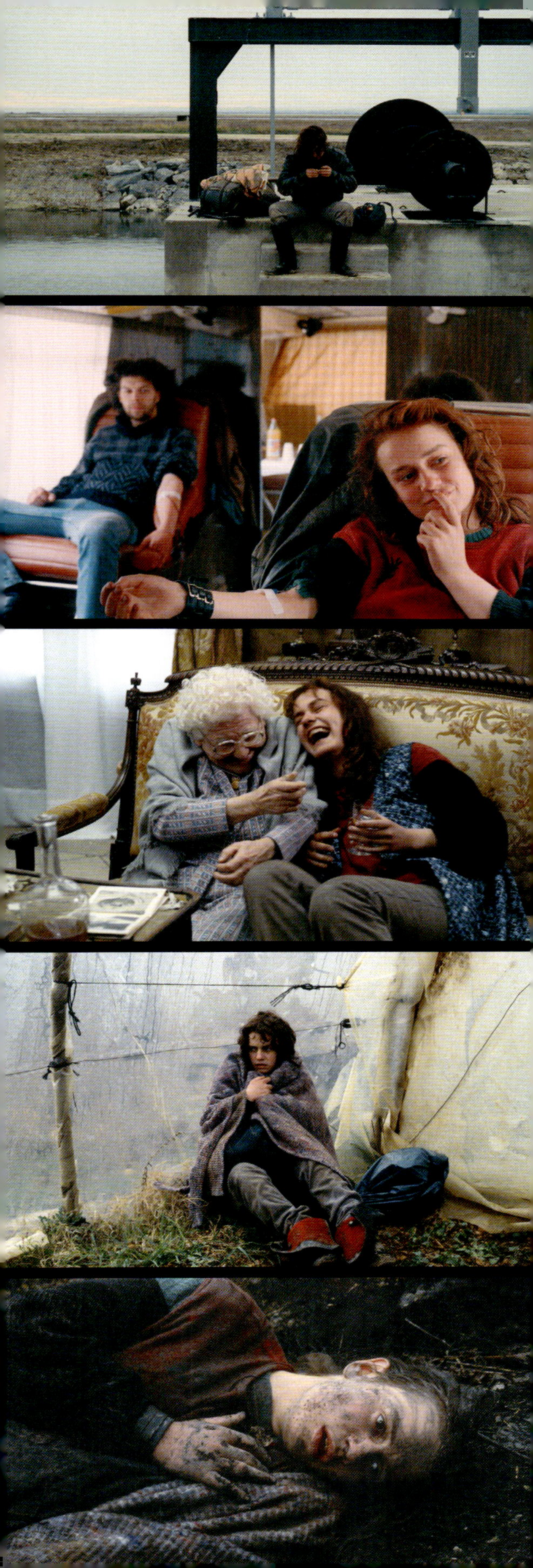

CHLOÉ ZHAO

I always had the desire to make a road movie, having been uprooted since childhood and moved around my whole life. There is something about the road that gives the illusion that life will go on forever because nothing is ever permanent and everything is always changing. What makes this lifestyle so attractive is exactly why it's so hard to capture on film. The aimlessness and meandering existence, the lack of controlled tension, are often the opposite of what we are taught in screenwriting classes.

I watched *Vagabond* for the first time while in film school, and I found myself rewatching it often during the long drives from NYC to South Dakota in the three years I was making my first film, *Songs My Brothers Taught Me*. I felt then that Agnès captured the road in a potent and truthful way that I rarely see on film. It echoed and lingered in me. I thought about it often at truck stops, motels, and nameless roadside diners as I watched and mingled with people I will never see again.

Vagabond tells the story of a young woman, Mona, who wanders through the countryside of France in the winter. We discover right at the beginning that she has died, after which the movie backtracks and takes us through the last couple of months of her life. As it unfolds, we find ourselves trying to figure out what happened to her while also hearing from the network of people she encountered on her travels. She's a mystery we must solve watching this film.

At first Mona's fate may seem like a tragedy, but repeat viewings have convinced me that there's also an element of joy in her death that I didn't get the first time. The older I got, the more I realized that if you stay in one place long enough, it inevitably becomes a big part of who you are—your family, house, job, neighbors, coworkers, daily routines, etc. The more stable you are, the more you will be shaken when you lose everything. But when everything you own fits in a backpack and everyone you know is who you find yourself with in the present moment, then you truly have nothing to lose. You stop fearing, even death.

I think that's what makes Mona's character so insufferable to other characters: they are envious of her and reject her because she doesn't share their fears. Her fearlessness scared me the first time I watched *Vagabond*. But this film, like all great art, grows and ages with its viewer. Now I can accept Mona's death after having made *Nomadland*. She's not a martyr. She chose to live this way in a world that doesn't support her way of life. Her death is inevitable, but it was a choice, nevertheless. She came out of the ocean at the beginning of the film like a myth. Maybe that was what she was, a mythological creature the others conjured in their imaginations because they can never be her. She never belonged in our world, not unless we really look at ourselves and make it better.

I believe voices like Varda's are essential because, just like the world we live in, masculine and feminine energy in cinematic storytelling is out of balance. It goes beyond gender. We all have masculine and feminine energies in us. The yin and the yang. Form, control, logic, and civilization are masculine qualities, while intuition, fluidity, emotion, and nature are feminine qualities. Linear is masculine. Cyclical is feminine. We, as an industry, are built on celebrating masculine qualities in storytelling and in life. There are people like Agnès who dared to find the balance before we even started to realize the danger of our collective imbalance. It's more important than ever right now to celebrate artists like her. Agnès's cinema is like the ocean—the most feminine of it all—expansive, deep, mysterious, ever flowing, ever changing and with the lasting power that can turn the most rugged mountains into beautiful, soft sand.

Previous spread: Scenes from *Vagabond*

I wanted to create a stimulating or bracing discomfort whereby the spectator shapes a portrait from fragments and realizes the film has no answer.

Vagabond (1985) traces the final days of Mona, a young drifter played by Sandrine Bonnaire, and the people she encounters as she wanders through the Languedoc-Roussillon wine country region of France one winter.

Right: US theatrical poster for *Vagabond*

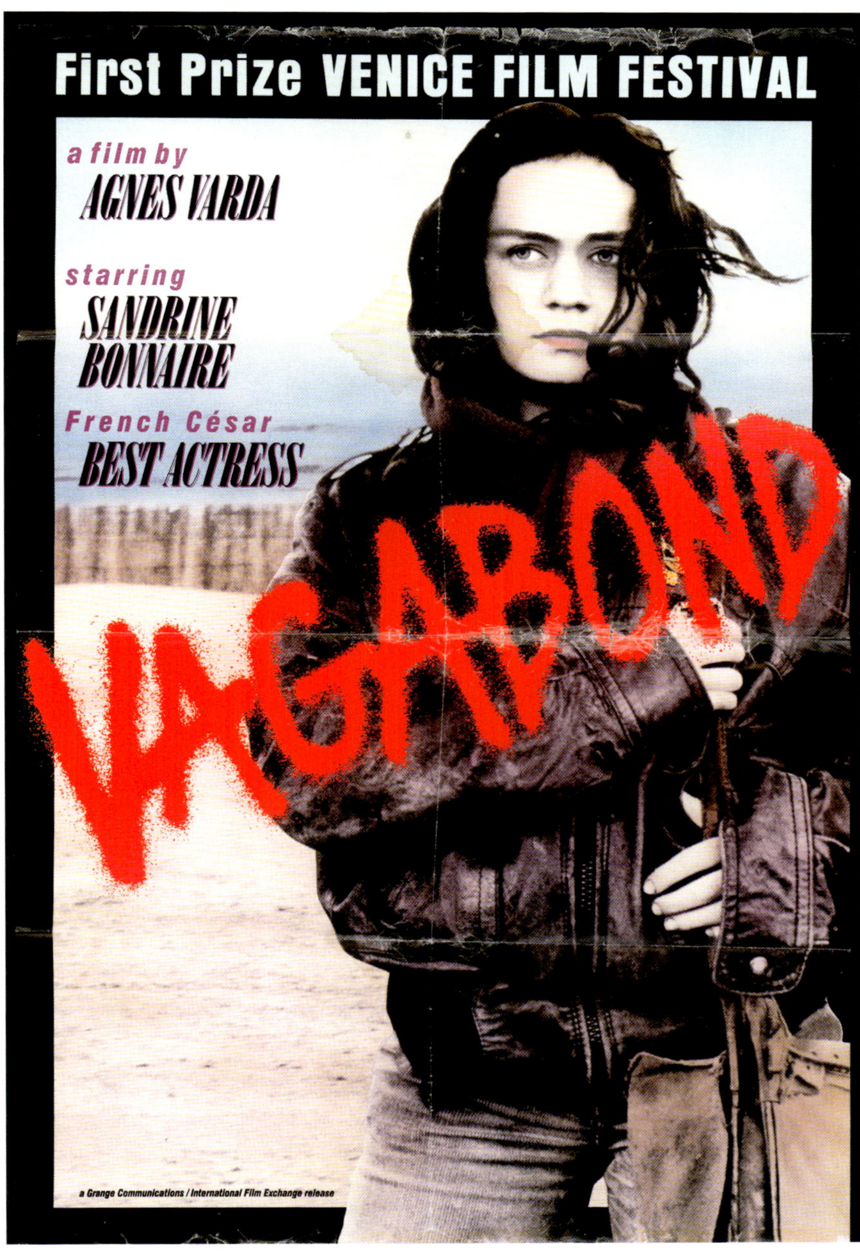

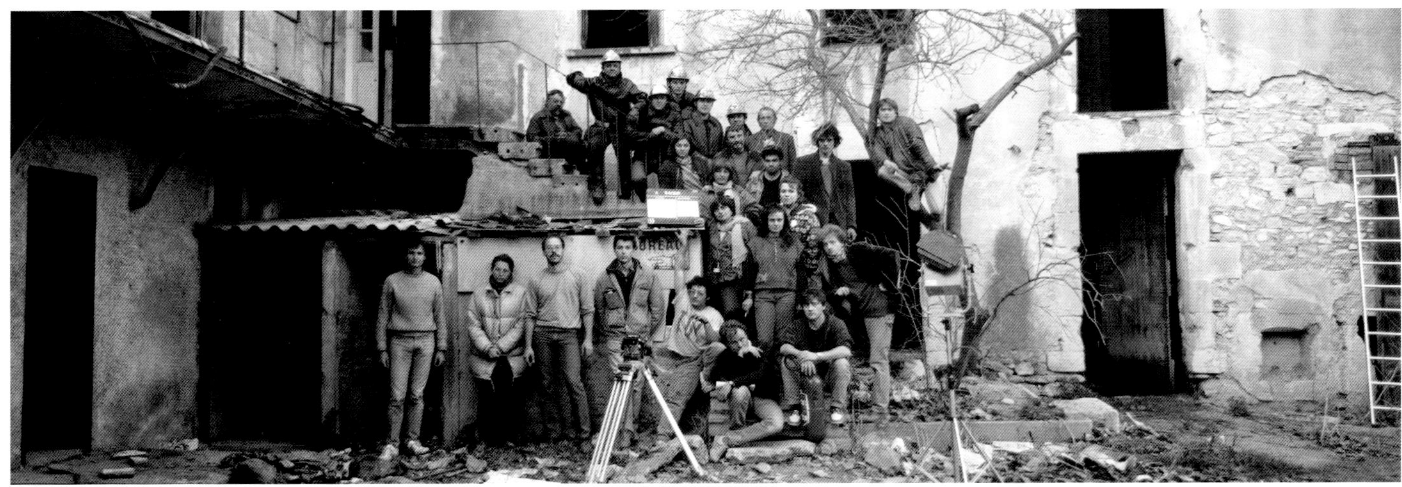

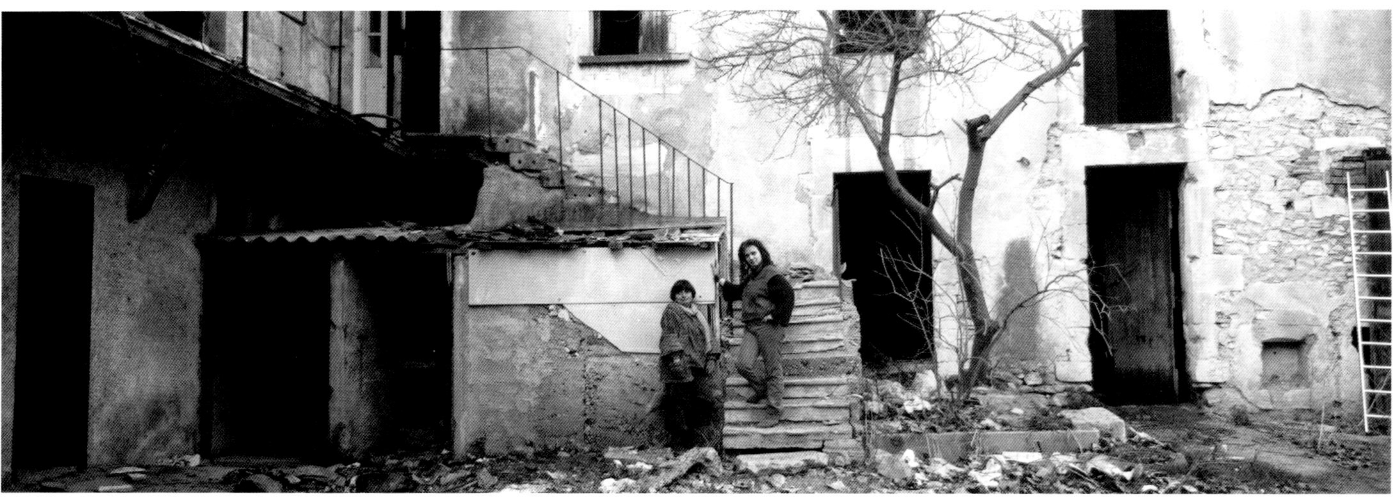

This page: Cast and crew during production of *Vagabond*

Opposite, top: Public transportation pass belonging to Djamila Arhab. Known as Setina, Arhab inspired the character of Mona.

Opposite, bottom: Flyer designed by Varda. The text above the title reads in English: "Would you take her in your car?" and "She's cute, she stinks, and she won't say thank you."

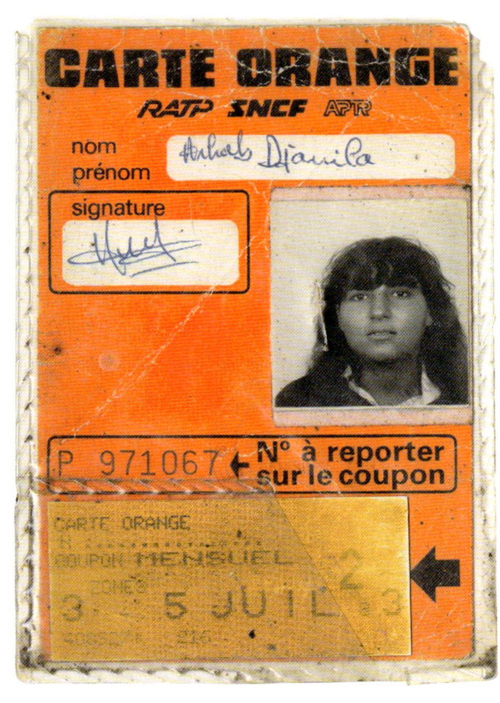

You bump into [Mona], know nothing about her, and all you can catch is what she is now. As a writer, I chose to forget about the writer's position and acknowledge that I don't know or understand her totally. I invented a character who eludes me.

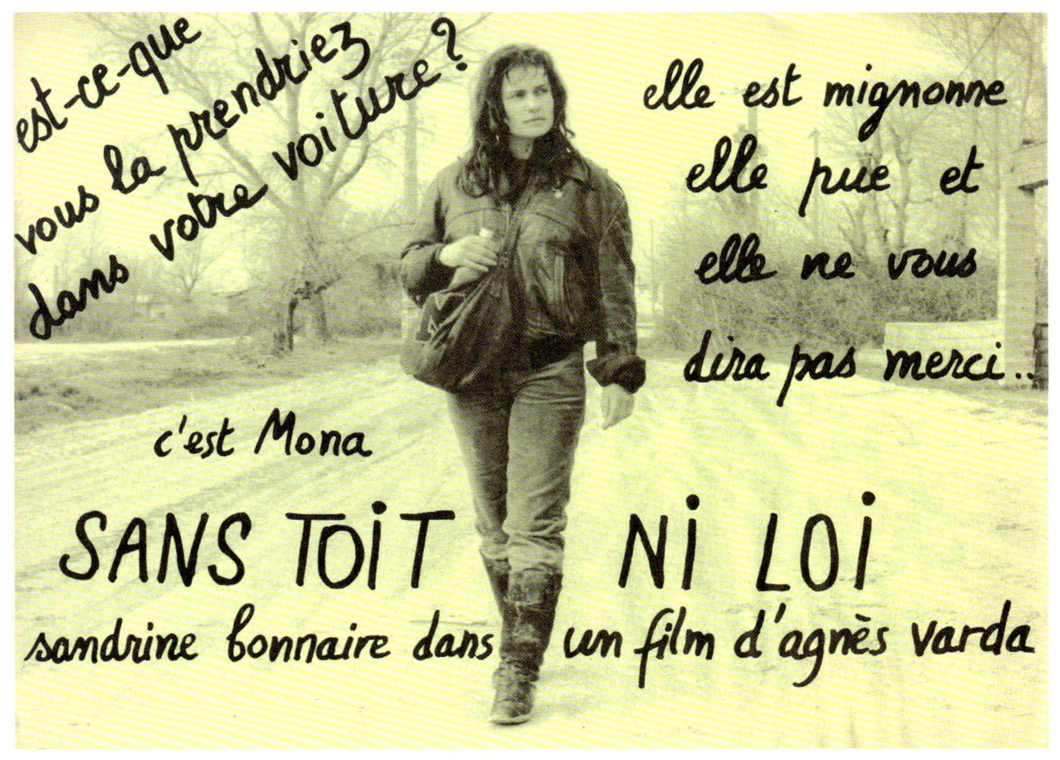

Would you give Mona a ride?
Would you let her sleep in your
car? Would you give her money?
It's not the question but the
questioning that matters.

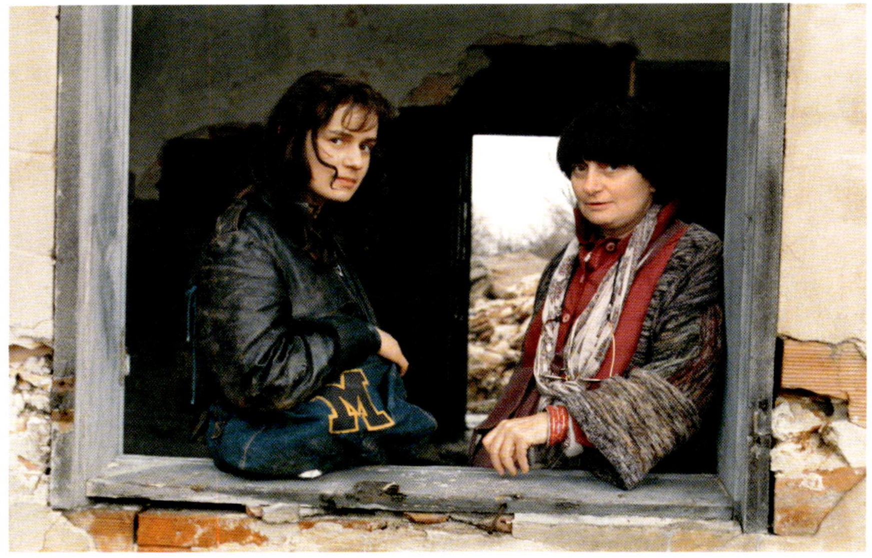

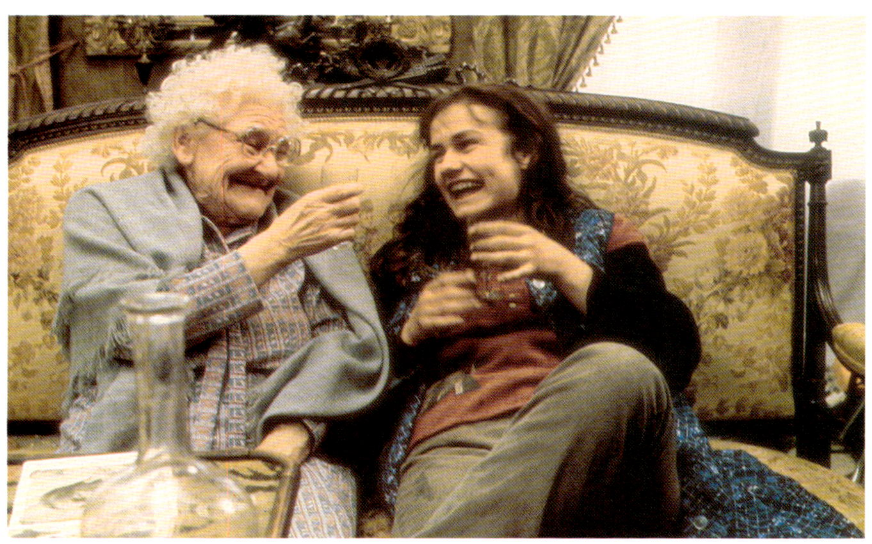

Top: Sandrine Bonnaire
and Varda on set

Bottom: Bonnaire
and Marthe Jarnias in
Vagabond

SANDRINE BONNAIRE

Agnès invited me to her home on rue Daguerre to discuss a part in her new film, which would become *Vagabond*. She said, "I have a movie, but there is no script. I'm offering you a character named Mona. She's thin, hungry. She's not polite or well educated. She smells, she's dirty, and she says 'Fuck off' to everybody. Do you want to do it?" And I said, "Yes, of course."

I had not seen her films, but I knew Agnès was very talented and smart. She had a special reputation as a hard woman, extremely tough, and she was. We had a fight on set once, I think because I was too young—I was 17—and I was looking for a mother. I'd had a father figure in Maurice Pialat, who directed me in *À nos amours* (1983). I wanted to be protected in the same way by Agnès, but she was not very tender. It was simple to work with her, though, because she had a strong vision.

Agnès arranged for me to camp for two nights in the countryside with a woman named Setina, who lived like Mona. I learned how to make a fire and build a tent like Mona would. For Agnès, these physical movements and behaviors were important. There was no psychology because Mona doesn't think. She doesn't feel anything anymore. She wants to eat, sleep, and drink. There is nothing else. I didn't wash my hair for twelve weeks.

Everything Mona does is suicide. That's my interpretation. She wants freedom, but, in fact, she's walking toward death. Near the end of the film, Mona falls into a ditch. Agnès had me do that fall twice. She said, "You'll fall there. This is the end of your life. It's very cold." When I was zipped into the body bag, it was as if I saw my own death. And when I came out of traumatic scenes like this, Agnès was not very comforting. She'd say, "Very good, we'll go on to the next scene now," and move on. She didn't discuss much with the actors or get into the emotional side of the work.

Agnès was, in fact, very tender, but she didn't want to show it. I learned that years later. With maturity, I understood who she was. At the end, we were very close, and she called every Sunday just to talk. So, that maternal figure I was looking for, I didn't get it at the beginning, but maybe I did at the end.

When I think of Agnès, I remember our visit the day before she died. She had shown me photographs she had made of people's hands placed together. I asked her, "Why don't you photograph your hand with someone else's?" And she said, "Because I'm not married anymore." So, I put my hand on her hand and said, "Well, neither am I, but we are married together because you changed my life."

Even though I had already done four movies by the time I met Agnès, I did not yet feel like an actress, maybe because of how I had started. I had no experience when I made my first films; I had not even taken any acting classes. I became an actress with *Vagabond*. The character was so far away from my life that I could feel I had done something special, and I became the youngest winner of the César Award for Best Actress. I am still very proud of the movie.

With Pialat, I was a flower. With Agnès, I became a tree with big, deep roots.

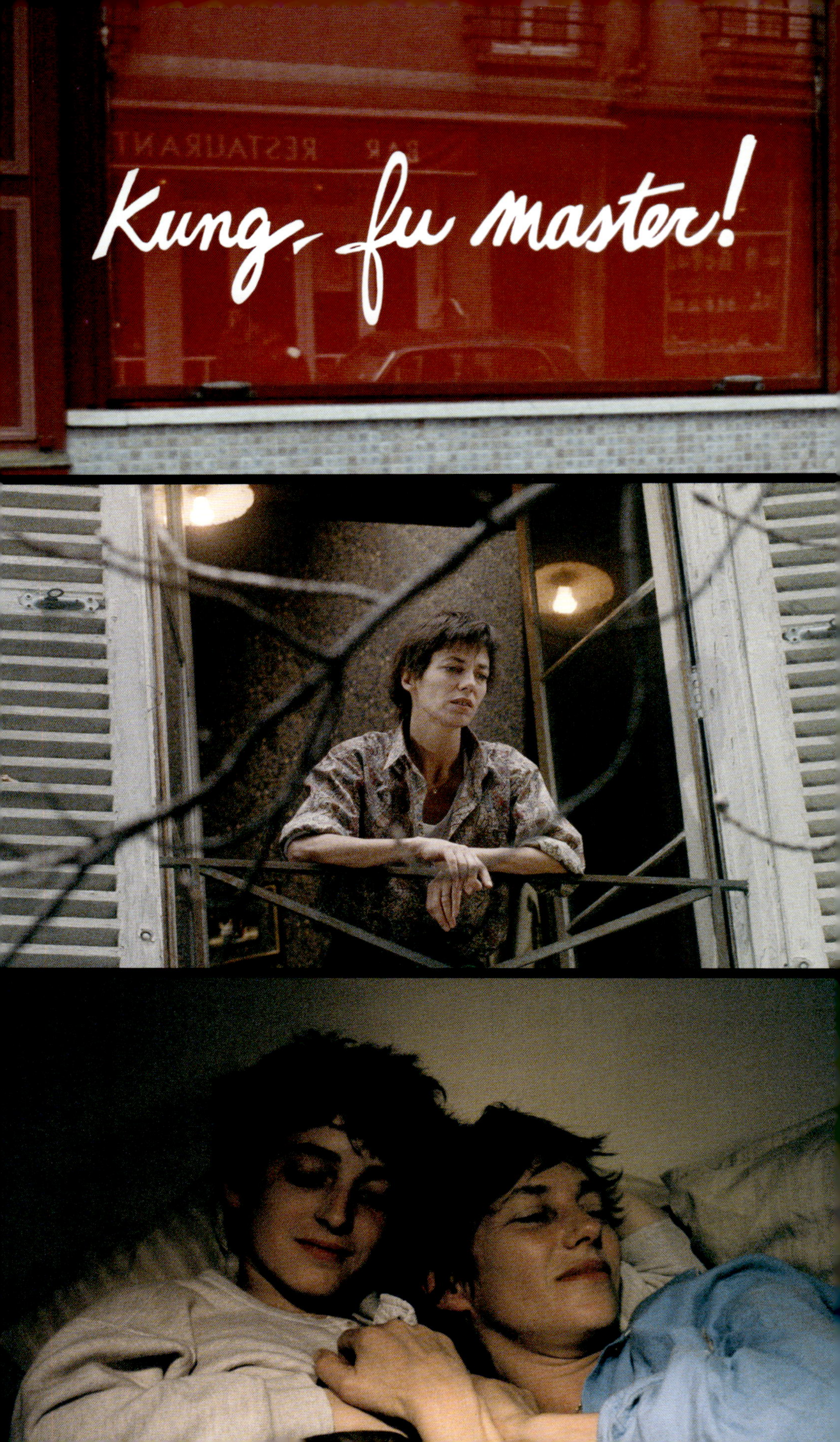
Kung-fu master!

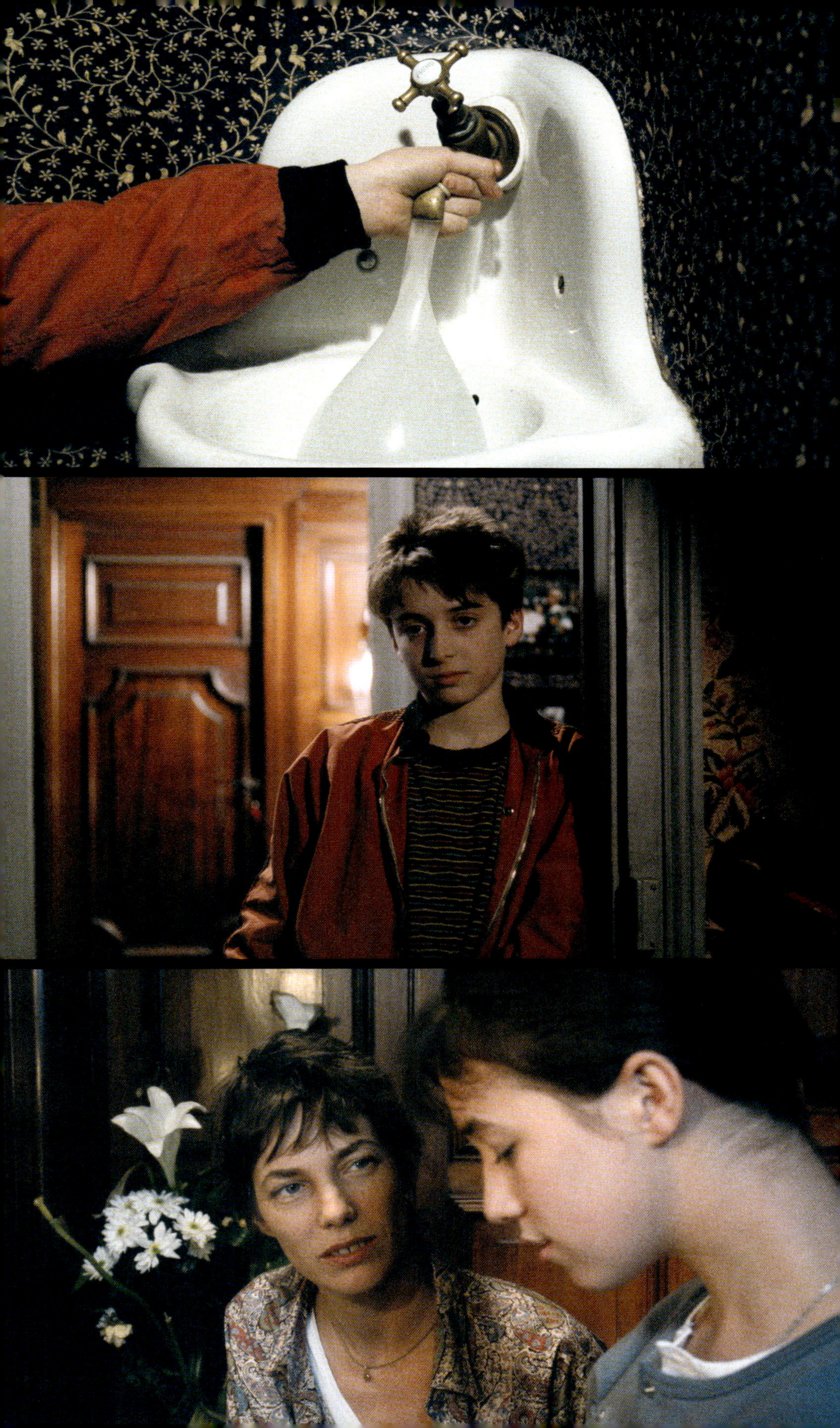

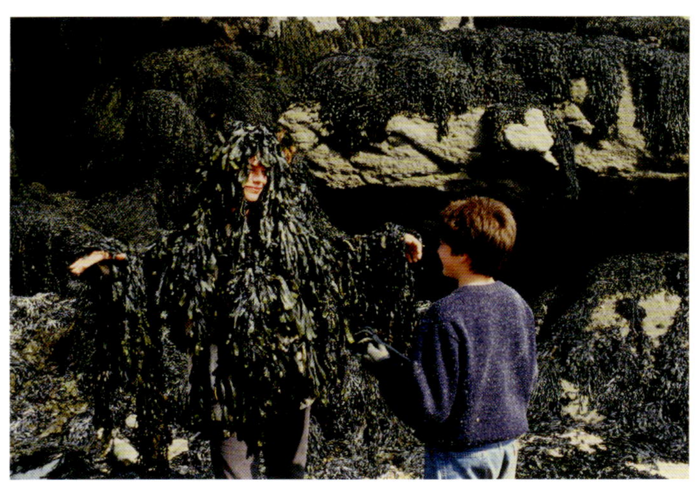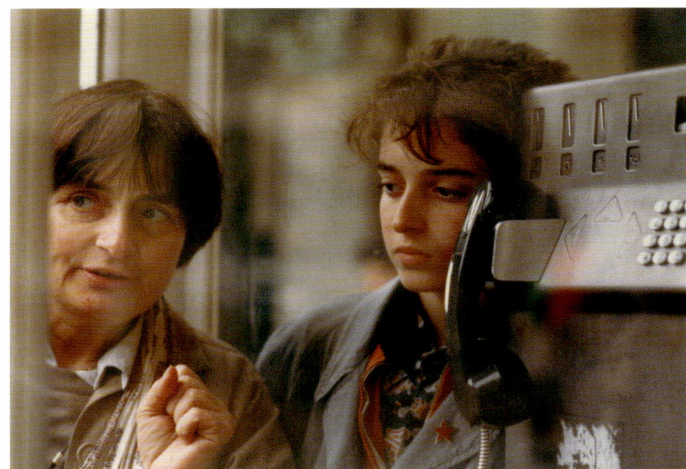

Jane Birkin conceived of and began writing *Kung-Fu Master!* while she and Varda were filming *Jane B. par Agnès V.* In the film, she plays a 40-year-old divorced mother of two who falls in love with her daughter's 14-year-old classmate. Varda and Birkin cast their respective children, Mathieu Demy and Charlotte Gainsbourg, and paused the production of *Jane B. par Agnès V.* to film them during an Easter school holiday.

Previous spread: Scenes from *Kung-Fu Master!* (1988) featuring Jane Birkin and Mathieu Demy

Above: Demy with Birkin (left) and Varda (right) during production

Right: Varda with her children, Rosalie and Mathieu, during production

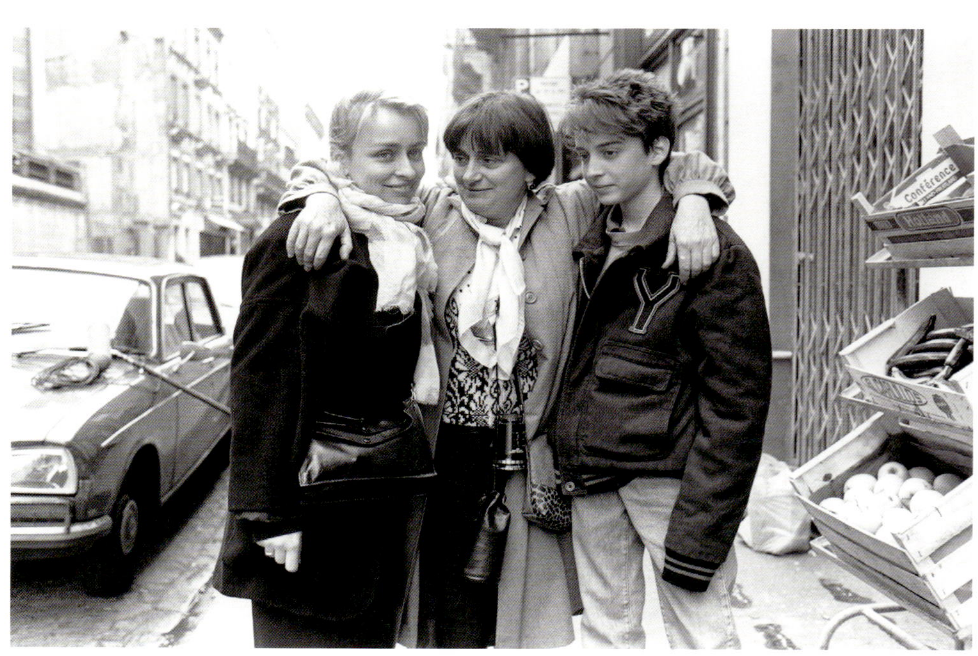

Kung-Fu Master! is about that time in adolescence where sexuality is very important, but at the same time it's very vague and hard to express. Older women can be very touched by this because they remember their own adolescence: their own vague confusion, the fear of daring and wishing and all of that.

```
MARY JANE    - JE NE SAIS  JAMAIS  RIEN..
             LUCY PARLE SI PEU..    VOUS JOUEZ À QUOI ?
   JULIEN  (OFF) - OH...ÇA DÉPEND...
             DES FOIS ON JOUE  A DONJONS ET DRAGONS...


   JULIEN
   ( ON) de très loin      " C EST UN JEU D'IMAGINATION..SI TU VEUX
                     ON DOIT SE METTRE DANS LA PEAU D'UN PERSONNAGE
                     ET ON DOIT VIVRE UNE AVENTURE QUI EST DÉCIDÉE PAR LE
                                             DONJON-MASTER

                     _ CELUI QUI DIRIGE LE JEU.

        (vite)       et IL FAUT JUSTE UN PAPIER ET UN CRAYON..
                        ET DES DÉS MULTIFACES.

   (ON)  ( à vue)  ALORS  MOI JE SUIS UN GUERRIER
                   UN GUERRIER DU MOYEN-ÂGE   ...OH NON..
                   PLUTÔT  UN ASSASSIN...UN VOLEUR ASSASSIN DU MOYEN-ÂGE

                   ET PUIS ON EST DANS UN DÉCOR
                   MOYENAGEUX

        OFF    ..ET PAR EXEMPLE LA MISSION EST DE DÉLIVRER UNE PRINCESSE
   ( et vite)      DANS UN CHÂTEAU
                   IL FAUT RÉUSSIR À LA DÉLIVRER  SANS SE FAIRE BROSSER LA TÊTE PAR
                   UN MONSTRE...PARCE QU'ON PEUT RENCONTRER DES MONSTRES EN COURS DE
                   ROUTE..DES  TROLLS..DES  GNÔMES  ET DES GOBELINS...
                   ON TIRE TOUT AUX DÉS, MÊME MA DEXTÉRITÉ, MA FORCE, MON INTELLIGENCE
                   ET MES ARMES...
                   DES ÉPÉES OU DES MASSES D'ARMES OU... ET DES ÉPÉES BÂTARDES...
                   BON. ALORS JE FRAPPE! JE VOIS SI JE LE TOUCHE OU PAS D'APRÈS LES DÉS
                   ET PAR RAPPORT À LA CLASSE D'ARMURES DE L'ADVERSAIRE.
                   ~~S'IL A UNE~~, UN BOUCLIER OU UNE COTTE DE MAILLES , S'IL A UN 2
                   IL FAUT QUE JE FASSE 18 OU PLUS AU DÉ À 20 FACES POUR LE TOUCHER.

                   ALORS SI JE LE TOUCHE DISONS AVEC UNE ÉPÉE QUI CORRESPOND À
                   UN DÉ À 6 FACES...ÇA FAIT 1 À 6 COMME DÉGÂTS
                   ...
                   SINON IL Y A LES P.D.V.


   MARY- JANE ( ON) - QU'EST-CE QUE C ' EST LES P.D.V.   ?
   JULIEN  ( ON )  - C EST LES POINTS DE VIE.. C'EST LE NOMBRE DE POINTS  QU'ON A...
                   ET QUAND IL N'Y EN....QUAND C'EST À ZÉRO  ON EST MORT.

   sur JANE
   JULIEN  ( OFF)  ET ON PEUT SE LES FAIRE RÉGÉNÉRER PAR UN MAGICIEN ..
                   SI ON A UN ANNEAU  REGENERATEUR
```

Annotated script page for *Kung-Fu Master!*

JANE BIRKIN

After watching *Vagabond*, I was so moved that I wrote two letters and sent them to rue Daguerre: one for Agnès and one for Sandrine Bonnaire, because I really didn't know who had done what in this extraordinary film. Agnès called and said she couldn't read a word of my handwriting, but would I like to meet? She arranged a rendezvous for us in the park. At the time, I was focused on music and didn't want to make movies. Agnès told me she wanted to make a film about seasons. I thought to myself, "What's she going to do? Dress me up with autumn leaves?" I was a little worried.

In the end, we did exactly what Agnès wanted me to do. We started meeting regularly in cafés and other places, and she would film me saying yes or no to her propositions. Her idea was for me to play parts that she wanted me to play or perhaps wanted to play herself. Then I realized I was making a film that was as much about her as it was about me, and I became putty in her hands. It was like being a teenager again. She would say, "Do you want to do a film where you'd be like a waif from Dickens?" "Oh yes," I said, "I long to." "Would you play Joan of Arc?" "Ah, I've always wanted to." "Will you play a Spanish dancer?" "Oh no, Agnès, I hate Spanish dancing and would be awfully bad at it."

I remember being Joan of Arc, sitting on a horse on rue de Rivoli. She put me in these pointed metal shoes they wore in the Middle Ages, which must have tickled the horse. I was in armor with a black wig on, if I remember right. The horse didn't like being tickled and shot off down the street. People cried out, "Oh! C'est Marie Laforêt!" They thought I was another actress entirely.

During this time, I wrote a very intimate script about a 40-year-old woman and a teenage boy. I called up Agnès, and she said, "Look, it's not really my thing. But I think it is a part of you, so I must do the film." That was her loyalty. The two films, *Jane B. par Agnès V.* and *Kung-Fu Master!*, came out together. She had made an enormous amount of money on *Vagabond* and lost it all on the two films she did with me.

We must have spent a year together, some of it shooting at my house. She set up lights in my kitchen that my family tripped over and reflective panels that kept falling off the walls. I could see it was annoying everyone except me. I was delighted. Agnès and I were truly happy. She'd put a ribbon all around my house; it was such fun, like playing charades forever.

While we were filming, Agnès did the most extraordinary feat of being a mother to Mathieu and looking after Jacques and her own mother, who had Alzheimer's and was wandering around the house with a fur toque on her head. Agnès was finishing up script pages she'd written that morning and handing them to all of us and the crew, then taking food over to Jacques, then picking up Mathieu from school. Doing all of this at the same time was Agnès's life.

Still, everything was more fun with Agnès. We traveled together to a film festival in North Africa and had a layover in Madrid. Instead of putting our feet up in the lounge and having a coffee, Agnès insisted we had enough time to go to the Prado. So, we took a taxi and went to see the work of Francisco de Goya and Diego Velázquez, even though we weren't supposed to leave the airport. There was an enormous queue, but Agnès was not to be deterred. She liked to live dangerously. If there were a bit of a risk, she'd take it.

I am so glad that she had enormous success with *Faces Places*. It was wonderful to see her rediscovered and celebrated. Watching her and JR rush from cinema to cinema together was like watching them win an Olympic race. He carried her high and brought out her best. That film paints a complete picture of Agnès. You see all of her good sides and her annoying sides too. And by the end of the film, you adore her.

German poster for *Jane B. par Agnès V.* (1988). Varda's unique documentary on Jane Birkin functions as a prism, showing the many facets of the beloved singer, actress, and style icon. "It's a surprise portrait in which Jane plays many roles, including herself, with a variety of partners. She was a good sport. She was funny, strange, magnificent, moving."

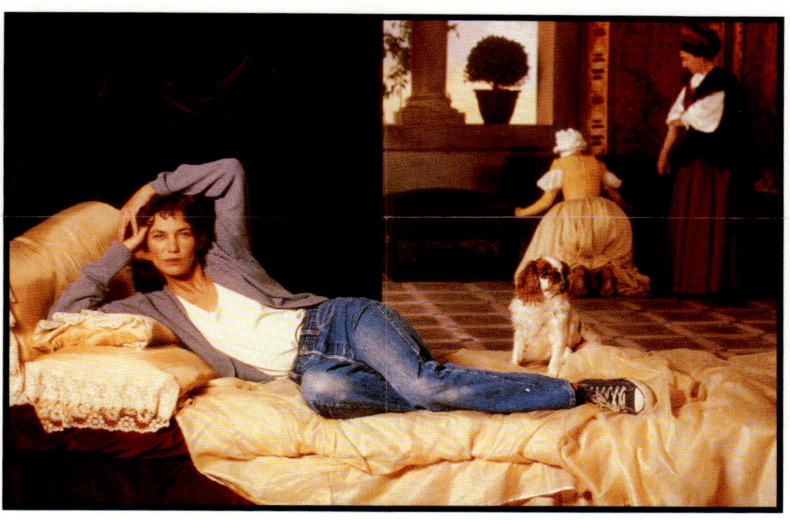

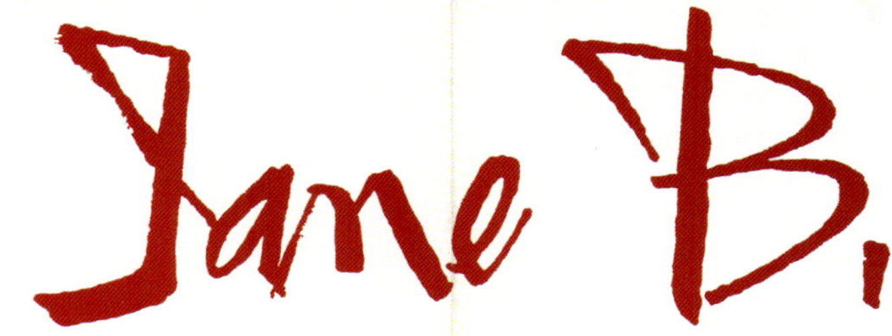

—

This film is an imaginary walk, a bulk, a collage.

Left: Scene charts for *Jane B. par Agnès V.*

Opposite: Scenes from *Jane B. par Agnès V.* featuring Varda, Birkin, and Serge Gainsbourg

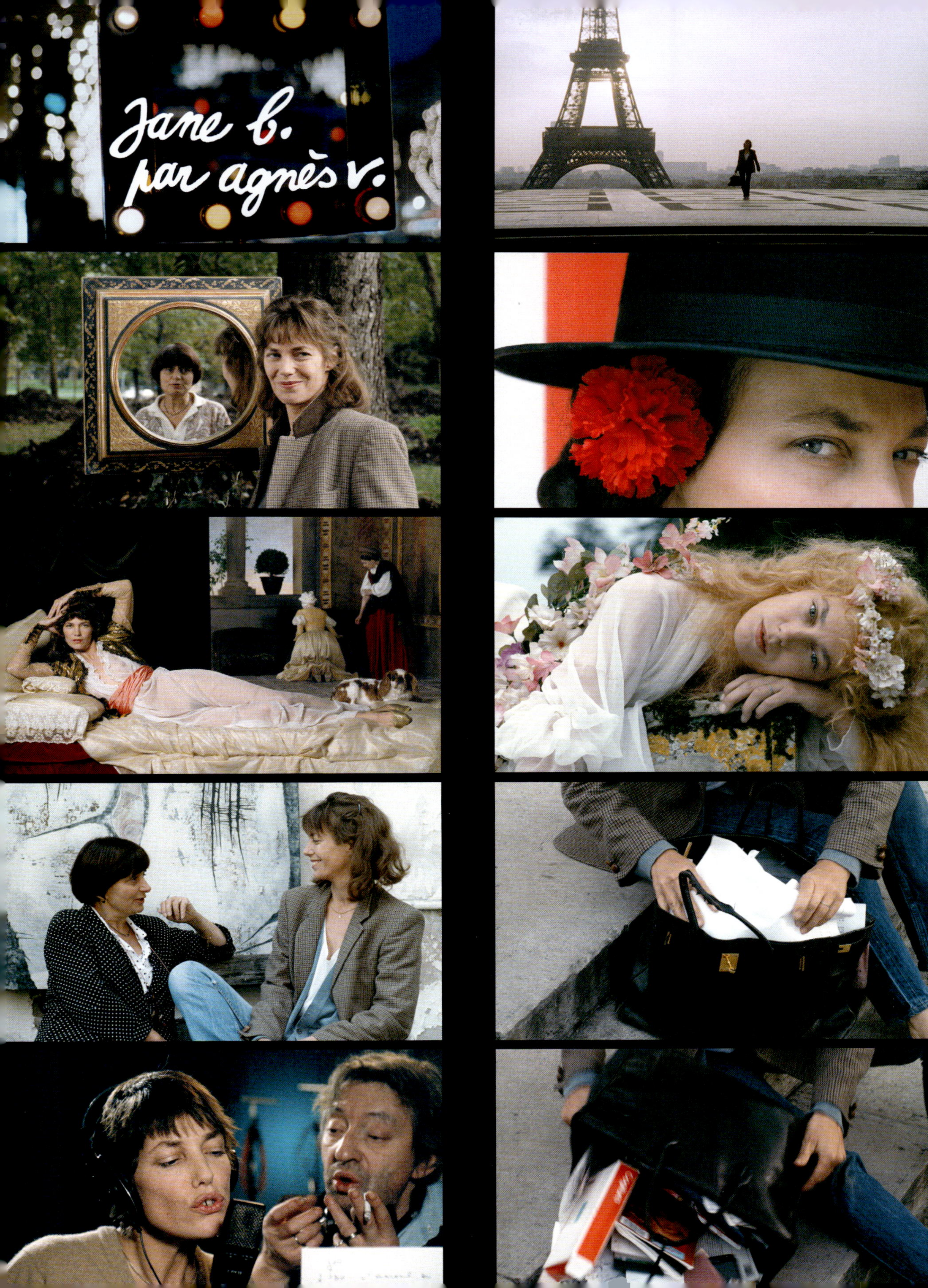

Jane B.
par agnès v.

JACQUOT DE NANTES

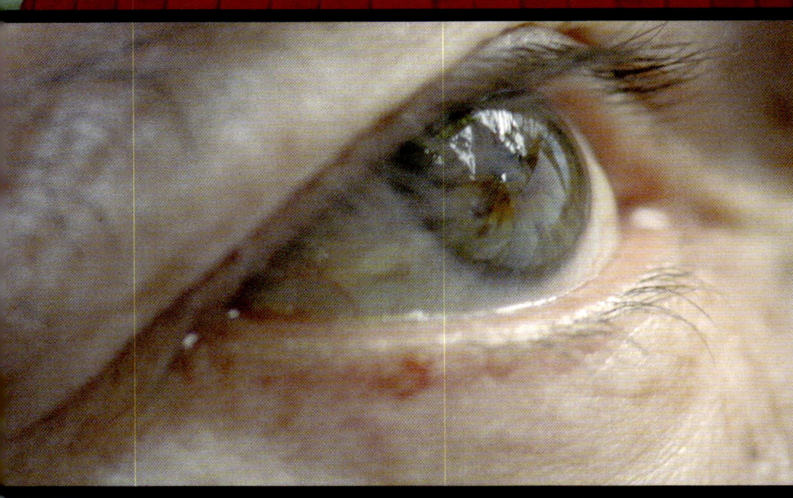

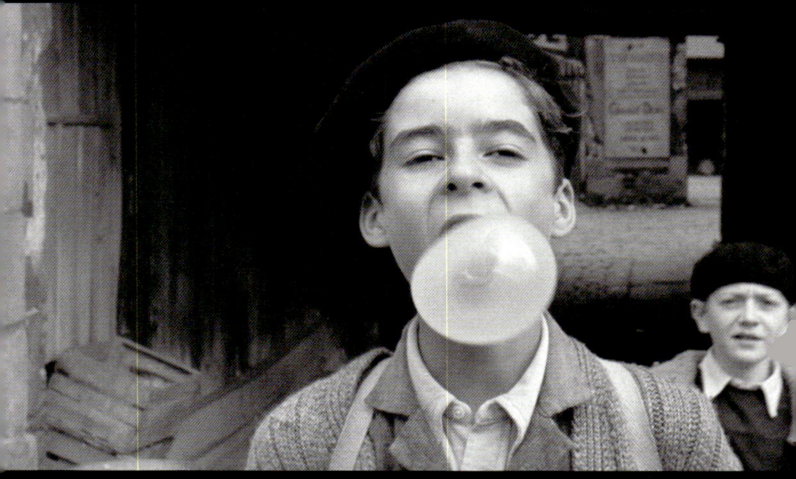

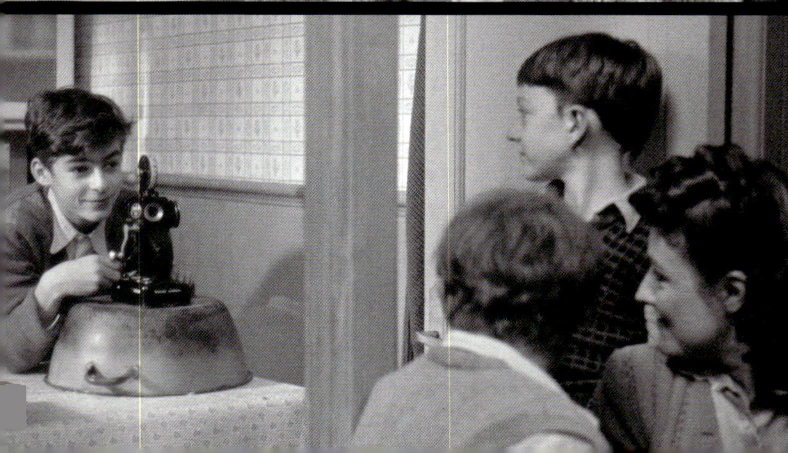

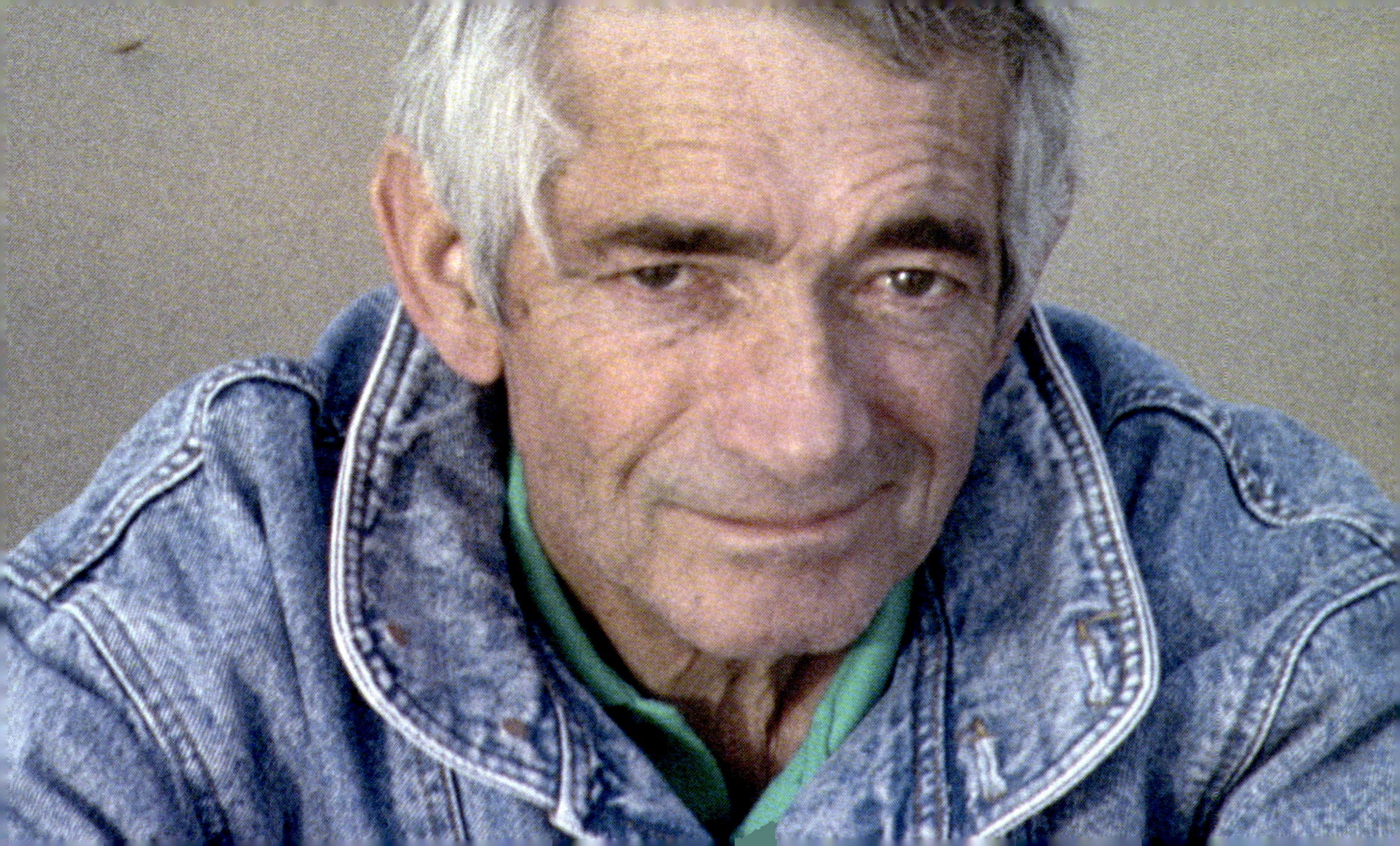

I met Jacques at a short-film festival in 1958.... We met as directors of short films and fell in love. Love came like a rain in spring.

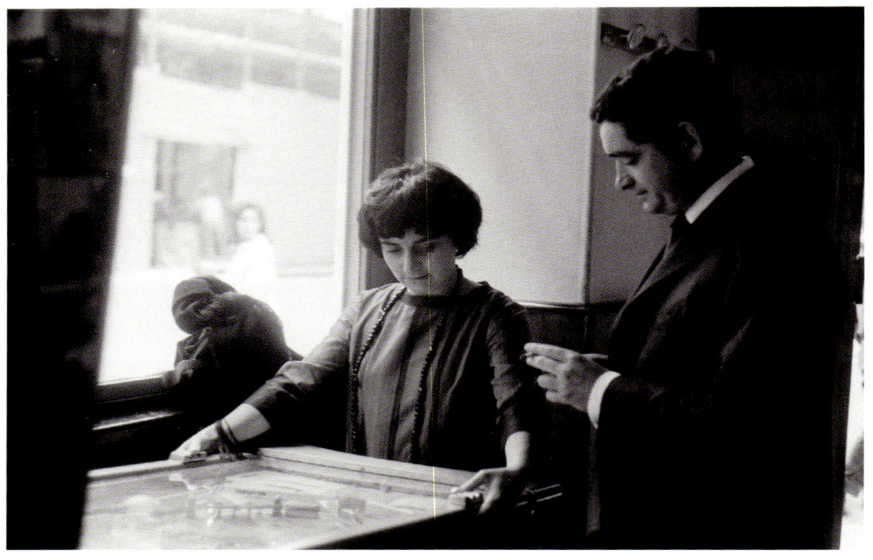

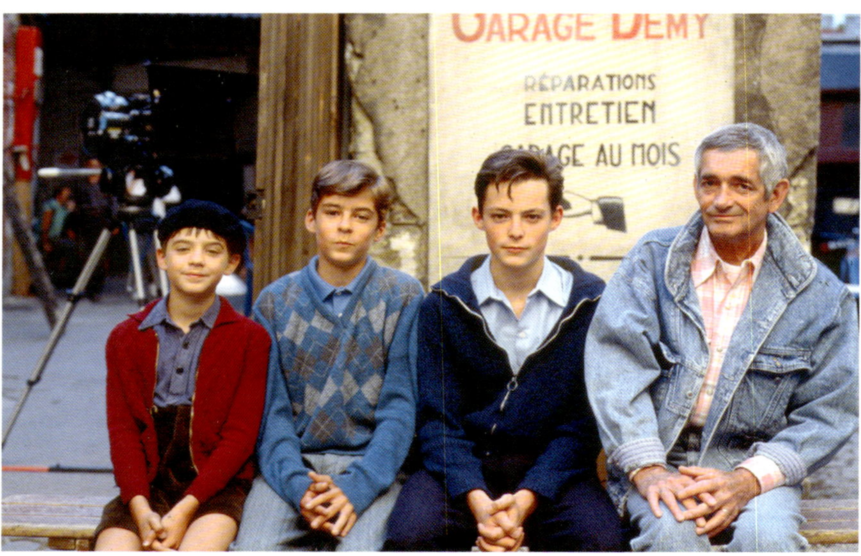

Jacquot de Nantes (1991), Varda's loving tribute to her husband, Jacques Demy, made near the end of his life, combines re-creations of his childhood in Nantes, clips from his films, and documentary footage of his later years.

Previous spread: Scenes from *Jacquot de Nantes*

Top: Varda and Demy, ca. 1958

Bottom: Demy (far right) with the three actors who play younger versions of him—Laurent Monnier, Edouard Joubeaud, and Philippe Maron—during production of *Jacquot de Nantes*

Opposite: Pages from a scrapbook made by Varda as a Christmas gift for Demy, 1962

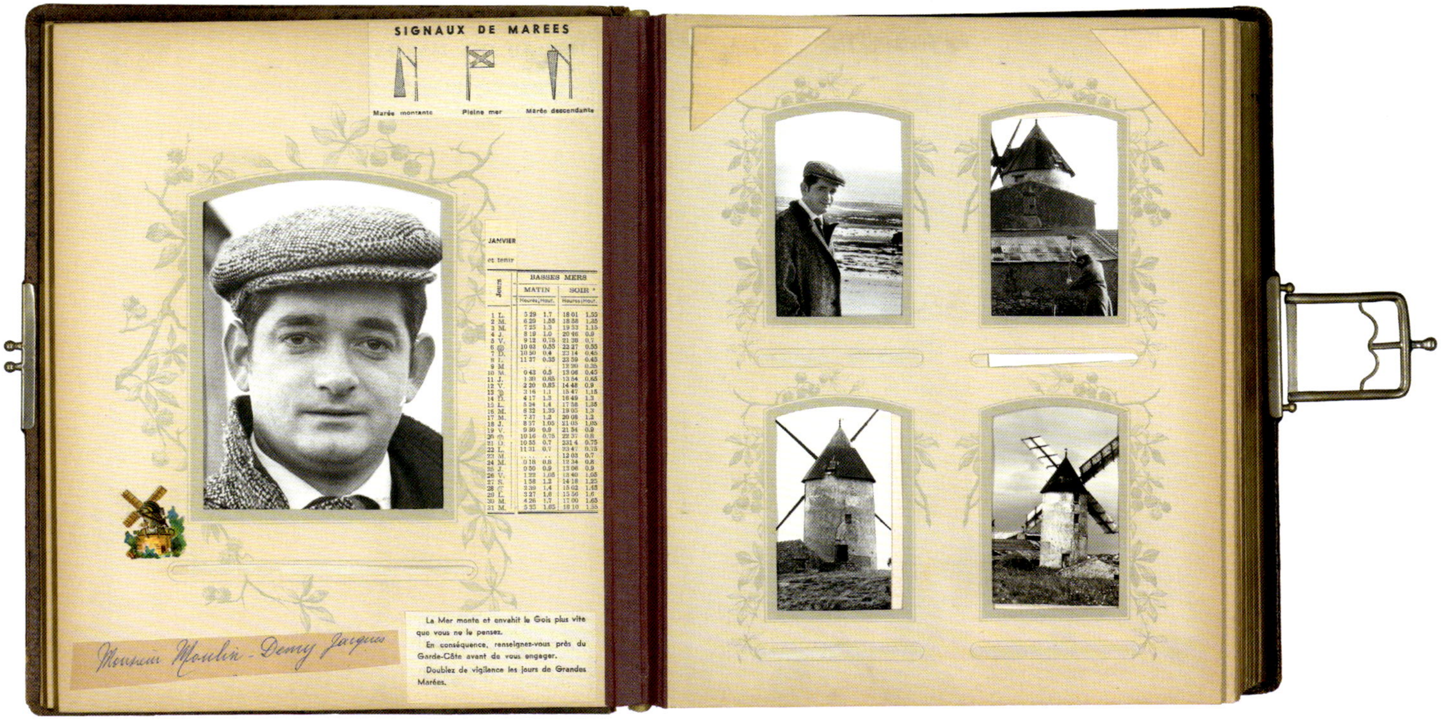

JANVIER
et février

JOURS	BASSES MERS			
	MATIN		SOIR	
	Heures/Haut.		Heures/Haut.	
1 L.	5.29	1.7	18.01	1.55
2 M.	6.25	1.55	18.58	1.35
3 M.	7.25	1.3	19.52	1.15
4 J.	8.18	1.0	20.46	0.9
5 V.	9.12	0.75	21.38	0.7
6 S.	10.03	0.55	22.27	0.55
7 D.	10.50	0.4	23.14	0.45
8 L.	11.37	0.35	23.59	0.45
9 M.			13.90	0.35
10 M.	0.43	0.5	13.06	0.45
11 J.	1.30	0.65	13.54	0.65
12 V.	2.20	0.85	14.48	0.9
13 S.	3.16	1.1	15.47	1.15
14 D.	4.17	1.3	16.49	1.3
15 L.	5.24	1.4	17.56	1.3
16 M.	6.32	1.35	19.05	1.3
17 M.	7.41	1.2	20.06	1.3
18 J.	8.37	1.05	21.03	1.05
19 V.	9.30	0.9	21.54	0.9
20 S.	10.16	0.75	22.37	0.8
21 D.	10.55	0.7	23.14	0.75
22 L.	11.31	0.7	23.47	0.75
23 M.			12.03	0.7
24 M.	0.18	0.8	12.34	0.8
25 J.	0.50	0.9	13.06	0.9
26 V.	1.23	1.05	13.40	1.05
27 S.	1.58	1.2	14.18	1.25
28 D.	5.38	1.4	15.02	1.45
29 L.	3.17	1.6	15.56	1.6
30 M.	4.26	1.7	17.00	1.65
31 M.	5.35	1.65	18.10	1.55

La Mer monta et envahit le Gois plus vite que vous ne le pensez.

En conséquence, renseignez-vous près du Garde-Côte avant de vous engager.

Doublez de vigilance les jours de Grandes Marées.

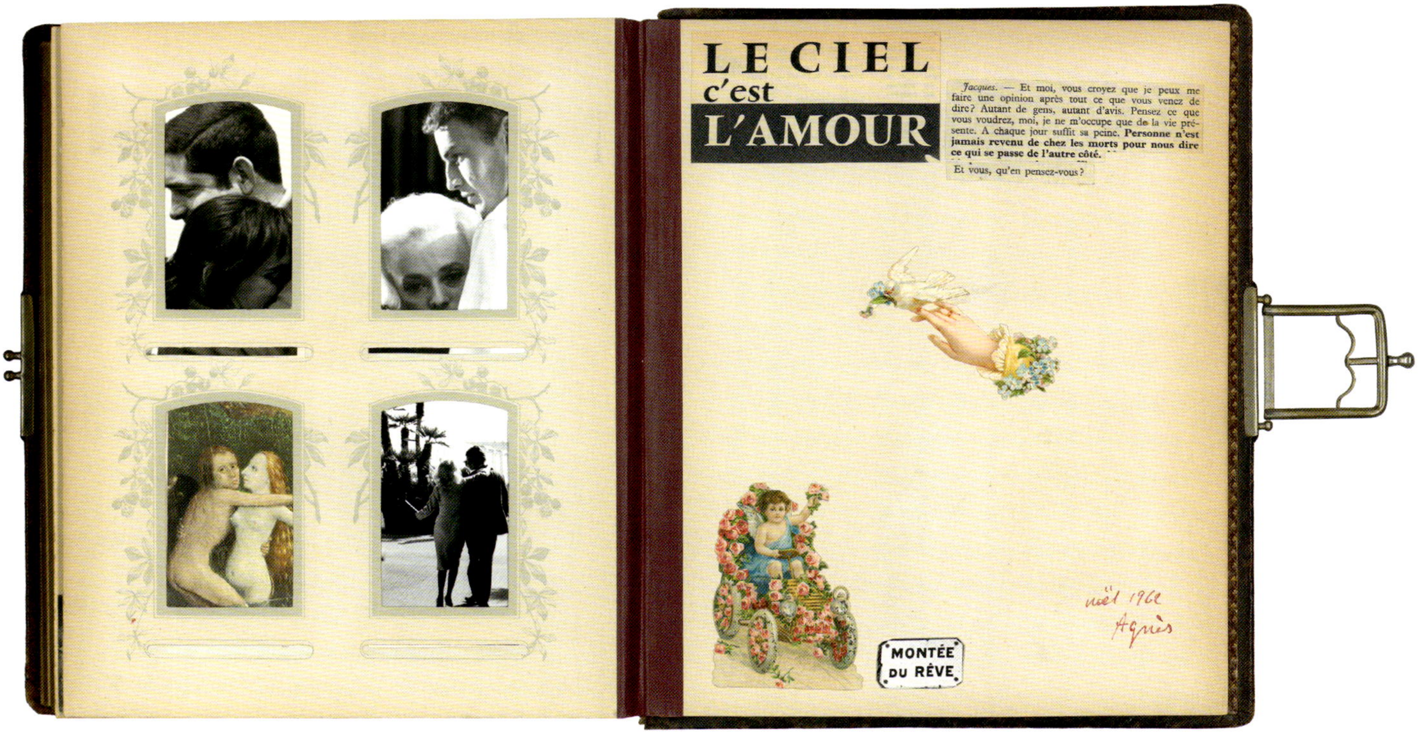

Monsieur Moulin - Demy Jacques

LE CIEL c'est L'AMOUR

Jacques. — Et moi, vous croyez que je peux me faire une opinion après tout ce que vous venez de dire? Autant de gens, autant d'avis. Pensez ce que vous voudrez, moi, je ne m'occupe que de la vie présente. A chaque jour suffit sa peine. **Personne n'est jamais revenu de chez les morts pour nous dire ce qui se passe de l'autre côté.**

Et vous, qu'en pensez-vous?

noël 1961
Agnès

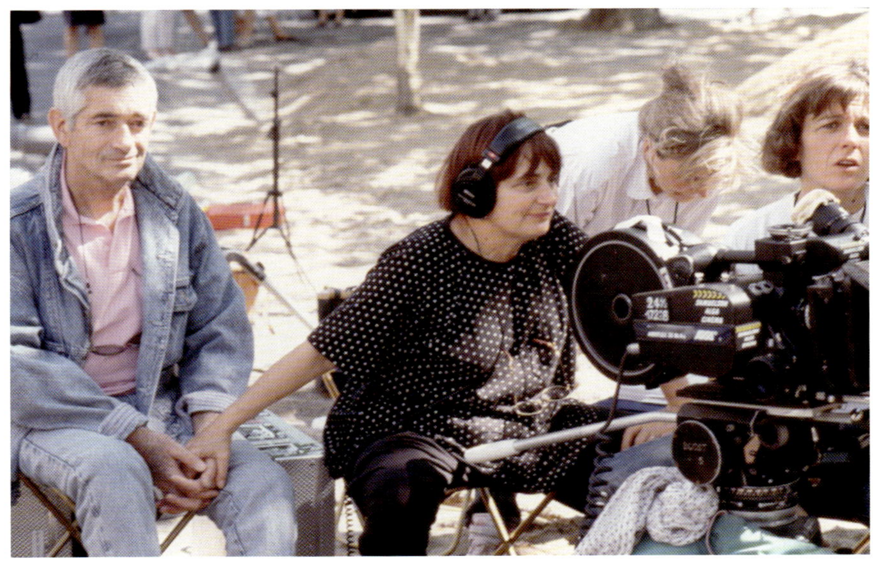

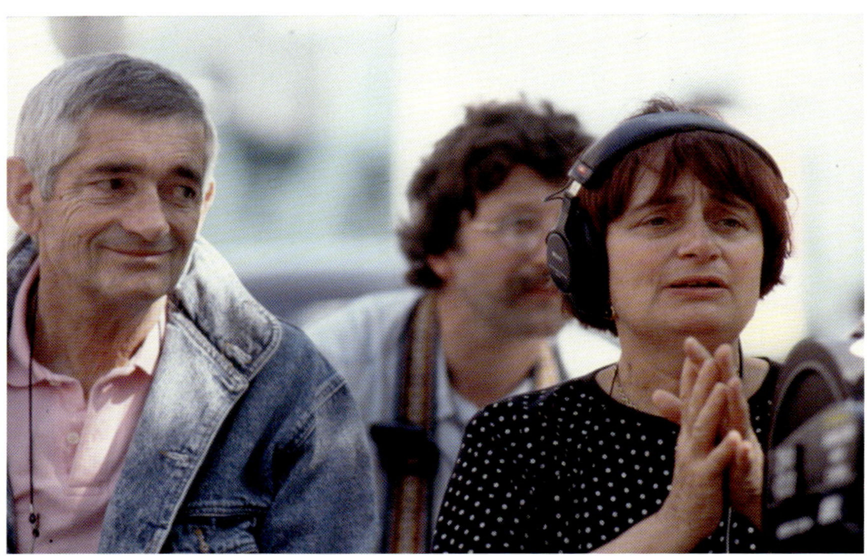

The real love is there.
I believe it is. I guess it's
in the film, and around
the film, like a little smoke.

Varda writes in her notes that the film "is the tale of a happy childhood and an evocation of what a vocation can be…told by the woman who shared his life."

Left: Varda and Demy during production of *Jacquot de Nantes*

DIDIER ROUGET

When Agnès hired me as first assistant director for *Jacquot de Nantes*, I didn't know it would be the start of a 30-year collaboration and friendship. The film is a distillation of Agnès's artistic approach: impulse, desire, urgency. Her husband was dying of an incurable disease. Agnès wanted to extend his life and perhaps thought making a movie could ease their shared suffering. The project required Jacques to write about his memories every morning, and he liked coming to the set to see the reconstruction of his childhood. They would hold hands while shooting, like a young couple in love. Agnès was anxious about his reactions, but he would reassure her. Shooting took over six months and extended Jacques's life by that amount. Agnès had won her gamble. That emotional project was the beginning of our indestructible friendship.

She asked me, naturally, to assist her with *One Hundred and One Nights*, a film celebrating 100 years of cinema. Although it was the biggest budget she had ever had, Agnès continued to create the way she always had: artisanally. She wanted to pay homage to the filmmakers and actors she admired, but their schedules were hard to coordinate. She slept on the set, and at night she would write scenes for the next day depending on which actors would join us. It was filmmaking in the present, seizing opportunities as they came. She wrote a garden party scene and sent out an invitation full of her playful spirit: "This Sunday, we'll eat, sing, dance, and we'll film a little bit." Actors came by the dozens, and we shot in this organized chaos. To pay homage to Fellini, she asked Mastroianni to reprise his role as Mandrake the Magician from *Intervista* (1987). But Marcello couldn't do any magic tricks, so she came up with an unexpected "Mandrake's assistant" character. Because Pierre Étaix had taught me some rudiments of magic, it would be me—so, here I am, assistant director and assistant magician to Mr. Mastroianni!

After *The Gleaners and I*, Agnès called me in a panic. "Didier, I'm going to be 80, and there's never been a film about me. Do you want to make one? I'll be your actress, and you'll be my director." Why me? Agnès liked my short films and the way I had filmed her for *The Gleaners and I*. We wrote *The Beaches of Agnès* together and rushed off to film on the Belgian beaches of her childhood. During the editing, she came to inspect my progress every day. She couldn't help but direct my choices, so I suggested filming her interventions in the editing room to complete her portrait. When she categorically refused, I realized that she wanted me to make a movie in the style of Agnès Varda. Impossible! I had to give it up. With her immense skill, she finished the movie and won the César Award for Best Documentary.

Our friendship remained, but we ceased to collaborate until one day, she called. She'd been filming *Faces Places* for eight months and admitted she was lost. Agnès and JR had become fast friends and artistic soulmates who shared the same desire: to make ordinary people larger than life. I offered my help, and they let me take charge of the set. Of course, Agnès took control in her favorite playground, the editing room. That's where she excelled in associating ideas, words, sounds, and images.

She thought this would be her last movie, but the ARTE channel asked her to make *Varda by Agnès*. She invited me to codirect it with her, and I agreed, even though I knew no one codirected with Agnès. You could make suggestions, support her, offer ideas—she had the talent to keep only the good ones. We wrote together and started filming with much joy and freedom. But soon we had to stop shooting because she was ill. Ultimately, this movie became a montage film primarily. As with our first encounter on *Jacquot de Nantes*, Agnès took her time finishing the film so she could extend her life as long as possible. Once again, art as savior. *Merci*, Agnès.

One Hundred and One Nights (1995) is Varda's whimsical salute to cinema's centenary. As his 100th birthday approaches, Monsieur Cinéma, who is played by Michel Piccoli and embodies the spirit of film, is visited by many of the medium's greatest stars: Anouk Aimée, Jean-Paul Belmondo, Sandrine Bonnaire, Robert De Niro, Alain Delon, Catherine Deneuve, Gerard Depardieu, Harrison Ford, Gina Lollobrigida, Jeanne Moreau, Hanna Schygulla, and many others.

Top: Sandrine Bonnaire on set. The actress enters the film in the clothes she wore as Mona in *Vagabond* and is magically transformed into a princess.

Bottom: Catherine Deneuve and Varda during production

Opposite: Scenes from *One Hundred and One Nights*

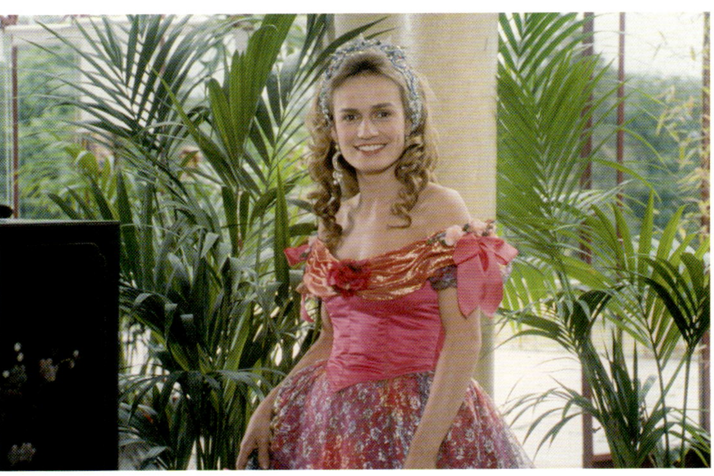

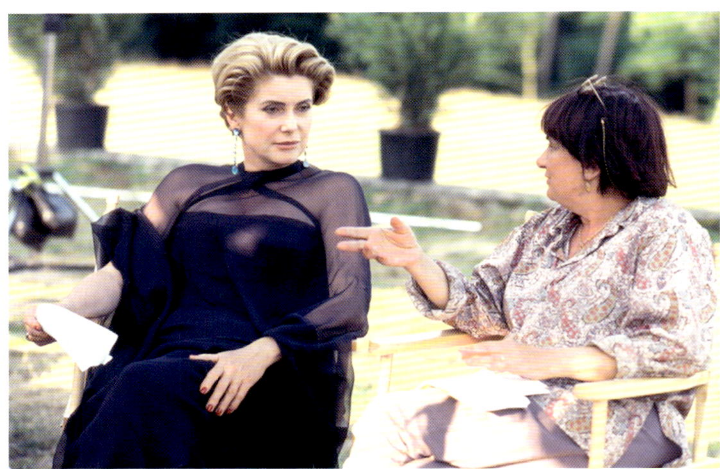

One Hundred and One Nights thumbs its nose at all the embalmers of the cinema. I wanted to celebrate the cinema by making a real film and not just doing another homage film. I agree with Buñuel, who said that commemorative gestures are dangerous.

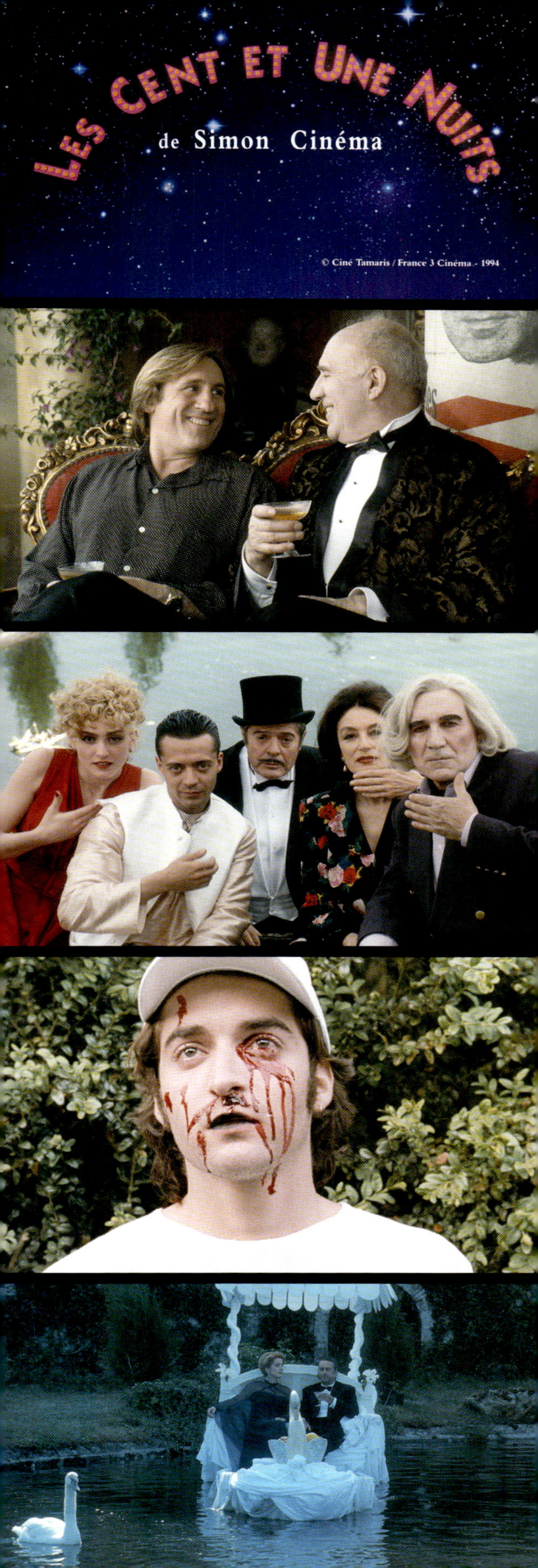

LES CENT ET UNE NUITS
de Simon Cinéma
© Ciné Tamaris / France 3 Cinéma - 1994

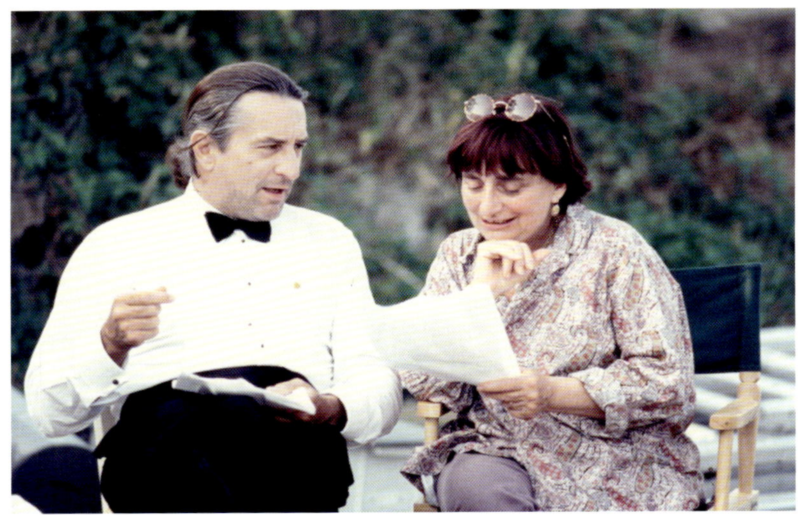

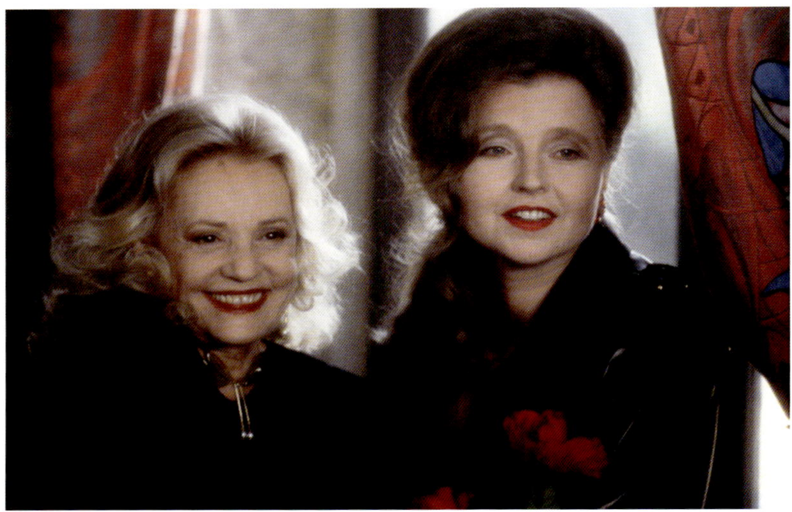

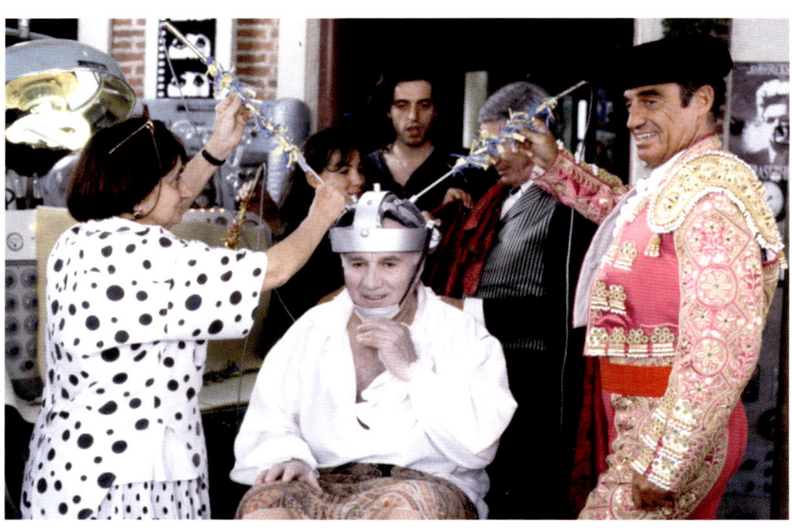

From top: Robert De Niro and Varda; Jeanne Moreau and Hanna Schygulla; and Varda with Michel Piccoli (seated) and Jean-Paul Belmondo during production of *One Hundred and One Nights*

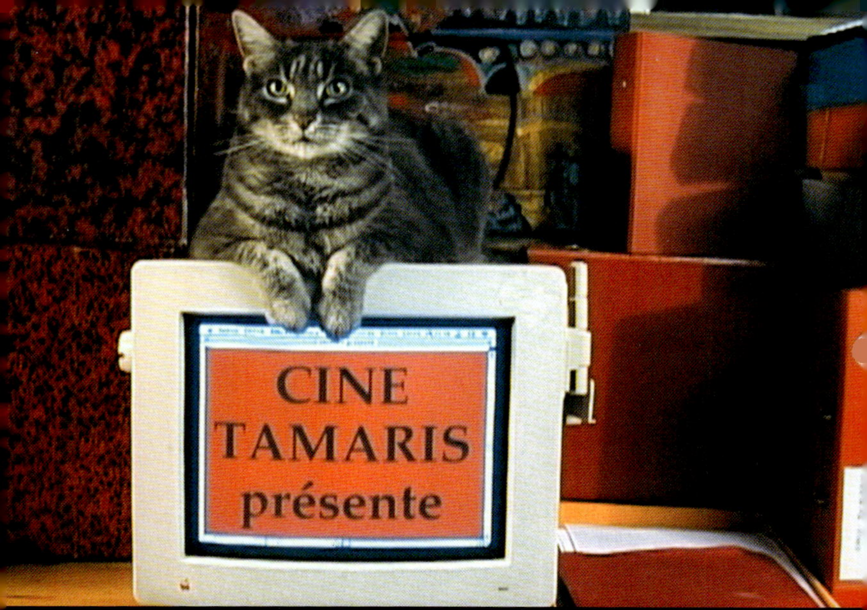

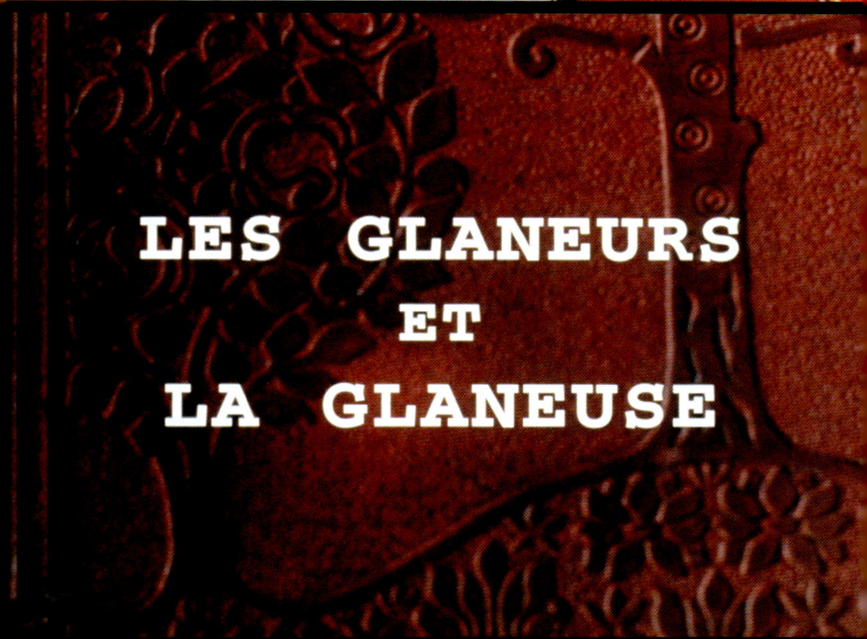

LES GLANEURS
ET
LA GLANEUSE

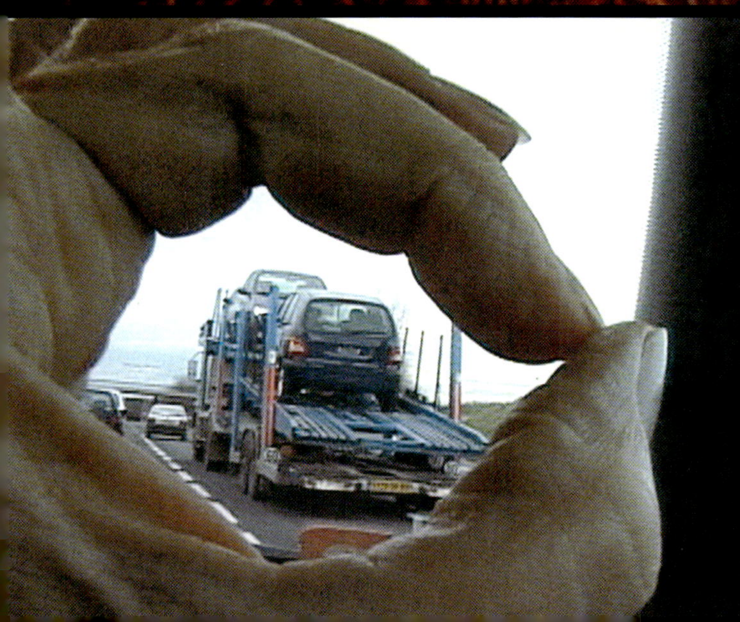

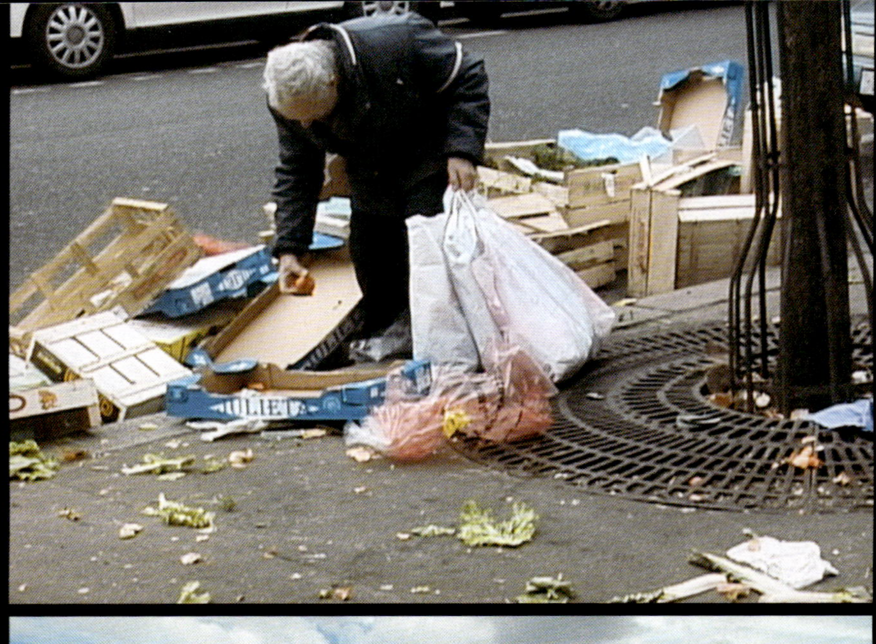

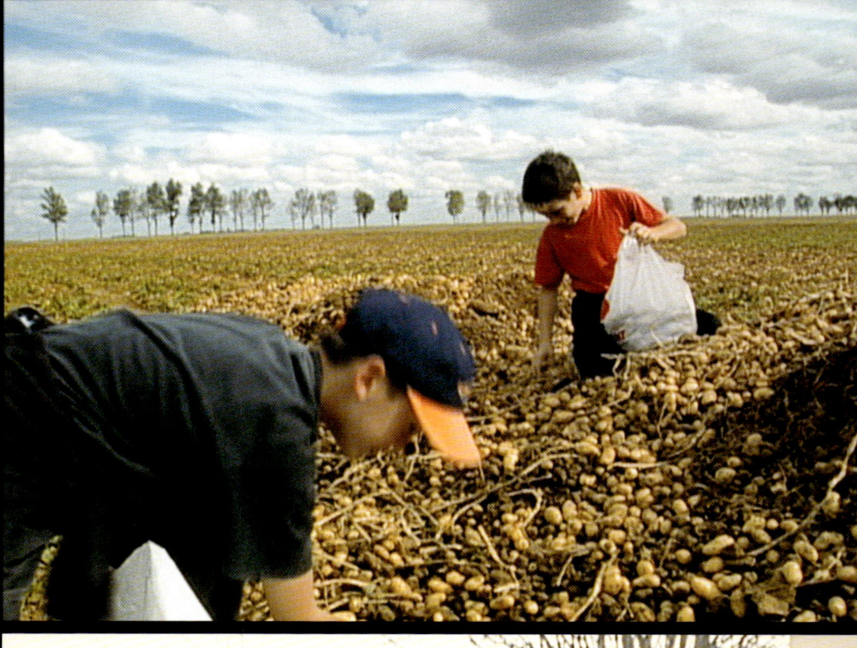

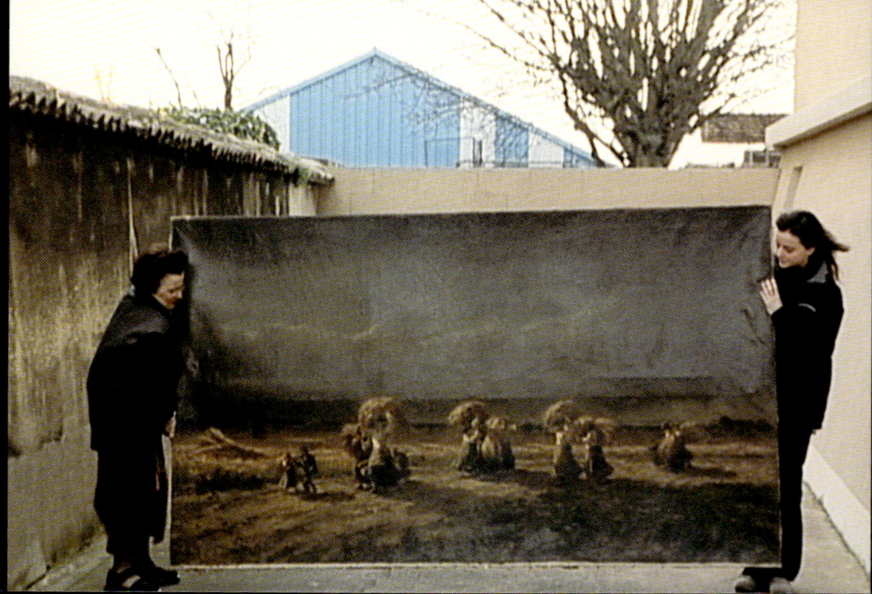

Utopia is the belief that by filming an old rotten potato you can express the beauty of the world. And looking at the potato is like looking at a face, at how different each person is and giving everyone the right to be themselves, to look beautiful in my camera.

The Gleaners and I (2000) is Varda's essay film on the French tradition of gleaning, the act of salvaging what others have discarded. It also incorporates her thoughts on aging and art, themes of special importance in her later works.

Previous page and opposite: Scenes from *The Gleaners and I*

Right: Varda's collection of postcards featuring *The Gleaners* (1857), a painting by Jean-François Millet

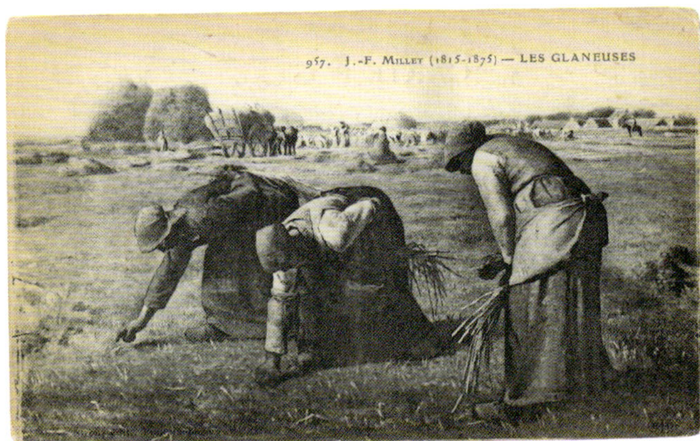

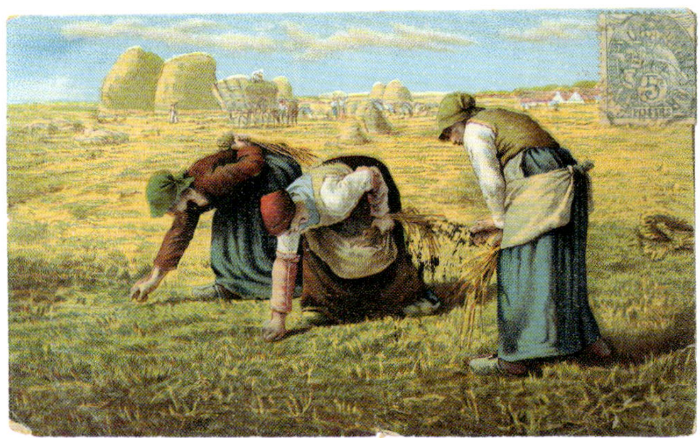

There are so many times in your life: Youth is a time, adolescence is a time, and being an adult is a time. Being a middle-aged woman is something else again and so is getting into a third age, the time of being old. It's interesting to mention it because I'm not sad, I'm not complaining. I don't depend on anything, I'm very free. I'm very alone too—that's part of it.

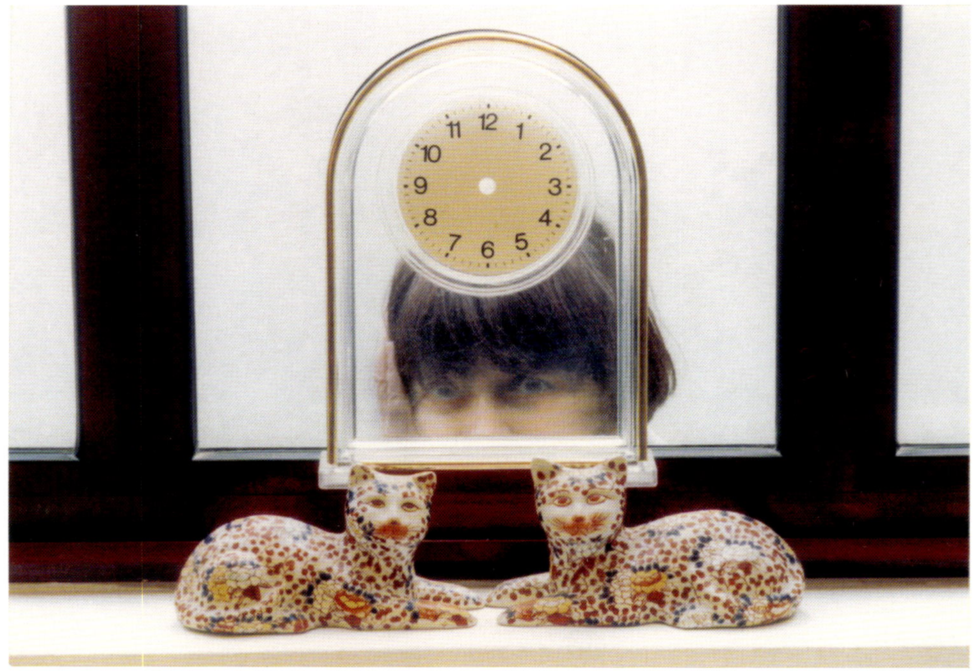

In one memorable line from *The Gleaners and I*, Varda says, "A clock without hands is my kind of thing."

Left: Varda during production of *The Gleaners and I*

MATHIEU DEMY

My mother wrote all the time. I can see her sitting at her desk in one of her offices at rue Daguerre—where pretty much every room was an office—writing. You'd think that the first image to come to mind would be her in the field on the go. Being part of the environment, understanding the people and the place, being present: this is how she worked as a filmmaker. But before you make a film, there's always that moment when you're just putting it all together and writing.

As a kid, you don't understand that your parents aren't doing the same job as everyone else. They're just your parents. As I grew up, I began to understand that my parents made art, the purpose of it—if there is one—and why they'd rather do this than anything else. When Agnès put me in her films, it was completely normal. It's like your parent bringing you to their grocery store and asking you to restock the fruit. You become a part of their world for a second. It was the same for me, except on a film set.

My father would never have put me in one of his films because he was all about fictionalizing things—creating sophisticated environments, sets, and songs. Agnès and Jacques viewed reality and fiction in opposite ways. Even their homes were opposite. At Agnès's house, we were surrounded by piles of books and objects from her work; it was a completely full house on the ground floor. Jacques's apartment across the street was on the eighth floor. It was very clean and white, decorated with marble and futuristic furniture. I would cross the street every Thursday to go see him.

My real childhood memories begin with *Documenteur*, when we were living in Venice Beach, Calfornia, and they're mixed up with the film. Usually what they say about acting is that the feelings have to be real; only the circumstances are fake. In this case, the circumstances of the story were precisely the ones we were living, with my parents being separated and money being tight. Most of my parents' lives was kept very private, but later in life, Agnès became more of a character in her films. Her haircut was an important turn in that matter. It took her public image and persona to another level and led to a more playful understanding of herself.

Just prior to *The Gleaners and I*, Agnès started to think about the fact that she was aging. We'd had her mother at rue Daguerre until she was very old, and Agnès took care of her—she always had a connection with the elderly. So, becoming older herself, she tried to wrap her mind around it. She started to question, "What remains?" That's when she got interested in the potatoes and the fruit—the things you throw away—and how that connects to the question, "What remains of myself?" She decided to make a film about what is left, and that became *The Gleaners and I*.

The last years were wonderful because she received every honor that could be given to a filmmaker. The Honorary Oscar and the Academy Award nomination for *Faces Places* were the peak of it. It's wonderful because she spent 70 years working in photography, cinema, and art, never chasing awards or success. When she was awarded the Légion d'honneur by the French government—the highest honor they can bestow—she sent them a fax saying, "I'll exchange my Légion d'honneur for some money to shoot a freaking film." She got a call back immediately. They gave her money to shoot, and she even got to keep the award.

That's the kind of thing she would do, always keeping front of mind what she was about and what she was chasing. When she got all the honors, she was happy, but she would say, "It's a dream. It's not real." The last years of her life, including the last moments with her friends, her family, and everybody at rue Daguerre were wonderful. Rosalie was a very important part of this process, being Agnès's producer for *Faces Places* and with her on all her adventures. I was back and forth from Paris to Los Angeles, but we were very close. At the end, Agnès was very much surrounded by love and family.

I wanted to be like a bird.
I wanted to be free in my
memory, to go from one part
to another and see what
I would find.

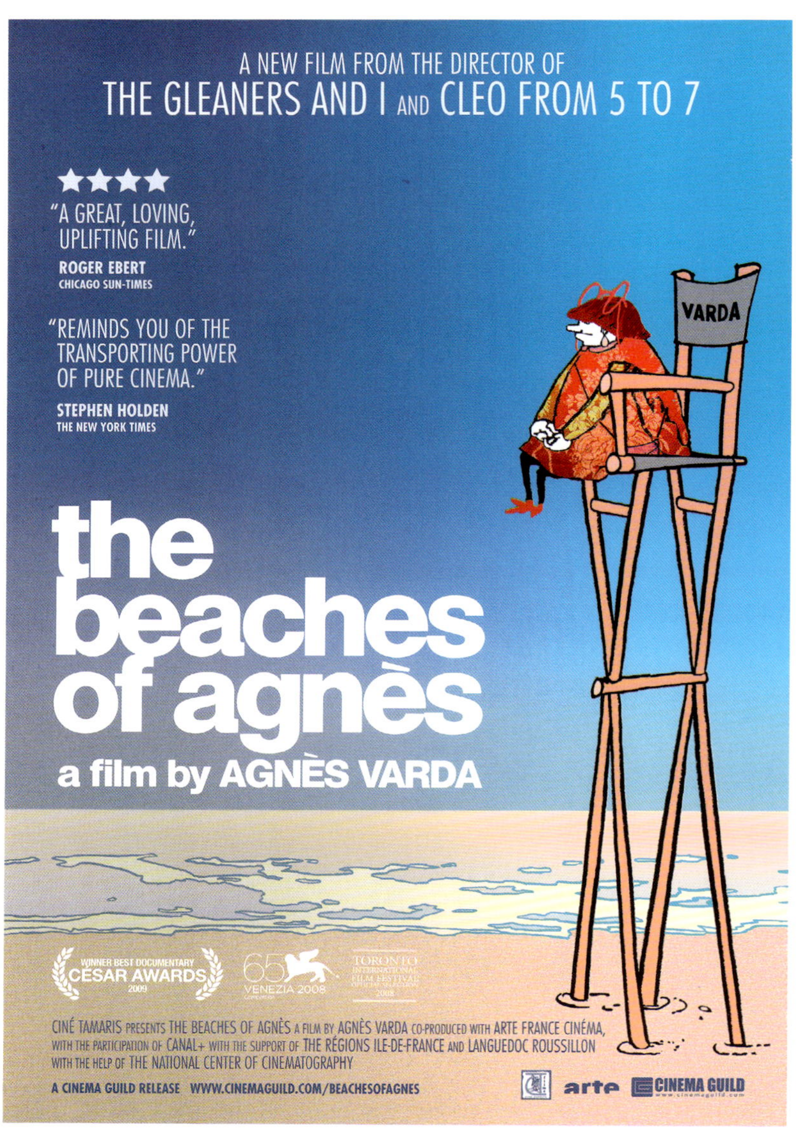

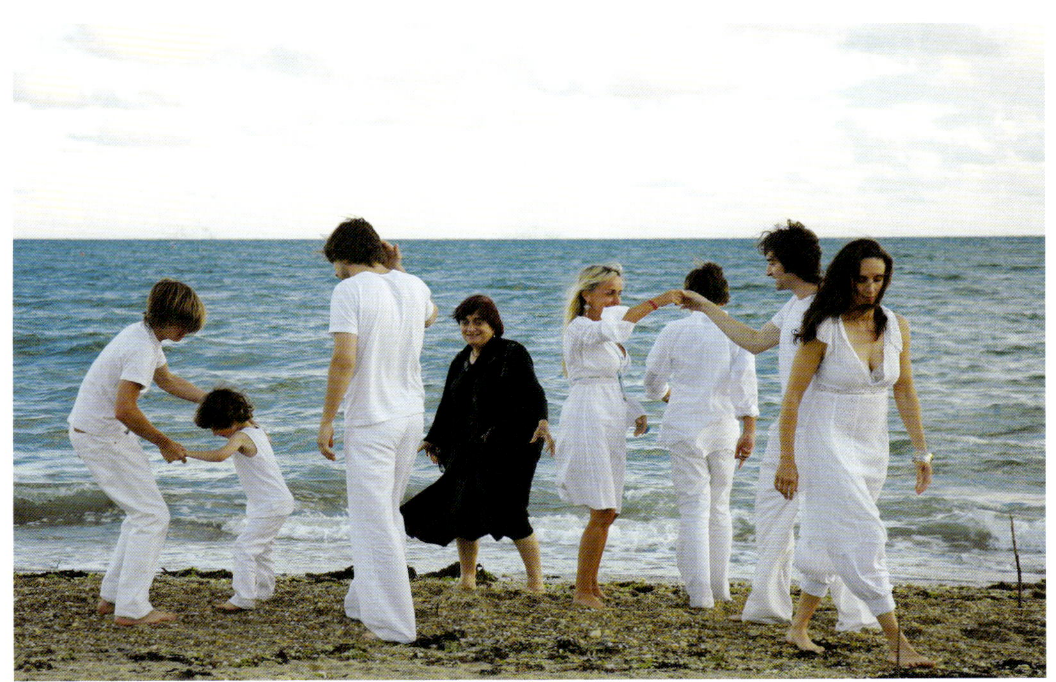

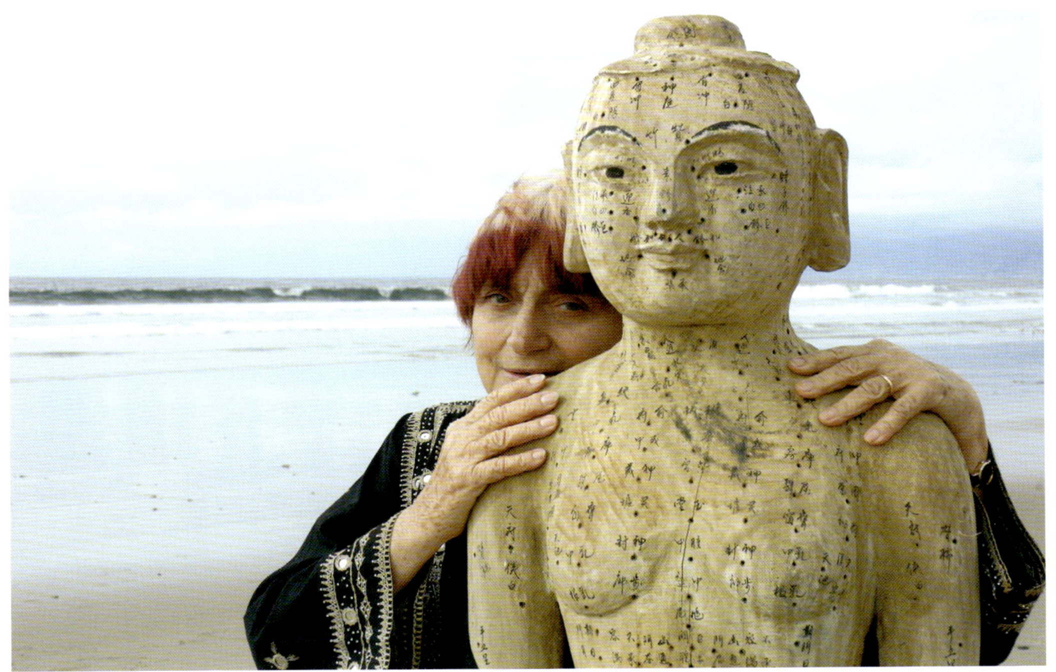

The Beaches of Agnès (2008) is Varda's playful autobiographical essay film. In an interview, Varda says she wanted "to invent a genre of story-collage; an auto-documentary, an illustrated filmography and moments of fantasy."

Opposite: US one-sheet poster for *The Beaches of Agnès*

This page: Varda and her family on La Guérnière Beach on Noirmoutier Island, France, during production. From left: Augustin Vignet, Constantin Demy, Valentin Vignet, Rosalie Varda, Corentin Vignet, Mathieu Demy, and Joséphine Wister Faure

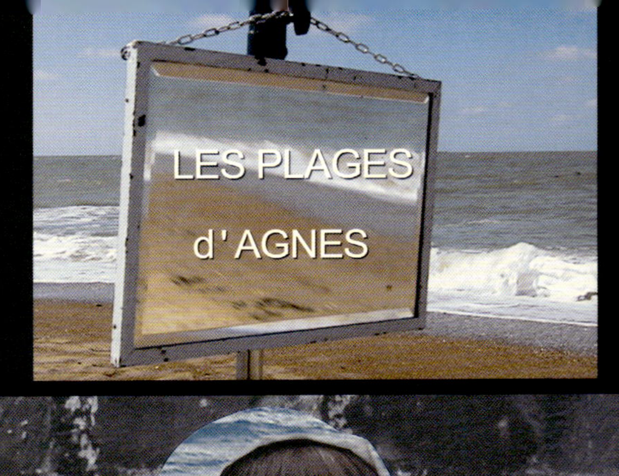
LES PLAGES
d'AGNES

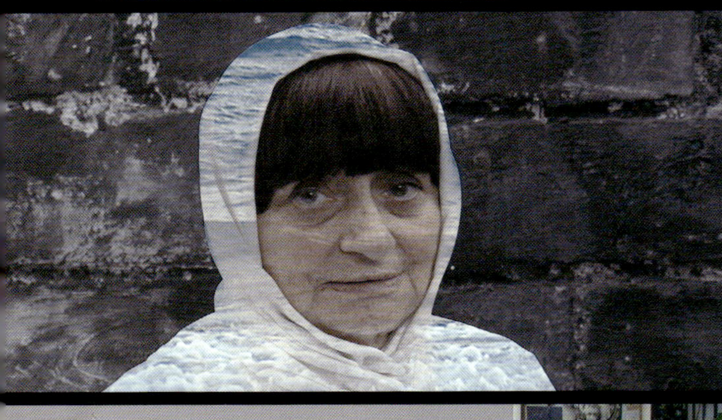

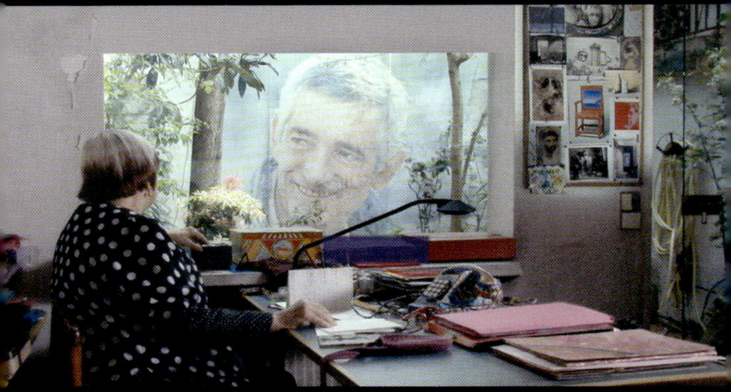

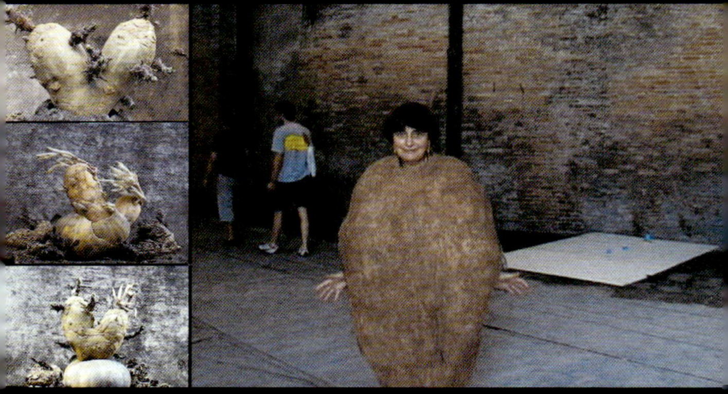

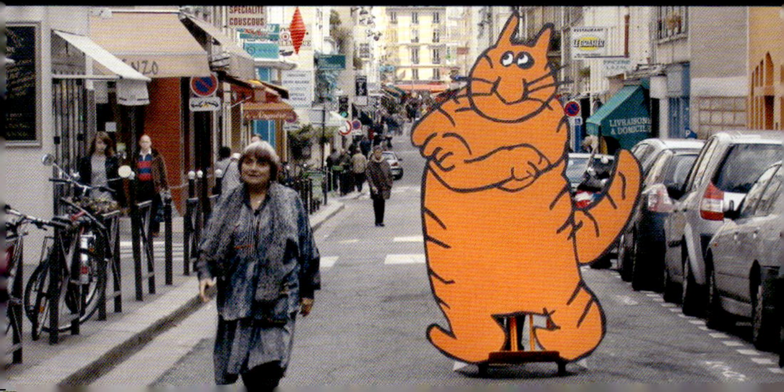

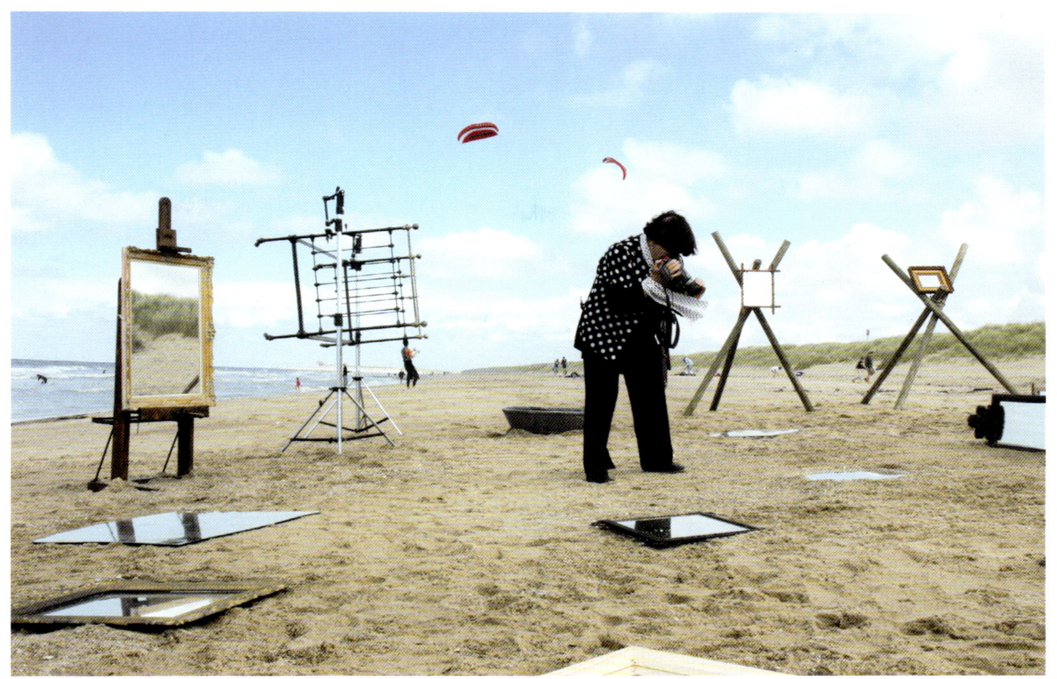

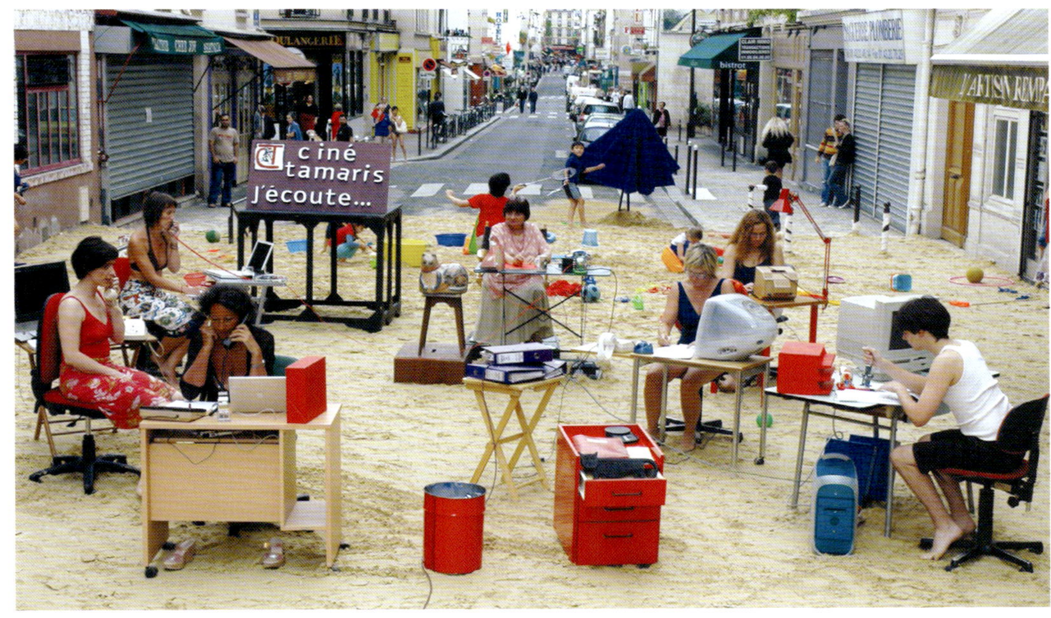

"These mirrors reflect the North Sea more than me," Varda says of the opening scene, "but the idea of this project as a self-portrait comes across clearly." For a later scene in the film, Varda created a beach office on rue Daguerre, unloading six truckloads of sand onto the asphalt in front of her home and the Ciné-Tamaris production offices.

Opposite: Scenes from *The Beaches of Agnès*

Top: Varda directing the opening sequence of *The Beaches of Agnès*

Bottom: Varda and cast during production

Our aims, on his side and on my side, had some common points, really: to be interested in other people, unknown people.... People that you can meet in villages.

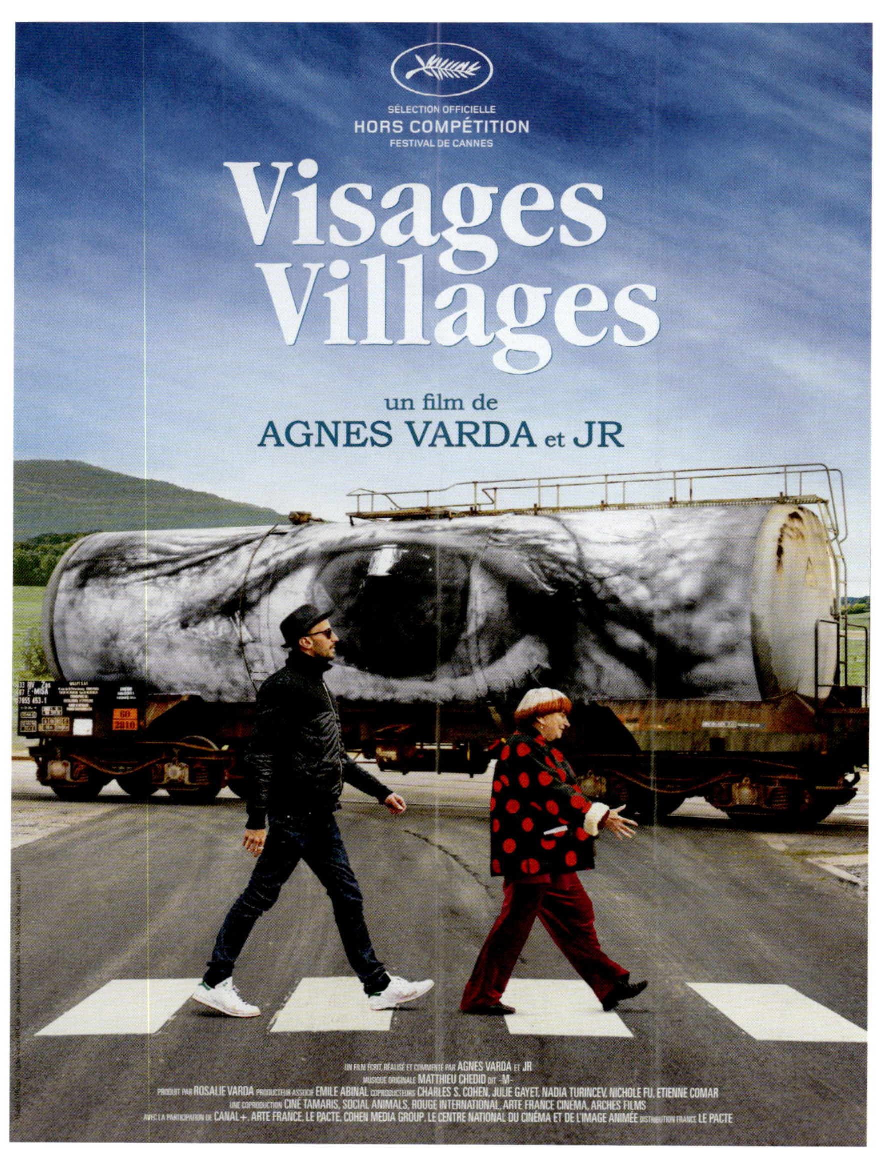

Faces Places (2017) is a collaboration between the 89-year-old Varda and the 33-year-old photographer and muralist JR. In this road movie, the duo travel to the villages of France, meeting locals, learning their stories, and producing epic-size portraits of them. The tender intergenerational friendship between these kindred spirits undoubtedly contributed to the film's critical and box-office success; Faces Places won numerous awards and received an Academy Award nomination for Best Documentary Feature.

Left: French theatrical poster for Faces Places

Opposite: Scenes from Faces Places

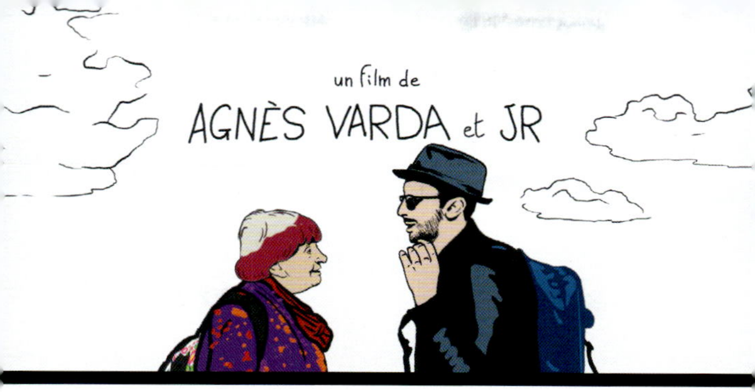

un film de
AGNÈS VARDA et JR

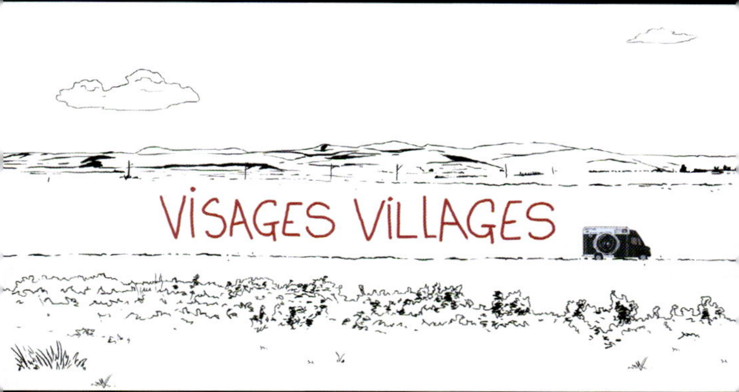

VISAGES VILLAGES

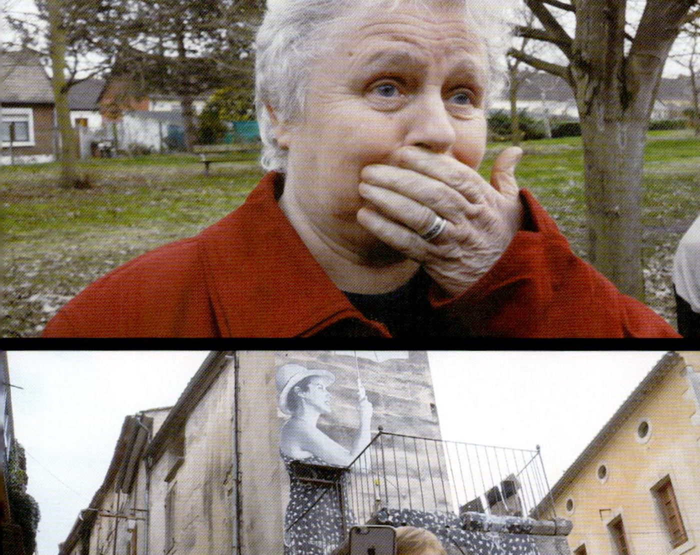

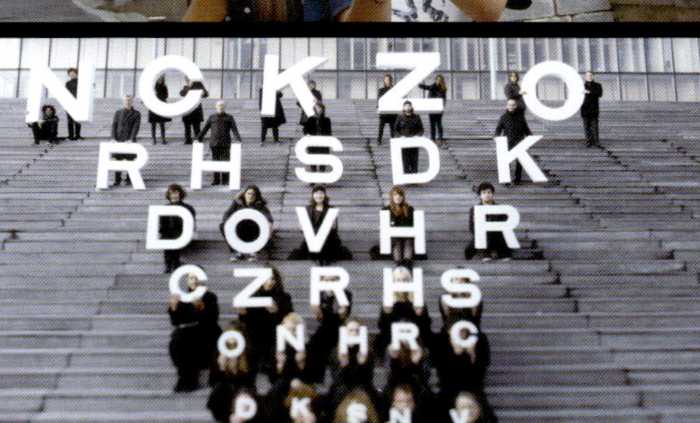

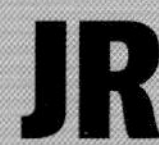

I received an email from Agnès's daughter, Rosalie, inviting me to meet with Agnès. We had tea, and I remember Agnès spilled some on my book, which was a book about wrinkles. She said, "Oh, now it's better because your book has wrinkles too!" Agnès was very funny, and we connected right away. We never discussed it then, but there was no question that we needed to work together.

The truth is, we didn't want to talk about a big project like *Faces Places* at first. The idea started small. We said we should travel to the villages in France, which was Agnès's idea. She loved that I could enlarge people; her eyesight was failing. I said, "The people we are meeting, I can make them bigger so you can see them." And that's how the project started. We did a couple of cities like that, and Agnès was like, "Where is this going? Why are we doing this here and not there?" And it's true: nothing connected those places but our journey.

We'd shoot a bit every month, which meant changing teams often. But I think that was a good thing because it allowed us to reflect on what we were doing. We had moments where we were very confident and moments when we were very lost, and that was good for us. We were starting to have enough footage that it could be a film. So, I was just like, "Let's see where this goes." But she was afraid of that becoming a film. If it was a short film, then OK—no one's really going to look at it. If it becomes a feature, possibly her last movie, then that becomes a real constraint, and we must take it seriously.

I had a lot of problems because she was so tough. She had 85 years of experience; I only had 30-something years. It was hard for me to say, "I think we should paste the image this way and not that way because visually, it will look better." She would say, "No, we'll paste it the other way." Each time my team would look at me like, "It's not

going to work." Then one day I went to her and said, "No, over my dead body. We'll do it this way." After that, something changed. She enjoyed that I challenged her because everybody was talking to her like a maestro; she wanted to be seen as an artist and confronted as such.

When I was working with Agnès, there was so much information that I knew she was giving me. She was really teaching me so much about filmmaking, about voice-over, all these things. It was hard for me to comprehend it all, but I knew it was important, so I was paying attention. I knew it would pay off at some point. On one of my recent projects, the editor, who also worked on *Faces Places*, said, "It's crazy. Now you are doing voice-over. It's like the cycle of life. I remember Agnès teaching you over and over, and now it finally hit you." And I was like, "It really did."

Agnès was in awe of life. I remember sitting with her at a restaurant, and there was a tablecloth with little flowers on it. I was looking at the menu, and she was like, "Oh, look at these little flowers. Can you believe how beautiful they are? And look at this color matching that color and how it matches that woman's collar over there." She would always stop to observe her surroundings and recognize the beauty of things.

At our screening in Bologna, there were six thousand people. I didn't realize how significant it was at the time. Agnès whispered in my ear, "You have to understand this is very special. Let's sit. Let's watch. Let's observe the people watching it. Let's watch the people walking by and not looking at the film. Let's watch it all."

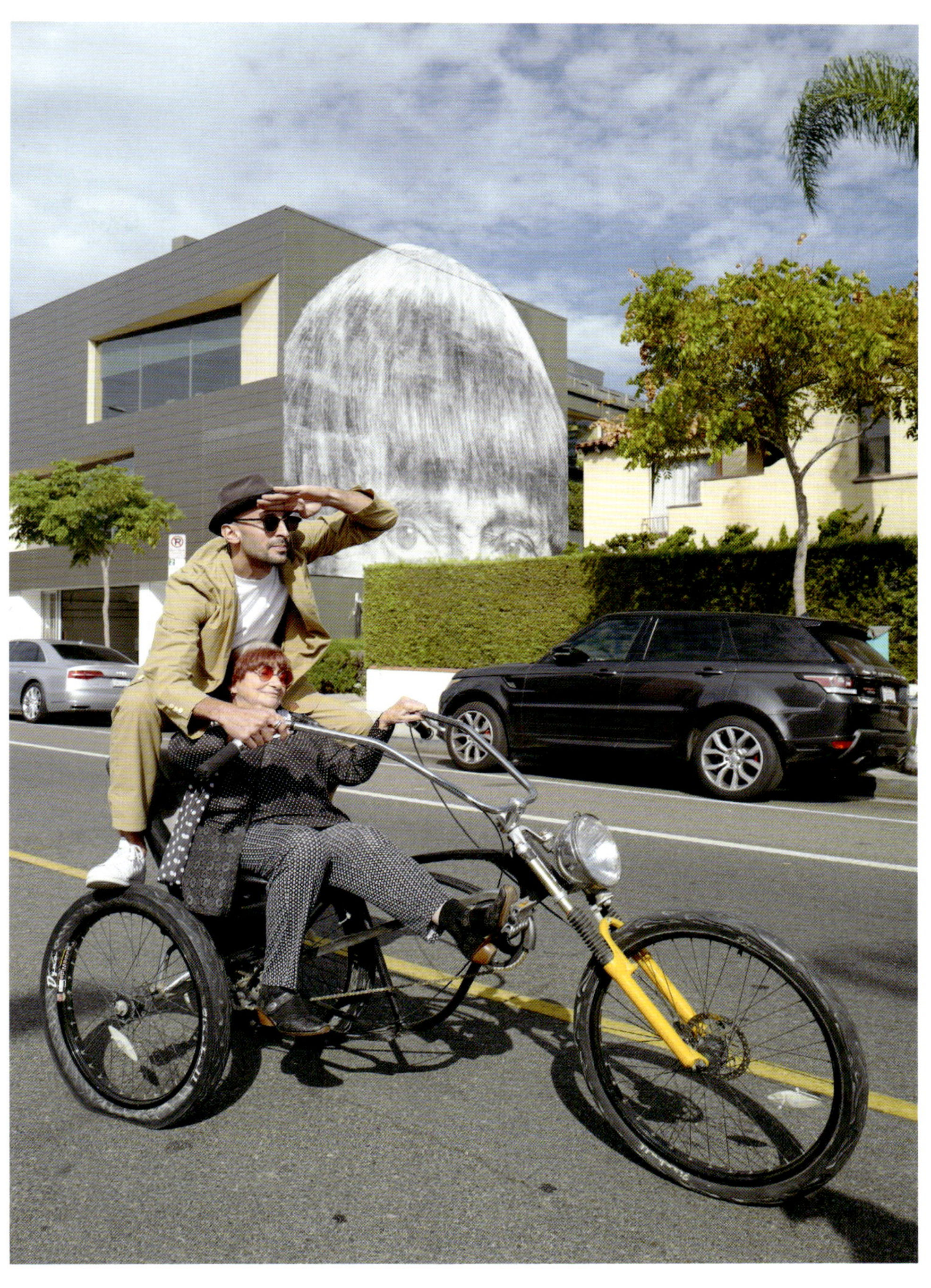

JR and Varda in Los Angeles, 2017. Varda says, "Do we always have to focus on our differences? Let's be peaceful. This movie is about togetherness. I hope that people feel this, too."

We have the same empathy for people. We like to make them be big.

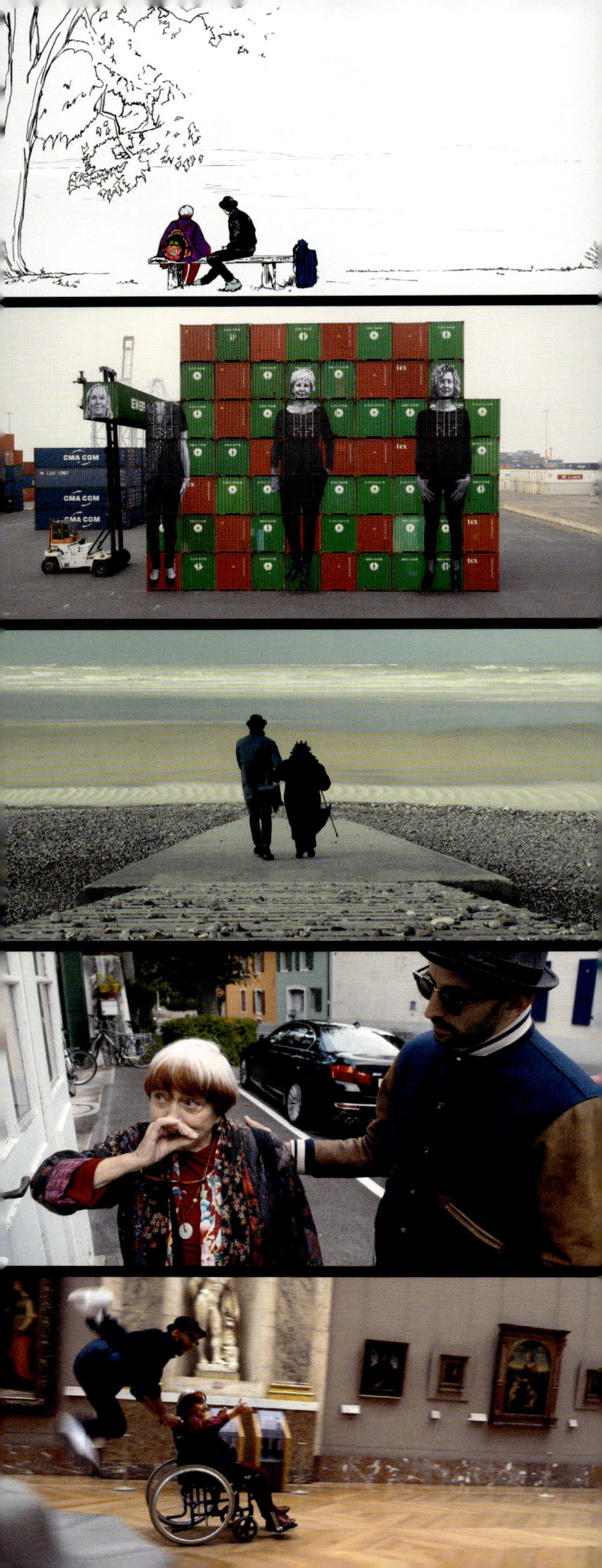

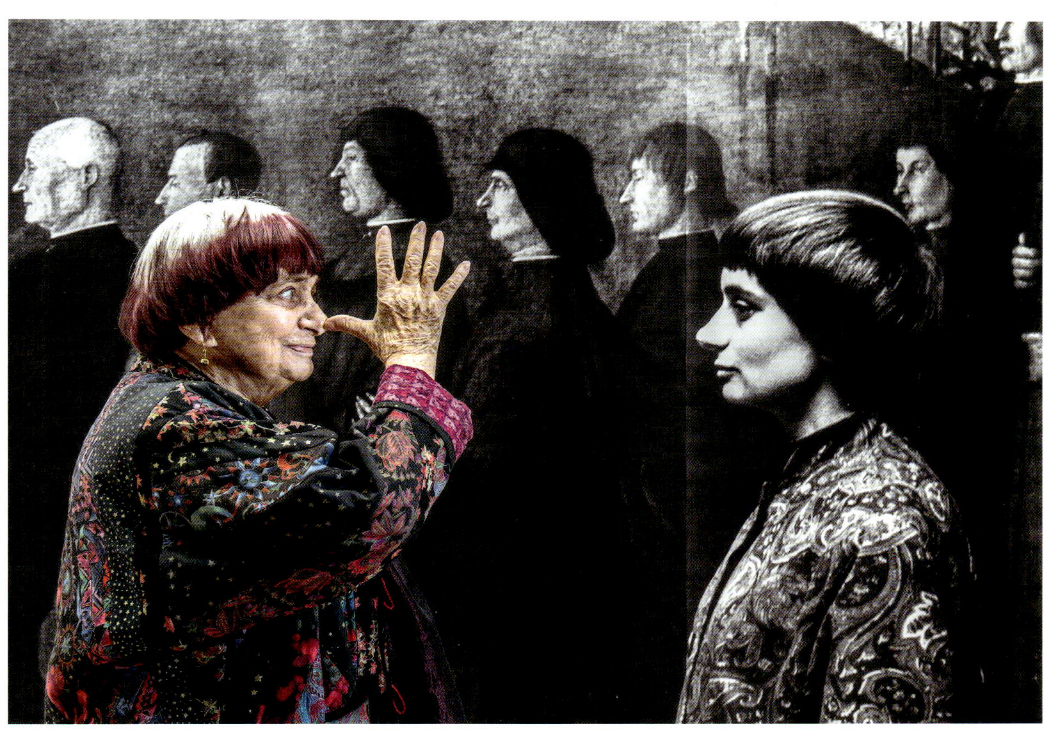

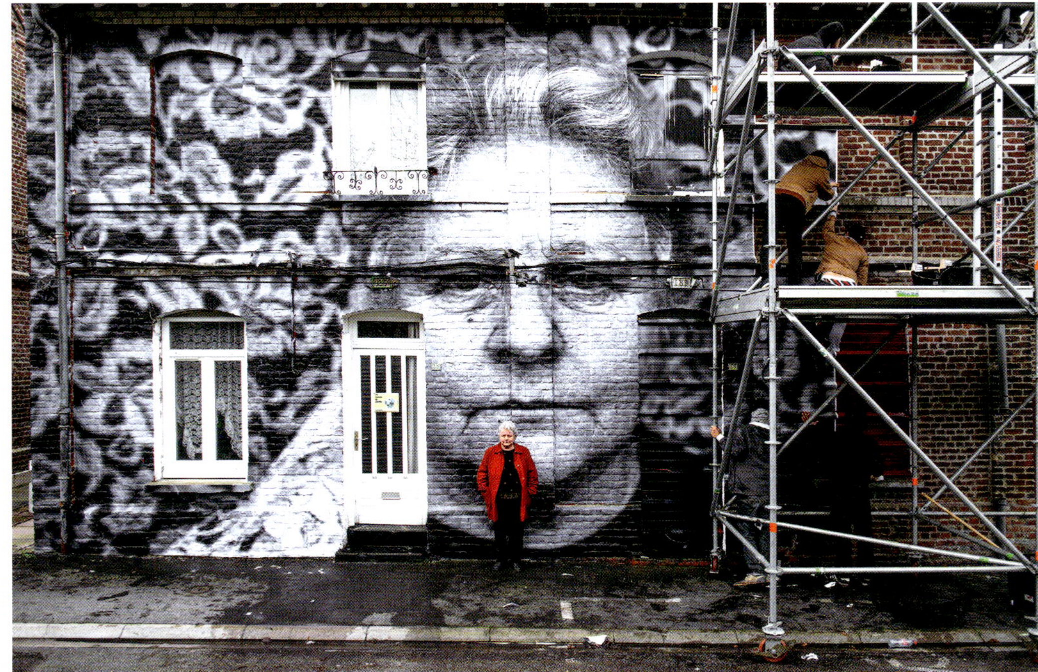

Opposite: Scenes from
Faces Places

Top: Varda with her
1962 self-portrait,
photographed by JR
during production of
Faces Places

Bottom: One of the
film's subjects in front of
her wall-size portrait

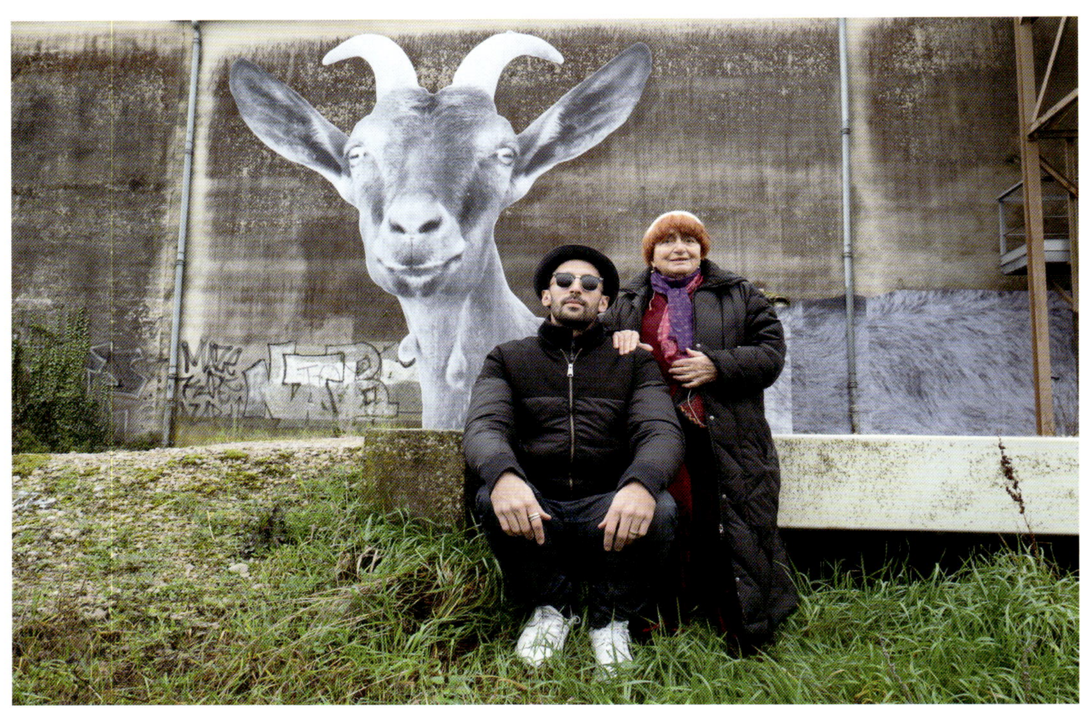

I'm very observant of life, observant of colors, observant of gestures of people. That's how you make documentaries—by observing, by being attentive.

Above: Varda and JR during production of *Faces Places*

Opposite and overleaf: Scenes from *Varda by Agnès* (2019). Varda's final film is a personal summation of her career as a photographer, filmmaker, and artist. In it she conducts a master class, revisiting important projects, moments, and people from her life. The scenes include a conversation with *Vagabond* star Sandrine Bonnaire and a visit to Varda's *Le Tombeau le Zgouzgou* (2006), an installation created in memory of her beloved cat.

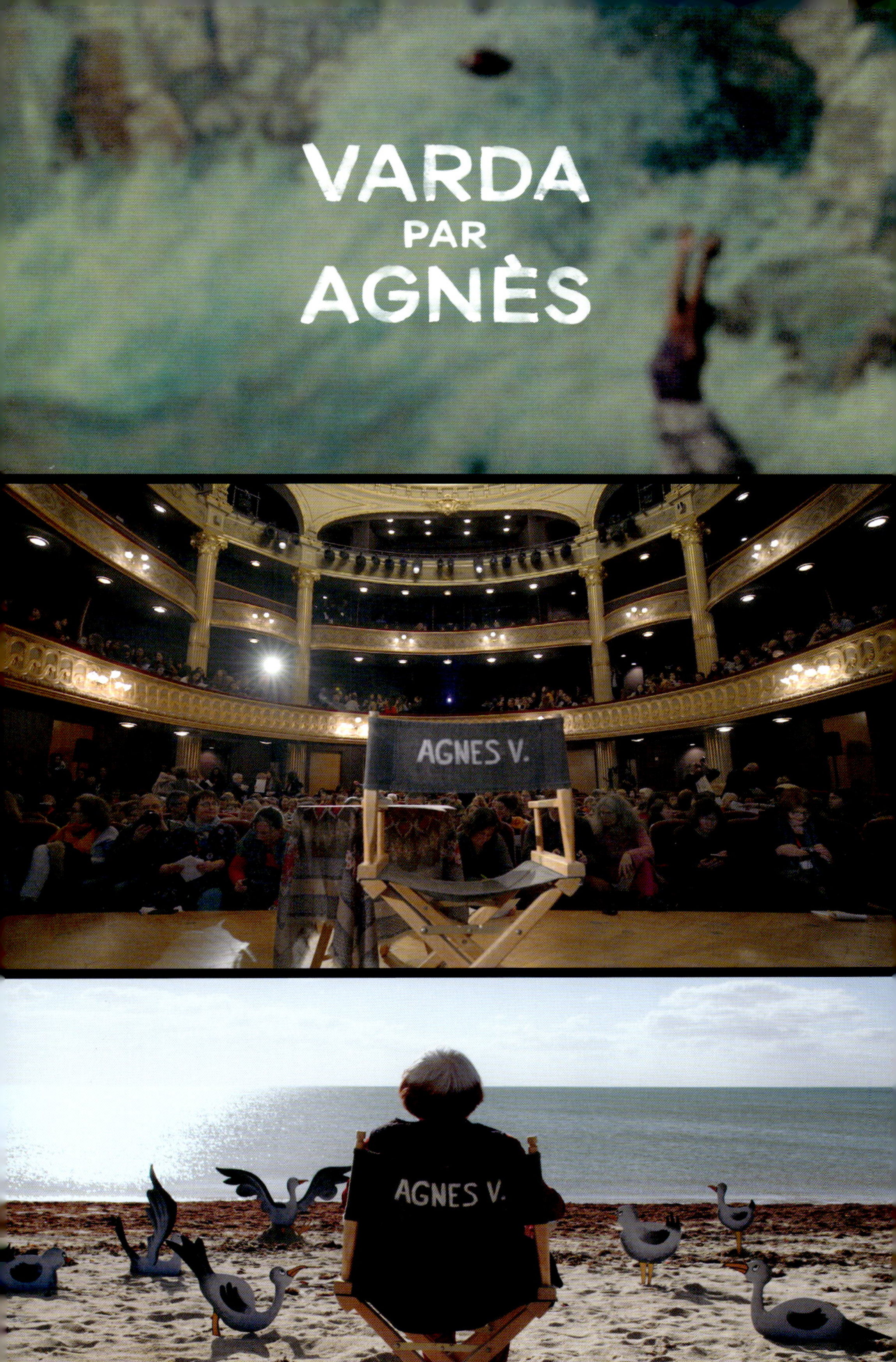
VARDA
PAR
AGNÈS
AGNES V.
AGNES V.

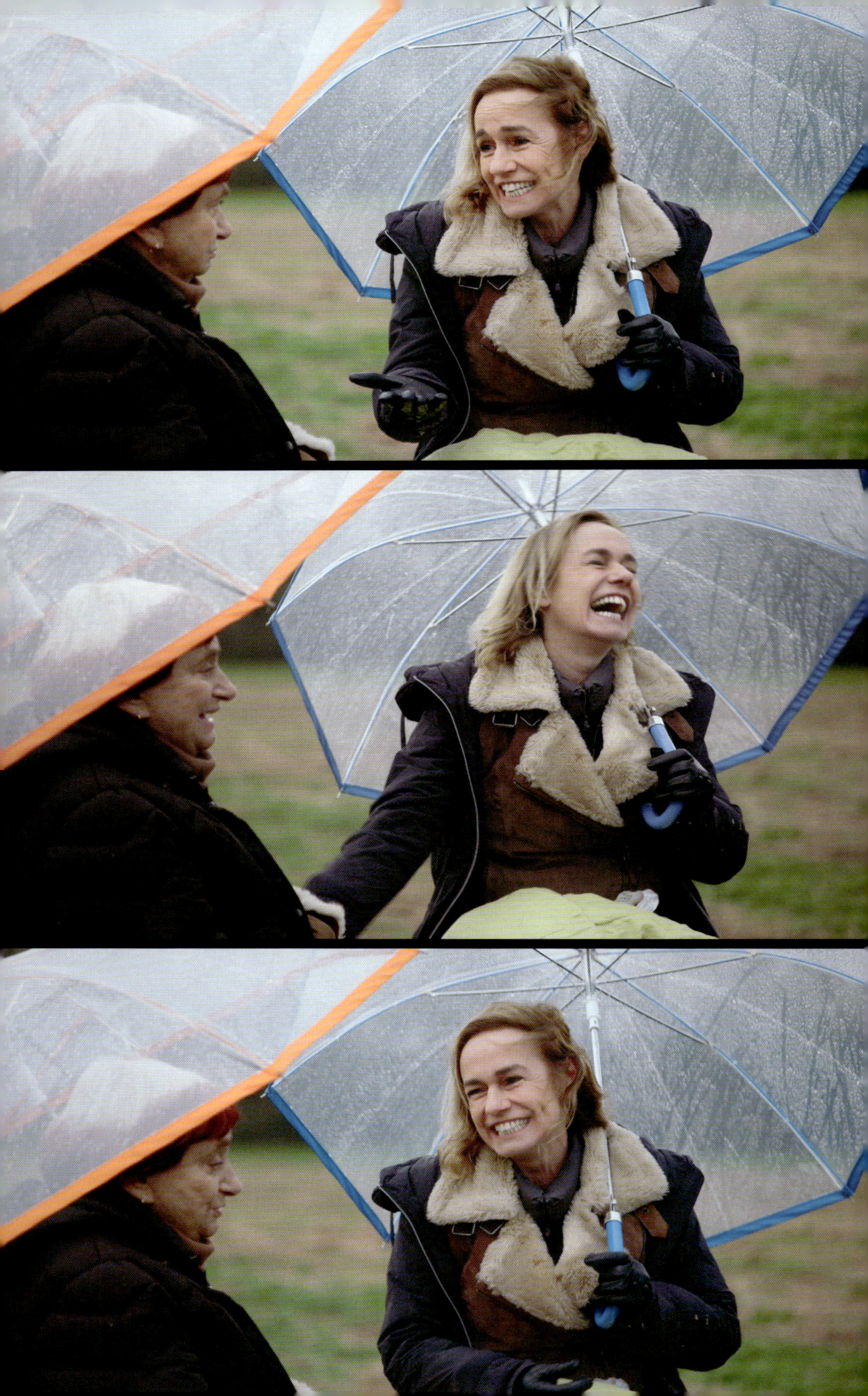

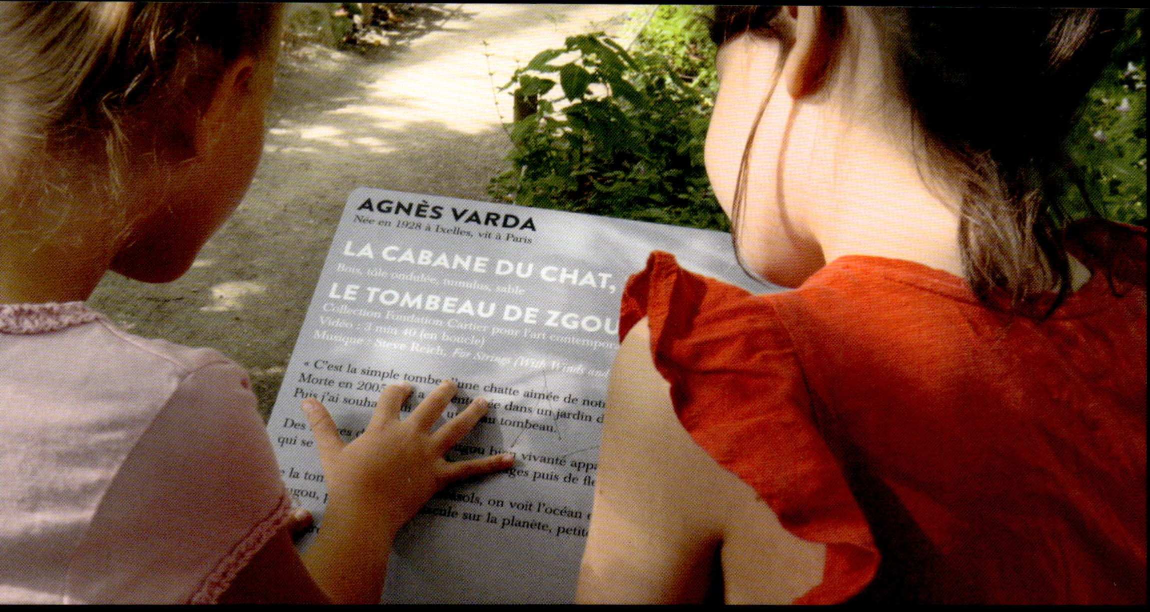

AGNÈS VARDA
Née en 1928 à Ixelles, vit à Paris
LA CABANE DU CHAT,
Bois, tôle ondulée, mosaïus, sable
LE TOMBEAU DE ZGOU
Collection Fondation Cartier pour l'art contempor
Vidéo : 3 min 40 (en boucle)
Musique : Steve Reich, For Strings (With Winds and
« C'est la simple tombe d'une chatte aimée de not
Morte en 2005 a été enterrée dans un jardin d
Puis j'ai souha un tombeau.
Des gou bien vivanté app
ges puis de fle
sols, on voit l'océan
cale sur la planète, petit

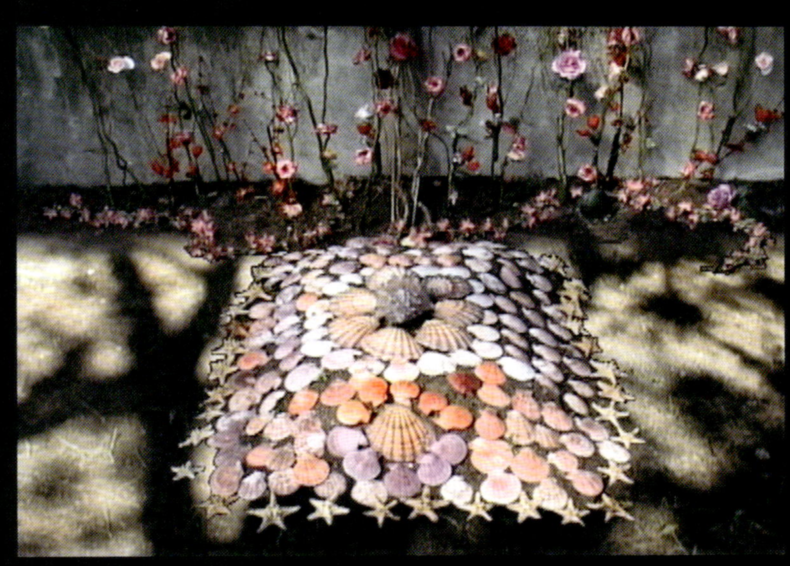

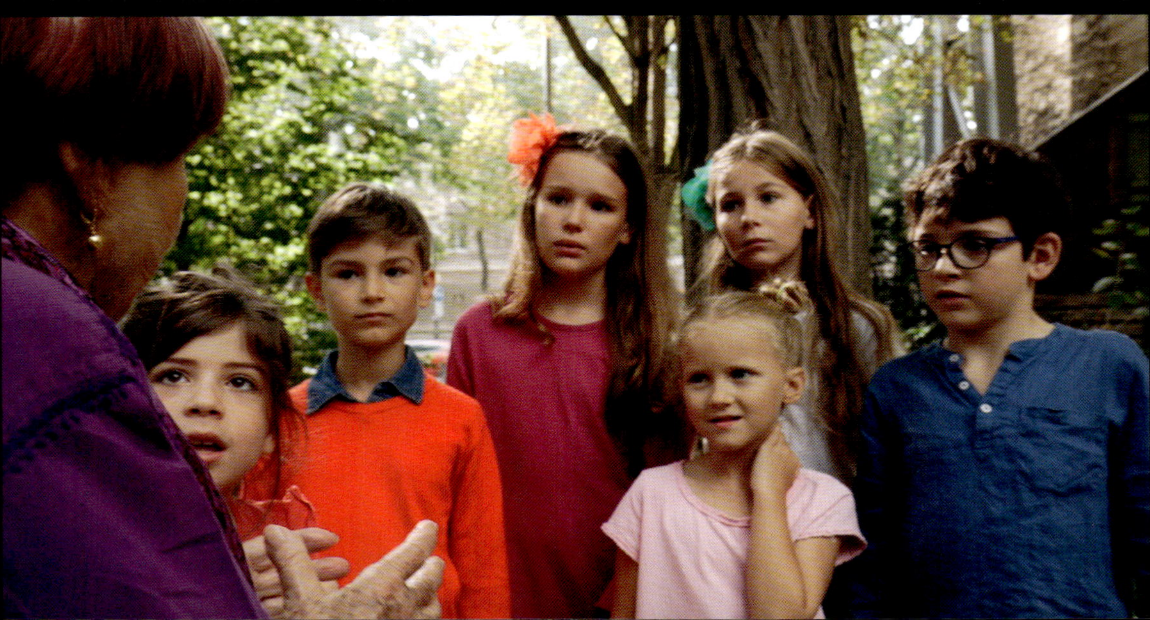

THIRD LIFE: VISUAL ARTIST

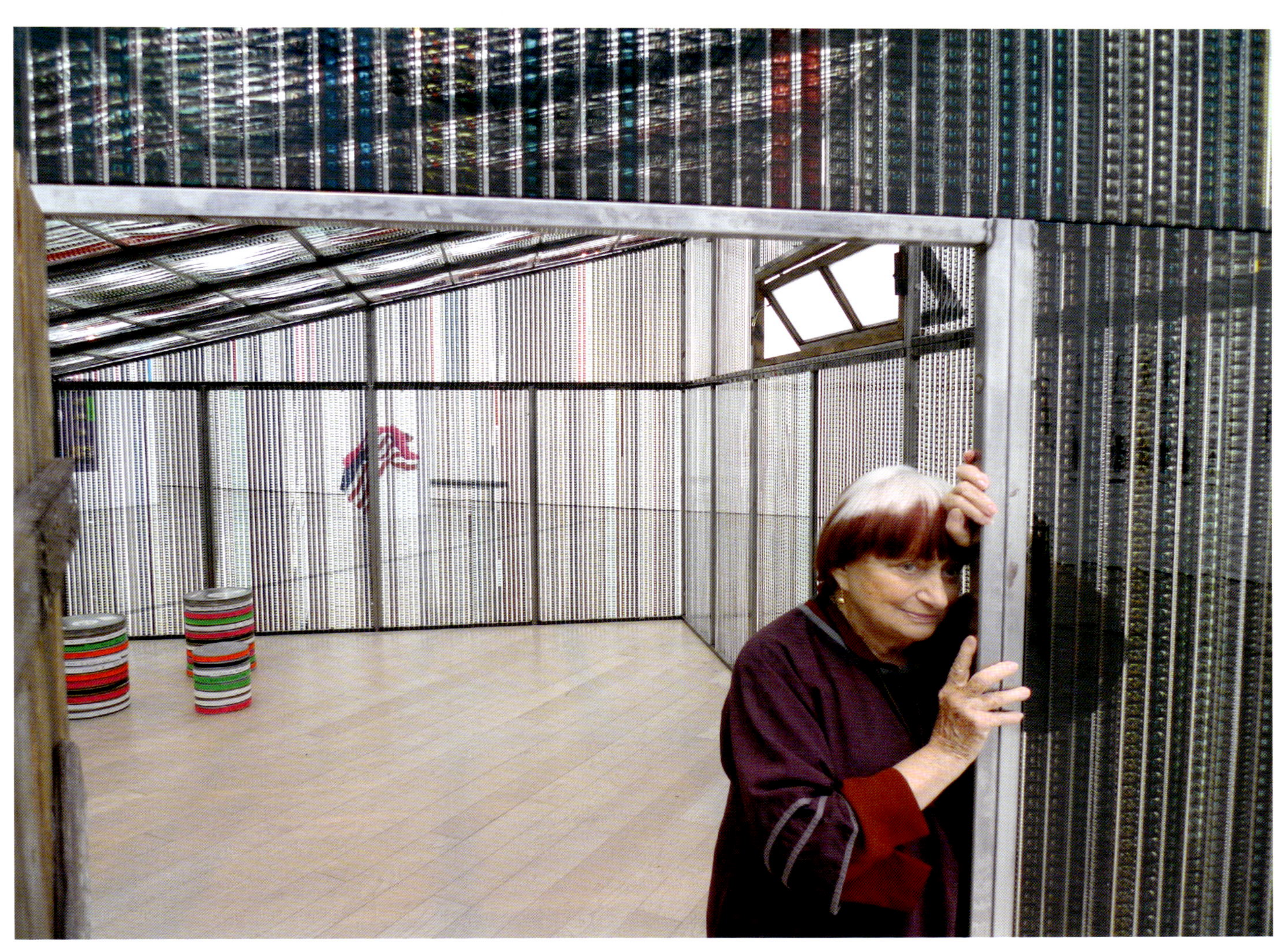

Agnès Varda at the
exhibition *Agnes Varda
in Californialand*, Los
Angeles County Museum
of Art, 2013

—

I've tried to listen to what comes naturally, whatever enters my mind in my desire to create, and to follow those inspirations. It seems to me that if you're an artist, you shouldn't plan. We should have confidence in what will come and the influences and impressions that impact us.

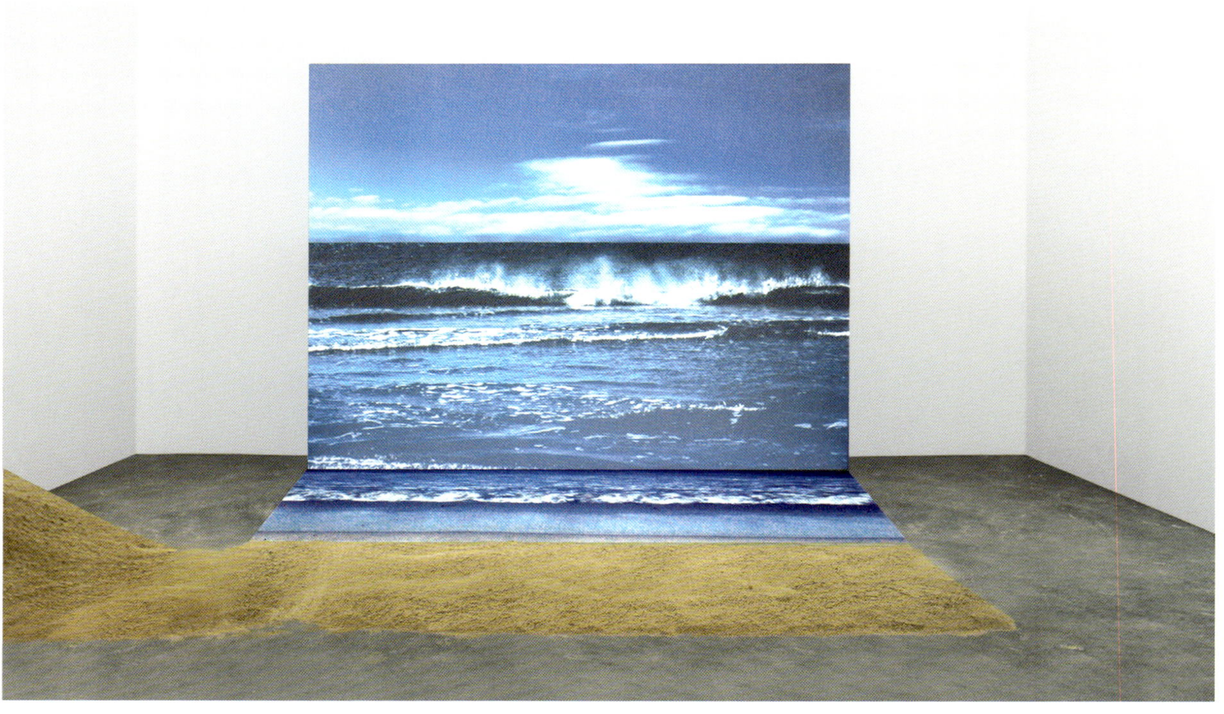

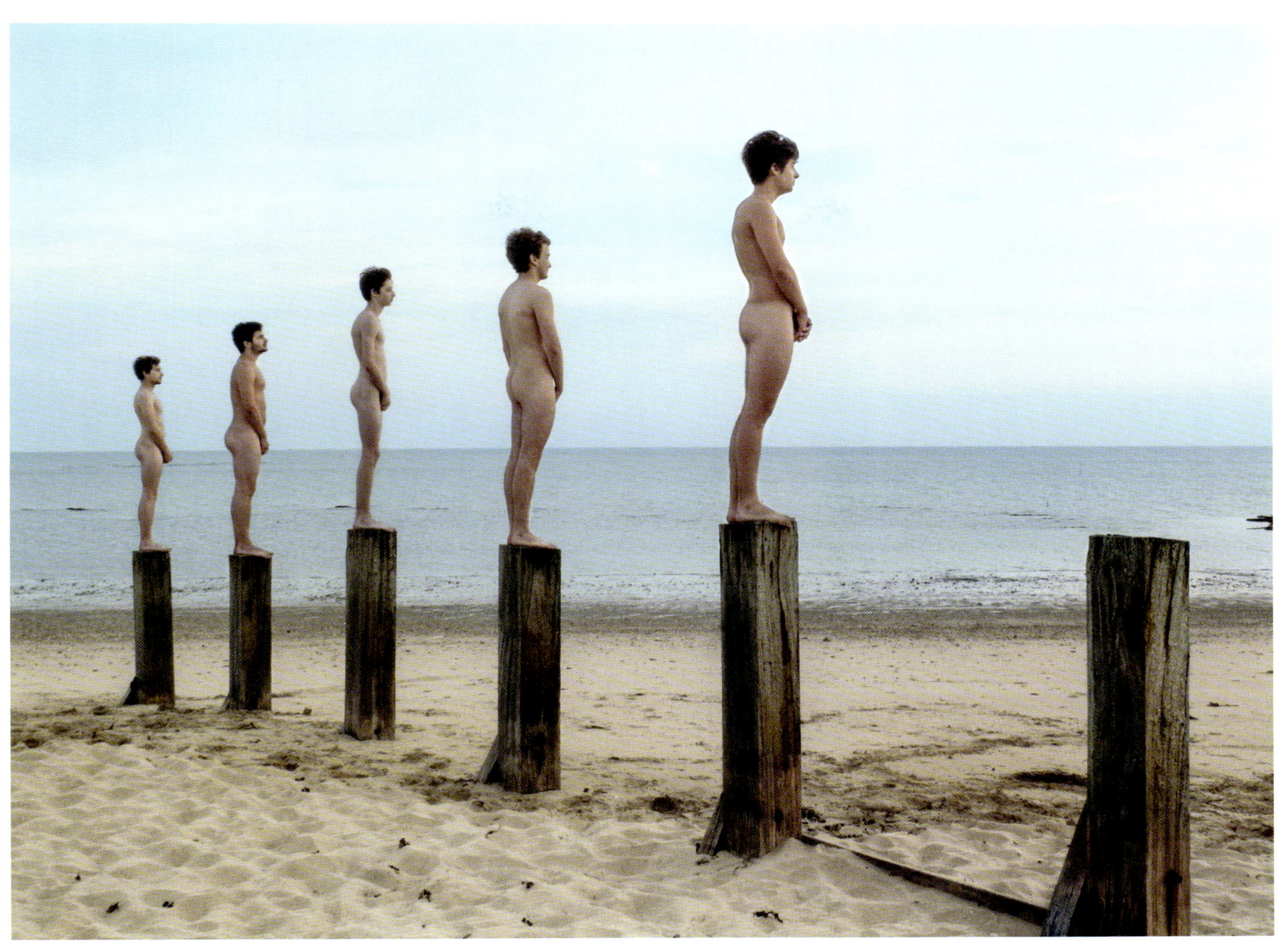

Opposite: *Seaside
(Bord de mer)*, 2009

Above: *Five Dreamers
(Cinq rêveurs)* (detail),
2016

JULIA FABRY

When I was a student at the Sorbonne, a teacher brought our class to meet Agnès. I remember this feeling of energy all around, even in the objects arranged in her house on rue Daguerre—eclectic souvenirs from her travels. A few months later, I saw *The Gleaners and I*, which reminded me of my childhood with farmers and times spent gleaning in the fields with my mother. I was so moved that I decided to write to Agnès. She called to thank me, and we remained in touch. Some years later, she invited me to work on *The Beaches of Agnès*, a movie as a self-portrait in five parts linked to the beaches of her past.

I assisted Agnès with the writing and also filmed images as second camera. I remember traveling with her to Los Angeles to shoot part of that film. We would drive every day from the murals that she filmed in *Mur Murs* to the seaside in Venice Beach, where she lived and filmed *Documenteur*, enjoying the light and trying to reconnect with her important memories from that time. We had similar interests and became fast friends; we were both passionate about images and how they could express life.

At that time, Agnès was an old filmmaker but a "young" visual artist. She had begun making installations and artworks, and my experience in that field was helpful to her. Soon my work on her films and exhibitions became coequal activities. I managed the production and documentation of her artwork and started to develop exhibitions for her as a curator. As she hated to waste time, we were always working on many different projects at once. I think it was easier for Agnès to enjoy herself while making exhibitions because she was freed from the financial pressures of cinema, where you are obliged to make money with ticket sales. She was always looking for freedom, so it made sense.

I have so many memories of making movies and installations with Agnès. The two practices intertwine in her Shacks of Cinema series, which began in 2005. Her concept was to recycle original 35mm prints and use them to build structures related to the content of her movies—a boat for *La Pointe Courte*, for example, or a tent for *Vagabond*. The shacks, for me, are among her masterpieces. They express how cinema is light passing through images and how Agnès felt living in this world. She approached the idea of recycling in a beautiful and poetic way that was ahead of her time, as always.

Since I was interested in film analysis, I particularly enjoyed it when she let me choose the images for the cinema shack created for the Los Angeles County Museum of Art in 2013. I selected the most meaningful and iconic scenes from *Lions Love (...and Lies)*: scenes of Andy Warhol; Robert F. Kennedy's assassination; the threesome of Viva, Rado, and Ragni naked in the swimming pool; the television, which was the fourth protagonist in the movie, as Agnès used to say; the streets she loved most; Hollywood icons; and of course, the brief moment when Agnès herself enters the frame to replace her alter ego, Shirley Clarke, and show her how to act.

Agnès was so special and impossible to categorize. She was a feminist fighting for women's rights to have their dreams and to be able to do what they want to do in life, but she was also interested in working with and understanding men. In the later years of her life, she was only fighting against time and trying to do all she wanted to achieve. One of the gifts of aging was that she could see her work reach its largest audience. She was not so interested in awards apart from the fact that they enabled her to share her work with more people. The most important thing I learned from my time with Agnès is that anything is possible with enough energy and faith. Her curiosity and desire to create kept her going until the end.

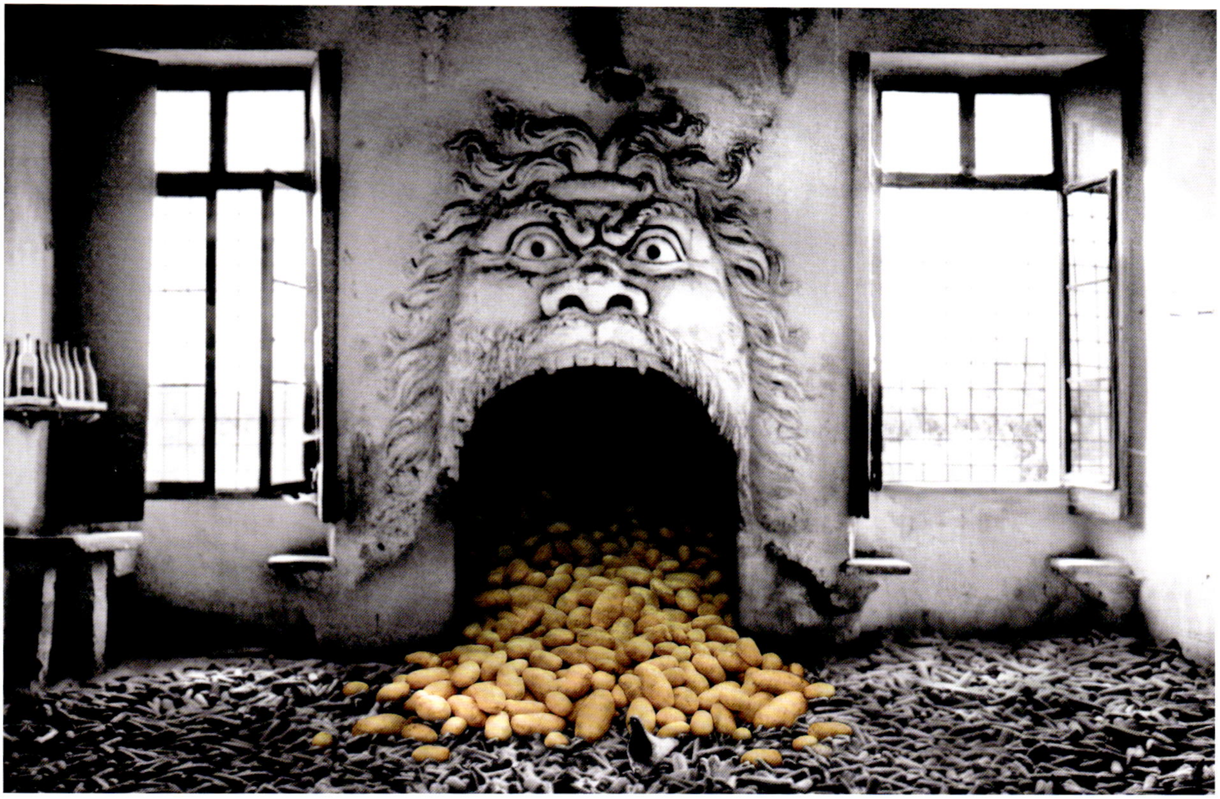

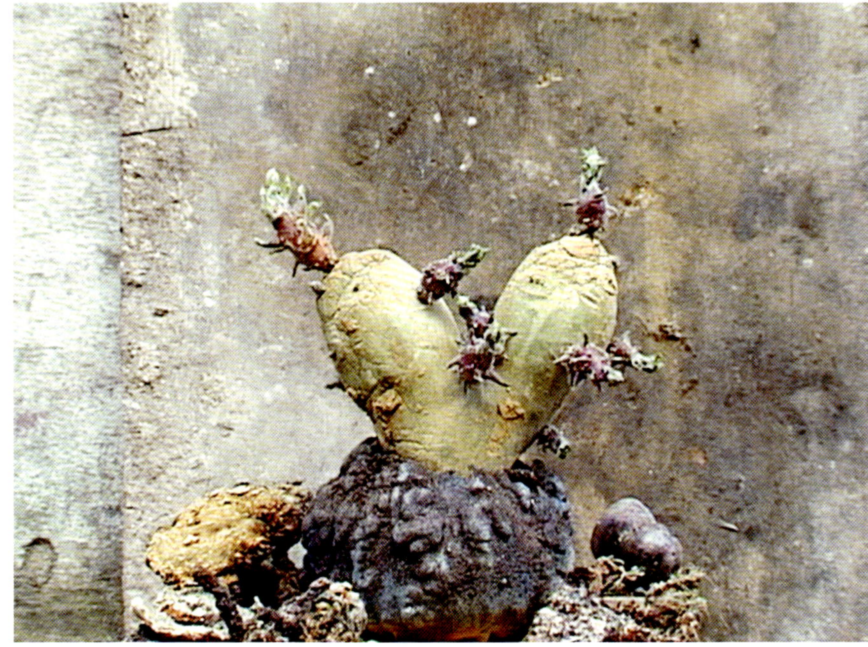

Above: *La cheminée patates*, 2003

Right: *Heartshaped potato no. 2*, 2002

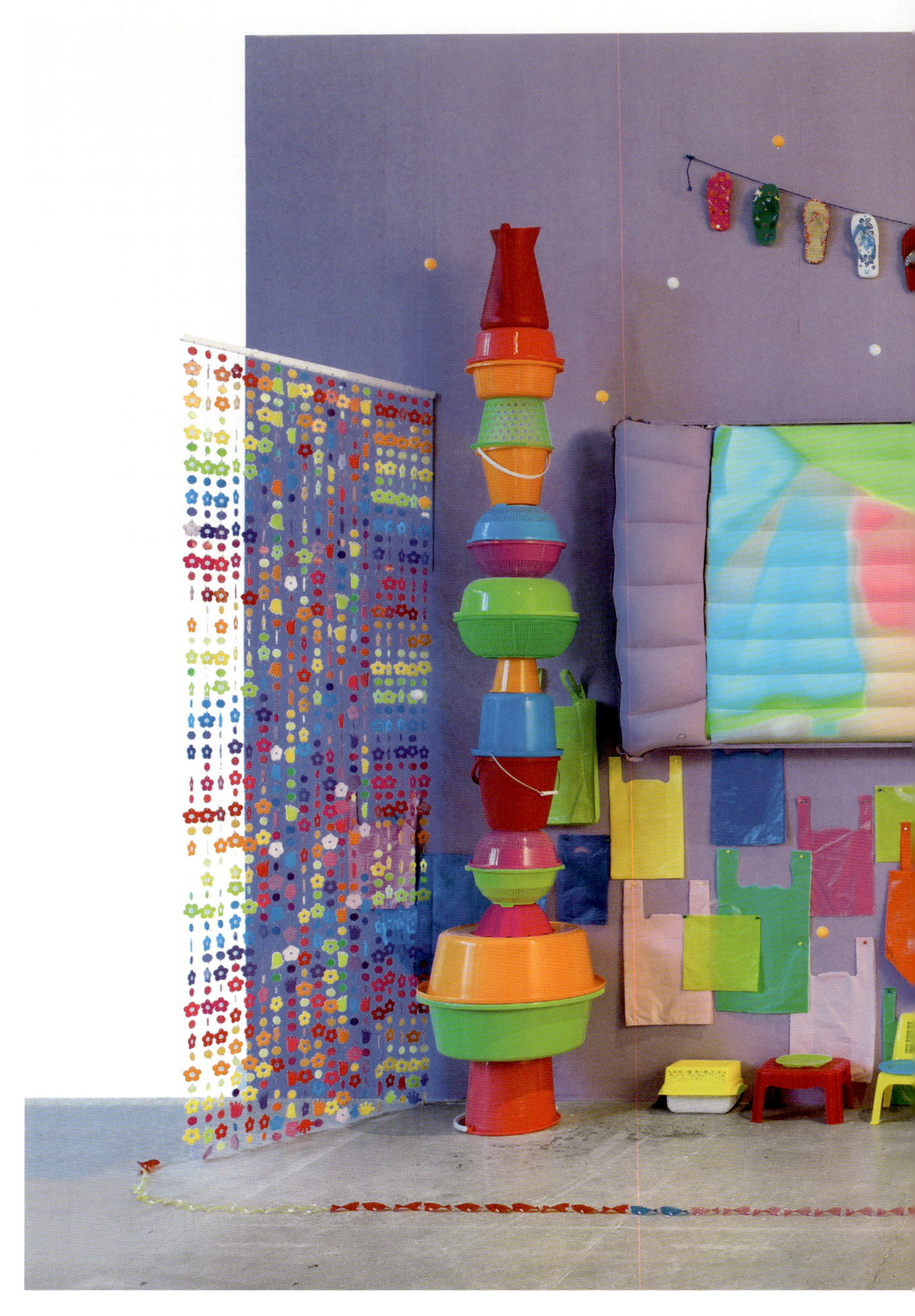

*Ping Pong, Tong et
Camping*, Fondation
Cartier pour l'art
contemporain, Paris,
2006

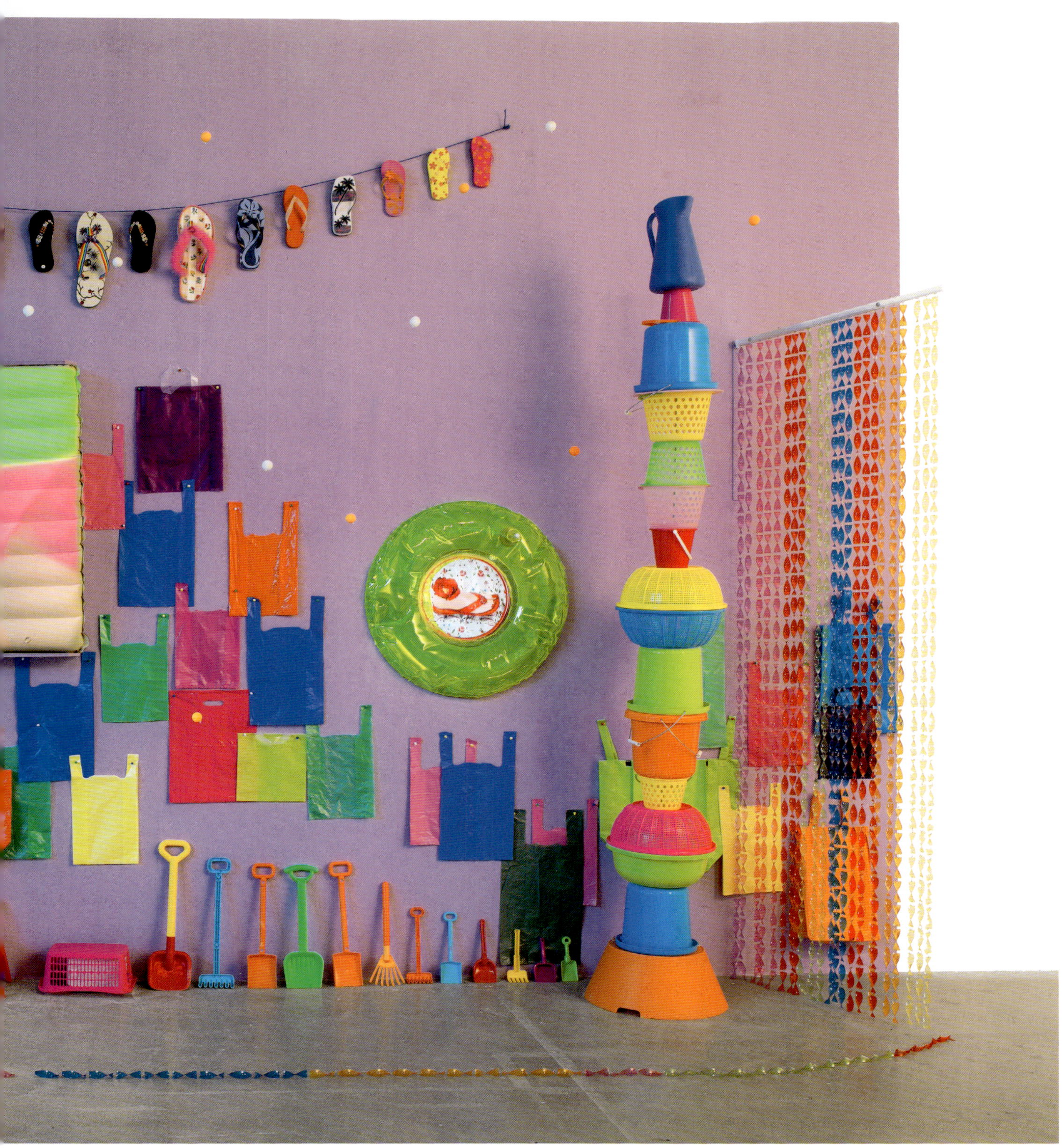

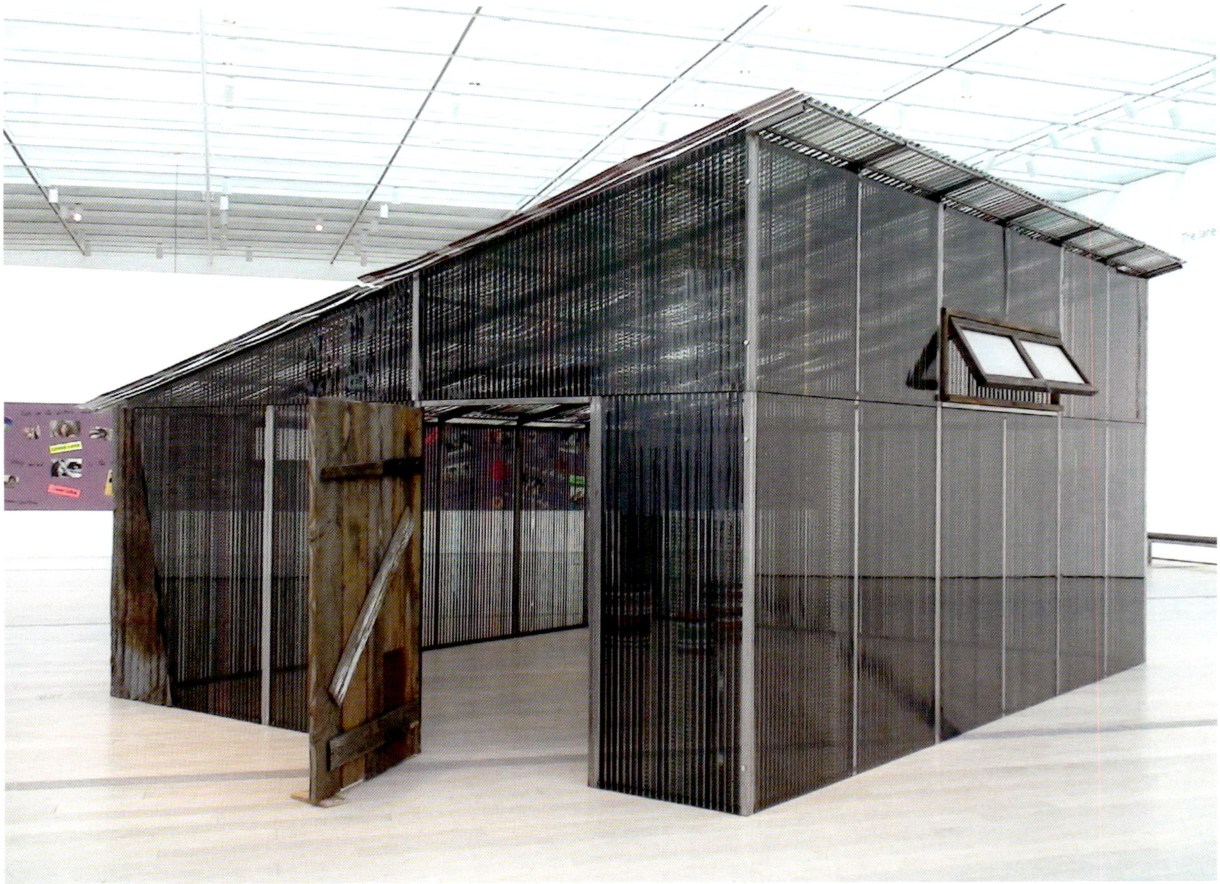

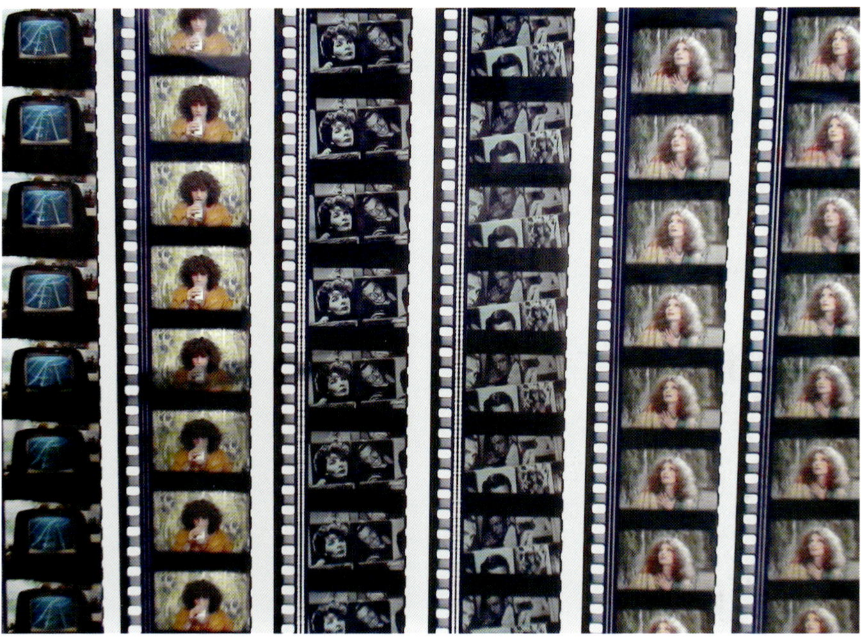

Above: *The Shack of Cinema (Lions Love...and Lies)*, Los Angeles County Museum of Art, 2013

Left: *The Shack of Cinema (Lions Love...and Lies)* (detail)

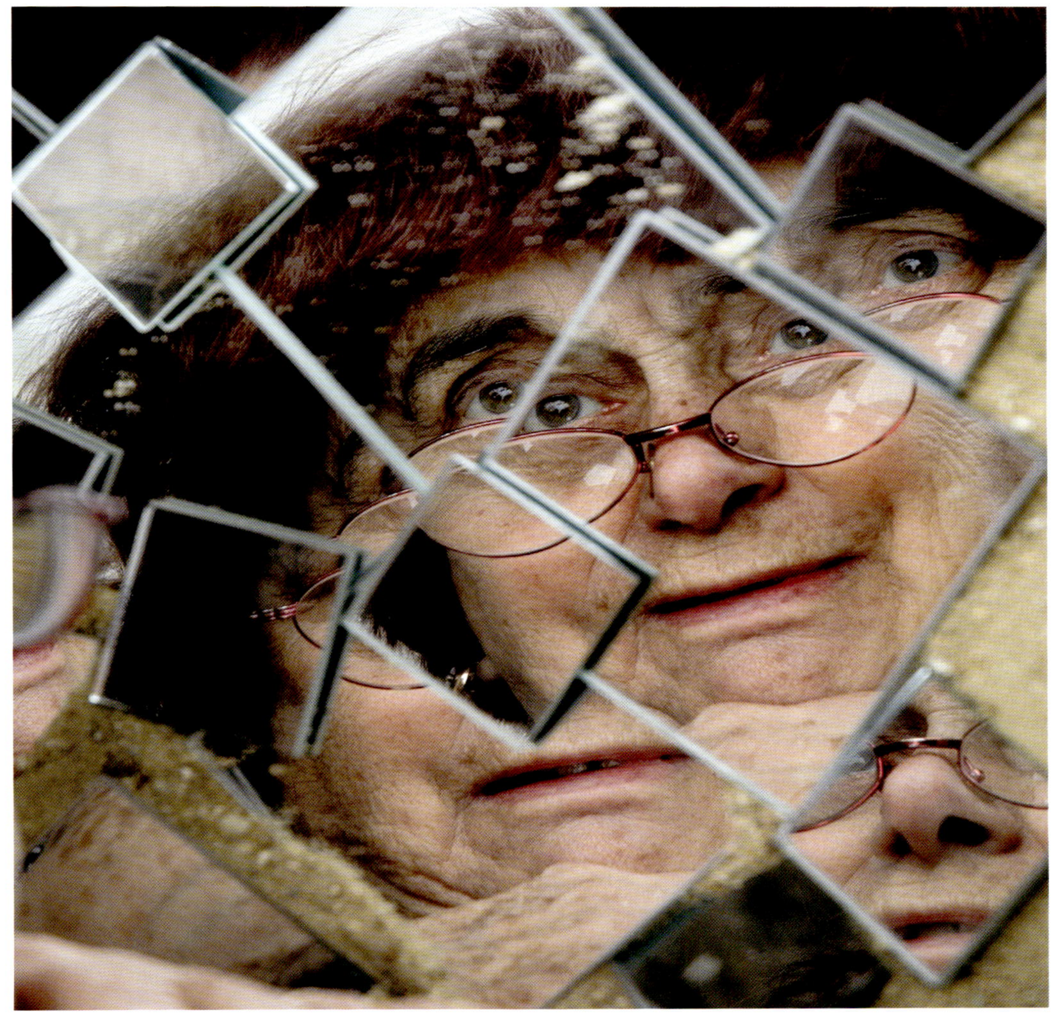

Autoportrait morcelé,
2009

INTERVIEW: AGNÈS VARDA
Manouchka Kelly Labouba

This conversation is an edited and condensed version of an Academy Visual History interview conducted on November 9, 2017, in Hollywood, California. It has been translated into English from the original French.

Manouchka Kelly Labouba: How did you learn to make films?

Agnès Varda: You can't jump right to films like that. When I was little, I dreamed a lot. I went to school just like everyone else, and I became a photographer. In truth, I've had three lives: I was a photographer, then a filmmaker, and then a visual artist, as they call it. My first life, as a photographer, started rather unintentionally. I'd not gone to school for that. I took some evening classes and immediately began taking pictures. I tried to capture some truly beautiful photographs just for my own pleasure. Those weren't the ones that sold, of course—everyone knows that. In the beginning, you do what you can to earn a living: I photographed trains for the train company, children, Santa Claus for a department store, things like that, pretty standard. But I still had a desire to create something beautiful. Even today, I can't really explain it.

I don't know how it evolved to filmmaking. In fact, I never watched movies when I was a child. My parents didn't go to the movies. In my early days as a photographer, I went to the theater. There was a man named Jean Vilar, who founded the Festival d'Avignon and was the director of Théâtre National Populaire—I learned so much there about the foundations of popular culture. When they put on high-quality productions, truly great works of theater, they'd open the doors to factory workers. They showed them Shakespeare, Molière, and Brecht. I understood that this man, Vilar, valued culture as something that should be accessible and appreciated. That's very important to me as well, as I've valued art all my life.

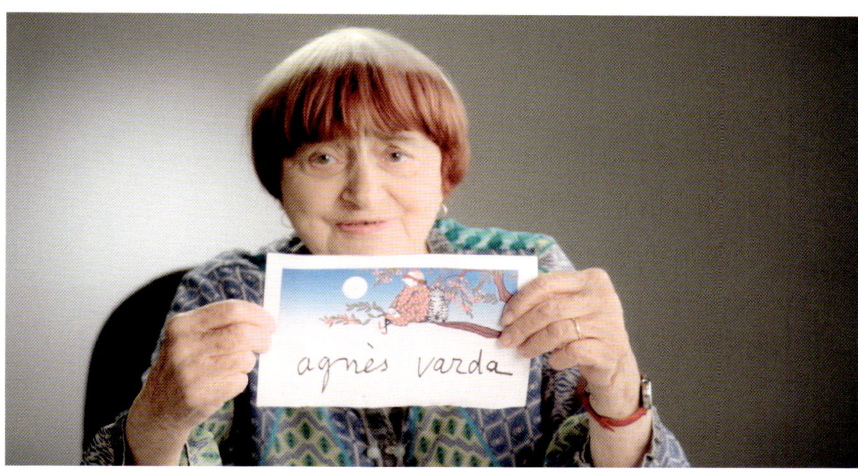

Academy Visual History interview, 2017. "My name is Agnès Varda. I was not born on a tree branch with a cat under the moonlight. I was born in Belgium to French parents in 1928."

I tasked myself with writing a script. I don't really know why. I read a lot, of course, and among the American authors I enjoyed reading Faulkner. One of his most important works, *The Wild Palms* [1939], was oddly constructed. There's a chapter about [a convict in] Mississippi, then a chapter about a couple, another about Mississippi, then the couple. I was confused by the structure, so I organized it for myself. I read chapters two, four, six, then one, three, and five, thinking that it would be easier to understand each story. Then I realized he'd deliberately created it this way, so I started over, reading [his book] in order. The challenge in following his format taught me you must create a film with a unique structure.

La Pointe Courte [1955], the first film I made, was formatted like that. The first day of filming, I was deliriously happy. I just knew I was a filmmaker. When people ask me, as you well may, who's influenced my work in film or elsewhere, well, I was only familiar with the films of Jacques Prévert, a poet that I adored who had written scripts. There was *Le quai des brumes* [*Port of Shadows*, Marcel Carné, 1938], there was *Les enfants du paradis* [*Children of Paradise*, Marcel Carné, 1945], which were so well written with magnificent dialogue. I was impressed by Giraudoux's works. As for art, it's always moved me; I was lucky to have seen Picasso's first exhibit, which was organized by the Communist Party. So, I was far removed from any education about the cinema. I'd not studied cinema, and I'd never been an assistant. Yet I jumped in feet first.

MKL: Could you tell me about how you were given your nickname, the Grandmother of the New Wave?

AV: Well, it's true that they call me [this] because when I filmed *La Pointe Courte*, it was 1954. I wrote it in 1953, and the great films that launched this wave of new filmmakers began in 1959 or 1960: obviously *Breathless* [Jean-Luc Godard, 1960], *The 400 Blows* [François Truffaut, 1959]. Rohmer, Demy, Chabrol—all of that group who were affiliated with the French film magazine *Cahiers du Cinéma*—they were called the Right Bank Group. I was in the Left Bank Group, along with Alain Resnais and Chris Marker. Marker was a guy who had a big influence on me because he began working on documentaries right away and including absolutely brilliant commentary. He was free-spirited but also very, very structured. He wasn't in the filmmaking milieu and neither was I; I didn't associate with other filmmakers. Jacques Demy wasn't in that world either. [Jacques and I] were happy living together. We both believed that it was wonderful to make films.

After his success with *The Umbrellas of Cherbourg* [1964], we were quite well off, and I made this film called *Le Bonheur* [1965]. I wrote it in three days. I have no idea what inspired it, but I knew I wanted to share the story of a happy couple with children, and they'd all love nature. The guy is in love with his wife, who's a charming, pretty blonde. He meets another woman, a postal worker, who is also charming and

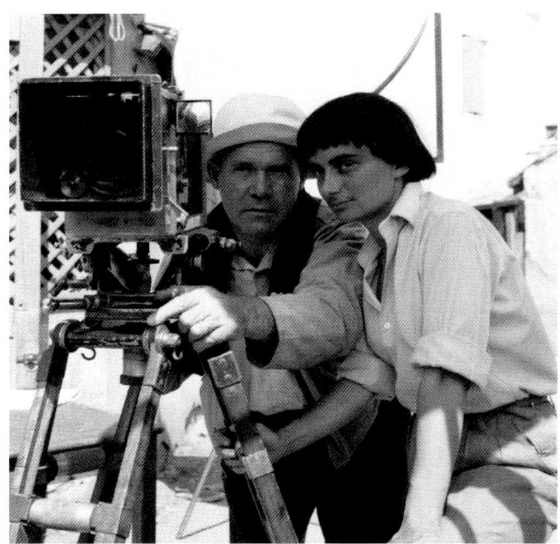

Cinematographer Louis Stein and Varda during the filming of *La Pointe Courte* (1955)

blond, and he falls in love with her. So, the question I was asking myself, and it's still a valid question: Is desire natural? How do we come to terms with desire in life? How is it viewed by society? Is the family unit more important than one's desire? Should we stifle our own desires?

I asked myself all of these questions, but I scripted them with the stunningly beautiful backdrop of the French countryside because I'd always loved the impressionists. We all know them, of course: Bonnard, Renoir, Vuillard, who created such beautiful works in the countryside surrounding Paris. I tried to capture tenderness through the grasses and the pale colors. You must remember that at that time, color film cost much more than black and white. So, this was my first full-length film in color. It was wonderful. And I was working with a cinematographer named Beausoleil, which means "beautiful sunshine." I thought that was extraordinary.

As I've said before, I like to film in natural light. I like to film in nature and on location, in real settings. We'd found some small houses, with virtually no lighting or hardly any. That was the revolution of a cinematographer named Raoul Coutard, who was most well known for making Godard's films. Coutard used very little lighting. Even with *Lola* [Jacques Demy, 1961], for example, he'd sometimes film in silhouette in front of a window or such. It was groundbreaking.

You must remember that when I began filmmaking, the classic cinematographers wouldn't even allow white shirts or white backdrops. They used sky-blue backdrops and wore sky-blue shirts so there wouldn't be any white—details like that—while we focused on contrasts, whites, blacks. This was also the result of the new film available after the war. During wartime there are always inventions, and they'd invented faster film stock—I think they called it Tri-X— that allowed you to film with less light.

All these new elements and techniques being used by this young generation of men—since I was the only female—who wanted to make less structured films with people who might be walking down the street, and dialogues that weren't always impressive, just naturally spoken dialogues with actions by unknown actors. Ten years later, it became known as the New Wave. That's how I came to be called the Grandmother of the New Wave. When I was 30 years old, I was already being called the ancestor of the New Wave. Now you understand why I say I'm a dinosaur of the New Wave, because it was such a long time ago.

* * *

It was in November 1967 that we came to Los Angeles for the first time. Jacques had been invited by Columbia. He'd written a film called *Model Shop* [1969], which he filmed here. And I discovered California with utter astonishment, I must say. Compared to France, which is so classic, prudent, and a little boring, it was a shocking culture clash. It's hard for you to understand the impact that has on a young French person.

Because everyone, even the men, wore flowered shirts. Everyone was saying "Peace and love," and they wore these huge medallions. There was love everywhere. We'd have these immense picnics in the parks, and people would bring their children and their dogs. We'd all share cherries. Music groups would come: the Doors, the Mamas and the Papas. There'd be no cost, of course.

I had a sense of extraordinary freedom. Obviously there was sexual freedom, and of course there were discussions about education. There were so many things we were trying to understand at that time. One topic that was quite new at the universities was women's studies. We'd already begun to feel strongly about feminist ideas. Of course I was quite happy about that. I immediately wanted to make a film on that subject because I was fascinated by all that was happening.

Like many of the people at that time, I'd seen the production *Hair* [1967], which was considered scandalous. It was written by James Rado and Gerome Ragni, who played themselves, completely naked, in the theater. I'd seen these guys, and I wanted to make a film with Viva. I'd met Andy Warhol. Warhol, in my opinion, was someone so significant to

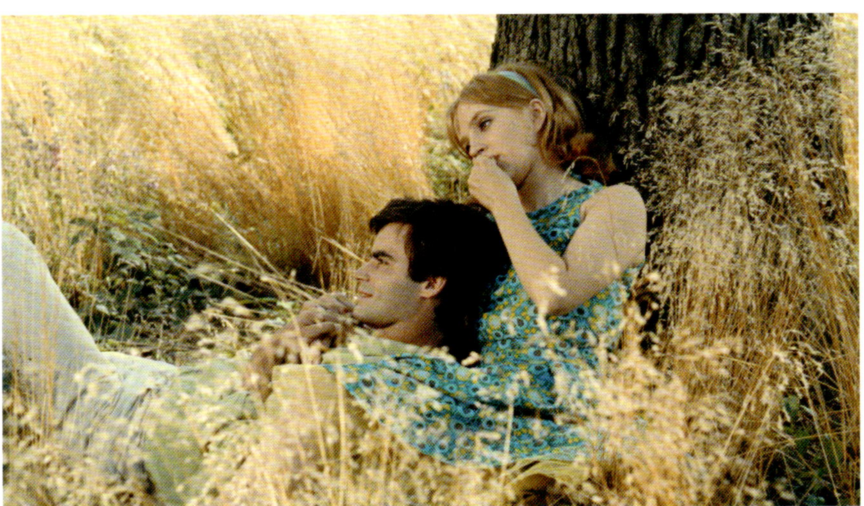

Jean-Claude Drouot and Claire Drouot in *Le Bonheur* (1965)

film, even though his films are unusual and sometimes boring to watch. He attacked the issue of duration, the challenge of time when making a film. I admired him enormously. I went to see him to ask if he'd mind my working with Viva, who was his star.

So, with Viva, Rado, and Ragni, I made a genuine hippie Hollywood film called *Lions Love (…and Lies)* [1969]. The characters were in a house with live plants and a few fake plants, and of course they were all naked most of the time. This took place just after [Robert F.] Kennedy was assassinated. I realized that the phrase that energized the American youth of 1967 was "sex and politics." Kennedy's assassination, which we saw almost live on TV, appeared in the film. I tried to express my shock at the California lifestyle, and I think that the film hit it right on. Of course, it wasn't a film that would be well received in America or France. It was produced by a very nice guy from Philadelphia. He'd produced a film by Nicolas Roeg and offered to pay me to make a film because he'd adored *Le Bonheur*. As you can see, my career succeeded thanks to happenstance and small acts of kindness.

I realized that what interests me is reinventing reality, not so much witnessing it. Can I find a structure for filmmaking that teases my observations from reality? Can I use things that have moved me, disturbed or pleased me? Since I was fascinated by the desire for disorderly freedom, I made [*Lions Love*], which is at the same time disorganized and amusing. Yet it also conveys reality as seen from TV, which had become so important. There are three people and a TV set. The TV is the star, smack in the middle of the room. They adorn it with a flag and crown it with feathers. I hope the film conveys that I was trying to understand the world around me. I didn't understand it more than anyone else, but I tried to understand it from a filmmaking perspective.

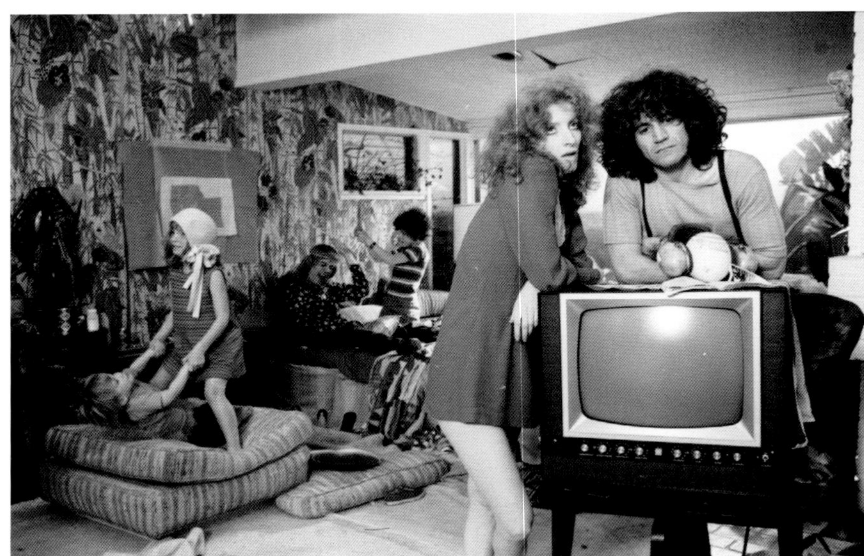

MKL: Prior to *Lions Love (…and Lies)*, you made other films while in California. Can you tell us about those films?

AV: Of course. Our arrival in California was so exciting. It began at the San Franciso International Film Festival, and [the film programmer and producer] Tom Luddy told me there was a man named Varda who lived on a houseboat in Sausalito. We went to see him, and it turned out he was my father's cousin. I was so happy and shocked to meet him and said, "This is amazing. I must film him right away!" We filmed two days later, and I re-created our encounter.

I [knew] I wanted to make a very specific montage. I also understood the degree to which the montage is a critical part in the writing of the film. So, I shot some footage that would allow me to show my encounter with Yanco in a pretty crazy way with some shots, retakes, repetitions. We were clapping and talking. I made a baroque montage because I wanted to capture the excitement, the pure joy. I wanted to show just how overjoyed I was to meet Uncle Yanco.

Viva and Gerome Ragni (with television) during production of *Lions Love (…and Lies)* (1969)

The cinematic writing of a film ends with the editing and with the mixing. How do we relay the events on film? So, the film *Uncle Yanco* [1967], which lasts 17 minutes, is first about the person, Yanco, who's adorable. It's also about the filmmaker as a go-between, which means that now other people get to love Yanco too. They might like the film, but I get to help them fall in love with the real person, the individual.

At the same time, we witnessed the emergence of the Black Panthers. They were a significant force at that time. They wanted self-determination regarding their future. They were making their voices heard and held demonstrations in Oakland because Huey P. Newton had been imprisoned. I filmed all of that and became acquainted with them. I filmed their demonstrations, everything they said. I'm so happy that I did, because what happened to the Black Panthers movement is quite sad. Just four years later, the movement had fallen apart. This is a significant work of documentation about a very significant time in the history of Black people, the peak of the Black Panthers movement. I've always felt it was important to bear witness to the period I'm in and invent formats for filmmaking. *Black Panthers* [1968] is a documentary. It's not especially creative, but it is well arranged, whereas *Yanco* was something I really wanted to do. Short films allow me to try different ways of sharing a story while using different techniques.

As for our lives in California, for both Jacques Demy and me, it was a childhood dream. We rented a little house. We also rented two white convertibles, every French child's dream. I drove around Los Angeles thinking, "It's the most beautiful city in the world." I still love this city and its unique spaces, its mixture of seaside and classic American city. All of it!

Afterward, I returned to France, as did Jacques. Life went on. But what do you think happened? What else had I discovered while in America? Feminism. The feminists there were much more radical than those in France. In France, the movement was growing bit by bit. But I actively lobbied with other women on the principles that we believed in: the right to have or not have children, the right to use contraception, the right to not accept bearing children that weren't wanted.

The battle for access to abortions was very difficult in France. There were women who were imprisoned. A particular group of women who were well-known intellectuals or in show business decided to sign a manifesto. It stated, "We have had abortions. Judge us." Delphine Seyrig asked me to join her by taking this letter to the courthouse. There was a hearing taking place to [try] some poor young girl who'd had an abortion because she was

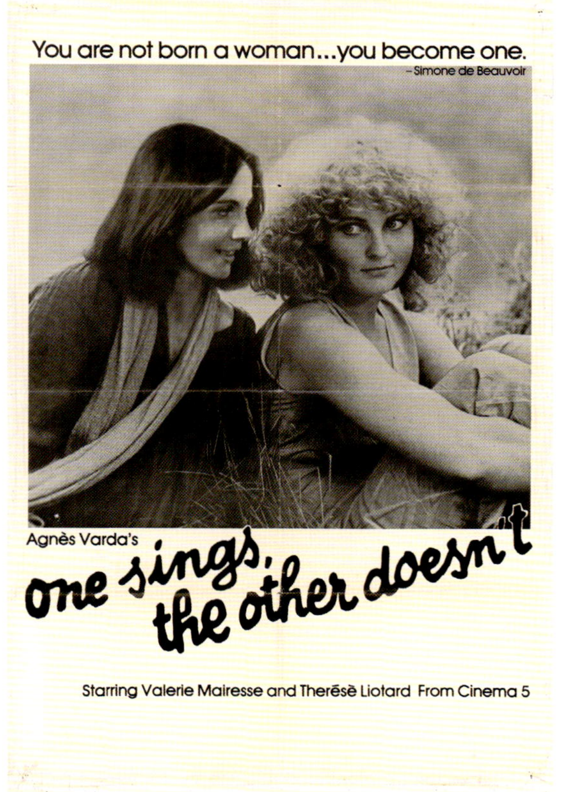

US theatrical poster for *One Sings, the Other Doesn't* (1977)

unable to care for a child. Clearly it was a trial of class and inherently unfair. These poor young girls were caught, while the bourgeoisie and those with money would just go to England or Holland or Switzerland. So, this manifesto was very important because it helped to change the law and led to the right to have an abortion.

I was so impressed by this that some years later I made a feminist film called *One Sings, the Other Doesn't* [1977]. I realized that when you explain feminist phrases to people, they are a bit harsh to say, so we created a musical in which the phrases were sung. We sung quotes from Simone de Beauvoir, who wrote [in *The Second Sex* (1949)], "One is not born, but rather becomes, a woman." *C'est magnifique!*

All these women I'd been associating with, with whom I'd joined forces—I wanted to bear witness that these were not enraged women. They'd not been beaten nor died from underground abortions. I wanted to testify to the profound friendship between women. So, *One Sings, the Other Doesn't* is not only a musical, but it sings of the solidarity among women. For me, it's a very important film because it tells of a 10-year battle. As for me, when I had my daughter, Rosalie, I wasn't married. It wasn't viewed as socially acceptable. I think I was always a little antisociety, fighting the bourgeoisie. This feminist film caused quite a ruckus.

MKL: Let's jump ahead a little. Since you mention being a nonconformist, I'd like you to talk to us about *Vagabond* [1985].

AV: That is quite a jump, indeed. What inspires these films? It's usually something that I've noticed and often something that revolts me. It's often something from real life that shocks me. In this case, I'd been struck because there was a lot of talk about the cold weather. There were some old women who'd died from the cold even while in their homes. I remember a country policeman shared with me that he'd discovered a young man who died of the cold under an apple tree. I kept wondering, "Why was he there?" I became very interested in the people we refer to as *les routards*, those who carry a backpack. And it wasn't just young men. More and more you'd see young women, which was a fairly new phenomenon around 1980 or 1981.

I documented this world quite a bit before writing a fictional story called "Vagabond." It's about a young woman who rebels and heads down the road. I didn't address the psychology, why she left or what drove her away, or where she came from. It was about her behavior: How does she live all alone with just a backpack? How does she set up her tent? What prompts her to spend the night by a cemetery in an effort to be left alone? How does she cope with the risk of being attacked? I knew [Sandrine Bonnaire] was the perfect one for this role. She was amazing. She swallowed the character whole, if I can say that. That's when I realized I didn't want to address psychology

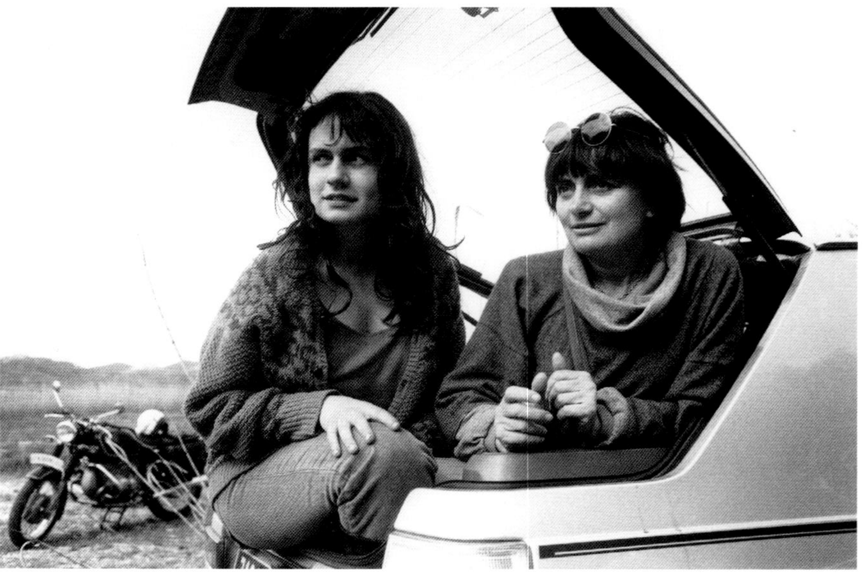

Varda with Sandrine Bonnaire during production of *Vagabond* (1985)

with actors. I wanted to work on behavior only: Exactly how do you carry your backpack? How do you break your bread, repair your shoes?

We know the film doesn't end well because we see in the beginning that she's dead. We witness the last two months of her life, which lead to her death. So, I knew it would be a difficult film, hard to watch. Oddly enough, it's my only film that was successful. At least it was in France. It had a very precise structure, and within that structure were emotions, encounters that were true to life. And the viewers were touched because, first, Sandrine was remarkable in her role. But also it was moving to watch the absurd battle of this young woman who keeps closing the doors around her. She didn't want to be helped. That raised a real issue: Are we able to help people who don't want to be helped? When you make films, when you create something, you're confronting questions you yourself have. The films don't provide the answers; they're just a means for asking the questions, a way to view the relationships we have with the world, with one another.

* * *

I've made 17 short films during my career. What I've noticed most is that when I've been disappointed in a film or anything I've created, it's always real life, life on the street, that reinspires me. I was in a café one day. It was about two in the afternoon, and there was a market there twice a week. People would come with their trucks, and while they were packing their baskets to put them back in their trucks—but before the street sweepers arrived with their green plastic brooms—there was a break of about 20 minutes. During this time, people came to gather items off the ground. I was astonished, so I began watching them after the markets closed. It popped into my head

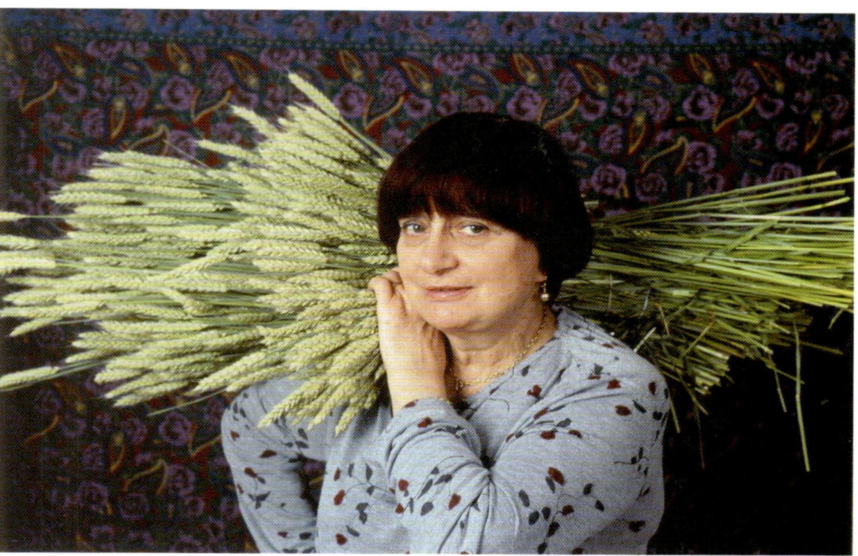

Varda in *The Gleaners and I* (2000)

rather suddenly. What struck me was, these people are going to eat what we've just thrown away.

I began to contemplate that. I thought about a word that's rarely used: *gleaning*. In days gone by, in the fields, once the harvest was done, there'd still be quite a lot of wheat in the ground, and people would come to gather the grains of wheat. They'd use it for their flour to make bread. They'd gather fruit. They'd gather corn. So, I decided to learn what I could about this. I wondered, "Who still gleans?" I became interested in this subject and the real lives of those who gleaned. I went to the countryside, and I asked their permission to film. I'd tell them how clever they were to do this. So much was being thrown away. People throw so much away.

It's interesting because cameras were dramatically changing [then]. It was the first time I'd used such a small camera, and it allowed me to film by myself. Because there's a challenge here. People are in such a difficult personal situation, you can't always come with a team. You don't want headsets, noise, and microphones. It was because of these small cameras that I was able to approach people in a more personal way, especially in situations like this, when they have nothing. They're eating things off the ground, which is still shocking in a society where there's so much wealth. This really confirmed for me that I've always been most interested by the disenfranchised. I've always filmed fishermen, farmers, or gleaners, people like that, because the others just don't interest me. That's why I've never filmed in a studio. I haven't even filmed scenes with rich people. On the other hand, I want to understand people and what makes some so different from others. That's what motivated me when I made *The Gleaners and I* [2000].

Something quite odd happened the second day of filming. We started following a trail of potatoes, because they'd throw out all the misshapen potatoes. That's another subject that interests me: we live in a structured society, so even our potatoes must follow a structure. They sell potatoes that are 2 to 3 inches long. If they're larger or smaller, they discard them. So, I was following the potato trail, and one day I saw a guy gathering these discarded potatoes. I stumbled upon a few in the shape of a heart. I immediately thought, "There's a message here. The message is that this modest but discarded vegetable is symbolic of people who deserve our love. We must learn to understand them."

I started keeping all the heart-shaped potatoes at my house. I'd put them in glasses and pots. You could say that I watched them age, but of course they began to shrivel and turn ugly. Obviously we couldn't eat them, so I put them in boxes in the cellar. Some of them took root with small sprouts. There was an extraordinary beauty in that, to think that these useless vegetables that were at the end of their lives were still living and still producing life. When I was invited to the 2003 Venice Biennale Art Festival, I already had the raw material I wanted to use.

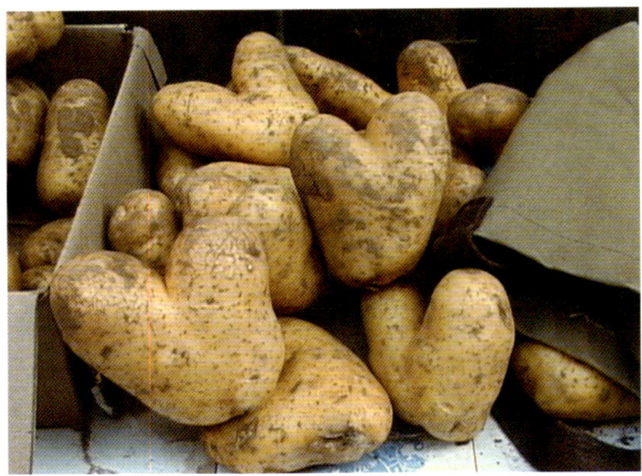

Heart-shaped potatoes from *The Gleaners and I* (2000)

* * *

I've always said there are three important words: *inspiration*, which is not a random thought that falls from the sky but an observation; then there's *creation* and *sharing*. Sharing films means finding people who love and understand the films, who share the emotions that have been elicited by the film through discoveries I've made, through the humanity of the people I've filmed or their situations. If all this can be shared, then I feel I've done my job, and that's good in the truest sense of the word. In a way, I've become a part of those I've filmed and those who've been moved by my filming.

If we can take time to reflect on life, to dream a little, create a little, then I think we're probably a little happier. Because we know full well that the world has its problems. We're in crisis. It's not just global warming. There's this enormous world migration taking place right now, leading to such tragic events—all these people drowning in an effort to find a better life, taking a boat because there's no food. We're in a world where there's so much sorrow. I often think about this, particularly during this last film [*Faces Places*, 2017] that I codirected with [the artist] JR. Do we need to contribute to the misery in the world? Do we need to add still more tragic information? We decided we didn't. Instead, we decided we'd go and talk with these people, be among them.

My ideas and JR's ideas were well meshed in our desire to make a film about sharing. For example, in a world that's so divided by politics, we never asked people for whom they'd voted. We thought, "Maybe we can make a film of one person meeting another." That's what happened in this film. It created a space for the public to experience tenderness, an overall empathy, because the people had opened their doors to us. We had nothing to offer other than, "Can we meet you? May we speak with you? Would you like to share something with us?" That worked very well. With JR—his team and his magic truck—we created small miracles in the villages. We were quite happy to make this film. At that time, it was very well received. By reaching out your hand, you're saying that everything is all right. Yet we know the world is not fine. But we can take a moment from our day, take time for sympathy, pleasure, and smiles even if what we're sharing isn't genuinely funny.

MKL: Do you think you could describe the essence of your filmmaking style?

AV: I don't know that I have a style. I know I have a desire to make films by using images and sounds in real ways. But to say that I have a style when filming, I don't know that there's a specific fabric to filmmaking, especially when making documentaries. With the ideal documentary, you put the camera just so, facing a certain way, and you allow it to film for 48 hours. In some ways, that's why I've said Andy Warhol is so important, because it was Warhol who said, "Leave it alone. Give it time. We want to capture something over the long term." There's another perspective, from Ozu, for example, who believed that a fixed scene filmed from below reconstitutes the space of life, of silence.

Quite a lot of research has been done on how we interpret through film, what we understand. For me personally, I don't know that I've contributed a single thing. Each time I film, I wonder, "Can I represent in one format or another what I'm trying to convey?" I've shared the story about editing *Yanco*. I was so exuberant that the editing is kind of crazy. With *Lions Love (...and Lies)*, I interviewed the hippies who were high, a little stoned. Frankly, they weren't in a normal state of mind. Do people understand that?

At the same time, can we try to share something while maintaining our own values? For example, I've never made a film in which women are mistreated or their bodies are exploited. God knows that desire exists in real life and is regularly shown in films, but we make choices as to how we represent that. For instance, there are many films that focus on the erotic zones of the body, and I don't think that's right. I think it's beautiful to acknowledge that the body is an entire entity, an entire person, whether man or woman. I remember making a film that involved a separation, and I filmed the woman naked and all alone, and I also filmed the man naked and all alone. It was as though that was the most effective way to show they weren't together, rather than

JR and Varda in *Faces Places* (2017)

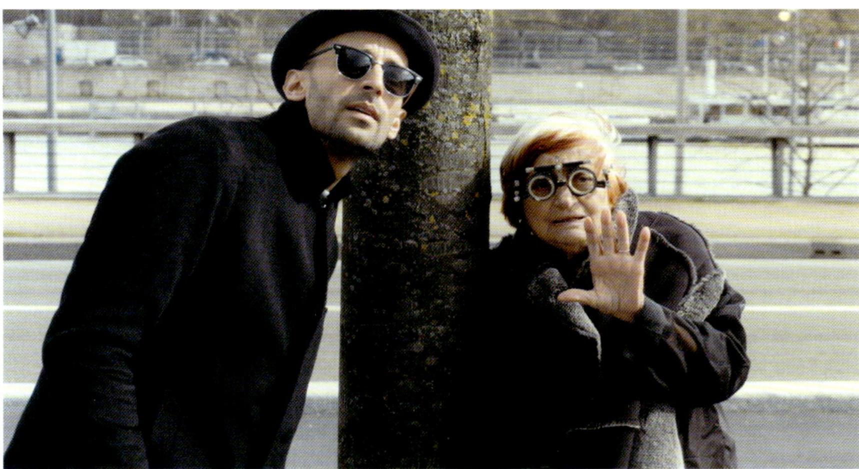

filming a scene where they're breaking up or walking away from each other.

So, we try to find a form—sometimes symbolic, sometimes metaphoric—to convey what we're trying to say. We see if some small shift can capture something for a public that is used to having everything explained. We explain it to them—A, B, C—except for a few exceptional filmmakers who know how to retain mystery. One of my mentors, though I never studied under him, is Buñuel. In his first surrealist films, Buñuel makes it clear in a wonderfully unique way that he mistrusts the bourgeoisie yet wants to share these extravagant tales. The film *The Discreet Charm of the Bourgeoisie* [1972] is an extraordinary creation! Then you have filmmakers who use subtlety and sorrow. I think that Cassavetes is an extraordinary director. He and Gena Rowlands created some beautiful films, so important. What's the name of the film where she was unbalanced?

MKL: *A Woman under the Influence* [1974].

AV: That's it. *A Woman under the Influence*, which is a critical film when studying the topic: psychological issues and so on. Personally, I adore Fellini's exuberance, his works brimming with imagination, capturing life as it is. Of course, we've learned from so many filmmakers. When we were young, for example, Bergman was very much in vogue. He brought psychology to the forefront. I didn't like it that much, but the work he did was very important. Later there were filmmakers from other countries. And that's beautiful, because film itself is a beautiful language. There are some films that don't interest me at all. I'm not interested in watching films about space travel, or in which manufacturing is explained to me. It's fine that they made *Gravity* [Alfonso Cuarón, 2013], but I really couldn't care less. It doesn't matter to me. But as soon as there's something that makes us agonize over life,

reconciles something within us, or helps us understand people or our emotions in a way we wouldn't have had we not seen the film—really, films offer a proposition. Not about life but for understanding things we don't yet understand. In the end, they open our hearts and maybe amuse us. Films might not be monuments, but they are living elements. They're just a little organic.

When people tell me they love my films, I don't necessarily know *why*. But I know they like them, which makes me so happy because, in the end, what I really want is for people to see the films. A film critic once said, "I'd like to take this film and keep it with me." That's a magnificent compliment because it means we've become a part of this person's imagination. We've entered their small world of memories, images, secrets. I, too, have seen films I'll never forget, and sometimes just a single scene I'll never forget. Sometimes I remember a film but can't recall the details or much of it at all. This shows that the impact films have is powerful. I don't mean to imply this is why we work, but we must keep that in mind when working. We must passionately create each project using every ounce of our skills.

I know there are many important films about very serious subjects. I've not chosen that path. I see some films that are important, and I think there's room for personal communication, which I try to have with each person watching the film. Can this viewer understand my thoughts and decisions? Can they accept the means I've used and the steps I've taken to please them? What are their reflections? I like films that make people think. Not right away, to the point of being tedious. They might be funny films, but they still make you think, and I believe we need to be thinking.

MKL: Had you not become a filmmaker, what would you have done with your life?

AV: I would have been a singer. I think it would be magnificent to have a part of your body that expresses your inner self. I've written lyrics for songs, but I've never sung because I don't know how. I only sang one time, when I made a film about widows. Since I'm a widow myself, I sang a small song for Jacques [Demy]. It was just a few words from Prévert.

I don't really know what else I would have done because when I began work as a photographer, I didn't know then I'd become a filmmaker. When I was a filmmaker, I didn't know that I'd dare to become an artist and put on exhibitions. This means that none of this was planned. I've tried to listen to what comes naturally, whatever enters my mind in my desire to create, and to follow those inspirations. It seems to me that if you're an artist, you shouldn't plan. We should have confidence in what will come and the influences and impressions that impact us.

I've already mentioned that I was greatly impacted by all the painters, the great artists that so positively affected me. When I see an exhibition or watch a beautiful film, I feel a stirring within: the desire to create. When I see a bad film, I think, "Films are disgusting!" When I see a beautiful film, I think, "That's what I must do. I must create a beautiful film!" So, we're all impressionable, and it's ever changing. I'm not a structured person, not organized. I'm fragile, although I might seem determined. I am also determined, but I think it's important to retain some fragility because it allows us to feel emotions. It stops us from shutting the door on an experience that might teach or offer us something.

MKL: How would you like to be remembered?

AV: Since I've changed my hairstyle, and I've chosen to add a little color to my white hair, they might remember my hair. Everyone says I'm very petite, so people will also remember that. People might also remember that I've aged, because I'll soon be 90 years old, which means that I've worked for more than 60 years. Really, what will become of it all, this body of work? It's a lifetime of accomplishments that fits in a bread box. I know that I'm loved by my children and some friends. They'll think of me a bit, just as I think of the people I've loved who are now dead. But can that be sustained for a body of work? I'm not sure. I've played a small role in the history of French cinema, but will I be remembered? I just don't know. I don't bother myself with these questions, but I'm happy to have persisted.

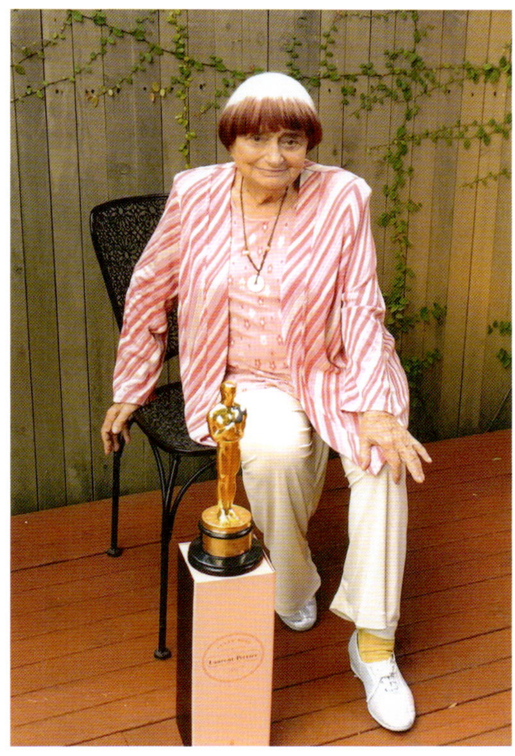

Varda with her 2017 Honorary Academy Award, which reads: "To Agnès Varda, whose compassion and curiosity inform a uniquely personal cinema"

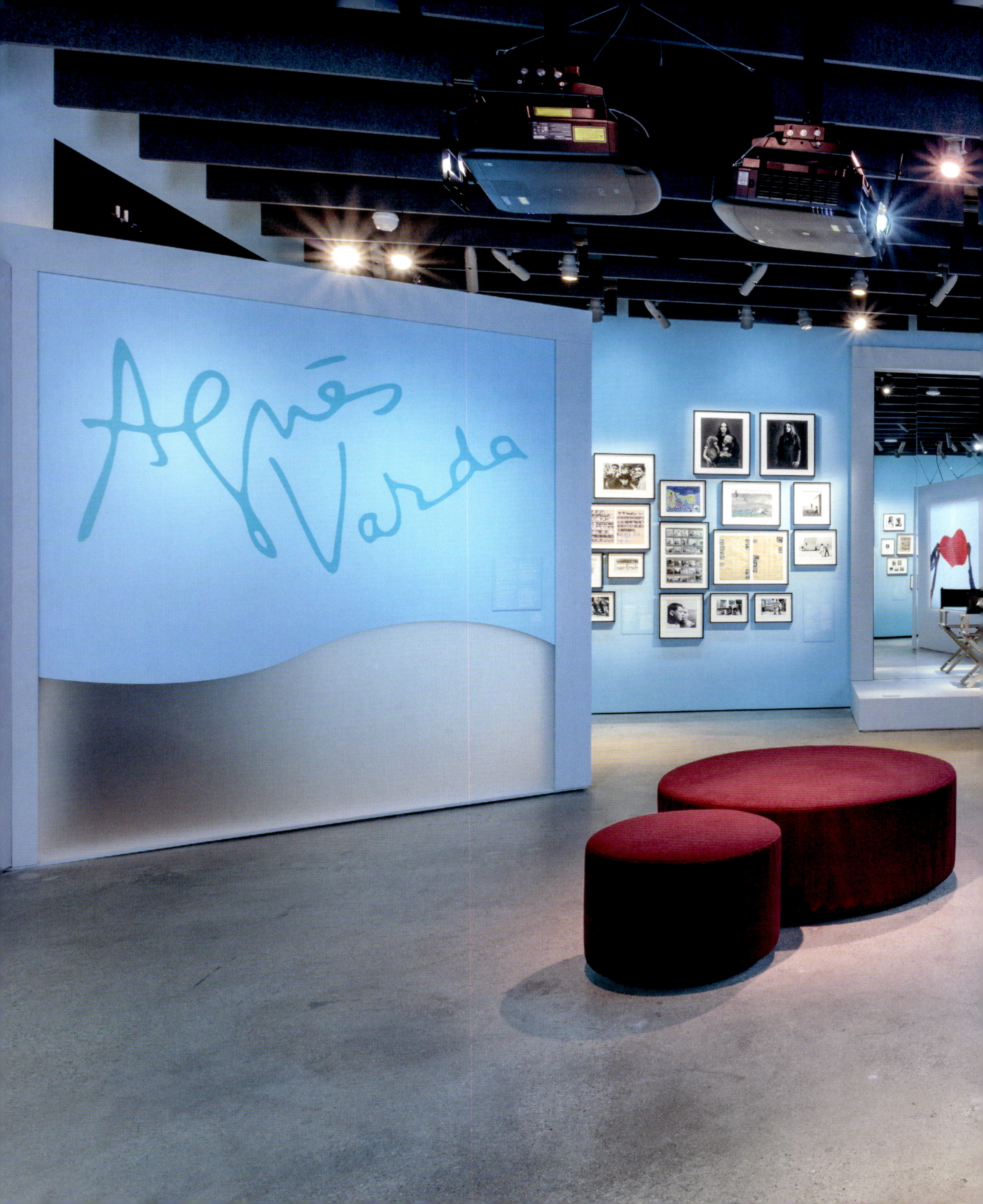

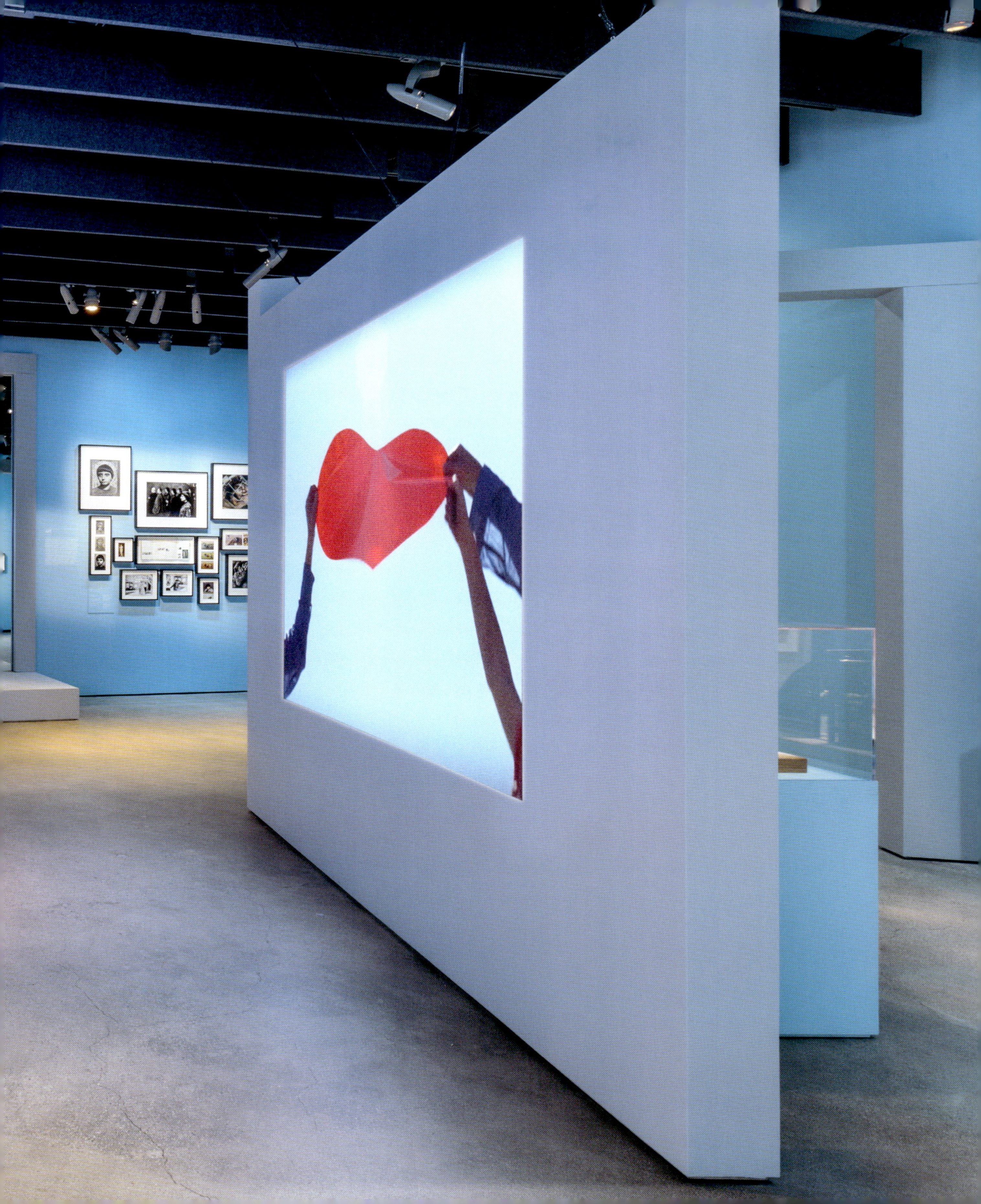

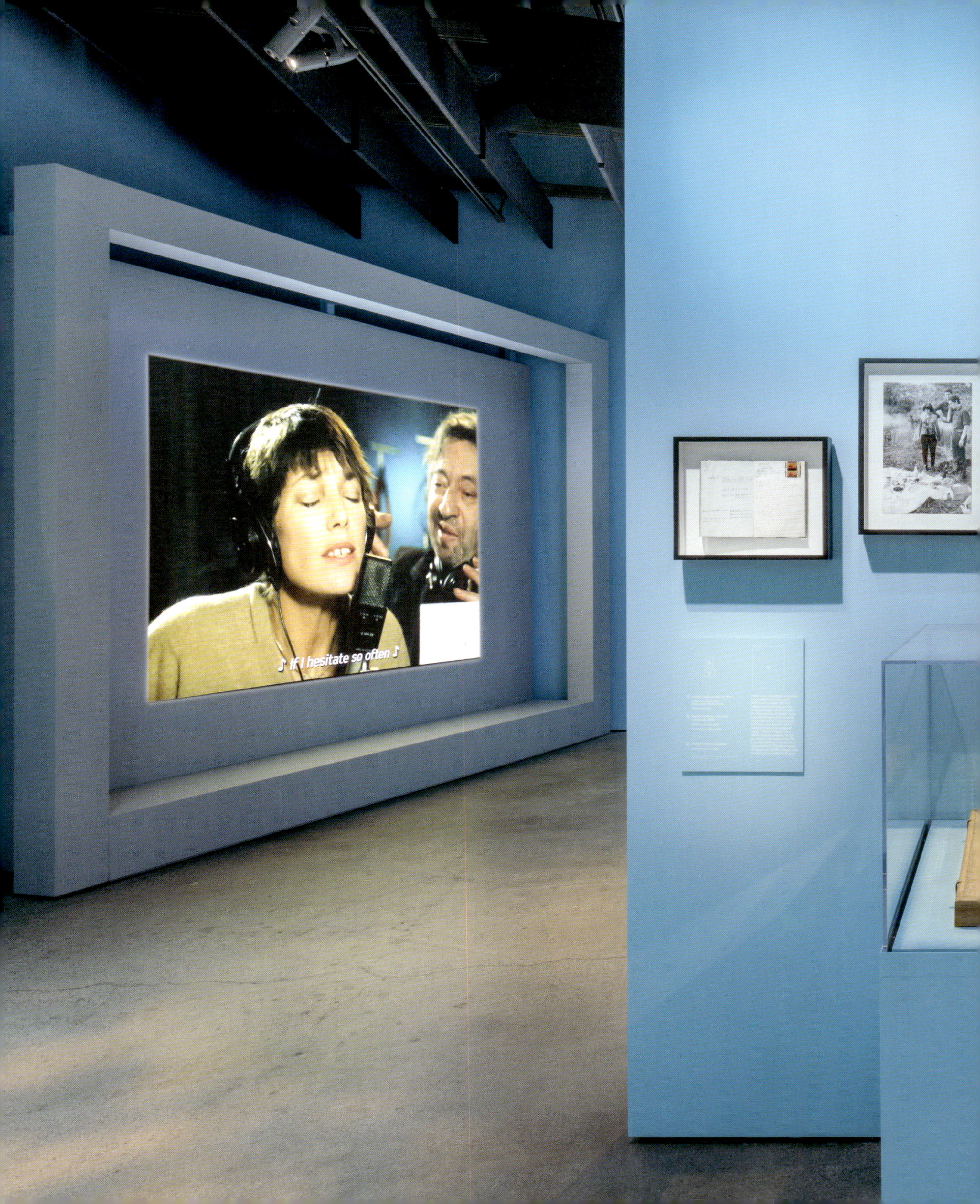

♪ If I hesitate so often ♪

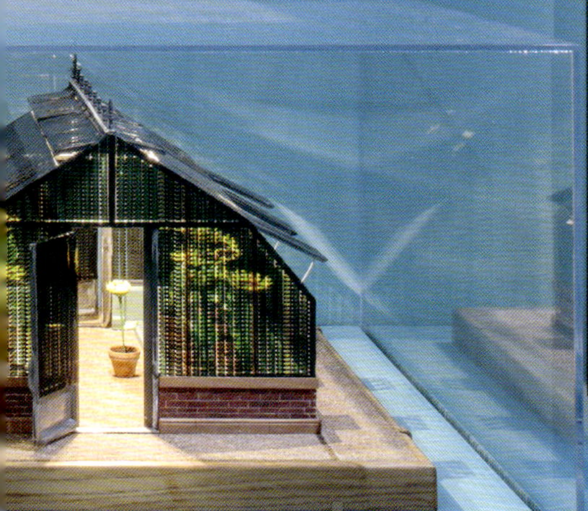

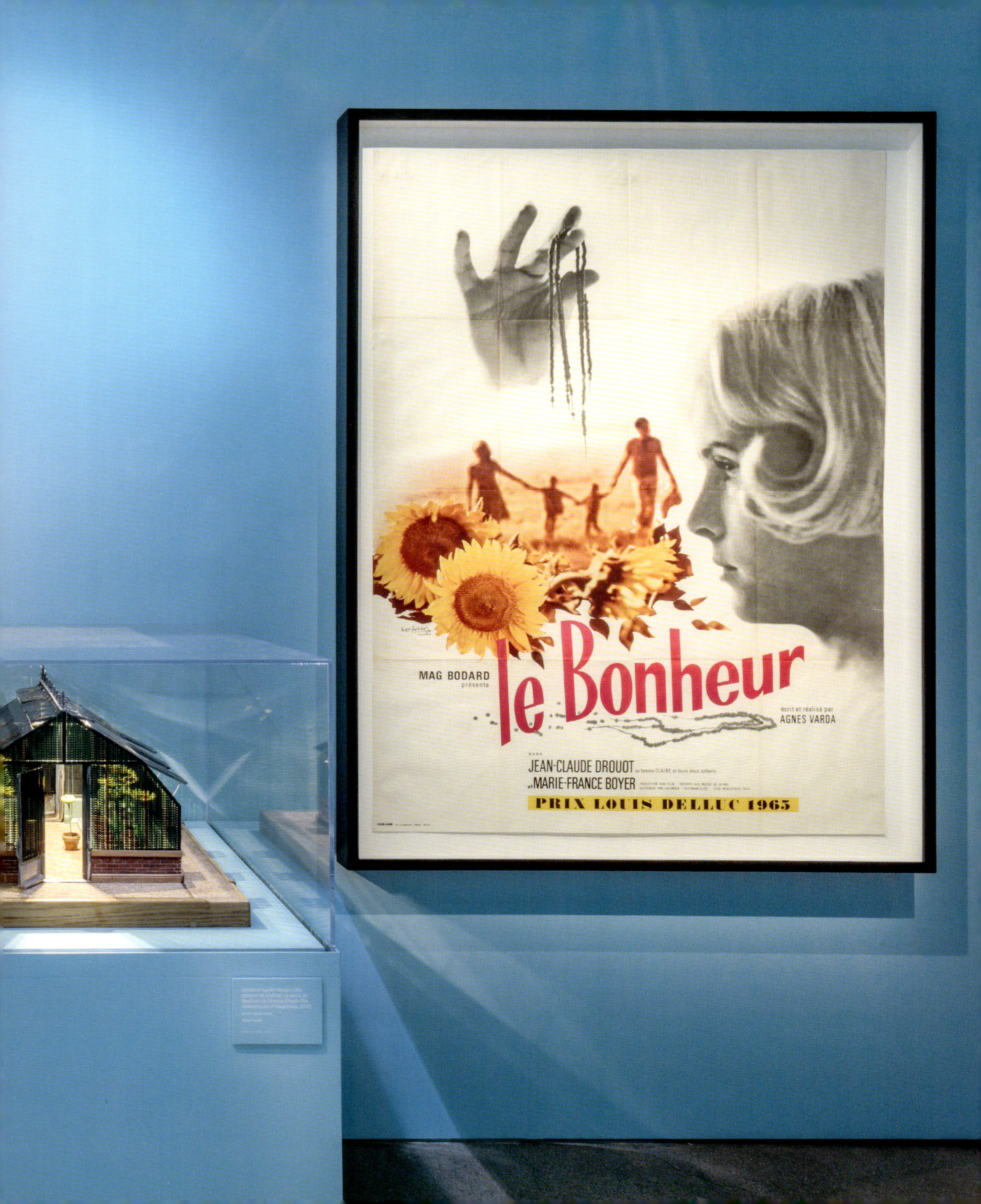

MAG BODARD
présente
le Bonheur
écrit et réalisé par
AGNES VARDA
avec
JEAN-CLAUDE DROUOT
et MARIE-FRANCE BOYER
PRIX LOUIS DELLUC 1965

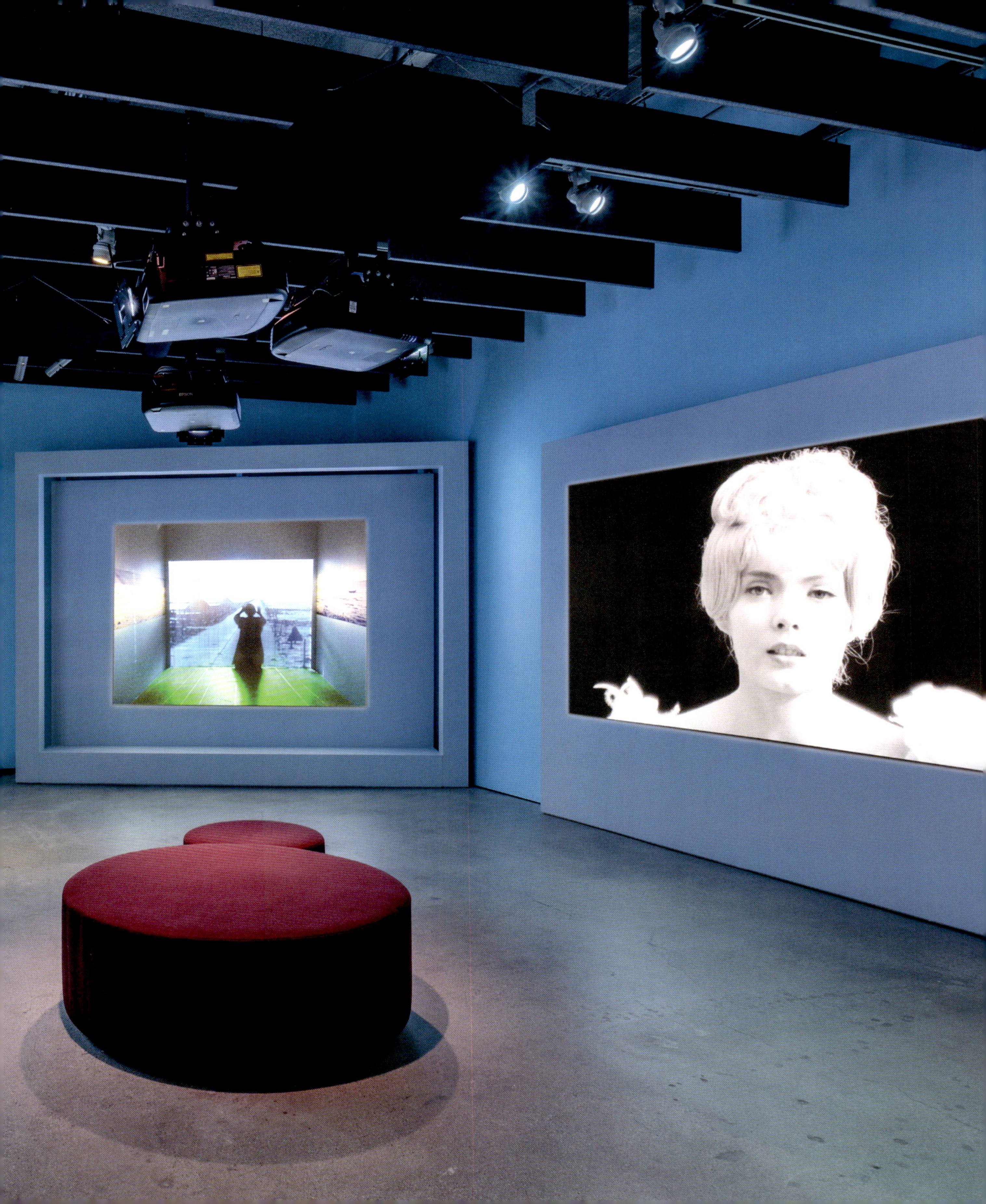

CONTRIBUTORS

Sasha Archibald writes and edits non-fiction. Her work has been featured in the *New Yorker*, *The Atlantic*, the *White Review*, the *New York Times, The Point,* and in many books and catalogues. She is a contributing editor at *Places Journal* and the *Public Domain Review*.

Jane Birkin is a singer, actress, and style icon. Her initial fame came as a result of her presence in the Swinging London scene of the mid-1960s, with appearances in Michelangelo Antonioni's *Blow-Up* (1966) and the French thriller *The Swimming Pool* (1969), as well as her partnership with Serge Gainsbourg, with whom she recorded "Je t'aime moi non plus" in 1968. Birkin's other film roles include *Death on the Nile* (1978), Varda's *Kung-Fu Master!* and *Jane B. par Agnès V.* (both 1988), *La Belle Noiseuse* (1991), and *A Soldier's Daughter Never Cries* (1998).

Sandrine Bonnaire is an actress, film director, and screenwriter who made her debut in Maurice Pialat's *À nos amours* (1983), for which she won the César Award for Most Promising Actress. Her work as Mona in Agnès Varda's *Vagabond* (1985) won her a second Cèsar, for Best Actress. Bonnaire's filmography also includes *Under the Sun of Satan* (1987), *Monsieur Hire* (1989), Rivette's *Joan the Maid* (1994), *Intimate Strangers* (2004), and Chabrol's acclaimed thriller *La Cérémonie* (1995), for which she shared the Best Actress award with Isabelle Huppert at the Venice Film Festival.

Manohla Dargis is chief film critic of the *New York Times*, which she joined in 2004. She grew up in the East Village of New York, where she attended public school and was a frequent attendee at both St. Mark's Cinema and Theater 80. She started writing about movies professionally in 1987 while earning her MA in cinema studies at New York University. A class with the longtime *Village Voice* critic J. Hoberman led to her being hired to write about avant-garde cinema for the *Voice*. She has written prolifically about film for numerous publications; her work has also been anthologized in several books. She lives in Los Angeles with her husband.

Peter Debruge is chief film critic of *Variety*, where he has written more than 1,700 reviews since 2005. How committed is he to world cinema? From 2014 to 2016, he relocated from Los Angeles to Paris, where he covered the festival circuit from Tokyo to Reykjavik to Cannes and befriended Agnès Varda. A cofounder of the Animation Is Film Festival, Debruge has taught at Chapman University and was knighted by France in the Order of Arts and Letters.

Mathieu Demy is an award-winning actor, director, and producer and the son of Agnès Varda and Jacques Demy. He began his career acting in films directed by his mother, including *One Sings, the Other Doesn't* (1977), *Documenteur* (1981), and *Kung-Fu Master!* (1988). Demy wrote and directed his first feature film, *Americano*, in 2011, which he also produced and starred in opposite Salma Hayek and Geraldine Chaplin. Demy's numerous performances include those in Céline Sciamma's *Tomboy* (2011) and the Netflix series *On the Verge* (2021) with Julie Delpy.

Julia Fabry is an independent curator with a PhD in fine arts from the Sorbonne. She is also a visual and video artist. Fabry worked with Agnès Varda on for more than 13 years, assisting with films and art installations, and curated several exhibitions of Varda's work in Spain, China, Sweden, Belgium, the United Kingdom, and France. She is coeditor, with Dominique Bluher, of *The Third Life of Agnès Varda* (2022).

This publication accompanies *Director's Inspiration: Agnès Varda*, organized by Ana Santiago and Jessica Niebel in collaboration with Ciné-Tamaris and presented at the Academy Museum of Motion Pictures, Los Angeles, November 3, 2022–January 5, 2025, as part of the exhibition *Stories of Cinema*.

Stories of Cinema is presented by PwC. Major funding is provided by Gerald Schwartz and Heather Reisman. Generous support is provided by Metro-Goldwyn-Mayer Studios, Ruderman Family Foundation, FotoKem, Barbara Roisman Cooper and Martin M. Cooper, Jocelyn R. Katz, John Ptak and Margaret Black, Lauren Shuler Donner, Randy E. Haberkamp, Kevin McCormick and A. Scott Berg, Chanel, and John and Lacey Williams.

Technology solutions generously provided by Panasonic and Sony Electronics Inc.

Powered by Dolby.

Academy Museum digital engagement platform sponsored by Bloomberg Philanthropies.

Published in 2023 by the Academy Museum of Motion Pictures and DelMonico Books • D.A.P.

Academy Museum of Motion Pictures
6067 Wilshire Boulevard
Los Angeles, California 90036
academymuseum.org

DelMonico Books available through ARTBOOK | D.A.P.
75 Broad Street, Suite 630
New York, NY 10004
artbook.com
delmonicobooks.com

Design: IN-FO.CO
Editing: Nikki Bazar, Chelsea Bingham
Proofreading: Dianne Woo
Color separations: Echelon, Los Angeles

Academy Museum of Motion Pictures
Director of Publications: Stacey Allan
Senior Editor: Chelsea Bingham
Publications Coordinator: Lars Eckstrom

DelMonico Books
Publisher: Mary DelMonico
Director of Production: Karen Farquhar

Printed and bound in China

ISBN: 978-1-63681-060-7
Library of Congress Control Number: 2023939457

Cover, top to bottom: Agnès Varda, *Self Portrait in front of Gentile Bellini*, 1960; *Uncle Yanco* (1967); *Le Bonheur* (1965)
Back cover: Agnès Varda, 1988